Alberto Cavalcanti
Realism, Surrealism and
National Cinemas

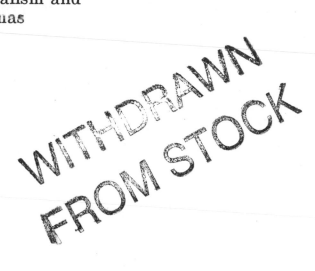

Alberto Cavalcanti

Realism, Surrealism and National Cinemas

Ian Aitken

FLICKS
BOOKS

A CIP catalogue record for this book is available from the British Library.

ISBN 1 86236 014 6 (Pb)
ISBN 1 86236 015 4 (Hb)

First published in 2000 by

Flicks Books
29 Bradford Road
Trowbridge
Wiltshire BA14 9AN
England
Tel   +44 1225 767728
Fax   +44 1225 760418
Email   flicks.books@dial.pipex.com

Printed and bound in Great Britain by MPG Books

Contents

Acknowledgments

This book has been written with the support of an Arts and Humanities Research Leave Award, and I would like to thank the AHRB, and the Research Committees of the Faculty of Art, Media and Design, University of the West of England, and the Faculty of Humanities and Social Sciences, De Montfort University for supporting this project. I would also like to thank those within the British Film Institute, the Cinemateca Brasileira, the Filmmuseum Amsterdam, the Bundesarchiv-Filmarchiv and the Centre National du Cinéma, Paris, for their help. I would also like to thank Christina Daniels, Nicholas Hodgkin, Maria Gemmel and my partner, Sylvie Gautheron, for their help with translations from the French, German and Portuguese. Special thanks must go to Christina Daniels here for her efficient and professional liaison work between England and Brazil, and for her journalistic and research skills. During the course of this research I have also had the pleasure of coming into contact with a number of people who have provided me with help and assistance. In this respect, I would like to thank Mário Audra, Wolfgang Klaue, Charles Drazin and Claudio Valentinetti. Valentinetti and Lorenzo Pellizzari's edited study of Cavalcanti has proved invaluable, particularly in relation to Cavalcanti's Brazilian period. I would also like to thank Sylvie Gautheron for putting up with me over what has been a particularly intense period of study. I would also like to thank Matthew Stevens of Flicks Books for the substantial role he has played in bringing this project to a successful conclusion, and, in particular, for the professional thoroughness which he has brought to bear upon the task of editing the manuscript. Finally, I would like to thank the man to whom this book is dedicated, Alberto Cavalcanti.

Preface

The origins of this book on Alberto Cavalcanti lie in my previous research into the British documentary film movement. My doctoral research, which focused on the historical context of the documentary film movement and on Grierson's theory of documentary film, paid little attention to Cavalcanti. Prior to that, however, I had carried out master's level research on the film *North Sea* (1938), a film directed by Harry Watt and produced by Cavalcanti. It was during the course of that research that it first became clear to me that Cavalcanti's contribution to the documentary film movement may have been at least as great as that of Grierson.

This belief was further reinforced when, after concentrating on Grierson during my doctoral research, and publishing that as *Film and Reform: John Grierson and the Documentary Film Movement* (1990), I turned my attention to other members of the documentary film movement. The outcome of this was *The Documentary Film Movement: An Anthology* (1998), which, in addition to reprinting works by Grierson, presented excerpts from the writings of Paul Rotha, Humphrey Jennings, Basil Wright and Cavalcanti. It was whilst working on this project that I became convinced of the need to undertake a comprehensive critical study of Cavalcanti, and this perception was later reinforced by viewings of Cavalcanti's films, some of which I had not seen before. I was immediately struck by how curious, complex and unpredictable many of these films were, and even more so by how little critical attention they had received. It will no doubt surprise many English readers to learn that Cavalcanti has been written about extensively in France, Germany, Italy, Portugal and Brazil, because in England only a few writers have written intelligently about him. I think that there are reasons for this lack of attention to Cavalcanti in England, and I will set these out in the book's conclusion.

In this book I have attempted to assess Cavalcanti's contribution as both a film producer and a film director. Thus, each chapter begins by examining the context of a particular period in Cavalcanti's career, before going on to examine the films which he produced and directed during that period. The ten chapters which make up the book follow the course of Cavalcanti's career from *Résurrection* in 1922 to *Um Homem e o Cinema* (*One Man and the Cinema*) in 1976. In the "Conclusion", I also establish the key thematic motifs and stylistic characteristics in Cavalcanti's films, and address the nature and quality of his contribution to the cinema.

This has been a fascinating but, at the same time, difficult, project to undertake. Cavalcanti was more nomadic than most filmmakers, and information about his films and activities is scattered across the world, from Rio de Janeiro to Paris, via London, Berlin, New York, Tel Aviv and numerous other cities. In addition, many of Cavalcanti's films are rarely, if ever, screened and have proved difficult to track down. Consequently, much time has been spent telephoning, faxing and writing to institutions in Paris, Berlin, Rio de Janeiro, São Paulo and elsewhere in an attempt to obtain both films and other primary source materials.

However, despite these difficulties, I was eventually able to view virtually all of Cavalcanti's films, including his entire Brazilian and British output, films which few people in the West have seen. Cavalcanti's output as a director was considerable. Between 1926 and 1976, he directed over 30 films, and also produced and co-produced many others. I hope that this book will do justice to this achievement, and help to bring these films the critical attention which they deserve.

1

Brazil-France

Alberto de Almeida Cavalcanti was born in Rio de Janeiro on 6 February 1897. His father, Manoel de Almeida Cavalcanti, came from the town of Palmeira dos Índios in the region of Alagoas in the north-eastern part of Brazil, whilst his mother, Dona Ana Olinda do Rego Rangel, came from the town of Olinda in the nearby region of Pernambuco. Manoel's family, which was originally of Italian extraction, had aristocratic descendants, but, by the time of Alberto's birth, their circumstances had become reduced to that of a middle-class family, living in one of the more affluent suburbs of Rio de Janeiro and enjoying a relatively prosperous existence. Despite this *bourgeoislfication*, however, the Cavalcantis retained a patrician and gentlemanly view of their own circumstances and condition, and this was to influence the later development of Alberto's character.

The Cavalcantis moved to Rio de Janeiro shortly before Alberto's birth, when Manoel obtained an appointment as a teacher of mathematics in the Escola Militar of Praia Vermelha. In addition to his career as a mathematician, however, Manoel was steeped in the French rationalist tradition and was an enthusiastic disciple of Auguste Comte, the 19th-century French positivist philosopher. The Cavalcanti household was consequently well-stocked with books on positivism, philosophy and social education. Manoel also attempted to instil a commitment to learning and the materialist tradition in Alberto by compelling him to take daily lessons in addition to his schoolwork. However, Alberto found this training, which was conducted with militaristic determination by his father, increasingly irksome, and turned instead to children's literature, with its tales of exploration and adventure.[1]

Manoel Cavalcanti's dedication to French intellectual culture was later to have a profound impact on Alberto. However, it was his mother's influence which was ultimately to shape his character most strongly. Alberto and Dona Ana were extremely close, and later Dona Ana would accompany Alberto when he left Brazil for England, Switzerland and France. When Alberto went to England in 1934, he lived with his mother until her death in 1945,[2] and this degree of closeness to his mother was later to shape Alberto's personality significant ways.

The earliest formative influences on Cavalcanti stemmed from this combination of intellectual rationalism, inherited from his father and influenced by French intellectual culture, and the maternal, feminine and conservative atmosphere which dominated the home through his mother, his grandmother Leocádia, and his two aunts (his mother's sisters) Manuela and Elisa. Cavalcanti spoke about growing up in a house filled with "positivism and old women",[3] and it seems that the household was dominated by Dona Ana and the matriarchal figure of Leocádia, who lived well into her nineties and whose "opinions were orders".[4] Cavalcanti's early childhood in this house of women and Comtean rationalism was a happy one, and the family enjoyed prosperous times, sustained by Manoel's salary from the Escola Militar, whilst Alberto was cosseted by Madalena, the black maidservant employed by Dona Ana. The house which the Cavalcantis occupied on the Rua Dona Marciana was large, with an even larger garden, and the family enjoyed good relations with neighbouring families. To complete the picture of an idyllic childhood, Alberto and his brother Milo even studied at a local public school which was situated on the beach.[5]

However, this idyllic situation changed suddenly and dramatically for the worse when Manoel became ill, and was forced to resign from his post. From then onwards, the Cavalcantis struggled to remain financially solvent, and Manoel was even forced to sell his beloved library. Soon, the house which had been full of books on positivism and mathematics was empty, and the books were dispatched to the far north of Brazil, never to be seen again. His father's sudden and calamitous illness and his mother's unstinting devotion to her husband thereafter marked Alberto's personality deeply, creating strong bonds between the three of them, and linking him particularly closely to his mother.

In 1908, at the age of eleven, Alberto entered the Colégio Militar which, according to Hermilo Borba Filho, was the only suitable destination for a child from such a traditional family as the Cavalcantis.[6] However, Alberto found the regime at the Colégio too strictly regulated for his liking, and, above all, he realised that he did not want to pursue a career in the military. Accordingly, in 1913, and at the age of sixteen, he persuaded his parents to allow him to transfer to the Faculty of Law at the Escola Politécnica at Rio de Janeiro. It was here that Alberto's interest in the arts first became stimulated, and where he gained his first experience of the cinema when he saw films starring the Swedish actress Asta Nielsen and the French comedian Max Linder.[7]

However, Alberto was soon in trouble at the Politécnica when, in a moment of youthful indiscretion, he was caught caricaturing one of the professors after being given a low mark for an essay on the philosophy of law. Alberto was expelled from class as a result of this behaviour, and Manoel then withdrew him from the Politécnica together.[8] Shortly after these events, and after a consideration of

Alberto's examination results from military college revealed a predisposition for the arts rather than law, Manoel and Dona Ana took the decision to send Alberto to Europe in order to study architecture.[9]

Later that year, Alberto left Brazil for Switzerland, where he studied architecture at L'École Technique de Fribourg. At Fribourg, situated between Bern and Lausanne, and within easy reach of Geneva and Milan, Alberto began to discover European culture at first hand for the first time, and made frequent visits to theatres, cinemas and art galleries in Geneva and Milan. Alberto left Fribourg in 1914 at the age of seventeen, in order to study architecture and art at L'École des Beaux Arts in Geneva. He was joined in Geneva by Manoel, Dona Ana, his brother Milo, and Madalena, to whom Alberto was particularly attached. This demonstrates how close the Cavalcantis were as a family, and how determined they were to remain together, despite the problems caused by what were the first of many manifestations of Alberto's characteristically nomadic inclinations. After obtaining his diploma in Geneva, Cavalcanti went on to study at L'École des Beaux Arts in Paris, and also registered at the Sorbonne, where he studied aesthetics. However, he left L'École des Beaux Arts after only a year, seemingly unwilling to cope with the constraints and disciplines of student life.[10]

Cavalcanti's decision to terminate his studies prematurely was significant and shaped his future development. One consequence of his decision to leave L'École des Beaux Arts and the Sorbonne was that he did not receive the kind of systematic education which would have provided a sound basis for his future development as an intellectual and cultural figure. His decision to cease studying was motivated by a desire to put the knowledge he had already acquired into practice, rather than to continue to engage in intellectual enquiry. From this point onwards, Cavalcanti's reputation as an educated man with a knowledge of European culture, a reputation which was later to impress those with whom he worked in the British film industry, was to be based largely on his own efforts at self-improvement. For better or worse, this meant that he did not enter into his maturity ideally equipped to become a major thinker or intellectual.

After spending some time looking for work, Cavalcanti eventually succeeded in gaining employment with the Parisian architect Alfred Agache, who was then developing an urban planning scheme for areas around Rio de Janeiro.[11] Cavalcanti did well in Agache's agency, but his family's financial situation continued to deteriorate, and, as a consequence, he was forced to leave Agache in order to take up a more prestigious and better paid post at the Compagnie des Arts Français, an organisation which traded in the import and export of French fine art and artefacts. Following this change of profession from architect to cultural entrepreneur, Cavalcanti conceived the ambitious idea returning to Brazil in order to establish a branch of the Compagnie Arts Français in Rio de Janeiro. Again, the main motive for decision appears to have been the need to raise money in or-support his family. However, the venture turned out to be a complete failure – an early indication, perhaps, of the lack of financial and business acumen which was to blight his career, particularly in its latter years.[12]

The disastrous failure of the experiment in Rio de Janeiro had important consequences for Cavalcanti, plunging his family into financial difficulties, and ending his embryonic career as architect and cultural entrepreneur. After four months, during which Alberto – the family's only breadwinner – was unable to generate any real income, and during which frequent and heated family discussions took place on how to resolve the situation, Manoel eventually managed to find him a highly implausible position: that of diplomatic aide in the Brazilian Consulate in Liverpool. This radical new direction was to be the third change of career for Alberto in as many years, and was also further to consolidate his nomadic inclinations. In the midst of these unlikely developments, however, and, before leaving for Britain, an event occurred which was to prove crucial for his career as a filmmaker.

In 1919, at a cinema in Rio de Janeiro, Cavalcanti saw Marcel L'Herbier's first major film, *Rose-France*. Produced by Gaumont with the assistance of the French military authorities, it was a heady mixture of nationalist propaganda, melodrama and "*fin-de-siècle* symbolism".[13] Like L'Herbier's second film for Gaumont, *Le Carnaval des vérités* (*The Carnival of Truths*, 1920), *Rose-France* was essentially a fantasy film, and one of a number of such to emerge from Gaumont between 1918 and 1922.[14] Although released after the war, and losing much of its topical appeal as a consequence, *Rose-France* was warmly praised by critics, and Cavalcanti was also strongly impressed by the film when he saw it in Rio de Janeiro. However, what struck him most, as a recent student of architectural design, was the realisation that, for all its qualities, *Rose-France* lacked appropriate and effective set designs. In an act of youthful enthusiasm, Cavalcanti wrote to L'Herbier, setting out his thoughts about *Rose-France*, the cinema and set design, although without much expectation of receiving a reply. However, to his delight, L'Herbier did respond and, moreover, he invited Cavalcanti to join him in France.[15]

In the meantime, Alberto and his family packed their bags again and left for Liverpool. There they felt completely out of place, and Alberto experienced particular difficulties in associating with the English and Brazilian personnel within the Consulate. The one exception to this was the Consul General, Dario Freire, who displayed the type of conservative *gravitas* which appealed to the Cavalcantis, and who was later to play a decisive role in the development of Alberto's career as a filmmaker. Alberto now felt himself completely cut ff from the kind of cultural life he had experienced in Paris, and his ͜sponse to this intellectual isolation was to go to the cinema as ⅂ularly as he could and, for the first time, and possibly with his ⅂t correspondence with L'Herbier in mind, critically examine the that he saw. However, whatever his avant-garde inclinations might have been at that point, it was mainly popular American cinema which he saw in Liverpool.

It was in the following, very harsh winter when Manoel Cavalcanti died. It was a sad time for the remaining Cavalcantis, and the family were particularly unhappy that, because of their financial circumstances, Manoel would have to be buried in Liverpool, a city which he had disliked, rather than in the family burial plot in northeastern Brazil. Shortly after Manoel's death, Dona Ana returned to Brazil with Milo in order to attend to the necessary legal matters, leaving Alberto behind. There followed one of the most unhappy periods in Cavalcanti's life. Alone in Liverpool, a city which he was later to describe as "an abomination",[16] and deprived of contact with both his father and his mother, from whom he had previously been inseparable, he became increasingly depressed about his predicament as a foreigner, forced to work in a profession in which he had no interest, and increasingly pessimistic about the chances of improving his situation.

Then, when things seemed to be at their worst, Cavalcanti was unexpectedly presented with the opportunity he needed, in the shape of a letter from Marcel L'Herbier, who had just founded a film company in Paris, Cinégraphic Films. In his letter, L'Herbier reiterated his earlier invitation and proposed that Cavalcanti come to work for him as a set designer. Cavalcanti immediately sought an audience with Dario Freire and pleaded with him to be allowed to leave the embassy in order to join L'Herbier in Paris. Rather surprisingly, Freire agreed and even offered to pay Cavalcanti's salary for a year, on condition that he chaperon Freire's two daughters, who were then staying in a Parisian boarding-house. However, Freire also held Cavalcanti to an agreement that, if he had not found suitable employment within twelve months, he must return to the Consulate in Liverpool.[17] Unsurprisingly, Cavalcanti quickly agreed to these conditions, and found himself with one year at his disposal in which to make or break his career as a filmmaker.

Cavalcanti returned to Paris with his mother in 1923, and went straight to work for L'Herbier. When he arrived at Cinégraphic, L'Herbier was making *Le Marchand de plaisirs* (*The Merchant of Pleasures*, 1923), and Cavalcanti took the opportunity to learn as much as he could as quickly as possible. He then went on to work with L'Herbier on a number of films between 1923 and 1926, including *The Merchant of Pleasures*, *Résurrection* (1922), *Don Juan et Faust* (1923), *L'Inhumaine* (*The Inhuman*, 1924) and *Feu Mathias Pascal* (*The Late Mathias Pascal*, 1925). This involvement with L'Herbier provided a platform for Cavalcanti's later development as a filmmaker, and L'Herbier's films also influenced Cavalcanti's early French films in a number of ways.

Although described as "perhaps the most consistently impressionist director", L'Herbier's films span a range of different genres.[18] As already mentioned, his first films – *Rose-France* and *The Carnival of Truths* – were influenced by Symbolism and Expressionism

However, his L'Homme du large (The Man of the Ocean, 1920) was grounded in the early realist tradition associated with figures such as André Antoine and Louis Delluc. The influence of 19th-century realism and naturalism on early French cinema is well-known. Prior to 1914, a tradition of location-shooting flourished in France, inspired by the novels of Emile Zola.[19] The first film versions of novels by Zola appeared as early as 1903, with Ferdinand Zecca and Lucien Nonguet's La Grève (The Strike, 1903) and Au Pays noir (In the Black Country, 1905), both adaptations of Zola's Germinal (1885). André Antoine began his career in the theatre, founding the Théâtre Libre (1887-96) and then the Théâtre Antoine (1897-1906) before beginning to direct films from 1914. He also adopted a naturalist style based on location-shooting in his films – La Terre (Earth, 1921), for example, is an adaptation of Zola's novel of the same name.

After the war, this realist tradition was reinvigorated, and directors such as Antoine, L'Herbier, Mercanton, Baroncelli, Delluc, Epstein, Gance, Renoir, Feyder and Cavalcanti worked productively within it. L'Herbier's The Man of the Ocean clearly falls within this tradition. Set and shot on the Normandy coast, it was part of a subgenre of films which focused on the relationship between regional communities and the power and grandeur of nature. Stylistically, this genre was also influenced by Impressionist painting, and particularly by the work of Millet, Corot and other members of the Barbizon School.[20] This realist tradition continued throughout the 1920s, and culminated in the work of the documentary avant-garde, in films such as Dmitri Kirsanoff's Ménilmontant (1926), Jean Grémillon's Tour au large (A Journey on the Ocean, 1927), and Cavalcanti's Rien que les heures (Nothing But the Hours, 1926) and En rade (Stranded, 1927).[21] It also influenced the development of the "city symphony" genre which appeared throughout Europe during the 1920s. For example, René Hervil's Paris (1924), a film which can be situated within the realist tradition, predated and influenced later works such as Nothing But the Hours, Berlin – Die Symphonie einer Großstadt (Berlin – Symphony of a Great City, Walter Ruttmann, 1927) and Čelovek s kinoapparatom (Man With a Movie Camera, Dziga Vertov, 1929) by a number of years.

Although essentially based in an aestheticised pictorial realism, The Man of the Ocean also contains features, such as subjective camera shots and optical effects, which can be identified with more avant-gardist cinematic practices, and L'Herbier's next three films, El Dorado (1921), Don Juan et Faust and The Inhuman, went even further along this more modernist direction, to some extent abandoning the realist tradition which had influenced The Man of the Ocean.[22] The Inhuman also marked a new departure for L'Herbier. Unlike his previous films, which had all been produced and financed by Gaumont, The Inhuman was made by L'Herbier's newly-established production company, Cinégraphic, and can be associated with the genre of the "studio spectacular", which evolved in the mid-1920s and was designed in order to break into the international – and particularly the American –

market. The basic subject-matter in these films was that of the young Parisian *nouveau riche* at play in nightclubs and restaurants, and the films took every opportunity to showcase the latest French designs and fashions. As with many of these films, *The Inhuman* was made almost entirely with American money and an international cast, and was a "fantasy of internationalism that denied the specificity of French culture and acceded to the hegemony of the American cinema".[23]

Although *The Inhuman* can be situated within the relatively superficial genre of the studio spectacular, it was a much more complex and ambitious work than most of the other films which fell into this category. For example, L'Herbier used the film's science-fiction plot as a pretext to experiment with the stylistic repertoire of cinematic impressionism. In addition, the sets, designed by Cavalcanti and the painter Fernand Léger, were deliberately extravagant and symbolic, and the film has even been described as "arguably the first great example in the narrative cinema of the so-called post-modernist aesthetic", because of its use of pastiche, parody and quotation.[24] Postmodern masterpiece or not, Cavalcanti had serious misgivings about his involvement with this film – as will be made clear later.

After *The Inhuman*, L'Herbier made what has been described as "the biggest fantasy film of the decade", *The Late Mathias Pascal*, based on Luigi Pirandello's novel, *Il fu Mattia Pascal* (1903).[25] Although *The Late Mathias Pascal* was far less extravagant than *The Inhuman*, it was exemplary of the French Impressionist avant-garde cinema in its combination of linear naturalistic narration and the exploration of subjective modes of representation. *The Late Mathias Pascal* is essentially concerned with notions of freedom and identity, and L'Herbier uses cinematic devices such as slow-motion, rapid juxtapositions and collisions of images to represent these notions.[26] The sets within the film, designed by Cavalcanti, also use multiple framing devices which suggest constraining environments, and which function as extensions of the states of mind experienced by the central characters, providing "an objective correlative that relates both a psychological state and an ideological problem to an exterior manifestation or symbol".[27] In addition to these modernist features, *The Late Mathias Pascal* continues the earlier pictorialist naturalist tradition embodied in films such as *The Man of the Ocean*.[28] In general, and over this period, L'Herbier's films exhibit both a reliance on the realist tradition and a concern to explore the formal properties of the medium, and it was this combination of realism and cinematic impressionism which was to influence Cavalcanti's first attempts at filmmaking when he came to direct *Nothing But the Hours* and *Stranded*.

As already mentioned, Cavalcanti's first venture into filmmaking was as an observer on the set of L'Herbier's *The Merchant of Pleasures*. His first active participation in a film was as a set designer and assistant director on L'Herbier's next film, *Résurrection*. During the course of this production, Cavalcanti also met the actress

Eve Francis, who had previously featured in both L'Herbier's *El Dorado* and Delluc's *La Femme de nulle part* (*The Woman from Nowhere*, 1921). *The Woman from Nowhere* had been a commercial failure and, as a consequence, Delluc was experiencing difficulty in raising finance for further film production. In order to aid his friend, L'Herbier offered Delluc the opportunity to direct *L'Inondation* (*The Flood*, 1923), and Francis then persuaded Delluc to appoint Cavalcanti as the film's set designer. Like L'Herbier's *The Man of the Ocean*, *The Flood* also drew on the pictorialist naturalist tradition, to some extent abandoning the style of modernist impressionism then being practised in the films of directors such as Abel Gance and Germaine Dulac.[29] The experience of working on *The Flood* and *Résurrection* had an important impact on Cavalcanti, and ensured that his earliest work in the cinema as a director was firmly grounded within the realist tradition.

However, and in stark contrast to *The Flood*, Cavalcanti's next project with L'Herbier was the science-fiction extravaganza *The Inhuman*, on which he worked as set designer alongside Léger and the designer Claude Autant-Lara. However, Cavalcanti was uncomfortable with the film's eccentric combination of French fashion displays, impressionist trickery and absurd plot, and also disapproved of its overt commercialism, which conflicted with his own developing convictions concerning the importance of the film medium as an art form.[30] Despite his reservations, however, Cavalcanti was unable to influence L'Herbier's plans for *The Inhuman*, and this lack of influence, and disagreement over the subject-matter of the film were to mark the beginning of the end of their collaboration.[31]

After *The Inhuman*, Cavalcanti worked as a set designer and assistant director on *La Galerie des monstres* (*The Gallery of Monsters*, Jacque Catelain, 1924). Following this, he worked as an assistant director, set designer and, for a short period, principal director on *The Late Mathias Pascal*. It was whilst filming this film that Cavalcanti's disillusionment with L'Herbier, which had first become apparent during the production of *The Inhuman*, began to re-emerge. As assistant director, he found it increasingly difficult to cope with L'Herbier's tendency to improvise during shooting, a practice which made strategic planning difficult, and which created organisational problems which became his responsibility to resolve.[32] However, his problems were unexpectedly eased when L'Herbier left the set in order to attend conferences in Rome and Madrid. Cavalcanti then took over as principal director of the film,[33] an elevation which marked an important new stage in his development as a filmmaker: the beginning of his career as a director.

After *The Late Mathias Pascal*, the co-producer of the film, the White Russian Oskar Kamenka, aware of the extent of Cavalcanti's contribution to the film's successful completion, invited him to direct his first feature film, *Un Chapeau de paille d'Italie* (*An Italian Straw Hat*, 1927), for his Albatros company. However, the project was then taken from Cavalcanti, and given to the more senior and experienced

René Clair, who was also involved with Kamenka and who had demanded to be awarded the project.[34] Following this, Cavalcanti was asked to submit a script for a production by Sasex, a production house founded by the White Russian emigré community in Paris. Cavalcanti accepted the invitation and suggested an adaptation of Pirandello's *Lontano*. However, Sasex collapsed before production could commence, and the film was never made.[35] Despite these set-backs, Cavalcanti became closely involved with the large emigré White Russian community in Paris during this period, an involvement strengthened by his friendship with Ivan Mosjoukine, the principal actor in *The Late Mathias Pascal*. Like the Russians, Cavalcanti also felt something of an outsider in France, and this caused him to identify with them and form a number of long-lasting friendships.

Cavalcanti's final project before directing a film himself was *Voyage au Congo* (*Voyage to the Congo*, 1927), a documentary directed by Marc Allégret. Earlier that year, Allégret had travelled through the Congo with his uncle, the writer André Gide, filming as they went. On his return, Gide saw *Nothing But the Hours* and asked Cavalcanti to edit the footage he had brought back from the Congo. Cavalcanti agreed to this, largely out of respect for Gide's reputation as a writer, but found the editing difficult because of the uneven quality of the material with which he had to work.[36] *Voyage to the Congo* was a collaborative work produced by Allégret, Gide and Cavalcanti, and was one of a group of films made between 1925 and 1930 which have been described as "avant-garde documentaries", and which include André Sauvage's *Etudes sur Paris* (1928) and Jean Vigo's *A Propos de Nice* (1930).[37] The principal importance of *Voyage to the Congo* in relation to Cavalcanti's later development as a filmmaker lies in the fact that it constituted his first real engagement with the documentary film *per se*.

By 1926, Cavalcanti had gained experience as a director, producer, set designer and editor on a range of films, from commercial "super-productions" to independently-produced documentaries. He had also become familiar with the work of directors such as Clair, Delluc and L'Herbier, and was beginning to formulate an approach to filmmaking grounded in the traditions of French realism and impressionism. He was consequently in a position to direct his first two films: *Nothing But the Hours* and *Stranded*.

Notes

[1]   Hermilo Borba Filho, "Une vie (1953)", in Lorenzo Pellizzari and Claudio M Valentinetti (eds), *Alberto Cavalcanti* (Locarno: Éditions du Festival international du film de Locarno, 1988): 90. The book was later published in Portuguese as *Alberto Cavalcanti: Pontos sobre o Brazil* (São Paulo: Instituto Lina Bo e P M Bardi, 1995). All subsequent references here are from the original 1988 publication.

[2]   Claudio M Valentinetti, "Les origines et le cinéma français (1897-1928)", in Pellizzari and Valentinetti (eds): 13.

3   Translated from the French: "Il y régnait une atmosphère de vieilles dames, d'histoires guerrières, de positivisme et de leçons à apprendre". Ibid: 13.

4   Translated from the French: "ses opinions étaient des ordres". Filho, in Pellizzari and Valentinetti (eds): 90.

5   Ibid: 92-93.

6   Ibid: 95.

7   Valentinetti, in Pellizzari and Valentinetti (eds): 14.

8   Charles Drazin, *The Finest Years: British Cinema of the 1940s* (London: André Deutsch, 1998): 113.

9   Valentinetti, in Pellizzari and Valentinetti (eds): 15.

10   Ibid: 17.

11   Ibid.

12   Filho, in Pellizzari and Valentinetti (eds): 113.

13   Alan Williams, *Republic of Images: A History of French Filmmaking* (Cambridge, MA; London: Harvard University Press, 1992): 104.

14   Richard Abel, *French Cinema: The First Wave, 1915-1929* (Princeton, NJ: Princeton University Press, 1984): 144.

15   Filho, in Pellizzari and Valentinetti (eds): 116.

16   Translated from the French: "La ville était une abomination". Ibid.

17   Ibid: 119.

18   Williams: 103.

19   Leo Braudy, *Jean Renoir: The World of His Films* (London: Robson Books, 1977): 26.

20   Abel: 97.

21   Ibid: 137.

22   Williams: 105.

23   Abel: 206.

24   Williams: 105.

25   Abel: 144.

26   Allen Thiher, *The Cinematic Muse: Critical Studies in the History of French Cinema* (Columbia; London: University of Missouri Press, 1979): 19.

27   Ibid.

28   Ibid: 18.

29   Williams: 99.

[30]   Noureddine Ghali, *L'Avant-Garde Cinématographique en France dans les Années Vingt: Idées, Conceptions, Théories* (Paris: Éditions Paris Expérimental, 1995): 107.

[31]   Filho, in Pellizzari and Valentinetti (eds): 121.

[32]   Ibid: 123.

[33]   Alberto Cavalcanti, "O Cenógrafo", in *Filme e Realidade* third edition (Rio de Janeiro: Editora Artenova, in collaboration with Empresa Brasileira de Filmes – Embrafilme, 1977): 126. Originally published in 1952.

[34]   Filho, in Pellizzari and Valentinetti (eds): 128.

[35]   Ibid.

[36]   Ibid: 138.

[37]   Translated from the French: "documentaires avant-gardes". Ghali: 44.

2

The French Avant-Garde: *Rien que les heures,* *En rade* and Other Films

Before turning to an analysis of Cavalcanti's two avant-garde films, it is first necessary to situate them within the constellation of filmmaking and film theory which made up the avant-garde of the time. As already mentioned, the French narrative avant-garde cinema emerged from an earlier tradition of filmmaking which has been described as pictorialist naturalism.[1] Influenced by 19th-century traditions of realism, naturalism and impressionism, this tradition was characterised by a concern for landscape and the picturesque.[2] More specifically, films such as L'Herbier's *L'Homme du large* (*The Man of the Ocean,* 1920), Louis Mercanton's *L'Appel du sang* (*The Call of Blood,* 1920) and Jacques de Baroncelli's *Ramuntcho* (1919) can be related to what Linda Nochlin has referred to as the tradition of "picturesque regional genre painting".[3] Many of these films, shot on location in regions such as Provence, Brittany and the Auvergne, attempt to invoke a landscape's atmosphere through a series of evocative impressions, and are centrally concerned with the relationship between regional communities and the natural environment.

A sense of lyricism, as well as veneration of the power and beauty of nature, pervades these films, as, for example, in Baroncelli's series of mountain films, or Antoine's *La Terre* (*Earth,* 1921), which draws on the pictorial lyricism of the Barbizon School, and the paintings of Millet and Corot in particular. In addition to what might be referred to as an "animated impressionism", clearly influenced by Impressionist and post-Impressionist painting, these films draw on subject-matter from the naturalist tradition. So, for example, L'Herbier's *The Man of the Ocean,* Antoine's *Earth,* Epstein's *La Belle Nivernaise* (*The Beautiful Nivernaise,* 1924) and Feyder's *Crainquebille* (*Old Bill of Paris,* 1922) all deal with typical naturalist issues of entrapment, obsession, mental illness and abuse.

The first French avant-garde, the French Impressionist school, although differing in significant respects from this tradition of naturalist pictorialism, also emerged from it, and the key development in the transition from one movement to the other lay in the use of film to evoke subjective experience, as well as mood and feeling. The transition can be seen in films such as Epstein's *The Beautiful*

Nivernaise which, in addition to evoking the spirit of a landscape, contains subjective point-of-view shots which express the state of mind of the principal characters. Similarly, an increasingly common concern with the representation of subjective experience can be found in films such as Epstein's *L'Affiche* (*The Poster*, 1925) and Abel Gance's *La Roue* (*The Wheel*, 1923).[4]

French cinematic impressionism, the school of cinema within which Cavalcanti began his filmmaking career, was influenced by 19th-century Symbolism, and this antecedent distinguished it as a movement from the naturalist pictorialist tradition of filmmaking, which was primarily influenced by 19th-century realism and naturalism. More specifically, cinematic impressionism can be associated with the late Symbolist aesthetic of Mallarmé, which emphasised the work of art's capacity for rendering the subjective vision of the artist through evocation, symbolic allusion and suggestion.[5] Epstein, for example, defined cinematic impressionism as an "aesthetic of approximation and the indefinite".[6]

This neo-Symbolist conception of art also privileged the importance of the artist's vision and imagination, and the Impressionists believed that, for film to evolve into a genuine art form, the filmmaker must transform the material reality before him or her in some revelatory fashion.[7] This degree of transformation necessitated a departure from the realistic style of the naturalist pictorialist tradition, in which the filmic representation of the external world retained a considerable degree of verisimilitude, and the emphasis on the transformative power of imagination and the need to render subjective experience led to the appearance of distorted images of external reality in impressionist films. In company with avant-garde movements such as *cinéma pur*, cinematic impressionism advocated an exploration of the specific properties of the medium of film for expressive ends, although, unlike *cinéma pur*, this was generally pursued as a means of expressing subjective experience and vision, rather than as an end in itself.[8]

One of the most fundamental concepts within cinematic impressionism was that of *photogénie*. Louis Delluc, whose book, *Photogénie*, was published in 1920, argued that the source of *photogénie* was located in the ability of the moving image to render an object in an expressive way,[9] whilst René Clair argued that *photogénie* was based in the transformative power of the camera. Through this power, he argued, "there is no detail of reality which cannot be extended here into the realm of the wondrous".[10] *Photogénie* was, therefore, a latent force within the moving image. However, "true" *photogénie* emerged when this latent material was used to express the vision of the filmmaker.

In addition to *photogénie*, two other important impressionist categories, both of which influenced Cavalcanti, were those of musical rhythm and musical structure. Impressionist film technique was grounded in musical rhythm, and this provided the basis for a style which emphasised rhythmic editing. This was also the basis for the rapid montage techniques for which impressionist films are perhaps most well-known. After 1923, and influenced by Gance's *The Wheel*, more films began to appear which included fast rhythmic editing, including Epstein's *L'Auberge rouge* (*The Red Inn*, 1923) and *The Beautiful Nivernaise*, L'Herbier's *L'Inhumaine* (*The Inhuman*, 1924) and *Feu Mathias Pascal* (*The Late Mathias Pascal*, 1925), Kirsanoff's *Ménilmontant* (1926) and Gance's *Napoléon* (1927).[11] However, as early as 1924, Epstein was arguing that rhythmic editing had become a superficial and clichéd cinematic device,[12] whilst Clair proclaimed that the whole cinematic model of impressionism, with its rapid editing, optical effects and cinematic trickery, had become "false art".[13]

By 1926, the aesthetic model of impressionism was beginning to fragment under the impact of a variety of pressures and changing circumstances. One of these was the stylistic diffusion which followed from the emergence of a number of small independent production companies after 1924. Until then all the impressionists had been employed in major production companies. However, in 1924, L'Herbier established Cinégraphic, Gance established Films Abel Gance, and Epstein established Les Films de Jean Epstein, whilst Renoir, Kirsanoff and Dulac also began to finance their own films.[14] This new context of relative freedom from commercial constraint influenced the stylistic diffusion which occurred after 1925, and many of the films produced after this, including those by Renoir, Kirsanoff, Epstein, Dulac and Cavalcanti, were shorter, more esoteric and more elliptical.[15]

The stylistic unity of impressionism was also fractured by the appearance of other modernist movements after 1926. For example, the impressionist concern with cinematic specificity and the centrality of rhythmic structures led to the development of *cinéma pur*, and to the emergence of films such as *Thèmes et Variations* (Dulac, 1928) which were primarily concerned with issues of formal composition and experimentation. Other modernist movements which also appeared in the late-1920s included Surrealism and Dada, and relations between modernist independents such as Luis Buñuel, Salvador Dalí, Germaine Dulac and Jean Cocteau, and impressionist filmmakers such as Gance and L'Herbier, were often strained.[16] The period between 1923 and 1928, in which figures such as Clair, Léger, Chomette, Dulac, Man Ray, Allégret and Cavalcanti were active, was a particularly diverse one, and, after 1928, Surrealism emerged as the most important movement. After 1930, this period of cultural proliferation came to an end as the avant-garde went into decline, primarily as a result of the arrival of the sound film, and the consequent rationalisation of the French film industry.[17]

Before turning to an analysis of *Rien que les heures* (*Nothing But the Hours*, 1926), one final category of films which must be considered is the group of poetic documentaries produced by directors such as Allégret, Sauvage, Vigo and Cavalcanti himself. *Nothing But the Hours* can be grouped alongside six other avant-garde documentaries made between 1925 and 1930. The other films were

Voyage au Congo (*Voyage to the Congo*, Allégret, 1927), *Etudes sur Paris* (Sauvage, 1928), *La Zone* (Georges Lacombe, 1928), *Nogent, Eldorado du dimanche* (Marcel Carné, 1929) and *A Propos de Nice* (Vigo, 1930). The documentary flourished in France during the second half of the 1920s, and theories about documentary aesthetics circulated freely between avant-garde filmmakers. For example, André Sauvage developed an approach to avant-garde documentary realism based on an objection to the categorical use of the term "documentaire".[18] Discussing Flaherty's *Nanook of the North* (1922), Sauvage argued that "documentaire" was a "vulgar" ("vulgaire") word, and that it would be more appropriate to use a term such as "poetic realism" when addressing such a film.[19] He also argued that no substantive distinctions should be made between the documentary and other types of filmmaking.

Nanook of the North was one of the key influences on the development of this genre of French poetic documentary filmmaking. For example, the filmmaker and critic Hubert Revol argued in 1930 that documentary films were an expression of "pure cinema" ("cinéma pur") and of a "poetic cinema" ("cinéma poétique"), and that *Nanook of the North* provided the model for the future development of the genre – a genre consisting of "visual poems which [would] touch the spectator through the beauty of their images":

> Documentary must be made by poets. Few of those within French cinema have understood that in our country we possess innumerable elements and subjects to make, not just insignificant ribbons [of film], but splendid lively and expressive films...The purest demonstration of pure cinema, that is to say of poetry which is truly cinematographic, has been provided for us by some remarkable films, vulgarly called documentaries...particularly *Nanook* and *Moana*.[20]

In addition to this belief in documentary as "pure cinema", Revol, Canudo and others believed that documentary films such as *Nanook of the North* and *Moana* (Flaherty, 1926) were particularly suited to represent the "formidable power" of natural forces, and that the relationship between documentary and the natural world was an important consideration for these filmmakers.[21]

Although critics and filmmakers such as Sauvage, Canudo and Revol were influenced by cinematic impressionism, they were even more influenced by pictorialist naturalism. This influence is revealed in Canudo's claim that the "mission of documentary" was "to show man's relationship with the world around him".[22] Such a mission clearly draws on the French naturalist and realist tradition, and illustrates the extent to which these documentaries constituted a bridge between impressionist modernism and naturalist pictorialism. Unlike cinematic impressionism, however, the concern with subjectivity in these films is mediated by the desire to evoke a poetic external reality, often located in the urban milieu of Paris. For example, Jean Dréville argued that it was in the documentary, rather than in the fiction film, that *photogénie* could best be realised, and he argued that Walter Ruttmann's *Berlin – Symphony of a Great City* (1927) "brought out the photogénie of urban life".[23] Here Dréville equates both documentary and *photogénie* with what Revol called "pure cinema".

As these statements suggest, the documentary provided an ideal form for the synthesis of the two traditions of pictorialist naturalism and impressionism, and the documentary style which emerged from this union was characterised by interlacing visual effects, impressionistic delineations of the urban or rural environment, indeterminate narrative structures, and fluid camerawork and montage, all of which were arrayed in order to create poetic and expressive effects. In these films, as in impressionist films, reality was transformed by the filmmaker using film technique, but the use of documentary footage also ensured that it was a primarily external, rather than a subjective, world which was evoked.

The constellation of filmmaking which existed in France between 1923 and 1930 provides the context within which Cavalcanti's films must be situated. It was a context in which impressionism was beginning to lose its stylistic coherence, and in which new modernist movements were emerging. Cavalcanti's films were made against this background of increasing stylistic diversity and divergence, and against both the gradual decline of the avant-garde and structural changes taking place within the French film industry. This unstable context, situated between the established aesthetic theory and practice of impressionism, and the emergence of the sound film, made it difficult for filmmakers such as Cavalcanti to form systematic approaches to their practice, and this was reflected in the films they made between 1926 and 1934.

Rien que les heures (*Nothing But the Hours*, 1926)

After working for L'Herbier on *Résurrection* (1922), *The Inhuman* and *The Late Mathias Pascal*, Cavalcanti began work on his first directed film, *Le Train sans yeux* (*The Train Without Eyes*, 1926), which was produced by Pierre Braunberger's Néo-Film company. *The Train Without Eyes* was based on a scenario by Louis Delluc, and was originally to have been directed by Julien Duvivier.[24] However, Duvivier withdrew from the project when he left Néo-Film in 1925 in order to join another production company, Film d'Art, and the commission was then handed over to Cavalcanti.[25] Shot in Germany at the Berlin Babelsburg Studios, *The Train Without Eyes* was withheld from distribution until 1928 because of Néo-Film's inability to cover the costs of using the studio. This was a disappointment for Cavalcanti, but he responded by immediately beginning to develop a second project, and so began work on the script of what would eventually become *Nothing But the Hours*. The finished film, which cost only FF35 000 to make, was premièred at the Studio des Ursulines in 1926, before being shown at the Film Society in London in 1928.[26]

Like *The Train Without Eyes*, *Nothing But the Hours* was produced by Pierre Braunberger. Braunberger regarded himself as an enlightened, idealistic entrepreneur, committed to the enhancement of French film culture.[27] He maintained close contact with the avant-garde during the 1920s, and in 1927 founded what may have been the world's first avant-garde film distribution house, Studio Film, and a production company, Néo-Film, which was committed to avant-garde filmmaking.[28] During the 1920s, Braunberger produced and distributed films by Cavalcanti, Ray, Dulac and Allégret, and played a significant role in assisting these and other filmmakers.[29] Braunberger first came into contact with Cavalcanti when he distributed Allégret's *Voyage to the Congo*, which Cavalcanti had edited. Braunberger went on to produce Cavalcanti's *The Train Without Eyes*, *Nothing But the Hours* (both 1926), *En rade* (*Stranded*), *Yvette* and *La P'tite Lilie* (all 1927).

Nothing But the Hours opens with an intertitle stating that "this film does not need a story, it is no more than a series of impressions on time passing".[30] Despite this assertion, however, *Nothing But the Hours* does contain a story, and it can be distinguished from a film such as Joris Ivens' *Regen* (*Rain*, 1929), which *is* structured in terms of a series of impressions.[31] Like later "city symphony" films such as Walter Ruttmann's *Berlin – Symphony of a Great City* and Dziga Vertov's *Čelovek s kinoapparatom* (*Man With a Movie Camera*, 1929), *Nothing But the Hours* is also structured chronologically. However, it differs from these films in two important respects. Firstly, *Nothing But the Hours* does not attempt to represent the experience of the city as a whole, as these other films do, but only part of that experience, that associated with the depiction and observation of a lumpenproletariat underclass. Secondly, *Nothing But the Hours* does not employ the dawn-till-dusk chronology typical of the city symphony films in a consistent or logical manner. Throughout the film, close-ups of a clock-face indicate the changing of the hours. However, these changes are neither chronological nor logical. For example, a shot of a clock showing 12.00 sometimes changes to one showing 13.00, and sometimes to one showing 24.00, yet no explanation is given for these discrepancies.

As mentioned above, in addition to its impressionistic evocation of the life of the city, *Nothing But the Hours* has a distinct narrative structure, containing characterisation and dramatic development. Within this, a number of characters can also be discerned, whose primary function appears to be to reinforce the central thesis of the film, which is that, underlying the apparently civilised façade of bourgeois society, there exists a darker reality marked by violence, inequality and brutality. This thesis, which is represented metaphorically in other sections of the film, is given substance through its embodiment in these characters, and in the sub-plot of criminality, violence and victimisation which gradually emerges around them in the latter half of the film.

The central characters in *Nothing But the Hours* are a prostitute, her pimp, a sailor, an old lame woman, and a female newspaper vendor. Initially, these characters are presented without connection to each other, and are integrated into the general flux of visual impressions which make up the film. However, connections between the characters begin to occur after about two thirds of the film have elapsed. One exception to this is the character of the old lame woman, who is first seen dragging herself forlornly through a narrow alley-way. At this point in the film, the old woman is represented alongside a series of other images which denote aspects of urban squalor, and her relationship to the other characters in the film remains unclear.

The next character to be introduced is the prostitute, who is seen soliciting in the street. This scene is followed by more images of urban wretchedness, including shots of foraging rats and rotting rubbish. The pimp is then shown for the first time, and, after another series of shots symbolising the unsavoury reality of bourgeois society, the newsvendor is shown selling her newspapers. This is followed by another series of shots of sleeping alcoholics, dead cats and other urban detritus. After this, the newsvendor is shown approaching a fortune-teller. To the newsvendor's dismay, the fortune-teller then predicts her imminent death. This scene is the first coherent unit of dramatic development in the film, and contrasts with the series of disconnected images and thematic motifs which make up the film to this point.

The next character to be introduced is the sailor, who is first seen in a run-down café. The next shot is of the prostitute with a client, and the next is of the pimp kissing the prostitute before sending her off to solicit. After a series of disconnected scenes showing various evening leisure pursuits, including scenes set in a funfair, the pimp, prostitute and sailor are seen together in the interior of the café shown earlier. The pimp waits patiently whilst the prostitute dances with the sailor at the bar. Then, in the street (it is now daytime, but the link to the previous events, which were set during the evening, remains unclear), the pimp and prostitute lie in wait for the newspaper vendor. As the prostitute acts as lookout, the pimp attacks and kills the newspaper vendor in order to steal her takings. Towards the end of the assault, the prostitute sees the sailor approaching and leads him to her room, where they prepare to have sex.

As *Nothing But the Hours* develops, various sequences showing the old lame woman are interspersed with other events taking place in the film, although these sequences have no apparent connection with those events. At about the same time that the story of the pimp and the prostitute is about to begin, the old woman is seen collapsing in a construction or dumping site close to the Seine, and a title reads "Indifferent to time passing". As the events at the café and in the alley unfold, shots of the old woman are intercut with the violence taking place. Unconnected to the narrative causality of the story, the old woman seems to function as a symbol, and metaphorical victim, of the degenerate world of which the criminal events taking place in the alley-way and the images of urban squalor which pervade the film are all representative. Although a sense of irony pervades much of *Nothing But the Hours*, particularly in the way in which playful juxtapositions and modernist special effects are used, the sequences involving the old woman appear strikingly harsh and harrowing, and the last time she is seen, sitting down in the abandoned rubbish yard, could be interpreted as signifying her approaching death.

At a retrospective of his work mounted at the National Film Theatre in London in 1977, Cavalcanti chose, rather surprisingly, to select a number of light Parisian songs to accompany a screening of *Nothing But the Hours*. This apparently had the effect of making the film appear largely ironic and even comic in parts, and of making the figure of the old woman appear parodic rather than tragic.[32] The reasons for Cavalcanti's decision to use popular songs to accompany the film are unclear, but it is difficult to imagine how the old lame woman in the film could have been rendered comic by such treatment. Whatever Cavalcanti's motives were in 1977, a careful viewing of the film suggests that this character is to be read realistically, rather than parodically.

The prologue of *Nothing But the Hours* states that the film is not concerned with conventional representations of Paris, such as its monuments or celebrities, but with "the common life of the lowly and downtrodden", and later, in the 1970s, Cavalcanti was to describe his film as being "about the lack of work, about the lives in miserable places".[33] However, although *Nothing But the Hours* does contain realistic representations, it does not adopt a social realist approach to film form. Another title states that "only a succession of images can reconstitute life for us", and Cavalcanti's approach in *Nothing But the Hours* is to use fragmentary and often contradictory conjunctions of images in order to evoke these "downtrodden lives in miserable places". This approach is also reinforced in the final titles of the film, which proclaim that "you can fix a point in space...and a moment in time...but space and time escape you", implying that it is futile to attempt to represent the experience of modern, urban existence in a linear, realistic way, and that only a fragmented, juxtapositional style of filmmaking will succeed.

Underlying *Nothing But the Hours* is a notion of reality as masked, and the film employs juxtaposition to render the impression that a gradual unmasking process is taking place as the film unfolds. *Nothing But the Hours* also employs a binary oppositional structure as part of this unmasking process, as conventional images based on clichéd perceptions of Parisian life repeatedly give way to others which subvert and contradict them. One example of this is a scene in which shots of food in a market-place are followed by glimpses of rubbish in a bin.

Another is a sequence showing an affluent young man eating a steak in a café, which is immediately followed by shots of cows being slaughtered in an abattoir. At one point, the scene in the abattoir is superimposed over the plate from which the man eats, indicating the existence of an inseparable relationship between bourgeois privilege and a more sordid, underlying reality. In yet another scene which emphasises the same thematic opposition, a shot of a limousine fades out to reveal an old man leading a heavily-laden donkey. All these sequences reinforce the film's attempt to demystify the conventional and unmask the darker realities hidden behind the façade of bourgeois normality.

The use of modernist devices in *Nothing But the Hours*, such as wipes, dissolves and superimpositions, also serves to emphasise the authorial source of the critique of bourgeois norms being mounted within the film, and, as is the case with impressionist filmmaking, the vision of the filmmaker is foregrounded here through the application of these explicitly modernist techniques. However, the modernism in *Nothing But the Hours* is not employed within the context of an experimental investigation into the properties of the medium *per se*, as is the case with *cinéma pur*, but as part of a demystifying exercise which seeks to subvert conventional forms of representation in order to critique bourgeois society. Writing in 1955, and looking back on his experience in the 1920s, Cavalcanti was to argue that, like other members of the avant-garde, he was:

> [I]nterested in telling a story by using to the maximum, with a liberty which the public considered revolutionary, the cinematic means of expression, and by going to extremes in the choice of analogies, comparisons and metaphors.[34]

However, in *Nothing But the Hours*, this concern with modernist experimentation is firmly anchored to an analysis and subversion of dominant discourses, and is not taken "to extremes" for its own sake.

The concern with debunking, parodying and unmasking which pervades *Nothing But the Hours* also characterises the film's representation of sexuality. The couplings between men and women in the film are all onerous in one way or another, and show those couplings taking place within a context of exploitation. The fact that the central relationship in *Nothing But the Hours* is that between a pimp and a prostitute reinforces this. Cavalcanti's own homosexuality may have influenced his view of heterosexual romance here, but it is more likely that the film's critique of sexuality is conditioned by its overall critique of bourgeois norms. Some critics have found the final sequences in the film, in which the violent murder of the newspaper vendor is immediately followed by a scene in which the prostitute and the sailor lustily prepare to have sex, to be disturbing and in poor taste,[35] and Cavalcanti also mentioned that the censors had problems with these aspects of the film at the time.[36] However, this jarring and disjunctive treatment of characterisation, which is carried out in conjunction with a sudden shift in tone from the tragic to the parodic, is a recurring feature within Cavalcanti's films, and one which would unsettle many other critics in years to come.

Critical reaction to *Nothing But the Hours*, as is the case with most of Cavalcanti's films, has been extremely varied. There is no doubt that *Nothing But the Hours* cemented Cavalcanti's reputation as an important avant-garde director. However, the film has often been regarded as an uneven, if pioneering work, rather than a project of substance, and even Cavalcanti described it as a "clumsy social document".[37] It is unquestionably an uneven film, which links elements of documentary naturalism, social realism, modernist experimentation and ironic parody within a mixture of styles which sometimes clash with each other. One critic has argued that *Nothing But the Hours* oscillates irregularly and confusedly between the "simple representation of a wretched milieu" and the portrayal of an "incoherent" reality.[38] Another has described the film as "an odd mixture of images".[39] Yet another writer, comparing *Nothing But the Hours* to Jean Grémillon's *Tour au large* (*A Journey on the Ocean*, 1927), a documentary about tuna fishing fleets, argues that Grémillon's is the better film, and that Cavalcanti's film is "uneven and rather lacking in warmth".[40]

It is difficult to compare *Nothing But the Hours* to other films of the period because, like many of Cavalcanti's later films, it is so unlike any of these other films. Although Siegfried Kracauer has compared *Nothing But the Hours* to Ivens' *Rain*, the two films are not really comparable.[41] The anarchic modernism of *Nothing But the Hours* also means that it cannot easily be classed as either an impressionist film or a work of *cinéma pur*. Similarly, the use of melodramatic characterisation in *Nothing But the Hours* makes it more difficult to identify the film with the "city symphony" genre than a film such as Vigo's *A Propos de Nice*. One film to which *Nothing But the Hours* might be compared is Clair's *Entr'acte* (1924), although Cavalcanti's film lacks the overtly Dadaist aspirations of Clair's film. *Nothing But the Hours* might also be compared to Buñuel's *Un Chien andalou* (1928). However, as with *Entr'acte*, Buñuel's film is far more overtly and deliberately linked to a theoretical position, in this case Surrealism, than is Cavalcanti's.

Although Cavalcanti drew on many of the above influences in making *Nothing But the Hours*, his film is best regarded as a unique distillation of those influences, rather than one which can be too closely associated with other films of the period. *Nothing But the Hours* was also, in many respects, the first and virtually last high-modernist film made by Cavalcanti, and he was only to return to this type of filmmaking once more during the course of his career, with the collaborative project of *Coal Face* in 1935.

En rade (Stranded, 1927)

Stranded, Cavalcanti's second film, differed from Nothing But the Hours in that its production budget was considerably higher, and in it employed prominent actors such as Catherine Hessling and Natalie Lissenko. Like Nothing But the Hours, Stranded was produced by Pierre Braunberger's Néo-Film company. However, unlike Nothing But the Hours, Stranded was distributed commercially by Super-Films, a larger distributor than the Louis Aubert organisation which had distributed the earlier film. Stranded was released immediately into the specialised cinema network, and was premièred at the Vieux-Colombier in November 1927, almost exactly one year after the première of Nothing But the Hours.[42]

Stranded is a far more linear and conventional film than Nothing But the Hours. Set in the old port area of Marseilles, the plot involves a young man who lives with his mother but seeks escape through travelling overseas. At the beginning of the film, he is seen at home, in the claustrophobic apartment which he shares with his mother. Later, at the dockyard, he meets a seemingly retarded vagrant who appears to spend most of his time on the docks and who, like him, also dreams of going to sea. Through the simpleton, the young man meets and falls in love with a local café waitress, and the young couple make plans to elope together. However, the mother discovers the couple's plans, and sets out to find her son. Coming across the simpleton, she attacks him, believing that he was responsible for encouraging her son to leave. Later, the son, apparently overcome by violent sexual passion, assaults the waitress, who then ends the relationship. At the close of the film, the son is seen back at home with his mother, whilst the simpleton sets out to sea in a small boat and is drowned.

Stranded begins by establishing an opposition between a claustrophobic domestic environment and the possibility of escape from that environment offered by the sea. The sea, ships and harbour represent these possibilities, whilst the apartment shared by mother and son, and the run-down café and adjoining streets symbolise an entrapping and confining environment. The central character in the film is referred to simply as "the son", and is played by Georges Charlia, whilst the central relationship in the film is that between him and his mother, who is referred to only as "the laundress", and is played by the White Russian actress Natalie Lissenko. This relationship is clearly depicted as problematic, based on the mother's need to control and dominate her son, and on the son's passive, even masochistic acceptance of this. Later, the son develops a relationship with the retarded vagrant (Philippe Hériat), and finally, through the vagrant, the son establishes a romantic relationship with the café waitress (Catherine Hessling). The film ends with the son and the waitress back once again within their own separate environments, but this narrative closure is not harmonious, and the death of the simpleton in the final scenes of the film parallels the spiritual dissolution of both the son and the waitress.

A number of similarities exist between the structures of characterisation in *Stranded* and those in *Nothing But the Hours*. For example, the vagrant in *Stranded* plays a similar role to that of the newsvendor in *Nothing But the Hours*, in that both function as counterpoints to the central characters within the two films. Both are also depicted as naïve, or detached from the intrigues which develop around the principal characters, and both also suffer unwarranted violence. The relationship between mother and son in *Stranded* is also analogous to that between the pimp and the prostitute in *Nothing But the Hours*, since, in both cases, this relationship is depicted as aberrant. In *Stranded*, this relationship is based on repression and manipulation, whilst in *Nothing But the Hours* it is based on exploitation and prostitution. The waitress in *Stranded* can also be seen as analogous to the sailor in *Nothing But the Hours* in that both become involved in a central relationship between a man and a woman. The central character relationship in both films is therefore based on exploitation, and, although other characters in both films threaten the stability of this central relationship, it prevails in the end. The similarity between the forms of characterisation in these two films indicates that Cavalcanti was experimenting with formats based around a central quartet of figures. Within this quartet, various relationships occur, develop and end, although it is the negative, destructive relationships which prevail, particularly in *Stranded*.

Stranded differs from *Nothing But the Hours* in that it is more realistic and less concerned with formal experimentation. Although both films deal with naturalist subject-matter, in *Nothing But the Hours* a more politicised avant-garde critique of bourgeois mores dominates the typical naturalist concerns of entrapment and the oppressive weight of the environment. Naturalist subject-matter is more evident in *Stranded* than in *Nothing But the Hours*, and, as with films within the earlier pictorialist naturalist tradition, this subject-matter is linked to an evocation of atmosphere and milieu. To this end, the interior sets of *Stranded* were deliberately designed so as to blend in seamlessly with the location-shooting used in the film, in order to achieve an overall impression of poetic naturalism. The film's location, a picturesque regional setting, is also typical of the pictorialist naturalist genre, and reveals the influence of films such as L'Herbier's *The Man of the Ocean* and *The Late Mathias Pascal*.

In addition to abandoning the high-modernism of *Nothing But the Hours* for a more realistic and linear form of film practice, *Stranded* abandoned the juxtapositional style of *Nothing But the Hours* in favour of one based on more conventional forms of narrative structure. However, the theme of the sudden emergence of violent behaviour, apparently originating within the naturalist "inner beast", and connected to both the abuse of power and aggressive sexuality, is apparent as a common theme within both films. Another common theme which emerges in both films is concerned with the difficulty, or impossibility, of achieving successful heterosexual romance. Yet another constant in both films is the emphasis placed on the melodramatic, and, in both films, the central structure of character relationships is melodramatic, rather than realistic. This use of melodramatic forms is more pronounced in *Stranded* than in *Nothing But the Hours*, and it was criticised at the time by some within the Parisian avant-garde who regarded such material, which was more generally associated with popular culture than with art cinema, as too trivial to form the basis of a film with artistic and authorial pretensions.[43]

    Stranded looks back to both Impressionism and the pictorialist naturalist tradition for its stylistic antecedents far more than does *Nothing But the Hours*. For example, when *Stranded* employs modernist montage, it is always within the context of representing subjective experience or point of view, as in the Impressionist tradition. One example of this is the scene in which the son assaults the waitress in the café. A series of staring eyes signify the obsessive fixation which the son has for the waitress, and this non-naturalistic use of imagery is clearly designed to express subjectivity rather than abstract ideas, as is often the case with *Nothing But the Hours*. Similarly, *Stranded* frequently draws on the pictorialist naturalist tradition in employing shots whose sole function is to show individual characters set against an imposing background of ships and monumental machinery. Although *Nothing But the Hours* became a far better-known film than *Stranded*, it was the latter film which provided Cavalcanti with the basic model for many of his later works.

Yvette and *La P'tite Lilie* (both 1927)

If *Stranded* was a more mainstream film than *Nothing But the Hours*, *Yvette* was even more so. *Yvette* was Cavalcanti's contribution to the studio spectacular genre, and was produced largely because Pierre Braunberger decided to cash in on the popularity of such films by asking Cavalcanti to direct his own version of one.[44] An adaptation of a short story by the French naturalist writer Guy de Maupassant, *Yvette* was also designed as a vehicle for its star, Catherine Hessling, who had earlier played the prostitute in *Nothing But the Hours* and the waitress in *Stranded*. *Yvette* largely conforms to the conventions of the studio spectacular genre, and, although it also displays an ironic critique of those conventions in some of its sequences, this is carried out in too understated a fashion to be particularly effective.[45] Although it did not do particularly well in France, *Yvette* did achieve some success in England and the United States, where it won prizes for photography and décor.[46] The only section of the film available for viewing today is that in which Yvette commits suicide through taking poison. The décor and photography in this scene are sumptuous, and the acting is melodramatic, whilst Cavalcanti also took the opportunity to use special effect techniques in order to render Yvette's subjective experience of her impending mortality.

Although Cavalcanti embarked on *Yvette* because of his relationship with Braunberger and because of his pressing financial difficulties, his involvement in the film created friction between himself and other avant-garde critics and filmmakers, who criticised him for making such an overtly commercial film.[47] Cavalcanti was offended by this criticism, and eventually distanced himself from many of his former associates within the avant-garde. He may also have had the fuss over *Yvette* in mind when he claimed in the 1970s that the French avant-garde of the 1920s "detested" each other: "We hated ourselves... We couldn't bear any of the others".[48] Although it is not clear exactly to whom Cavalcanti was referring here, it was at about this time that he became closely, but briefly, involved with some members of the Surrealist Group, and it was the Surrealists who took a leading role in criticising *Yvette*. This probably explains why Cavalcanti's relationship with the Surrealist filmmakers was a distant and rather brittle one after 1927.

Cavalcanti's third film of 1927 was *La P'tite Lilie*, a short film shot during a break in the shooting of *Yvette*, which eventually became a critical and commercial success in itself, running for over six months at the Studio des Ursulines in Paris. The film was based on a little-known French song of the same name dating from 1900, and was Cavalcanti's first venture into the comedy genre.[49] Like *Stranded*, *La P'tite Lilie* is concerned with the evocation of atmosphere. However, the dominant tone of *La P'tite Lilie* is more lyrical, light-hearted and ironic. The gloomy weather in which the film was shot enhances this predominant lyrical quality, giving the film a restrained visual quality, an effect further heightened by the use of a canvas filter placed over the camera lens during shooting.

Writing about *La P'tite Lilie*, the Hungarian film theorist Béla Balázs argued that this use of a filter emphasised the representational surface of the film, and also provided it with a degree of "visual homogeneity".[50] In addition to its evocation of atmosphere and mood, therefore, *La P'tite Lilie* foregrounds its use of cinematic devices, and this reflexivity is further reinforced by the fact that the film is essentially a parodic comedy. It is this conjunction of formalism and the comedic, a combination which appears in many of Cavalcanti's later films, which gives the film what Balázs described as its "ironic and bizarre style".[51]

La P'tite Lilie, like *Yvette*, received a mixed critical and commercial response when it first appeared. According to Cavalcanti, the film was a significant commercial success, which more than recouped its production costs. However, in a denunciation which also reflected the adverse reaction to the melodramatic content of *Stranded*, *La P'tite Lilie* was also criticised by Jean Cocteau – then a relatively little-known figure within the avant-garde – for its use of trivial subject-matter.[52] One of the differences which began to emerge between Cavalcanti and others in the avant-garde during this period, and which is illustrated by Cocteau's criticism, was over the use of popular cultural forms, such as the song of "La P'tite Lilie" in Cavalcanti's film. However, such a use of popular culture later became a central aspect of Cavalcanti's filmmaking.

La P'tite Lilie reveals Cavalcanti attempting to evolve an eclectic and ambitious cinematic style by 1927, one which sought to integrate realism, popular formats and a degree of innovative formal experimentation into an overall aesthetic synthesis. Given the difficulty inherent in successfully combining such disparate elements, it is hardly surprising that his early films were uneven and only partly successful. Unfortunately, circumstances were soon to dictate that Cavalcanti would have little additional opportunity to develop his work further between 1927 and 1934. During this period, Cavalcanti was forced to accept a succession of commercially-orientated commissions, and this made it difficult for him to evolve a more mature or integrated style.

One of the most significant personal and professional relationships which Cavalcanti formed between 1927 and 1929 was with Jean Renoir. Unlike Cavalcanti, Renoir was relatively comfortable financially, having inherited the estate of his late father, the Impressionist painter Auguste Renoir. As a consequence, Renoir was able to fund his first major production, Nana (1926), himself.[53] Shortly after making Nana, Renoir became involved with Pierre Braunberger's Néo-Film company. At the time, Cavalcanti was developing a film for Braunberger entitled Tire-au-flanc (The Idler, 1928), a military comedy based on a long-running boulevard play, and starring the young Michel Simon, who would become one of the most important French actors of the 1930s. However, for reasons which remain unclear, Cavalcanti ceded the direction of the film to Renoir, and remained on the project only as set designer. It is possible that Cavalcanti was, in fact, actually eased out of the project by Renoir,[54] who had known Braunberger for a number of years, and may have used his influence to have the project handed over to him.[55] Whether or not this was the case, the fact is that, from that point onwards, relations between Cavalcanti and Renoir were often tense.

Another cause of this tension can be attributed to the part played in both their lives by Catherine Hessling. Hessling, who had been married to Renoir and had also starred in the critical and commercial disaster of Nana, was divorced from Renoir when he decided that he wanted to marry Dida Freire, one of the two daughters of Dario Freire, the Consul General at the Brazilian Consulate in Liverpool. This difficult situation was made even more complicated by the fact that Hessling and Cavalcanti quickly became close friends, a factor which provoked a certain amount of jealousy on Renoir's part. Yet another factor which contributed towards the strained relations between Renoir and Cavalcanti during this period was that, unlike Renoir's unsuccessful treatment of Hessling in Nana, Cavalcanti managed to obtain an effective performance from her in La P'tite Lilie.

Matters were strained further when Cavalcanti later "gave"

another Néo-Film project, *Le Tournoi dans la cité* (*The Tournament in the City*, 1929), to Renoir. *The Tournament in the City* eventually became a commercial success,[56] although at one point Renoir came close to giving up the project because of misgivings he had about working within the genre of the historical reconstruction film.[57] Afterwards, Renoir complained that his involvement with this film, which, like *Nana*, went well over budget and behind schedule, contributed to the widespread perception that he was an unreliable filmmaker, and made it difficult for him to find a producer for his first sound film, *La Chienne* (*The Bitch*, 1931).[58] All this exacerbated the tensions between Renoir and Cavalcanti.

Nevertheless, Renoir went on to collaborate with Cavalcanti on two films, *La P'tite Lilie* and *Le Petit chaperon rouge* (*Little Red Riding Hood*, 1929), and between 1927 and 1929 the two filmmakers also collaborated closely in making a number of other short films with a small group of actors, which included Catherine Hessling, William Aguet, André Cerf and Pierre Prévert.[59] In fact, Cavalcanti may have been closer to this community of actors and film people than to any other group, including the Surrealists, during this period; if this is the case, it strengthens the argument for relating his French films more closely to strains of relatively untheorised lyrical naturalism than to the Impressionist or Surrealist traditions. Cavalcanti's move from the avant-garde into the less intellectual circle around Renoir also reveals a predisposition to engage in his own personal filmmaking preoccupations, rather than become involved in theoretical debates about contemporary cinema.

Le Capitaine Fracasse, La Jalousie du Barbouillé (*The Jealousy of the Barbouillé*), *Tire-au-flanc* (*The Idler*) (all 1928) and *Le Petit chaperon rouge* (*Little Red Riding Hood*, 1929)

Cavalcanti's final six films of the silent period began with *Le Capitaine Fracasse*. The origins of this film must be traced back to changes occurring within the French industry during the mid- to late-1920s. During this period, Hollywood's dominance of the French market led French producers to experiment with new forms and types of film production. In opposition to the American super-productions with which the French could not compete, lower-budget films were produced, and a number of new production and distribution companies emerged to make them.[60] Some of these concentrated on making films for the French market, but others attempted to develop co-production strategies with European and American companies aimed at the international market. Two major genres of filmmaking emerged from this context: the modern studio spectacular, and the historical reconstruction film. The modern studio spectacular genre has already been discussed. The films produced within the parameters of the historical reconstruction genre, of which *Le Capitaine Fracasse* is an example, focused either on the adventures of royalty and the feudal élite, or on more recent historical events. These films also employ lavish set designs, and considerable attention was bestowed upon costume and décor.[61]

One of the companies which came into being specifically to produce historical reconstruction films was Lutèce Films, which in 1928 produced L'Equipage (The Crew), a major production set during the First World War and directed by Maurice Tourneur. The success of The Crew encouraged Lutèce to develop a similar project based, as in that film, on the same formula of spectacle and costume, and this eventually became Le Capitaine Fracasse. Although Maurice Tourneur had been the original choice to direct Le Capitaine Fracasse, this turned out to be controversial. During the First World War, Tourneur had left France in order to live in the United States and, despite the success of The Crew, was greeted by a "violent campaign" in the press, in which he was accused of lacking patriotism, when he returned to direct Le Capitaine Fracasse. As a consequence, Tourneur was forced to give up the project, and the Managing Director of Lutèce Films, Charles Schneider, who had been impressed with Cavalcanti's Yvette, then offered the project to Cavalcanti.[62]

By 1928, Cavalcanti was eager to work in the new medium of the sound film, and saw the Lutèce project as an opportunity to realise his ambitions. With this in mind, he accepted the commission, and then attempted to persuade Schneider to make Le Capitaine Fracasse as a synchronised sound production. However, Schneider was dissuaded from this course of action by the cost of sound production, and insisted that the film remain silent. After this initial disappointment, Cavalcanti ran into more problems during the shooting of Le Capitaine Fracasse when other members of the production team began to question whether such a relatively inexperienced person should have directorial responsibility for what was, in effect, a relatively large-budget film. The outcome of this was that Cavalcanti lost his position as director on the film, and his contribution thereafter was limited to one of adapting the scenario in collaboration with the newly-appointed director, Henri Wulschleger.[63]

Following this series of disappointments, Cavalcanti became even more determined to move into sound filmmaking. However, his next film, La Jalousie du Barbouillé (The Jealousy of the Barbouillé, 1928), was again destined to be silent. Based on a similar approach to the historical construction film as Le Capitaine Fracasse, The Jealousy of the Barbouillé was adapted from a play by Molière and produced by the Studio des Ursulines. Cavalcanti directed and edited the film, and also designed the set. Produced on a far lower budget than Le Capitaine Fracasse, The Jealousy of the Barbouillé even boasted costume designs by Cavalcanti's mother.[64] Like La P'tite Lilie, The Jealousy of the Barbouillé is essentially comedic, although based on the traditions of the commedia dell'arte, rather than popular song, as La P'tite Lilie had been. Essentially a generic film, The Jealousy of the Barbouillé is firmly grounded in theatrical convention, contains little of the experimental and avant-garde qualities of *La P'tite Lilie*, and cannot be counted as anything other than a routine minor work.

Cavalcanti eventually achieved his goal of producing a sound film with *Little Red Riding Hood*, which was produced by Jean Renoir and distributed by the Société Française de Gestion Cinématographique. However, *Little Red Riding Hood* was not a true sound film. It was initially shot silent because synchronisation equipment was not available, and dialogue and music were added later at the studios of Tobis d'Epinay.[65] As a consequence, the use of both dialogue and music in *Little Red Riding Hood* had to be restricted, and this imposed limitations on the ambitions which Cavalcanti had originally entertained for this film. Like *La P'tite Lilie*, *Little Red Riding Hood* was based on popular folk traditions, this time on the story of Little Red Riding Hood, and once again Cavalcanti was able to draw on the same group of close collaborators who had appeared in his previous films. Catherine Hessling played the title role, Renoir the part of the wolf, and Pierre Prévert and William Aguet also appeared in minor roles.

Although *Little Red Riding Hood* was well-received in Paris, it was not widely taken up for commercial exhibition. Released in either late-1929 or early 1930, its mixture of folklorism and avant-gardism fell foul of the new demand for the Hollywood-style sound film. As with many other members of the avant-garde at the end of the 1920s, Cavalcanti found that his approach to filmmaking was out of step with the development of the commercial sound film, with its emphasis on naturalistic dialogue and theatrical conventions. In fact, the commercial failure of *Little Red Riding Hood*, coming in conjunction with the rise of the sound film, left Cavalcanti in a difficult position, to the extent that he was unable to find work for over a year.[66]

The transition to the sound film and the Paramount experience: *Toute sa vie (All His Life)*, *A Mi-chemin du ciel (Halfway to Heaven)*, *Les Vacances du diable (The Devil's Holidays)* (all 1930) and *Dans une île perdue (On an Island Lost, 1931)*

Between 1930 and 1931, Cavalcanti made a number of sound films for Paramount Studios. He had been interested in the sound film since it first appeared in 1927, and by 1930 this interest had grown to become one of his chief concerns. However, his experience at Paramount was to prove a disappointing one, and the films which he produced or directed there did little to advance his knowledge and understanding of filmmaking. Before turning to an analysis of these films, however, it is first necessary to situate Cavalcanti in relation to the critical debates and responses to the emergence of the sound film which characterised this period of French cinema.

Between 1929 and 1930, film production in France almost doubled under the impact of the introduction of the sound film.[67] Most of these films were little more than filmed versions of successful boulevard stage plays. The first fully integrated French sound production was André Hugon's *Les Trois masques* (*The Three Masks*, 1929). Based on a stage play, *The Three Masks* had to be shot at Twickenham Studios in London because of the shortage of sound synchronisation resources available at that time in France.[68] The first talking picture filmed entirely in France was probably L'Herbier's *L'Enfant de l'amour* (*The Love Child*, 1930), based on a play by Henri Bataille, which L'Herbier had originally planned to make as a silent film. Both these films suffered from the poor quality of sound synchronisation available at that time.[69]

This rapid expansion in sound film production soon led to the emergence of critical debates within the avant-garde over the implications which the sound film posed for an aesthetics of film which, until then, had been founded on a belief that cinematic specificity was grounded in the visual. Critics and filmmakers such as Clair, L'Herbier, Epstein and Benjamin Fondane initially reacted with suspicion and apprehension to the emergence of the sound film, whilst Surrealists such as Antonin Artaud argued uncompromisingly that this unwelcome development constituted a threat to the survival of film as an art form.[70]

Despite this adverse critical reaction, however, others argued that the sound film provided the basis and potential for new and significant developments. For example, one critical response to the advent of sound in film was based on the notion that the silent film was an immature aesthetic form which had reached maturity with the advent of sound. So, for example, in a 1929 paper entitled "Les possibilités d'un art élargi" ("The Possibilities of a Broadened Art"), Jacques Feyder argued that the lack of sound had arrested the development of film, making it "an incomplete instrument".[71] In a similar vein, Marcel Pagnol argued that sound would enable film to communicate a degree of psychological realism which the silent film had been unable to achieve.[72]

In addition to those who believed that the cinema had reached maturity with the emergence of the sound film, other French filmmakers, theorists and critics acknowledged, with varying degrees of enthusiasm, that the sound film would soon be a permanent addition to the cultural landscape, and that a new aesthetic language would have to evolve in order to accommodate it. Consequently, in the writings of Clair, Epstein, Feyder, Gance and others, increasing emphasis began to be placed on the need to experiment with new sound image relationships in an attempt to maximise the aesthetic potential of the sound film. For example, Clair argued that language should be considered as "organized sound", and used as one formal element amongst others,[73] whilst Epstein argued that the sound film should "prospect" the natural sounds found in the contemporary environment in order to create a new tapestry of sound effects.[74] A similar approach to the experimental use of sound was adopted by Jean Renoir, who used natural sounds in an attempt to capture the "distinctive accents and timbres" of urban life in *The Bitch*.[75]

One outcome of the advent of the sound film was a revival of earlier debates on the specific character of French national cinema. It was argued in some quarters that the French rationalist tradition, based on dialogue and debate, provided an ideal basis for the growth of a successful French national sound cinema, and that the sound film was more suited to French cultural traditions than the silent film.[76] Another development closely related to this concern about the relationship between cinema and national culture was the way in which the sound film helped to revive the practice of adapting great works of literature and theatre for the screen, which had been a staple of the French film industry since its origins. Within this tradition, adaptation was not seen as a lesser category of filmmaking, as it had been by the Impressionists, but as a valid way of augmenting and revitalising the historical legacy of French culture.

One important part of that legacy was the realist and naturalist heritage, and filmmakers active within that tradition also believed that the sound film, with its capacity for verisimilitude, could reinvigorate and complement some of the central concerns of realism. For example, Epstein argued that image, music and sound effects should be used to evoke atmosphere and environment, just as purely visual effects had in the earlier films of the pictorialist naturalist tradition.[77] Epstein later put his ideas into practice in his "Breton trilogy": *Finis terrae* (*Land's End*, 1929), *Mor Vran* (1931) and *L'Or des mers* (*The Gold of the Seas*, 1932).[78] Closely related to this concern with realism and naturalism was the belief, held by Marcel Carné and others on the Left, that the sound film could make possible a new and more realistic portrayal of working-class experience.[79] These ideas became increasingly important during the 1930s, as internal political division grew in France, and as both Left and Right attempted to use the cinema to promote their respective agendas.[80]

Cavalcanti can be placed alongside filmmakers such as Renoir, Grémillon, Feyder and others in that he embraced the creative possibilities offered by the sound film. Like Epstein and Clair, Cavalcanti argued that speech must be fully integrated into the image track of the film, rather than dominate it, and that, whilst the image was a "medium of statement", sound was a medium of "suggestion", and so should be used to render the facticity of the image less determinate.[81] Speaking in 1935 in an interview with Alistair Cooke, Cavalcanti also argued that, during the late-1920s and early 1930s, he had sought to use sound in films in ways which would be "specific" to cinema.[82]

The influence of modernist musicians such as Maurice Jaubert, Erik Satie, Kurt Weill and Darius Milhaud led Cavalcanti to advocate a contrapuntal, non-synchronised approach to the use of film music and film sound.[83] The most important influence on Cavalcanti during this period was that of Jaubert, who wrote the music for *Little Red Riding Hood*. Jaubert had been involved with the avant-garde from the early

1920s, had been a member of Ricciotto Canudo's Club des Amis du Septième Art from its founding in 1921, and had associated with filmmakers, writers and musicians such as Cavalcanti, Dulac, Epstein, Delluc, L'Herbier, Jean Cocteau, Alexandre Arnoux, Arthur Honegger and Maurice Ravel.[84] He also contributed to Canudo's journal *La Gazette des Sept Arts*, and was involved in the expositions of film screenings set up by Canudo between 1921 and 1923, which attempted to set out the basis for the development of cinema as an art form.[85] Together with Debussy, Satie and Honegger, Jaubert contributed music for Jean Grémillon's *Maldone* (1928),[86] before working on *Little Red Riding Hood* in 1929 and Cavalcanti's *Au Pays du scalp* (*In the Country of the Scalp People*) in 1931. Later, Jaubert would provide musical scores for Jean Vigo's *Zéro de conduite* (1933) and Marcel Carné's *Le Jour se lève* (1939) before his death during the war.[87] Cavalcanti enjoyed a particularly close relationship with Jaubert between 1927 and 1933, and this association played a crucial role in making the creative use of sound and music one of the central concerns of his filmmaking career.

Another important influence on Cavalcanti's approach to the creative use of sound during this period was a conference on music which he attended at Baden-Baden in 1928. Cavalcanti travelled to the festival with the directors of *Voyage to the Congo*, André Gide and Marc Allégret, and he also came into contact there with Kurt Weill, Bertolt Brecht, Paul Hindemith and Darius Milhaud.[88] Part of the festival was concerned with the relationship of music to the sound film, and, during the proceedings, a version of *La P'tite Lilie* was screened with a soundtrack composed for the occasion by Milhaud. However, despite the best efforts of Cavalcanti and Milhaud, this version of the film was never exhibited in a French cinema, because its use of avant-garde pictorial effects, contrapuntal music and lack of spoken dialogue made it unattractive to French distributors at the dawn of the age of the sound film.[89] Cavalcanti's ambitions to make innovative sound films were ultimately to remain unfulfilled until he left France for England in 1934 to join the British documentary film movement. Before that, however, he was to gain practical experience of commercial sound film production through working at the Paris studios of Paramount Pictures.

In 1929, Cavalcanti was approached by the theatre director Marcel Pagnol, who asked him to become involved in making film versions of Pagnol's successful stage plays *Topaze* (1928) and *Marius* (1930). *Marius* shares some remarkable similarities with *Stranded* in that it is also about a young Marseillais torn between his love for a woman and his desire to go to sea, and in that it shared the same poetic evocation of fatalism and entrapment which characterised Cavalcanti's film.[90] These resemblances were so great that, at the time, many believed Pagnol had drawn on *Stranded* as the source for *Marius*, without sufficiently acknowledging it.[91] This may or may not be the case, although, if it were so, Cavalcanti did not appear to be overly concerned, as there is no record that he ever commented on the matter in any of his writings. Nevertheless, the striking similarities between *Stranded* and *Marius* would have been an important factor in leading Pagnol to invite Cavalcanti to help make the film version of his play.

Pagnol's invitation provided Cavalcanti with a singular opportunity to direct a feature-length sound film. However, he decided to decline Pagnol's offer in the belief that the resulting film would only be a form of filmed theatre, a type of cinema to which, in company with others within the avant-garde, he was philosophically opposed.[92] However, *Marius* was far more than just filmed theatre. The film was produced at Paramount by the Hungarian-born producer Alexander Korda, and Korda's authority within the organisation ensured that Pagnol enjoyed an unusual degree of autonomy in the development of his project.[93] *Marius* was also made after Paramount had decided to abandon the formulaic production of vacuous international studio spectaculars, and to adopt a strategy of making films with a more local orientation for the French market. This, together with the film's use of naturalistic location photography and unusually authentic set designs (designed by Alexander Korda's brother Zoltan), marked the film out from other Paramount productions of the period.[94]

Although Cavalcanti's decision to turn down the opportunity to direct *Marius* contributed to the year of inactivity he suffered following the making of *Little Red Riding Hood*, he did not regret his decision, as he believed that both *Marius* and Pagnol's later *Fanny* (1932) were far too dependent on theatrical convention. However, Cavalcanti was more sympathetic to Pagnol's *Jofroi* (1934), *César* (1936) and *La Femme du Boulanger* (*The Baker's Wife*, 1938), which were more firmly situated within the pictorialist naturalist tradition and also anticipated the appearance of postwar Italian neo-realism.[95] Cavalcanti was influenced by these films, and was later to draw on them when developing his own filmmaking, first in England and then in Brazil.

By the end of 1929, Cavalcanti's financial position was once more becoming precarious, and, in order to support both himself and his mother, he accepted a second offer from Paramount to produce films at Joinville. Cavalcanti did not join Paramount willingly. He had already turned down Pagnol's offer of work, and during 1929 had tried repeatedly, but without success, to obtain suitable filmmaking commissions. His decision to join Paramount should also be seen within the context of what was happening elsewhere within the French avant-garde during this period. Under the impact of the sound film, many avant-garde filmmakers were forced into associating with forms of commercial filmmaking which compromised their earlier ideals and aspirations: for example, L'Herbier went on to make a series of unremarkable films within the mainstream industry after 1930, whilst Germaine Dulac ended her career producing routine newsreels for Pathé. The work carried out by Cavalcanti at the Paramount organisation at Joinville in 1930 and 1931 was as far removed from his aspiration to develop an autonomous film practice as possible, but, like

L'Herbier and Dulac, he had little alternative but to accept the inducements of Mammon.

The aim of the French Paramount operation, which was inaugurated in 1930, was to make foreign-language versions of American films, and to produce filmed versions of popular French boulevard plays. Teams of actors and directors, fluent in up to fourteen different languages, were employed on the foreign-language films, and up to half a dozen foreign-language versions were made of each Hollywood film. Production methods within Joinville adhered unwaveringly to the then-dominant production strategy within Hollywood of scientific management or "Taylorism".[96] This strategy, which was aimed at maximising the efficiency of mass film production, consisted of breaking down the production process into its constituent elements, and ensuring that all members of the production team carried out instructions to the letter. At Joinville, scripts derived from Hollywood films were translated into various European languages and then handed to directors, who were instructed to develop films in close conformity with the scripts. When Joinville first began operation, the dominant practice within the studio was one of making several versions of a film on the same set, with different groups of actors acting the different foreign-language versions. Later, as sound-recording technology advanced, films would be remade only once, whilst groups of translators, housed in glass booths alongside the sets, translated the scripts into their own languages. Unsurprisingly, the resulting synchronisation was often crude and unconvincing.[97]

The studios at Joinville operated 24 hours a day, completing feature-length pictures in multilingual versions in less than two weeks:[98] by 1932, the studio's output had reached a peak of 24 films, or one film per fortnight over that period.[99] Fortunately, many of the more labour-intensive and repetitive practices of multiple-version film production at Joinville were abandoned after 1932, when post-synchronous dubbing became available.[100] In the same year, and in response to a French audience demand for more films with a French orientation, Paramount also abandoned the strategy of remaking Hollywood films, and concentrated instead on adapting frothy "boulevard-style" comedies for the screen. By the end of 1932, only two of the studio's 24 films were made in a language other than French. These manoeuvres did not, however, succeed in saving the French Paramount operation, and in 1933 most of it was closed down.[101]

Cavalcanti was employed to make French and Portuguese versions of American films at Joinville, and had no say in the choice of film to be duplicated, nor the manner of duplication.[102] His first film for Paramount was *Toute sa vie* (*All His Life*, 1930), one of six parallel remakes of Paramount's *Sarah and Son* (1930), initially directed by Dorothy Arzner and starring Fredric March. *Sarah and Son* was a routine melodrama about a mother's search for her lost child, and reputedly not one of Arzner's better films.[103] *Sarah and Son* was also remade in 1930 in an Italian version, *Il Richiamo del cuore*; a Spanish version, *Toda una vida*; a Swedish version, *Hjartats rost*; and in 1931 in a Polish version, *Glos Serca*. Cavalcanti also directed the Portuguese version of the film, *A Canção do Berço* (*Song of the Cradle*, 1930).

After *All His Life*, Cavalcanti directed and adapted the screenplay for *A Mi-chemin du ciel* (*Halfway to Heaven*, 1930), based on the 1929 American title of the same name, a melodrama set in a circus, about the travails of trapeze artists, and starring Jean Arthur. German (*Der Sprung ins Nichts*), Spanish (*Sobras de circo*) and Swedish (*Halvvags till himien*) versions of this film were also produced in 1931. Cavalcanti then directed and adapted the screenplay for *Les Vacances du diable* (*The Devil's Holidays*, 1930), a French version of Paramount's 1930 film of that title, directed by Edmund Goulding and starring Nancy Carroll, about a model who marries a wealthy young aristocrat from a conservative background. German (*Sonntag des Lebens*), Spanish (*La Fiesta del diablo*) and Italian (*La Vacanza del diavolo*) versions of this film were made in 1930, and a Swedish version (*En kvinnas morgondag*) in 1931. Finally, in 1931, Cavalcanti directed *Dans une île perdue* (*On an Island Lost*), an extremely free adaptation of Joseph Conrad's novel *Victory* (1915), via William A Wellman's equally free 1930 film version of the same novel, entitled *Dangerous Paradise*, a film about the adventures of a hotel violinist and her lover on a small island near Malaysia, and again starring Nancy Carroll. German (*Tropennächte*), Italian (*La Riva dei bruti*), Swedish (*Farornas paradis*) and Polish (*Niebezplczny raj*) versions of this film were all produced in 1930.[104]

Although Cavalcanti considered *On an Island Lost* the best film of this series, he had a generally low opinion of all of them, and his distaste for the whole experience of working for Paramount led him to cancel the contract for the second series of films which he had originally been commissioned to direct.[105] Unfortunately, having given up Paramount, Cavalcanti then found himself yet again unable to find suitable work, and he was forced into accepting a commission to direct a series of commercial, "boulevard-style" comedies which were as superficial as the films with which he had been involved at Joinville.

The first of these comedies, *Le Truc du brésilien* (*The Game of the Brazilian*, 1932), was an implausible, melodramatic love story concerning a young husband who, wishing to get rid of an inconvenient mistress, impersonates a rich Brazilian in order to seduce the mistress, thus ridding himself of the inconvenience. This was followed by two other boulevard-style comedies, *Le Mari garçon* (*The Married Batchelor*) and *Coralie et cie* (both 1933). In *The Married Batchelor*, a young couple hiding in the countryside are discovered by guests from whom they had been trying to escape. Their relationship breaks down as a result, but they are eventually reunited and the film ends happily. *Coralie et Cie* is similarly frothy. Set in a provincial town, the film concerns Madame Coralie, a seamstress who turns her establishment into a discreet meeting-place for romantic liaisons. Husbands, lovers and mistresses exchange partners in the resulting mêlée, but all are happily reunited in the end.

After these three undistinguished projects, Cavalcanti provided the set designs for another musical comedy, *Votre sourire* (*Your Smile*, 1934), which was co-directed by Pierre Caron and the English director Monty Banks. Cavalcanti's last significant commercial film of his French period was *Pour un piano* (*For a Piano*, 1934). The plot concerns two young female musicians who have their house, including their piano, repossessed. The remainder of the film, which is liberally interspersed with comic routines and musical interludes, concerns their attempt to find another piano.

Cavalcanti was later to refer to these films as "table and bedroom" films because of the way in which the narrative moved inexorably from dinner table to drawing-room to bedroom, according to firmly established generic conventions.[106] Although he later claimed that these comedies were "terrifically successful commercially", and had provided him with invaluable experience as a director and producer within the commercial film industry,[107] it was his despair at being forced into making such films which ultimately led him to leave France and join the documentary film movement.

In addition to making these commercial films, Cavalcanti saw out the remainder of his time in France by making a number of short films over which he enjoyed more artistic autonomy. These include *In the Country of the Scalp People*, *En lisant le journal* (*On Reading the Newspaper*, 1932), *Le Jour du frotteur* (*The Day of the Scrubber*, 1932), *Revue montmartroise* (1932), *Nous ne ferons jamais de cinéma* (*We Will Never Pretend to Make Cinema*, 1932), *Plaisirs défendus* (*Forbidden Pleasures*, 1933) and *Tour de chant* (*Tour of Song*, 1933). These films are a mixture of short reviews and boulevard comedies. *Tour of Song*, for example, consists of three short stories, each linked by musical vignettes, songs and dances.

Of all these films, by far the most interesting is *In the Country of the Scalp People*, a travelogue shot in South America by the amateur cinematographer the Marquis de Wavrin. The film was edited by Cavalcanti, and the music composed by Maurice Jaubert. In many respects, *In the Country of the Scalp People* is similar to *Voyage to the Congo*, the silent travel documentary which Cavalcanti had edited for Allégret and Gide in 1927. Although basically a conventional travelogue, *In the Country of the Scalp People* also contains numerous surrealistic episodes based around sequences showing the primitive customs and religious festivals of the people of the scalp country. A concern with the bizarre, the exoticism of primitive cultures, and the power of natural forces in the Amazon rain forest also pervades the film, making it similar in some respects to Buñuel's slightly later surrealistic documentary *Las Hurdes* (*Land Without Bread*, 1932). However, perhaps the most interesting aspect of the film lies in its use of sound and music. Jaubert's music is often dissonant and contrapuntal, and reminiscent of the work of Kurt Weill in *Die Dreigroschenoper* (*The Threepenny Opera*, G W Pabst, 1931) and *Kuhle*

Wampe, oder wem gehört die Welt? (*Kuhle Wampe, or Who Does the World Belong To?*, Slatan Dudow, 1932). Sound is also used in an effective and sometimes contrapuntal way, creating tensions between the sound and image tracks. A little-known film, *In the Country of the Scalp People* prefigures the attempts to integrate music, image and sound which was to become a feature of Cavalcanti's later work, particularly in films such as *The Song of Ceylon* (1934) and *Coal Face*.

Notes

[1]   Alan Williams, *Republic of Images: A History of French Filmmaking* (Cambridge, MA; London: Harvard University Press, 1992): 113.

[2]   Richard Abel, *French Cinema: The First Wave, 1915-1929* (Princeton, NJ: Princeton University Press, 1984): 97.

[3]   Cited in ibid.

[4]   David Bordwell, *French Impressionist Cinema: Film Culture, Film Theory and Film Style* (New York: Arno Press, 1980): 118.

[5]   Ibid: 96.

[6]   Ibid.

[7]   Ibid: 110.

[8]   Ibid: 122.

[9]   Ibid: 105.

[10]   Ibid: 108.

[11]   Ibid: 232.

[12]   Ibid: 236.

[13]   Ibid: 237.

[14]   Ibid: 240.

[15]   Ibid: 242.

[16]   Williams: 140.

[17]   Noureddine Ghali, *L'Avant-Garde Cinématographique en France dans les Années Vingt: Idées, Conceptions, Théories* (Paris: Éditions Paris Expérimental, 1995): 48.

[18]   Ibid: 287.

[19]   Ibid: 288.

[20]   Translated from the French: "poèmes visuels qui touchent le spectateur par la beauté des images"; "Le documentaire demande à être traité par des poètes. Il n'y a actuellement aucun homme de cinéma français qui ait compris

que même dans notre pays, nous possédions d'innombrables éléments de constructions pour faire, non pas des rubans insignifiants, mais de splendides films vivants et expressifs...Les plus pures démonstrations de cinéma pur, c'est-à-dire de poésie qui soit réellement cinégraphique, nous ont été fournies par quelques films remarquables, vulgairement dénommés documentaires... particulièrement *Nanouk* et *Moana*." Hubert Revol, cited in ibid: 288-289.

21   Ricciotto Canudo, "Chronique du Septième Art: Films en couleurs", *Paris-Midi* 4131 (31 August 1923): 2.

22   Translated from the French: "fondre la vie de l'homme dans la vie des milieux". Ibid.

23   Translated from the French: "faisent ressortir la photogénie de la vie urbaine". Jean Dréville, "Le Documentaire, aimé du cinéma", *Cinémagazine* 2 (February 1930): 51.

24   Abel: 402.

25   Williams: 192.

26   Abel: 402.

27   Dudley Andrew, *Mists of Regret: Culture and Sensibility in Classic French Film* (Princeton, NJ: Princeton University Press, 1995): 101.

28   Ibid.

29   Abel: 271.

30   Quotations are taken from the English print of this film.

31   Ian Aitken, "Distraction and redemption: Kracauer, surrealism and phenomenology", *Screen* 39: 2 (summer 1998): 129.

32   Elizabeth Sussex, "Cavalcanti in England", *Sight and Sound* 44: 4 (autumn 1975): 208, reprinted in Ian Aitken (ed), *The Documentary Film Movement: An Anthology* (Edinburgh: Edinburgh University Press, 1998): 188.

33   Sussex: 207, reprinted in Aitken (ed): 188.

34   Quoted in Emir Rodriguez Monegal, "Alberto Cavalcanti", *The Quarterly of Film, Radio and Television* 9: 4 (summer 1955): 344.

35   Abel: 407.

36   Sussex, in Aitken (ed): 188.

37   Ibid.

38   Abel: 406.

39   Sussex, in Aitken (ed): 188.

40   George Morrison, "The French Avant-Garde", in Lewis Jacobs (ed), *The Emergence of Film Art: The evolution and development of the motion picture as an art, from 1900 to the present*, second edition (New York; London: W W Norton & Company, 1979): 114.

[41]   Siegfried Kracauer, *Theory of Film: The Redemption of Physical Reality* (New York: Oxford University Press, 1960): 31.

[42]   Abel: 408.

[43]   Ibid.

[44]   Lorenzo Pellizzari and Claudio M Valentinetti (eds), *Alberto Cavalcanti* (Locarno: Éditions du Festival international du film de Locarno, 1988): 411.

[45]   Abel: 216.

[46]   Hermilo Borba Filho, "Une vie (1953)", in Pellizzari and Valentinetti (eds): 139.

[47]   Charles Drazin, *The Finest Years: British Cinema of the 1940s* (London: André Deutsch, 1998): 115.

[48]   Sussex, in Aitken (ed): 184.

[49]   Filho, in Pellizzari and Valentinetti (eds): 141.

[50]   Béla Balázs, *Theory of the Film (Character and Growth of a New Art)*, translated by Edith Bone (London: Dennis Dobson, 1952): 221-222.

[51]   Ibid.

[52]   Filho, in Pellizzari and Valentinetti (eds): 140.

[53]   Williams: 137.

[54]   Filho, in Pellizzari and Valentinetti (eds): 141.

[55]   Leo Braudy, *Jean Renoir: The World of His Films* (London: Robson Books, 1977): 200.

[56]   Ibid: 199.

[57]   Filho, in Pellizzari and Valentinetti (eds): 142.

[58]   Jean Renoir, *My Life and My Films*, translated by Norman Denny (London: Collins, 1974): 104.

[59]   Braudy: 200.

[60]   Abel: 36.

[61]   Ibid: 35.

[62]   Filho, in Pellizzari and Valentinetti (eds): 142.

[63]   Ibid: 143.

[64]   Pellizzari and Valentinetti (eds): 413.

[65]   Filho, in Pellizzari and Valentinetti (eds): 145.

[66]   Ibid. Unfortunately, as copies of *Souvenirs de Paris* (1928) and *Vous verrez la semaine prochaine* (1929) have been lost, it was not possible to discuss

them here.

67   Roy Armes, *French Cinema* (London: Secker & Warburg, 1985): 68.

68   John W Martin, *The Golden Age of French Cinema 1929-1939* (London: Columbus Books, 1987): 26.

69   Ibid: 27.

70   Richard Abel, *French Film Theory and Criticism: A History/Anthology 1907-1939. Volume II; 1929-1939* (Princeton, NJ: Princeton University Press, 1988): 47.

71   Quoted in ibid: 38.

72   Ibid: 57.

73   Ibid: 40.

74   Ibid: 66.

75   Andrew: 104.

76   Abel (1988): 9.

77   Ibid: 20.

78   Armes: 69.

79   Abel (1988): 21.

80   Ibid: 10.

81   Alberto Cavalcanti, "The Sound Film" [1938], in Jacobs (ed): 185.

82   Alberto Cavalcanti, "Discussion sur le film sonore (1935)", in Pellizzari and Valentinetti (eds): 217.

83   Jacobs (ed): 180.

84   Ghali: 56.

85   Abel (1984): 252.

86   Ibid: 421.

87   Williams: 248.

88   Filho, in Pellizzari and Valentinetti (eds): 138.

89   Ibid.

90   Williams: 201.

91   Filho, in Pellizzari and Valentinetti (eds): 144.

92   Ibid: 145.

93   Andrew: 97.

94   Ibid.

95   Williams: 204.

96   For a comprehensive account of scientific management, or "Taylorism", see Harry Braverman, *Labour and Monopoly Capitalism: The Degradation of Work in the Twentieth Century* (New York; London: Monthly Review Press, 1974).

97   Andrew: 97.

98   Martin: 27.

99   Armes: 69.

100   Ibid: 72.

101   Williams: 177.

102   Filho, in Pellizzari and Valentinetti (eds): 146.

103   Williams: 175.

104   Pellizzari and Valentinetti (eds): 416.

105   Filho, in Pellizzari and Valentinetti (eds): 147.

106   Translated from the French: "la table et le lit". Ibid: 149.

107   Sussex, in Aitken (ed): 185.

3
The Documentary Film Movement

As already mentioned, Cavalcanti's principal reason for leaving France in 1934 was his reluctance to continue with the boulevard-style comedies which he had been directing:

> After Paramount, I made a series of French comedies, which were awful, not only because they were talkies, but because they were sort of boulevard talkies in which people went from bed to table to supper and then back to bed. I was sick and tired. I had done four or five of these comedies and had signed for one more and then I didn't have the courage to go on. So I did what I have done many times in my long life, I said I was sick and I came to London to recover.[1]

Cavalcanti was attracted to London for a number of reasons. He had, of course, lived in England during his brief stay in Liverpool during 1921-22. He had also worked with British filmmakers prior to 1934, firstly on George Pearson's *The Little People* (1925), where he worked alongside Thorold Dickinson, and then on *Les Vacances du Diable* (*The Devil's Holiday*, 1930), where half the actors were English. One of Cavalcanti's closest collaborators in France, the cameraman Jimmy Rogers, was also active within the British film industry, and in a position to help him. Cavalcanti was also aware that *Rien que les heures* (*Nothing But the Hours*, 1926) had received a warm reception when the film was screened at the London Film Society in 1930, and that many involved with the Society regarded him as an important new director.[2]

In fact, the Film Society played a pivotal role in drawing Cavalcanti to London. At a time when the French avant-garde had gone into a period of decline under the pressure of the sound film revolution, the London Film Society was playing an important role in stimulating the growth of film culture in England. Founded by Ivor Montagu and others, the Film Society screened over 500 films between 1925 and 1939, including work by European directors such as Vigo, Dreyer, Dulac, Ruttmann, Eisenstein, Pudovkin, Renoir and Cavalcanti.[3] These screenings, and the debates which followed them, provided a foundation upon which many aspiring film directors and producers, including Michael Balcon, George Pearson, Thorold Dickinson, Alfred Hitchcock and Adrian Brunel, were later to build their careers. Various members of the documentary film movement, including John Grierson, Basil Wright, Arthur Elton, Sidney Cole and Cavalcanti, all of whom were members of the Film Society Council at one time or another, were also influenced by these screenings and debates.[4]

John Grierson, the leader of the documentary film movement, whose own *Drifters* was premièred at the Film Society in November 1929, saw *Nothing But the Hours* when it was first screened at the Society in 1930. Between 1930 and 1934, Grierson sought to reinforce his team of young documentary filmmakers at the EMB Film Unit with the addition of more experienced practitioners, and, with this in mind, he commissioned Robert Flaherty to make *Industrial Britain* in 1931.[5] By 1934, Grierson was particularly interested in appointing someone with expertise and interest in the sound film, as the newly-formed GPO Film Unit had just acquired both a sound system and a sound-recording studio.[6] Although *Nothing But the Hours* was a silent film, Cavalcanti had by this time already acquired a reputation as something of an authority on the creative use of sound in the cinema, and this made him particularly attractive to Grierson.

It was Jimmy Rogers, Cavalcanti's former cameraman, who first put Cavalcanti in touch with Grierson. Rogers, a regular attender at Film Society screenings, knew of the growing reputation of the documentary film movement, a reputation which, at that time, was based on the success of Grierson's *Drifters* and Flaherty's *Industrial Britain*, and on the critical platform provided by one of the movement's house journals, *Cinema Quarterly*.[7] Cavalcanti was impressed by the documentary film movement's association with Flaherty, whose *Nanook of the North* (1922) had been instrumental in influencing the growth of a documentary avant-garde practice in France,[8] and also believed that involvement with the documentary film movement might afford him the best opportunity available to become involved in creative and rewarding filmmaking activity in England. All this predisposed him to accept Grierson's offer of employment when it came, although it is unlikely that Grierson would have had much difficulty in persuading Cavalcanti to accept. Cavalcanti was desperate to leave the commercial industry in France at that time, and Grierson held out the prospect of something in which he, Cavalcanti, had been trying to become involved since 1929 – creative work with the sound film:

> Grierson told me about the documentary work that he was doing. I told him that there were great possibilities with sound which I wanted to work on but had not been able to do in France. Grierson said come to London for two or three months and teach the boys here about sound the way you understand it for

they know nothing about it. They had small studios in
Blackheath where I installed myself and began sound
experiments...We did lots of experimenting and the
results were very good.[9]

Nevertheless, Cavalcanti's decision to leave France for England
should not be regarded lightly. He was 37 years old in 1934, no longer
a young novice, and his decision to leave represented a decisive shift of
career and a turn away from the film culture within which he had
passed his formative years. Nor was it at all clear at the time that his
decision would ultimately prove to be a wise one.

The documentary film movement, 1929-36

The development of the documentary film movement has been
examined extensively elsewhere, and this is not the place to engage in
another inclusive account. Nevertheless, a summary and overview of
the movement's development up to 1939 will be necessary here in order
to situate Cavalcanti within that context. In particular, it is important
to understand the condition of the documentary film movement when
Cavalcanti joined in 1934, and how he fitted into the more general
picture of expansion and development up to 1937, when he replaced
John Grierson as head of production.

In 1924, Grierson was awarded a Guggenheim scholarship to
undertake research in the United States.[10] Although his research
project was initially concerned with the study of immigration, he soon
became more interested in issues of mass communication, and
broadened his project to include these.[11] One of the most significant
influences on him at this stage was Walter Lippmann, a writer on
public relations and propaganda issues, who argued that a
contradiction existed between the egalitarian principles underlying
democratic theory and the hierarchical nature of modern mass society.[12]
Lippmann's ideas were influenced by a more general context of
conservative ideology, prevalent in America at the time, which
questioned the validity of democratic processes. However, Grierson
disagreed with this view and argued that modern democratic structures
could work if adequate public information systems, which would both
service the state and inform the public, could be developed. From that
point onwards, Grierson's theory of documentary film was based on the
notion that public information, communicated through the medium of
film, could play a central role in sustaining democracy.

As his period of tenure in the United States came to an end,
Grierson became aware that, in Britain, the Empire Marketing Board
(EMB) had become one of the largest public information organisations
of its kind. In 1927, he contacted the EMB seeking employment, and
was eventually appointed there as Assistant Films Officer.[13] Between
1927 and 1929, Grierson produced a plan for film production at the
EMB, and the first film to emerge from this was *Drifters*. The EMB

The Documentary Film Movement · 45

Film Unit was established in the following year, and Grierson hired his first two apprentice filmmakers, Basil Wright and John Taylor. These were closely followed by J D Davidson, Arthur Elton, Edgar Anstey, Paul Rotha, Marion Grierson (John's younger sister), Evelyn Spice, Margaret Taylor (John Taylor's sister), Stuart Legg and Harry Watt.

However, the expansion of filmmaking activities at the EMB was soon undermined by other events taking place within the organisation. Grierson had initially been attracted to the EMB as a potential source of documentary film production because of its apparent size and importance. However, the EMB proved to be an untenable and transient institution, and anything but a secure foundation for the documentary film movement. Originally founded in 1924 as a half-hearted response to calls for effective protection for British trade within the Empire, the EMB largely failed to appease the proponents of protectionism, and the introduction of major tariff reform legislation in 1932 and 1933 rendered it irrelevant to the point where it was finally abolished in September 1933.[14] However, just prior to abolition, Stephen Tallents, the Secretary of the EMB and the man who had initially appointed Grierson, managed to secure a new appointment as Public Relations Officer at the Post Office. As a condition of his new appointment, Tallents insisted that the EMB Film Unit should also be transferred to the GPO and, in 1934, Grierson and his filmmakers moved to new premises in order to take up positions as employees of the Post Office.[15] It was also at this point that Cavalcanti joined the documentary film movement.

The films of the EMB Film Unit, 1929-34

By the time that Cavalcanti arrived in 1934, the documentary film movement had already built up four years of film production experience. However, Grierson's policy of recruiting young and relatively inexperienced novices meant that the overall level of technical and professional skill evident within the films produced between 1930 and 1934 was relatively low. These films fell into two distinct categories. Firstly, a number of routine advertising and publicity films were made which promoted aspects of Empire trade. Secondly, a smaller number of more innovative and experimental films, which explored the possibilities of film form, were also made. Although this latter group of films was sponsored by the EMB or by external organisations for specific commercial purposes, Grierson and his filmmakers sought opportunities to introduce an aesthetic and creative dimension whenever possible.

The first two films to emerge from the documentary film movement were short productions on pedigree cattle and herring fishing. The film on pedigree cattle was eventually dropped, and the herring film became *Drifters*. However, *Drifters* was very different from the straightforward publicity film which EMB officials had expected, and was a poetic montage documentary which drew heavily on the filmmaking styles of Eisenstein and Flaherty, and on Grierson's understanding of avant-garde aesthetics.

Drifters was followed by Conquest (Grierson/Wright, 1930), a compilation film of footage from Hollywood films, and then by a series of short films made by Basil Wright and Paul Rotha with titles such as Scottish Tomatoes and Butter (both 1930).[16] A number of other, relatively simple, single-reel films were also made during 1930, including South African Fruit and Canadian Apples (both Wright/ Rotha). The films produced in the following year were more advanced. Basil Wright directed The Country Comes to Town and O'er Hill and Dale; Arthur Elton made The Shadow on the Mountain and Upstream; Edgar Anstey made Uncharted Waters and Eskimo Village; and Robert Flaherty shot Industrial Britain.[17] However, all these films, with the exception of Industrial Britain, were relatively routine, commissioned projects which bore little relation to the groundbreaking Drifters.

One of Grierson's principal strategies for circumventing restrictions on filmmaking within the EMB was to seek commissions from outside organisations, and the final group of films to emerge from the EMB Film Unit, some of which were completed after the Board's demise, were largely commissioned by such organisations. Stuart Legg directed the first of these, New Generation (1932), for the Chesterfield Education Authority. Donald Taylor made Lancashire at Work and Play (1933) and Spring Comes to England (1934) in association with the Ministries of Labour and Advertising. Marion Grierson made So This Is London (1933) and For All Eternity (1934) for the Travel and Industrial Association. Evelyn Spice made a number of short films for schools on the English seasons, and Stuart Legg made two films for the GPO: The New Operator and Telephone Workers (both 1933). Basil Wright made Cargo from Jamaica and Windmill in Barbados (both 1934) for the EMB and the Orient Line, and then went on to make The Song of Ceylon (1934) for the Ceylon Tea Company. Arthur Elton made Aero Engine (1933) and The Voice of the World (1934) for HMV, and Harry Watt made Six Thirty Collection and B.B.C. Droitwich (both 1934) for the GPO and the BBC, respectively.[18]

A number of underlying themes can be identified in these early films. There is a general concern with issues of rural and regional identity, and with representations of working-class culture and craft skills. Work, as a distinct physical activity, embedded within the social relations of the small production unit and the rituals and techniques of skilled labour, constantly emerges as a recurrent theme, particularly in Drifters and Industrial Britain. In contrast, there are few representations of large-scale industry or mass labour. Similarly, representations of metropolitan life and culture, which become more common in the films made during the late-1930s, are conspicuously absent in these early films. A concern with indigenous cultures – particularly in Basil Wright's Cargo from Jamaica, Windmill in Barbados and The Song of Ceylon – can also be identified in this body of work.

This nascent tradition of filmmaking appears quite different from the films which Cavalcanti made between 1923 and 1934. During this period, Cavalcanti's films, particularly those over which he was able to exercise a degree of autonomy, were grounded in a realistic approach inherited from the pictorialist naturalist tradition, and overlaid by the influence of Surrealism, Impressionism and popular melodramatic traditions. The characteristic themes and preoccupations found in these films were also quite different from those found in the films produced by the EMB Film Unit between 1929 and 1934. In particular, the central preoccupation of the EMB films, that of the representation of working-class manual labour and craft skills, was entirely absent from Cavalcanti's films.

These dissimilarities soon led to the emergence of tensions between Cavalcanti and others within the GPO Film Unit, and these tensions were further exacerbated by a number of disagreements which quickly emerged between Cavalcanti and Grierson. One such disagreement concerned the attitude the two men adopted towards the commercial cinema. Grierson made a clear distinction between the state-sponsored documentary and commercial filmmaking, and rejected the idea that the documentary film movement should become involved in commercial feature filmmaking. However, although Cavalcanti's decision to join the documentary film movement had originally been motivated by his own disillusionment with the commercial film industry, he did not share Grierson's fundamentalist rejection of the commercial film, and his training in set design, editing, production and direction made him sensitive to the possibilities of operating effectively within the commercial industry.

Some critics have fastened onto Cavalcanti's willingness to work within the feature film to argue that he only joined the documentary film movement because he thought it might provide a useful stepping-stone to the British film industry. At their first meeting in 1934, Grierson himself told Cavalcanti outright that he only expected him to stay for approximately three months, before moving on to the commercial sector.[19] However, Cavalcanti always denied the charge that he used the documentary film movement in this way, and the evidence suggests that his denial should be believed. As has been shown, he had been seeking an opportunity to make small-scale innovative sound films since 1928, and the GPO Film Unit presented him with such an opportunity. Cavalcanti was also impressed by Grierson's *Drifters*, and hoped that his own involvement with the documentary film movement would afford him the opportunity to make films of a similar quality. The fact that Cavalcanti was also to stay with the documentary film movement for six years, rather than three months, also indicates that his commitment to the movement was a substantial one.

In addition to their difference of opinion over distinctions between the documentary and the commercial feature film, Grierson and Cavalcanti differed over the definition of documentary itself.

Grierson regarded the documentary as a special type of film, substantially different from the feature film, and his early theory of documentary disregarded distinctive aspects of the feature film such as characterisation and psychological motivation.[20] However, during the 1920s, Cavalcanti and other avant-garde filmmakers in France rejected the term "documentary" as insufficient to categorise films such as Flaherty's *Nanook of the North*, and argued instead that no fundamental distinction should be made between documentary and the feature film.[21] Although Cavalcanti agreed with Grierson that the documentary was an important film genre, he rejected the notion that it was fundamentally different from the feature film.

Cavalcanti's involvement with, and influence by, forms of cinematic realism differed significantly from Grierson's encounter with realism. Unlike Cavalcanti, Grierson was not particularly influenced by either French realist culture or French realist cinema. There is no evidence to suggest that he was familiar with the pictorial naturalist tradition embodied in the work of filmmakers such as André Antoine and Jacques de Baroncelli, or with the work of Louis Delluc, Marcel L'Herbier and Jean Epstein. In addition, there are few, if any, references in Grierson's writings to 19th-century French realism. Grierson was, in fact, far more influenced by the German, rather than the French, intellectual tradition and by the Russian, rather than the French, cinema.

In contrast, Cavalcanti was strongly influenced by French culture, firstly through his father's obsessive interest in Comte and the French rationalist tradition, and secondly through his stay in Paris between 1919 and 1920, when he became acquainted with the concert halls and art galleries there. Cavalcanti was also influenced by the French realist and naturalist filmmaking tradition. As we have seen, his earliest involvement in filmmaking was in realist films such as L'Herbier's *Résurrection* (1922) and *Feu Mathias Pascal* (*The Late Mathias Pascal*, 1925), and Delluc's *L'Inondation* (*The Flood*, 1923), and he carried on this tradition in his own *En rade* (*Stranded*, 1927). However, the themes and stylistic characteristics of the French realist and naturalist tradition were far removed from Grierson's concerns and interests at the time. For example, unlike that tradition, the theory of epic cinema which Grierson developed in the mid-1920s was essentially optimistic and positive in tone, and his theory of documentary film also contained little room for the darker preoccupations of the naturalist tradition.

In addition, although Grierson was influenced by the German philosophical tradition, he was opposed to the German Expressionist cinema, regarding it as too fatalistic and introverted in theme,[22] and it was the action-orientated and "heroic" tone of such Soviet films as *Turksib* (1930), a film about the construction of the trans-Siberian railway, rather than the avant-garde Expressionism of films such as Fritz Lang's *M* (1931), which provided the model for his own approach to filmmaking. In contrast, and in company with other members of the

Parisian avant-garde, Cavalcanti was strongly influenced by German Expressionist films, and the concern with *mise en scène*, luminous chiaroscuro and fatalistic subject-matter in such films fitted well with aspects of the naturalist tradition.

In terms of personality, Grierson and Cavalcanti were also very different: Grierson the abrasive, didactic Scot, fired by a missionary zeal concerning the nature of mass society, democracy and documentary film, who was also homophobic; Cavalcanti the cultivated Francophile intellectual with Third World sensibilities, who also happened to be homosexual. Nevertheless, despite these differences, Grierson and Cavalcanti did have some things in common. Both shared a degree of disillusionment with the more extreme excesses of the commercial film industry, and also a common antipathy towards extreme avant-garde practices. Finally, whatever differences may have existed between Cavalcanti and Grierson, the fact is that, during this period, the two men were mutually dependent upon each other. Whatever his personal feelings about Cavalcanti, Grierson depended on the latter's professional knowledge of film technique, a knowledge which the documentary film movement lacked in 1934, whilst Cavalcanti was perceptive enough to realise that his involvement with the documentary film movement probably constituted the most satisfying work he could have obtained in England at the time.

Cavalcanti and the documentary film movement, 1934-39

The operation which Cavalcanti joined in 1934 was, indeed, a small one, but it was growing fast. On transfer to the Post Office, the documentary filmmakers took up new residence in larger premises in Soho Square, where they remained until the outbreak of war in 1939. In addition, an old art studio in Blackheath, south London, was acquired for sound-recording purposes.[23] However, although these were important developments, facilities at the studios remained modest. For example, although the Post Office provided the Film Unit with a sound-recording system, they were also obliged by the Treasury to purchase a British Visatone system which was inferior to the more sophisticated American and German systems available at that time. As a consequence, many of the films made by the documentary film movement during the 1930s suffered from inferior sound quality.[24]

In 1935, Stephen Tallents left the GPO in order to take up an appointment at the BBC. Around the same time, Grierson and a number of the other filmmakers also decided to leave in order to develop the documentary film movement outside the public sector. Edgar Anstey was the first to go, establishing the Shell Film Unit in 1934. He was followed by Donald Taylor, Paul Rotha and Stuart Legg who set up the Strand Film Unit in 1935, and then by Basil Wright who established the Realist Film Unit in 1937.[25] Grierson himself finally resigned in June 1937 in order to set up Film Centre, an organisation dedicated to the coordination of documentary film production. By 1937, the documentary film movement consisted of four production units (the GPO Film Unit, Shell, Strand and Realist), the journal *World Film News*, which was launched in 1935, and Film Centre. Underlying this apparent expansion, however, was the fact that a significant division had emerged between those filmmakers remaining inside the GPO, including Cavalcanti, and those who had left.

These events also led to Cavalcanti's promotion to the post of production supervisor within the GPO Film Unit. One of the reasons why Grierson decided to leave in 1937 was that a Post Office Committee, which had been considering the future of the Film Unit, was due to report in 1936. Grierson expected the final report to place new restrictions on his room for manœuvre, and he was proved correct in this when the Committee of Enquiry, which reported in October, demoted his post of Films Officer to the less important one of production supervisor, which was then offered to Cavalcanti. From the Post Office's point of view, Grierson had always been a difficult employee who frequently ignored established civil service rules and procedures. Cavalcanti, on the other hand, was perceived more favourably as an experienced director and producer who could be relied upon to engage only in film production, rather than the constant proselytising characteristic of Grierson.

The administrative changes imposed on the GPO Film Unit in 1936 had the effect of establishing a more tightly regulated control of its operations than had previously been the case.[26] Initially, the filmmakers remaining at the Film Unit, including Cavalcanti, were apprehensive about these developments, fearing that their ability to make innovative films would now be more restricted than ever. However, this did not turn out to be the case, and, in fact, the new administrative structures put in place allowed Cavalcanti, Humphrey Jennings, Harry Watt and the others to concentrate more on filmmaking, and cast off the other responsibilities which Grierson had imposed upon them.

Between 1936 and 1939, with Cavalcanti at the helm as head of production, the GPO Film Unit continued to enjoy a reasonable degree of autonomy and to make a number of innovative films. Cavalcanti was now in a position to put his own ideas into practice far more than had been the case prior to 1936, and this led to the gradual appearance of films which differed significantly from those being made by documentary film units based outside the GPO. Despite this degree of autonomy, however, as was the case prior to 1936, the ability to make innovative films remained limited by the need to produce routine promotional films for the Post Office.

Cavalcanti as producer, 1934-39

The principal difficulty faced by any attempt to assess Cavalcanti's contribution to the films produced at the GPO Film Unit between 1934 and 1940 is that the credits attributed to those films are often unreliable, because Grierson and his filmmakers did not keep clear records of individual contributions. This is a particular problem in relation to Cavalcanti, because he was involved in so many films made by the documentary film movement over this period. Nevertheless, one initial distinction which can be made in order to assess Cavalcanti's contribution is between those films for which he is credited as producer, and those which, although he is not directly credited, nevertheless reveal his influence. Even here, however, a degree of uncertainty prevails, as some films contain no production credits at all.

Over the 1934-40 period, Cavalcanti has production credits for the following films: *S.O.S. Radio Service* (1934), *Book Bargain* (Norman McLaren, 1935), *Big Money* (Pat Jackson, 1935), *B.B.C.: The Voice of Britain* (1934), *Rainbow Dance* (Len Lye, 1936), *Calendar of the Year* (Evelyn Spice, 1936), *Roadways* (Legg and Coldstream, 1937), *The Saving of Bill Blewitt* (Harry Watt, 1937), *Mony a Pickle* (Norman McLaren, 1938), *N or NW* (Len Lye, 1938), *Happy in the Morning* (Pat Jackson, 1938), *Forty Million People* (John Monck, 1938), *North Sea* (Harry Watt, 1938), *Men in Danger* (Pat Jackson, 1938), *The City* (Ralph Elton, 1938), *Love on the Wing* (Norman McLaren, 1938), *Speaking from America* (Humphrey Jennings, 1939), *Spare Time* (Humphrey Jennings, 1939), *Spring Offensive* (Humphrey Jennings, 1939), *The Tocher* (Lotte Reiniger, 1939), *The HPO* (Lotte Reiniger, 1939), *Oh Whiskers* (Brian Pickersgill, 1939), *Squadron 992* (Harry Watt, 1939), *The First Days* (Jennings, Jackson and Watt, 1939) and *Men of the Lightship* (David Macdonald, 1940).

Cavalcanti also shares production credits with other members of the documentary film movement in a number of these films. The films in question are: *B.B.C.: The Voice of Britain*, co-produced by Cavalcanti, Grierson and Legg; *Rainbow Dance*, co-produced by Cavalcanti and Basil Wright; *Mony a Pickle*, co-produced by Cavalcanti and Richard Massingham; and *Forty Million People*, co-produced by Cavalcanti and Harry Watt. In addition to these production credits, Cavalcanti is credited for sound and editing on *The Song of Ceylon*, sound on *Coal Face* (Cavalcanti, 1935), and editing on *A Midsummer Day's Work* (Cavalcanti and others, 1939).

Cavalcanti's overall production credits within the GPO and Crown Film Units over the 1934-40 period are actually greater numerically than those of Grierson. Between 1934 and 1937 (when he left the GPO Film Unit), Grierson has production credits for between seventeen and twenty films. Over the same period, Cavalcanti has credits for between six and eight films, but, over the 1938-40 period, he has credits for a further sixteen. This means that Cavalcanti's overall contribution from 1934 to 1940 was greater than that of Grierson. These statistics also show that, whilst Cavalcanti's impact on the documentary film movement can be seen from as early as 1934, his impact was at its greatest between 1938 and 1939.

Cavalcanti's first engagement as producer at the GPO Film Unit was on a short film promoting the emergency radio service for shipping, *S.O.S. Radio Service*, a short, silent precursor of *North Sea*. However, his most important intervention as producer in 1934 was undoubtedly on Basil Wright's *The Song of Ceylon*. Cavalcanti's credit on the film is as production supervisor, but his main role was in working with the film's director, Basil Wright, and music composer, Walter Leigh, to produce the film's sound and music track, and to synchronise that to the image track.[27] *The Song of Ceylon* was one of the most aesthetically accomplished films ever to be made by the documentary film movement, winning the Prix du Gouvernement Belge at the Brussels Film Festival in 1935, and gaining widespread critical praise, both at the time of its release and afterwards.[28] As Wright has, quite reasonably, been given the major credit for *The Song of Ceylon*. However, it is worth bearing in mind that Wright had made nothing of equivalent stature prior to 1934, and would make nothing of comparable quality afterwards. Similarly, the impressive use of sound and music in the film cannot be attributed to the intervention of Walter Leigh alone, because he, like Wright, had no track record of producing work of such quality prior to this.

Although Wright and Leigh certainly made important contributions to *The Song of Ceylon*, the fact that the appearance of such an outstanding film coincided with the recent arrival of Cavalcanti indicates that the latter's involvement was a major factor in the film's success. The often discordant contrapuntal and non-synchronised use of sound and music in *The Song of Ceylon* closely accords with the views on the use of sound and music in films which Cavalcanti had expressed during the early 1930s, and is also similar in some respects to the soundtrack of *Au Pays du scalp* (*In the Country of the Scalp People*, 1931). However, the last word on the matter should go to Basil Wright:

> I was enormously grateful to him and always shall be,
> apart from his friendship which I managed to obtain,
> for all the things he did on the films I was working on,
> like *Song of Ceylon* and *Night Mail*. His ideas about
> the use of sound were so liberating that they would
> liberate in you about a thousand other ideas.[29]

In the following year, Cavalcanti worked as producer on Norman McLaren's *Book Bargain* and *Big Money*. However, his most important intervention in 1935 was, like *The Song of Ceylon*, on another production carried over from the EMB period: Stuart Legg's *B.B.C.: The Voice of Britain*. As with *The Song of Ceylon*, Cavalcanti contributed suggestions for the film's soundtrack, which contained extracts of Adrian Boult conducting the BBC Symphony Orchestra, and Henry Hall conducting the BBC Dance Orchestra. The film also contained a montage of interviews with writers such as George Bernard Shaw and J B Priestley, all of which were edited by Cavalcanti. Cavalcanti's involvement as producer on *B.B.C.: The Voice of Britain* was greater than it had been on *The Song of Ceylon*, and this probably reflected both his increasing involvement within the GPO Film Unit, and the extent to which his particular expertise in sound was brought to bear on a film which was centrally concerned with that subject. Despite this, however, Cavalcanti is not credited as the sole producer on *B.B.C.: The Voice of Britain*, but shares this credit with Grierson and Legg.

In 1936, Cavalcanti produced Len Lye's *Rainbow Dance*, Evelyn Spice's *Calendar of the Year*, and Harry Watt and Basil Wright's *Night Mail* (1936). Clearly, the most important of these films was the latter, although the precise nature of Cavalcanti's contribution to *Night Mail* remains unclear. Photographed and directed by Harry Watt, with directorial assistance from Basil Wright, and produced by John Grierson, *Night Mail* also features music by Benjamin Britten, poetry by W H Auden and editing by Basil Wright and R Q McNaughton. Cavalcanti's credited involvement is as general supervisor for the soundtrack, which was put together by A E Pawley. However, Cavalcanti argued that his credit for "sound direction" on the film does not do justice to his overall contribution, and he also claimed that his ideas on sound and image relationships permeate *Night Mail*. Cavalcanti also argued that *Night Mail* depends for the success of its techniques on the earlier *Coal Face*, which he directed.[30]

Cavalcanti was credited as producer on only two films in 1937, Stuart Legg and William Coldstream's *Roadways* and Harry Watt's *The Saving of Bill Blewitt*. The first of these examines the development of the modern road transport system and is largely journalistic in tone. Although there are some interesting sequences in the film dealing with the life and work of itinerant lorry drivers, and the development of the road haulage industry in the aftermath of the First World War, the film does not show Cavalcanti's imprint particularly strongly, and is much more the typical product of its principal director, Stuart Legg.[31]

The Saving of Bill Blewitt, is more significant in that it marks the beginning of the collaboration between Cavalcanti and Harry Watt which ultimately led to the development of major wartime story-documentaries such as *Target for To-night* (1941). Prior to 1936, Cavalcanti and Watt had discussed the possibility of adapting the documentary so as to include aspects of the feature film, and, after Grierson's departure, these discussions continued with renewed vigour. Cavalcanti and Watt wished, in particular, to develop a type of film which, whilst remaining dependent on actuality footage, would dispense with voice-over commentary, and employ forms of characterisation and dramatic development normally associated with the feature film. This, in some respects, marked a return to the tradition of narrative realist filmmaking with which Cavalcanti had begun his career, although, like its successor, *North Sea*, *The Saving of Bill Blewitt* still differed in a number of important respects from films such as L'Herbier's *Résurrection* and Delluc's *The Flood*. *The Saving of Bill Blewitt* concerns two sailors whose boat has been wrecked, and who, as a result of using the Post Office savings scheme, find themselves able to buy a new one. The film's narrative contains a modicum of dramatic development, and also attempts, with mixed results, to build characterisation through the use of humour and colloquial dialogue. This type of film, the product of both Cavalcanti's and Watt's dissatisfaction with the Griersonian distinction between documentary and the feature film, departed fundamentally from Grierson's montage-based theory of documentary film. As with the later *North Sea*, however, the general tone of the film, and its use of actors, dialogue and character traits are more accurately identified with Watt than with Cavalcanti. Cavalcanti clearly supported these projects and wished, like Watt, to develop this hybrid form of film further, but few of his characteristic themes and stylistic techniques can be found in the two films.

Cavalcanti took over fully from Grierson as the effective leader of the GPO Film Unit in early 1938, and, as a result of this change of role, the number of films on which he worked as producer that year grew from two in the previous year to eight. At the same time, Cavalcanti directed only one film in 1938: *Alice au pays romand* (*Alice in Switzerland*), a promotional film on Lausanne, commissioned by the Association des Intérêts de Lausanne. In 1937, he had directed four films: *We Live in Two Worlds*, *Who Writes to Switzerland?*, *Message from Geneva* and *Four Barriers* (1937). Like *Alice in Switzerland* and both *Line to Tcherva Hut* (1936) and *Men of the Alps* (1939), these films were set in Switzerland, and commissioned by the Swiss government. The shift from direction to production which took place in Cavalcanti's activities in 1938 therefore marks an important development in his relationship with the other filmmakers at the GPO Film Unit, in which his role as overall production supervisor and leader of the GPO Film Unit became firmly established.

The films which Cavalcanti produced, or co-produced, in 1938 included *Mony a Pickle* (Norman McLaren and Richard Massingham), *N or NW* (Len Lye), *Happy in the Morning* (Pat Jackson), *Forty Million People* (John Monck), *North Sea* (Harry Watt), *Men in Danger* (Pat Jackson), *The City* (Ralph Elton) and *Love on the Wing*. These films cover a variety of subjects. *Happy in the Morning* was made for the Gas Council, and shows how modern gas fires eliminate the drudgery of making up coal fires. *Mony a Pickle* was, like *The Saving of Bill Blewitt*, made for the Post Office Savings Bank, and is about ways of saving up to buy a house. *Forty Million People* was made for the Ministry of Health, and concerns the development of social services in Britain from the Industrial Revolution to the present day. Both *Men in Danger* and *North Sea* promote the Post Office telecommunications systems, and depict dramatic events at sea, whilst *The City* is concerned with the problems of traffic congestion and urban development in London. Some of these films, including *The City* and *Forty Million People*, employ complex sociological and historical frameworks, whilst others use a range of approaches, from comedy in

N or NW, to psychological characterisation and drama in *North Sea*.

Two films amongst this group which reveal Cavalcanti's distinctive, somewhat anarchic stamp, are *Mony a Pickle* and *N or NW*. In the latter film, about the virtues of using the correct postal address, Lye and Cavalcanti employ a whimsical story about two lovers who almost separate as a result of using the wrong postcode on their letters of reconciliation. The rather thin story-line is embellished with elaborate special effects, including shots of postboxes and letters seen spinning through the sky. *N or NW* also employs superimpositions, a background jazz score, non-synchronous sound effects, and a highly complex editing structure which uses partial repetition and extreme camera angles. One shot, reminiscent of paintings by the Surrealist artist René Magritte, shows an eye looking at the viewer through a hole cut in a letter which the viewer is reading. The overall tone of this scene and the film as a whole is playful and ironic, and the use of songs and music recalls Cavalcanti's earlier *La P'tite Lilie* (1927) and *Le Petit chaperon rouge* (*Little Red Riding Hood*, 1929).

In *Mony a Pickle*, Cavalcanti and McLaren use comic forms, local dialect and humorous characterisation to embellish another thin tale, this time about thrifty Scots, their savings, and the Post Office Savings Bank. Again, as in *N or NW*, animation is employed, particularly in a scene in which kitchen appliances shuffle around in the kitchen and become transformed into new, updated versions of themselves. *Mony a Pickle* also uses subjective point-of-view shots. For example, in one scene, a young couple, dreaming of a new house, have their dreams turned into reality. As the couple imagine their future, the dowdy furniture in their room becomes transformed into more desirable modern products. Then the couple unexpectedly, and disorientatingly, see new "ideal" versions of themselves. As the imaginary becomes real, the couple take fright, and leave the room in alarm. Such elaborate use of a double diegesis and subjective view-point betrays Cavalcanti's French Impressionist background here, and illustrates the ironic and comic stance which he often adopted within his films.

The most important film which Cavalcanti produced in 1938 was undoubtedly Harry Watt's *North Sea*. Although, in theory, a promotional film for the Post Office's ship-to-shore radio communications system, *North Sea* is essentially a short dramatic adventure film about a fishing trawler which becomes damaged during a storm. The film adopts what Watt refers to as a "rhetorical" structure, consisting of a "prologue" in which the men prepare to go to sea, a "thesis" in which the journey to sea develops unproblematically, an "antithesis" in which the vessel is stricken by the storm, and a "synthesis" in which the danger is resolved and the ship returns to harbour.[32] The actors employed on the film were local fishermen, and most of the shooting was filmed on location. Like the earlier *The Saving of Bill Blewitt*, *North Sea* employs a combination of documentary and dramatic conventions, and, like the earlier film, it is uneven and often unsuccessful, particularly in establishing characterisation.

Although, in some respects *North Sea* could be considered as constituting a significant step towards Cavalcanti's aspiration to establish a realist, rather than solely documentary, cinema, in other respects the film is quite different from the realist style of filmmaking with which he had become familiar prior to 1934. The overall tone of *North Sea* is colloquial and relatively unsophisticated, and, in general, the film reflects the influence of Watt, rather than Cavalcanti. In addition, although *North Sea* provided the model for the story-documentaries which Watt went on to make during the 1940s, it should be borne in mind that, unlike Watt, Cavalcanti abandoned the story-documentary approach after 1940.

One aspect of *North Sea* which can clearly be related to Watt, rather than Cavalcanti, is an ideological discourse around the exercise of authority and leadership. Although the film depicts the interactions and tensions between a group of men caught up in a crisis on board a stricken trawler, it privileges the role of the captain:

> [The] skipper [was] the lead player, and utterly vital to the whole story...while the others just had to be themselves, he had to act...He had to be authoritative, resourceful...He had to slave-drive the crew when they were all dropping with fatigue, yet give them hope and cheer.[33]

Such an emphasis on the necessity of leadership, and on the exercise of gritty, pragmatic and down-to-earth authority can be found in many of Watt's films, including *North Sea, Nine Men* (1943), *Eureka Stockade* (1949) and *Where No Vultures Fly* (1951). Although these themes are rarely explored with much sensitivity and imagination, they nevertheless remain part of Watt's authorial signature. However, no such emphasis can be found in films directed by Cavalcanti, and, in fact, given the latter's predisposition for the ironic, one can only imagine him parodying such themes, rather than treating them as serious objects of study.

Cavalcanti's influence on *North Sea* can be seen most clearly in the film's use of non-synchronous sound and formalist editing devices. Although *North Sea* is, in general, linear and naturalist in style, it uses over 60 formal linking devices, including wipes, fades and dissolves, a large number for a film of only 30 minutes' duration. One scene in the film which also appears to show the imprint of Cavalcanti particularly strongly occurs towards the end, when verses of the hymn "Eternal Father" are sung over a series of shots showing the fishing town (Aberdeen) during the evening. The complexity of sound-image relationships used here marks the scene out from the remainder of the film, and is reminiscent of sequences from both *The Song of Ceylon* and *Night Mail*.

If the directors of all the films mentioned previously are taken as a group, a clear shift in the balance of power within the GPO Film Unit can be observed following Grierson's departure and Cavalcanti's accession to the post of production supervisor. Watt, of course, had been employed by Grierson during the EMB period. However, between 1936 and 1940, when Grierson, Anstey, Rotha, Wright, Taylor and others left the GPO Film Unit, Watt remained and became increasingly associated with Cavalcanti. Similarly, Lye, McLaren, Elton and Jackson were all GPO Film Unit appointees, and consequently were more influenced by Cavalcanti's ideas than by those of Grierson. Between 1938 and 1940, these directors worked under Cavalcanti's leadership, taking the documentary film movement in a different direction to that then being urged by the movement's founder. Initially, no clear breach was evident between the filmmakers at the GPO and those outside it. However, by 1939, the differences between the two camps had increased significantly, and reached a peak in 1942, when Grierson, Rotha and others began openly to criticise Cavalcanti.

Between 1938 and 1940, Cavalcanti was also responsible for the production of the following films: *The Tocher, The HPO, Oh Whiskers, Speaking from America, Spare Time, Spring Offensive, The First Days, Squadron 992* (all 1939) and *Men of the Lightship* (1940). Of these, four were directed by Humphrey Jennings, indicating the growing closeness of the relationship between the two men over this period. In contrast, Harry Watt, often thought to be closest to Cavalcanti at this time, has sole directorial credits for only one film.

The most important of these nine films are the four directed by Jennings, and Macdonald's *Men of the Lightship*. The two animation films made by Lotte Reiniger, a German emigré filmmaker who came to Britain in 1936, are untypical of the work of the GPO and Crown Film Units during this period, and the same applies to Pickersgill's *Oh Whiskers*, another short animation piece. Watt's *Squadron 992* is concerned with the operation and maintenance of the wartime barrage balloon fleet. Despite the praise given to it then and afterwards by Grierson, particularly over the edited sequence in which shots of a greyhound chasing a rabbit are cut against shots of a Spitfire pursuing a German bomber, it is a routine film: in retrospect, even the greyhound sequence now appears laboured and rather wooden, and was probably the work of R Q McNaughton, rather than Watt.[34]

The fact that four of these final eight films were directed by Jennings, and only one by Watt, indicates that Cavalcanti's most important relationship during his final period at the GPO Film Unit was with Jennings. However, Cavalcanti's approach to filmmaking between 1938 and 1940 encapsulated and reached beyond the work of both Watt and Jennings. Cavalcanti made films in association with Watt which employed location-shooting, "social actors" and linear, dramatic narratives, whilst he made other films in collaboration with Jennings in which he developed a more modernist cinematic practice, based on non-linear narrative structures and the non-synchronous, symbolic use of sound and image relationships.

Spare Time, the first major collaboration between Cavalcanti and Jennings, was also responsible for bringing the growing breach between those members of the documentary film movement associated with Cavalcanti, and those with Grierson, to a head. Like Jennings' and McAllister's later *Listen to Britain* (1942), with its images of undernourished factory workers, *Spare Time* makes no attempt to idealise the working-class people it depicts, but, on the contrary, presents them as ordinary, and as engaged in mundane, often trivial pursuits. However, Grierson and others within the documentary film movement interpreted this attempt at impartial observation differently, and believed that, rather than merely describing the working class, Jennings and Cavalcanti were mocking them. One episode in particular, in which Jennings filmed a kazoo band performing in Manchester, was particularly strongly criticised in this respect.[35] Writing about this episode later, Basil Wright reiterated these criticisms when he argued that "Humphrey seemed to show, in our opinion, a patronizing, sometimes almost sneering attitude towards the efforts of the lower-income groups to entertain themselves. I'm thinking particularly of the kazoo band sequence".[36]

These criticisms of *Spare Time* were, in some respects, understandable, given that the documentary film movement had struggled for so long to make and endorse films containing positive representations of working-class people. However, such criticisms also underlined the degree of division which existed within the movement by 1939, and the extent to which criticism was being increasingly focused on Jennings and Cavalcanti, particularly by Grierson, who later described Cavalcanti as a "fellow traveller" and Jennings as "a minor poet...stilted...and fearfully sorry for the working class".[37] However, what Grierson and Wright interpreted as the expression of a patronising attitude towards working-class people was, in fact, the consequence of the influence of anthropology on Jennings, with its emphasis on impartial and disinterested observation, and the influence of the French realist tradition on Cavalcanti, with its characteristic concern for placing individuals, warts and all, within their social and cultural environment. It was the combination of these influences which placed *Spare Time* "far outside the mainstream of British documentary",[38] and which caused so much unease amongst Grierson and his associates in 1939.

Another aspect of *Spare Time* which baffled Grierson and the others was the way in which the film employed ambivalent conjunctions of images. For example, one of Grierson's closest associates, Edgar Anstey, claimed that he was troubled by the prevalence of "the curious, the eccentric, the inexplicable, the mysterious" in *Spare Time*.[39] This aspect of the film suggests the influence of Surrealism, an influence shared by both Jennings and Cavalcanti, and the film's latent surreality was also reinforced by its remit, which was to:

[S]how that workers of all grades have a secondary
life, over and above their working life, in which
colliers may become musicians, musicians may become
engineers, engineers may become dog-fanciers and so
on.[40]

Spare Time therefore is centrally concerned with the way in
which popular cultural activity emerges from a working life which is
quite different from it, and it is this depiction of the degree of difference
between these two spheres of existence which is partly responsible for
the film's ambivalent surreality. The final voice-over, which proclaims
that "as things are, spare time is a time when we have a chance to do
what we like, a chance to be most ourselves", also appears to elevate
this sometimes eccentric leisure culture above the world of work, an
elevation which flatly contradicted the Griersonian imperative to
celebrate the value of manual labour.

Cavalcanti's contribution to *Spare Time* was considerable. As
the film's producer, he was closely involved with Jennings in its
development, and also contributed many ideas which eventually found
their way into the final version of the film. A scrutiny of the way in
which the script for the film evolved also reveals that Cavalcanti's
original conception of it differed from that of Jennings. Cavalcanti
began work on the scenario for *Spare Time* in 1938, at a time when
Jennings was absent working with Len Lye at the Shell Film Unit.[41]
Cavalcanti's initial suggestions for the film include the following:

Female mill worker, machine tending or some such
repetitive work, rehearsing her lines for a play in which
she is to appear, perhaps a pretentious passage in great
contrast to her actual work...Pigeons might yield a
sequence...by a tie-up with a football match. Pigeons
can be seen fluttering up from the crowds at any big
match, carrying half-time results to the distant home of
the spectator...When a Tynesider stayed indoors for
some weeks, he gave the explanation that his dog had
died, and a man 'looks daft without his dog'.[42]

Cavalcanti's suggestions indicate that he wanted *Spare Time*
to be a more ironic and surreal study of popular culture than the final
version, made in mid-1939, turned out to be. The final version of the
film dispenses with such themes as the banality of repetitive labour
and the pretentious nature of high-cultural aspirations, replacing them
with a more lyrical and elegiac tone which expresses Jennings', rather
than Cavalcanti's, interpretation of the English character. Here, as in
later films, a distinction can be made between Jennings' ardent and
pensive preoccupation with the meaning and character of English
national identity, and Cavalcanti's more anarchic, quirky and parodic
approach.

Before working on *Spare Time*, Cavalcanti produced *The HPO* and *The Tocher*, two animated films directed by Lotte Reiniger. Reiniger, who had made animated films in Germany from as early as 1921, specialised in a technique based on the use of cut-out silhouettes placed against painted backdrops. *The HPO* uses cartoon images of angels perched on clouds to illustrate the theme that "it's heaven to receive a greetings telegraph, be an angel and send one". The spurious nature of the attempt to link the film, which is basically an exercise in slightly camp cartoon animation, to a Post Office service (the telegraph) is even more overt in *The Tocher*. Described in the credits as a "film ballet", with musical themes from Rossini arranged by Benjamin Britten, *The Tocher* is a fairy tale set in a Gaelic fantasy world, in which young Angus wins his true love, Rhona, despite the protestations of her father, the Laird, and with the help of the "wee folk". The wee folk present the brooding Angus, rejected by Rhona because of his lack of wealth, with a treasure chest within which is a Post Office savings book. Angus then rides back through a Celtic landscape shrouded in mist to present his book to the Laird, just as Rhona is about to be married to a rather dumpy-looking kinsman. The savings book does the trick and the two live happily ever afterwards.

The quirky humour and non-naturalistic music and sound combinations in these two films situate them alongside other "fantasy" films produced at the GPO Film Unit following Cavalcanti's arrival, and upon which he had a considerable influence. These include Cavalcanti's first film for the documentary film movement, *Pett and Pott* (1934), subtitled "A Fantasy of the Suburbs"; *The Fairy of the Phone* (Coldstream, 1936), described in the credits as a "fanciful comedy with musical sequences"; *Love on the Wing*, a colour animation film involving flying horses; and Len Lye's *A Colour Box* (1935). Lye's *Kaleidoscope* (1935), *Rainbow Dance*, *Trade Tattoo* (1937) and *N or NW* also fall into this category. All these films share a predisposition towards an anarchic and often camp antirealism, which sets them apart from the more serious, journalistic documentaries produced by Grierson and his associates, and which also reveals the influence of Cavalcanti. A prime example of this is *The Fairy of the Phone*, which uses a phantom telephone operator (the "fairy") who materialises alongside telephone users, offering advice on how to use the telephone properly. In one scene, which purportedly attempts to illustrate the way in which different types of people answer the telephone differently, a young dandy becomes transformed, first into a maid, then into a rather camp businessman. Parodic contrapuntal music is also used throughout the film alongside a series of special effects techniques which include wipes, fades and superimpositions.

One of Cavalcanti's important, although little-known, contributions to the documentary film movement was therefore to this group of films which includes *The Fairy of the Phone* and most of the films directed by Reiniger, Lye and McLaren at the GPO Film Unit between 1934 and 1939. These parodic, surreal and often camp films are also modernist in their use of montage and other special effects techniques, and, when grouped together, constitute an alternative tradition of filmmaking within the documentary film movement – and one which can be directly associated with Cavalcanti.

Cavalcanti, the GPO Film Unit and the Ministry of Information

At the outbreak of war, the GPO Film Unit was put at the service of the newly-formed Ministry of Information (MoI), although it was not formally incorporated into the Ministry's Films Division until April 1940. This initial, arm's-length administrative arrangement reflected apprehensions concerning the documentary film movement, and Grierson in particular, held within the civil service.[43] As a consequence, and in opposition to the demands for full inclusion of the Film Unit within the MoI then being made within the pages of one of the documentary film movement's house journals, *Documentary Newsletter*, measures were put in place to block the immediate entry of the Film Unit into the Films Division.[44]

The complicated institutional position in which the GPO Film Unit found itself between August 1939 and April 1940 unsettled Cavalcanti and the other filmmakers. The Film Unit had initially suffered as a consequence of the fact that the first Head of Films Division, Joseph Ball, the former Director of the Conservative Party's Research Department, was unsympathetic to the approach taken by the documentary film movement, and unimpressed by the claim that the movement produced better films than those made within the commercial sector.[45] It was not until Ball's dismissal in December 1939, and his eventual replacement by Kenneth Clark, that the GPO Film Unit was fully incorporated into Films Division, an event which occurred on 1 April 1940.[46] Despite this change of status, however, and somewhat anomalously, the unit retained its original title of the GPO Film Unit. The change of title to Crown Film Unit did not occur until December 1940, after Cavalcanti had left.[47] Clark stayed for four months as Head of Films Division before he was replaced by Jack Beddington towards the end of April 1940.[48] Beddington was sympathetic to the general aims of the documentary film movement, and had been associated with elements of it as early as the start of the 1930s, when, as Director of Publicity for Shell-Mex, he had commissioned Paul Rotha's *Contact* (1933).[49] In August 1940, Beddington also blocked an attempt to sack Watt, Cavalcanti and Jennings, who some within the MoI thought could be replaced by cheaper and more commercially-orientated directors.[50]

Despite the arrival of Beddington, Cavalcanti announced his intention to leave the GPO Film Unit.[51] Cavalcanti claimed that his decision to leave was made in response to demands from civil servants that he relinquish his Brazilian citizenship and become a British citizen: "They wanted me to get naturalised, and I didn't want to get naturalised...I don't believe I could be English just by changing my passport".[52] Elsewhere, Cavalcanti claimed that it was because he refused to relinquish his Brazilian citizenship that Ian Dalrymple was given his job: "The GPO people...put someone [Dalrymple] in my place... It was very silly on their part. I had been practically in charge at the GPO and they put someone in my place".[53] Although Cavalcanti first announced his decision to leave the GPO Film Unit in April 1940, he did not actually leave until August. However, in July, Ian Dalrymple, a commercial film producer who had worked for Alexander Korda as a scriptwriter, editor and associate producer during the 1930s, was appointed to Cavalcanti's post as Director of Film Production.[54]

Cavalcanti's claim that he left the GPO because he was under pressure as a foreign national is also supported by Harry Watt, who has described Cavalcanti as "the alien, whom some Blimps always suspected".[55] Cavalcanti's successor, Ian Dalrymple, also believed that he left for the same reasons:

> [H]e was a Brazilian, and as there was a state of war it was considered that they couldn't very well have an official government unit, which the GPO became under the Ministry of Information, run by a Brazilian.[56]

However, there are a number of problems with these accounts of Cavalcanti's departure. Although there may well have been some within the MoI who were concerned about the fact that he was not a British national, there is no evidence, other than the anecdotal recollections of those mentioned earlier, to suggest that any serious attempt was ever made to force him to change nationality. Although having a foreign national in charge of a government unit during wartime was unusual, the fact that this particular unit was involved in filmmaking would have made the situation less of an issue, given that so many other foreign nationals were employed in the film industry at the time. In addition, foreign nationals were frequently employed within the propaganda service because of their language skills, and the fact that Cavalcanti was from a neutral country and had been a resident in Britain for six years by 1940 would also have made his nationality less of an issue. There is also evidence to suggest that, contrary to Cavalcanti's recollections, some officials within the MoI were extremely keen that he should remain in the post. Cavalcanti was not regarded as untrustworthy in the way in which Grierson was, and he was widely admired, both within the Post Office and the MoI, as a competent and successful film producer. In fact, even after he had announced his decision to leave the GPO Film Unit MoI officials continued their attempts to persuade him to change his mind.[57]

Another reason given by Cavalcanti for wanting to leave the Film Unit was that he felt ill at ease with some of the people appointed to the Films Division of the MoI in 1940. According to Michael Balcon, Cavalcanti was disappointed by the increased bureaucracy at the MoI, and worried about the fact that the GPO Film Unit's future had once again been placed in question.[58] There is no doubt that the position of the GPO Film Unit remained precarious throughout the duration of the war. MoI policy regarding film propaganda was based on a strategy of developing projects in collaboration with commercial film producers, rather than one of making its own films, and only one feature film, Michael Powell's *49th Parallel* (1941), was produced by the MoI during the war. It is not surprising, therefore, that, in the light of this policy, some within the MoI came to question whether the existence of Crown as a government film unit was acceptable or tenable at all. Such deliberations clearly threatened the very survival of the Film Unit, and must have unsettled Cavalcanti.

Another reason for Cavalcanti's departure from the Film Unit was that he had only joined the documentary film movement by default in the first place, and had been waiting for his opportunity to join the commercial feature film industry. Writing in 1977, Rotha puts this point of view particularly bluntly, if not testily:

> Cavalcanti was working at the GPO Film Unit. He merely came to this country because he wanted to work in the field of feature films. But Korda and everybody else would not give him work, so Grierson gave him a job in the GPO Film Unit.[59]

However, Rotha's ungenerous account does not do Cavalcanti justice. Whilst it is true that Cavalcanti joined the documentary film movement because he wanted to experiment with sound filmmaking rather than make documentaries, this does not mean that he was merely exploiting the documentary film movement for his own self-interest. Cavalcanti had never really been a committed documentary filmmaker, and even *Nothing But the Hours*, often regarded as a documentary, cannot really be classed as such, whilst *Stranded*, which is far more typical of his work, is definitely not a documentary. The fact is that Cavalcanti's work in the cinema whilst in France contained elements which could not be fruitfully developed within the framework of the documentary, and the move back into feature filmmaking was, therefore, a logical step for him to take, and one which allowed him again to pursue the approach to filmmaking which he had last explored in France. In addition, when Cavalcanti left the Film Unit in 1940, it was not to join just any commercial company, but Ealing Studios, a small company which paid its staff a pittance, but which was also committed to quality, realist filmmaking.

In the spring of 1940, Cavalcanti took advantage of a clause in his contract which allowed him to leave the GPO Film Unit temporarily.[60] Shortly after commencing this leave of absence Cavalcanti made contact with Michael Balcon, the Head of Production at Ealing Studios, and entered into discussions with him over a plan whereby the GPO Film Unit would make a feature film at Ealing under

Cavalcanti's supervision.[61] Balcon then wrote to Jack Beddington in August 1940, outlining his and Cavalcanti's plans for a programme of films which would be made alongside the regular Ealing programme of production, three of which, it was hoped, would be made by the GPO Film Unit. The first of these films was to be called *Spitfire*, and was to be directed by Walter Forde. The second film was to be called *ENSA*, and was probably to have been directed by Harry Watt, whilst the third was to be based on an unspecified story by Louis Golding, and was to have been directed by Jack Holmes.[62] There seems no doubt that Cavalcanti was completely committed to this project, and to the eventual relocation of the GPO Film Unit at Ealing. Balcon was equally pledged to the project because he wanted to initiate his own programme of propaganda film production at Ealing. Like many within the film trade, Balcon believed that the MoI ought to commission films from commercial studios such as Ealing, rather than make its own in competition with the commercial sector, and the transfer of the GPO Film Unit to Ealing would, accordingly, advance both Balcon's strongly held convictions regarding this issue, and Ealing's commercial ambitions. However, despite Cavalcanti and Balcon's endorsement, Beddington rejected their plan out of hand, because he refused to allow the GPO Film Unit to be "taken over" by Ealing.[63] Although Cavalcanti had originally announced his intention to leave the GPO Film Unit in April, he had held on in the hope that he and Balcon's plan would be successful. He must have been disappointed, therefore, when his bluff was called, and Dalrymple was appointed as his successor before he had actually left. Cavalcanti's position in the three weeks or so between Dalrymple's appointment and his own departure from the GPO Film Unit must have been a difficult one, and he left within days of learning about Beddington's decision.

In many respects, Cavalcanti's departure from the GPO Film Unit marked the beginning of the end of the documentary film movement as a creative force. After 1940, the most aesthetically successful films made at the Crown Film Unit were all directed by Humphrey Jennings, and even Jennings' and McAllister's canonic *Listen to Britain* was strongly influenced by Cavalcanti. After Cavalcanti's departure, the most important type of filmmaking developed at Crown during the war years was the story-documentary. However, although films such as *Target for To-night*, *Coastal Command* (Jack Holmes, 1942), *Close Quarters* (1943), *Fires Were Started* (Jennings, 1943) and *Western Approaches* (Pat Jackson, 1944) were extremely popular during the war, they do not, with the important exception of *Fires Were Started*, stand up particularly well to the passage of time. Furthermore, shortly after Cavalcanti left, the Crown Film Unit entered into a slow and gradual spiral of decline which continued more or less unabated until the unit was finally abolished in 1952.[64] Cavalcanti's departure from the GPO Film Unit was, therefore, a decisive event which had considerable consequences for both himself and the documentary film movement. It could also be argued that, without his involvement, the movement quickly became a spent force.

The First Days (1939) and *Men of the Lightship* (1940)

After *Spare Time*, the second important film made during the final period of Cavalcanti's time within the documentary film movement, and the first major film to emerge from the GPO Film Unit during the war, was *The First Days*. The First Days was made under the direct initiative of Cavalcanti during a period in which the documentary filmmakers at the Crown Film Unit were under-employed by the MoI.[65] Although co-directed by Humphrey Jennings, Harry Watt and Pat Jackson, *The First Days* reveals the influence of Jennings and Cavalcanti, rather than that of Watt and Jackson. This is apparent, for example, in the opening sequences, in which people are shown listening to Chamberlain's announcement of the declaration of war against Germany. The use of non-synchronous sound, lyrical visual imagery, popular music and a *cinéma-vérité* observational style here is typical of both Jennings' and Cavalcanti's work, although the solemn, sometimes elegiac concern with national identity here and in much of the remainder of the film is more accurately associated with Jennings alone.

Although Cavalcanti's overall influence on *The First Days* was probably not as great as that of Jennings, there are a number of episodes in the film, all of which contain elements of irony and incongruity, which seem to suggest his authorial presence. During his stay in Britain, Cavalcanti sometimes felt the foreigner's typical sense of estrangement and distance from the culture around him, and used his filmmaking activity as an opportunity to depict some of the more parochial aspects of English culture. This concern with the oddities of Englishness should be distinguished from Jennings' preoccupation with an English national identity lying beneath the apparently incongruous and trivial façade of everyday life. Whilst Jennings wished to show the unity underlying apparently disjunctive associations, Cavalcanti had no such ambition, and preferred them to remain irrationally disjunctive.

The First Days contains a number of such episodes of incongruous irony. For example, there is a shot of a "hanged" statue being hoisted off its pedestal, and another of the "living cockney monument" of the "rock of Gibraltar", a mock sandbag fortress erected in the East End of London. A noirish element in *The First Days*, present in shots of the City of London at night, can also be attributed to Cavalcanti, rather than to Jennings, although the influence of Harry Watt may have been a factor here as well, as the visual composition of the shots of searchlights raking the night sky are similar to scenes in his later *London Can Take It!* (1940) and *Target for To-night*. Despite the fact that *The First Days* was directed by three directors, therefore, Cavalcanti's influence on this impressive wartime debut for the GPO Film Unit seems indisputable.

The final important film produced by Cavalcanti at the GPO

Film Unit, and one which reveals his influence considerably more than *The First Days*, was *Men of the Lightship*, a dramatisation of the German bombing of the *East Dudgeon* lightship on 29 January 1940. The bombing of such lightships was, in theory, contrary to the normal rules of wartime engagement, and the film dwells on this in order to build up a sense of outrage at the German action. *Men of the Lightship* carries on the tradition of the story-documentary initiated by *North Sea*, but, unlike that film, does not possess an entirely self-contained diegesis. Instead, a voice-over is used alongside naturalistic characterisation in order to provide information about the military context in which the film's story is set. Much of the film is competent, if somewhat pedestrian, and marred by the overbearing tone of the commentary. Despite this, however, after Harry Watt's *Target for To-night*, *Men of the Lightship* was the most commercially successful film to be produced by the GPO/Crown Film Unit during the war.[66]

Men of the Lightship clearly exhibits the influence of Cavalcanti in some of its scenes. In one sequence, where a German dive-bomber attacking the lightship has wounded a lightshipman, a series of rapidly edited subjective point-of-view shots, the recollected memories of the wounded man, flash across the screen. The metaphor used here is clearly the familiar one of past life flashing before the eyes of a dying man, but the use of rapid editing and subjective view-point is also reminiscent of shots from *Stranded* and *Nothing But the Hours*, as well as from French Impressionist films by L'Herbier, Gance and others.

In an almost abstract piece of filmmaking from this sequence, a shot of a burning piece of film is used metaphorically to suggest the notion of a disintegrating life. This series of shots also have a reflexive aspect, in that the metaphor of "dissolution" is linked to the medium – film – through which the fictional diegesis of *Men of the Lightship* is itself being produced. Cavalcanti could have used other visual metaphors to suggest the draining away of life here, but the reference to film, added to the use of this kind of intellectual metaphor, suggests a playful, knowing complexity in the film, which could only have originated from Cavalcanti, and definitely not from the film's David Macdonald. Before working for the GPO Film Unit, Macdonald had worked in the commercial industry, making films such as *Meet Mr. Penny*, *Dead Men Tell No Tales* (both 1938) and *This Man in Paris* (1939). None of these routine suspense films contains anything approaching the intellectual complexity of the scene from *Men of the Lightship* discussed above.

Another scene in *Men of the Lightship* which can be linked to Cavalcanti is set in a lifeboat, after the lightship has been sunk. As the men row their boat through the night, a series of shots superimpose their faces, one after the other, over a background of the boat. The superimposed images of the men's faces fill the screen, and stare blankly and directly into the camera. In its formal, slightly mystical solemnity, this scene is reminiscent of scenes from *Stranded*, as well as the scene from Abel Gance's *Napoléon* (1927), in which Gance superimposes the face of Napoléon over a background of a storm at sea, as Napoléon flees Corsica in his small boat. *Men of the Lightship* contains some extremely impressive pieces of filmmaking, most, if not all, of which were influenced by Cavalcanti. It was also the last major film which Cavalcanti produced for the documentary film movement.

Notes

1   Gavin Lambert, "Alberto Cavalcanti", *Screen* 13: 2 (summer 1972): 36.

2   Paul Rotha with Richard Griffith, *The Film Till Now: A Survey of World Cinema* (London: Vision Press, 1949): 310.

3   Jen Samson, "The Film Society, 1925-1939", in Charles Barr (ed), *All Our Yesterdays: 90 Years of British Cinema* (London: British Film Institute, 1986): 308.

4   Ibid: 312.

5   Forsyth Hardy, *John Grierson: A Documentary Biography* (London; Boston: Faber and Faber, 1979): 65.

6   Ibid: 74.

7   *Cinema Quarterly* was published between 1932 and 1936.

8   Alberto Cavalcanti, "The British Contribution (1950)", in Ian Aitken (ed), *The Documentary Film Movement: An Anthology* (Edinburgh: Edinburgh University Press, 1998): 205-208.

9   Lambert: 36.

10   Ian Aitken, *Film and Reform: John Grierson and the Documentary Film Movement* (London; New York: Routledge, 1990): 2.

11   Hardy: 31.

12   Aitken: 52-53.

13   Ibid: 91.

14   Ian Aitken, "John Grierson and the Documentary Film Movement 1898-1972", in Aitken (ed): 3.

15   Hardy: 71.

16   Paul Rotha, *Documentary Diary: An Informal History of the British Documentary Film, 1928-1939* (London: Secker and Warburg, 1973): 49.

17   Hardy: 65.

18   Ibid: 68.

19   Ibid: 74.

20   Ian Aitken, "Grierson's theory of epic cinema": in Aitken: 64-89.

21   Noureddine Ghali, *L'Avant-Garde Cinématographique en France dans les Années Vingt: Idées, Conceptions, Théories* (Paris: Éditions Paris Expérimental, 1995): 287-288.

22   John Grierson, "Better Popular Pictures", *Transactions of the Society of Motion Picture Engineers* 11: 29 (August 1927): 240.

23   Hardy: 73.

24   Aitken: 127.

25   Ibid: 136.

26   GPO Archives: Post Office Film Committee Memorandum, "Reorganization of Composition and Control", POST 33 P16682/37.

27   Lambert: 37.

28   Aitken: 132.

29   Elizabeth Sussex, *The Rise and Fall of British Documentary: The Story of the Film Movement Founded by John Grierson* (Berkeley; Los Angeles; London: University of California Press, 1975): 50.

30   Elizabeth Sussex, "Cavalcanti in England", *Sight and Sound* 44: 4 (autumn 1975): 206, reprinted in Aitken (ed): 183.

31   Ian Aitken, "The Documentary Film Movement: The Post Office Touches All Branches of Life", in John Hassard and Ruth Holliday (eds), *Organization Representation: Work and Organizations in Popular Culture* (London: Sage Publications, 1998): 29.

32   Harry Watt, *Don't Look at the Camera* (London: Paul Elek, 1974): 114.

33   Ibid: 116-117.

34   Dai Vaughan, *Portrait of an Invisible Man: The working life of Stewart McAllister, film editor* (London: British Film Institute, 1983): 36.

35   Aitken (1990): 147.

36   Sussex, *The Rise and Fall of British Documentary: The Story of the Film Movement Founded by John Grierson*: 110.

37   Ibid: 111.

38   Vaughan: 37.

39   Ibid: 41.

40   Ibid: 42.

41   Eva Orbanz, *Journey to a Legend and Back: The British Realistic Film* (Berlin: Volker Spiess, 1977): 183.

42   Vaughan: 43.

43   Nicholas Pronay, "John Grierson and the Documentary – 60 years on", *Historical Journal of Film, Radio and Television* 9: 3 (1989): 237.

44   James Chapman, *The British At War: Cinema, State and Propaganda, 1939-1945* (London; New York: I B Tauris, 1998): 116.

45   Rotha: 122.

46   Margaret Dickinson and Sarah Street, *Cinema and State: The Film Industry and the Government 1927-84* (London: British Film Institute, 1985): 114.

47   Chapman: 126.

48   Paul Swann, *The British Documentary Film Movement, 1926-1946* (Cambridge; New York; New Rochelle; Melbourne; Sydney: Cambridge University Press, 1989): 154.

49   Rotha: 88.

50   Chapman: 116.

51   Swann: 157.

52   Sussex, reprinted in Aitken (ed): 191.

53   Lambert: 45.

54   Swann: 157.

55   Watt: 128.

56   Sussex, *The Rise and Fall of British Documentary: The Story of the Film Movement Founded by John Grierson*: 120.

57   Charles Drazin, *The Finest Years: British Cinema of the 1940s* (London: André Deutsch, 1998): 121.

58   Sussex, reprinted in Aitken (ed): 192.

59   Quoted in Orbanz: 35.

60   Drazin: 121.

61   Chapman: 121.

62   Ibid: 271.

63   Ibid: 122.

64   Aitken (1998): 24.

65   Watt: 128.

66   Information on commercially distributed GPO VHS videotape entitled *The GPO Film Unit Presents*.

4

Pett and Pott to Film and Reality

The Glorious Sixth of June: New Rates and John Atkins Saves Up (both 1934)

Prior to Cavalcanti's arrival within the documentary film movement, the films made by the EMB Film Unit were all silent and generally earnest in tone, and used compilation footage and montage editing alongside written intertitles. However, Cavalcanti's debut film for the documentary film movement, *The Glorious Sixth of June: New Rates* (1934), was radically different from these earlier films, and the conjunction of his arrival, together with the introduction of sound-recording equipment, had an immediate impact on film production at the new GPO Film Unit. Made during the late spring of 1934, ostensibly in order to promote new telephone rates, *The Glorious Sixth of June: New Rates* is made in the same parodic vein as the slightly later *Pett and Pott* (1934), and has been described as being "on the level of amateur charades".[1] *The Glorious Sixth of June: New Rates* employs a highly whimsical and parodic story-line which basically debunks the institutions of the Post Office, and it also contains a cameo performance by the then newly-arrived Humphrey Jennings as "special GPO messenger Albert Goodbody". The overall style of *The Glorious Sixth of June: New Rates* is, in many respects, similar to one of Cavalcanti's last French films, the burlesque *Tour de chant* (*Tour of Song*, 1933). As in that film, *The Glorious Sixth of June: New Rates* employs overstated acting, parodic editing and conventions derived from the music-hall or boulevard farce.

Made at about the same time as *The Glorious Sixth of June: New Rates*, Arthur Elton's *John Atkins Saves Up* (1934) shares many of the characteristics of that other film, and, although he is not credited as its director, Cavalcanti must have played a central role in its realisation, particularly in the light of the fact that Elton is not normally associated with such "flights of fancy".[2] Like *Pett and Pott*, *John Atkins Saves Up* has, as its central character, a bowler-hatted suburban commuter – in this case, the John Atkins of the title. The film follows John's attempt to organise a holiday, one made possible by his sensible use of the Post Office savings scheme. As John leaves for work, a voice-over commentary describes his dreams of a holiday at Summersea. Later in his office, John is shown at work, with a commentary of "how doth the little busy bee". An invisible bee then enters the room and, echoing scenes from *Pett and Pott*, the office workers follow its course in pantomime unison as it circles the room. John Atkins' dream of a holiday then takes wing with the bee, as it departs through the window, and a series of subjective point-of-view shots, presumably from the view-point of the bee, of holiday scenes, including sea and skyscapes, are shown. Earlier in the film, John Atkins had seen a picture of a woman posing on the front cover of a holiday brochure for Summersea. Later, the same woman is seen again, but this time as a real person, walking in slow-motion through a holiday landscape.

In its use of formal devices and special effects techniques such as slow-motion, subjective imagery, parodic characterisation, a romantic sub-plot and a focus on desire and the comedic, *John Atkins Saves Up* can be clearly linked to Cavalcanti, and associated with the two other films which he is credited with directing at the GPO Film Unit in 1934. In addition, *John Atkins Saves Up* can be linked to some of Cavalcanti's final French films, including *Tour of Song, Pour un piano (For a Piano,* 1934) and *Votre sourire (Your Smile,* 1934).

Pett and Pott (1934)

Cavalcanti's second directed film for the GPO Film Unit was, like *The Glorious Sixth of June: New Rates,* made in order to promote the development of the Post Office telephone service. However, *Pett and Pott* does far more than this, and is a richly parodic and extravagant work which makes only fleeting reference to its supposed promotional purpose. The plot of *Pett and Pott* is centred around two suburban families: the Petts and the Potts. The Petts and Potts live next to each other, but they are also very different from each other. Whilst the Potts are decent, responsible citizens, the Potts live in a house called Kismet, and are easy prey to enticement and distraction.

We first see Mrs Pott draped languidly over an armchair, reading a bodice-ripper novelette, whilst a voice-over provides a reading of the contents of the book. These contain fairly overt sexual references ("the beloved fires were leaping up through her body", and so on). After this, Mr Pett and Mr Pott are seen leaving for work and we learn that, whilst Mr Pott is a debt-collector, Mr Pett is a "family solicitor". In the train going to work, the carriage is occupied by identically-dressed men wearing pinstripe suits and bowler-hats, all of whom are reading newspapers. Cavalcanti then introduces a surreal touch, as the uniformed office workers fall asleep, one by one, under the rhythm of the train. Non-synchronous music and rapidly spoken verse are also used here to create a formally composed and highly organised sequence.

The film then returns to suburbia to show Mrs Pett ordering shopping by telephone. Cavalcanti uses a split-screen effect to show the telephone transaction, which is, the film's commentary suggests, a modern and efficient means of carrying out such business. However, rather than subscribe to the telephone, Mrs Pott prefers to employ a maid to carry out her chores. This strategy backfires, however, as the maid turns out be to be both dissolute and "sluttish".[3] As the situation between Mrs Pott and her maid deteriorates further, arguments break out, and dissonant, raucous music is heard in the background, metaphorically evoking the growing tensions between the two women. In marked contrast to the melodramatic scenes next door, Mrs Pett is then shown continuing to chat happily over the telephone, and Cavalcanti goes on to make a parodic association here by intercutting shots of her alongside shots of a bird sitting on a telephone wire, singing cheerfully.

Mrs Pott then gives up her attempt to reform the maid, and is forced to do her own shopping herself. As she returns home on foot, laden down with goods, she begins to tire, and Cavalcanti uses slow-motion photography to suggest her gradual loss of momentum. A montage of pages from calendars is also superimposed over these scenes – perhaps as a parodic reference to Hollywood conventions which typically use such techniques to signal the passing of time.

In the meantime, Mr Pott has turned bohemian, and taken to partying late into the night with his office friends. Consequently, he is rarely at home, which means that Mrs Pott has to deal with her dissolute maid alone. Late one night, we see the maid trying on Mrs Pott's lipstick. Her friend, a thief dressed in traditional villain's clothing of a black-and-white stripped shirt, whom she addresses as "big boy", then appears. The maid encourages "big boy" to steal Mrs Pott's fur coat. An argument ensues between the two, and we see Mrs Pott cowering in bed upstairs, as the maid and her friend, whom she now refers to as a "big sausage", fight below. The situation is finally resolved when Mrs Pett's daughter (the Potts have no children), hearing the commotion next door, uses the telephone to call the police. The police arrive looking like the Keystone Cops, and apprehend the thief against an unexpected background of choral music.

The final scenes of the film take place in a mock courtroom, where a pompous Lord Justice Porridge presides over a cartoon court. In his final address to the court, Justice Porridge haughtily proclaims:

> These thieves have been apprehended by judicious use
> of the Post Office telephone. The good and just user
> appreciates the telephone service, whilst the evil and
> unjust despises it.

The final captions of *Pett and Pott* continue in the same exaggerated tone which characterises the remainder of the film, and also comment laconically on the difficulty inherent in producing creative work within the limitations imposed by sponsorship, by reflecting that the film is, after all, only "an advert".

Pett and Pott is one of Cavalcanti's least well-known films and is rarely screened. The reason for this obscurity does not, however, lie in the film's lack of merit, but in the negative campaign mounted against it by Grierson and his close associates. For example, Paul Rotha described the film as "an [error] of judgement...pretentious... show[ing] Cavalcanti's influence at its most mischievous, and...best mislaid".[4] Forsyth Hardy has also referred to *Pett and Pott* as "Cavalcanti's grotesque comedy",[5] whilst Stuart Legg has characterised it as "lighthearted rubbish".[6] Moreover, John Taylor believed that *Pett and Pott* illustrated Cavalcanti's unsuitability as a member of Grierson's documentary film movement, and also argued that the film revealed the first signs of the detrimental impact which, according to Taylor, Cavalcanti was later to have:

> That was the beginning of the division. I mean, looking back on it, it was a great mistake to have Cavalcanti, really, because he didn't understand what documentary was supposed to be doing.[7]

Cavalcanti himself seemed to have been retrospectively convinced by this barrage of criticism, or at least put on the defensive by it, stating, for example, that he "never liked" *Pett and Pott*, which was "not quite a film. It's a sound lesson, you know",[8] a "demonstration film".[9] *Pett and Pott* has also been ignored in much of the critical writing on the documentary film movement, and in more general studies of the history of the documentary film, where it is usually seen as a minor, diversionary experiment.

However, although the negative critical paradigm which has developed around *Pett and Pott* has defined the film as marginal and irrelevant, this was not how it was perceived at the time. For example, Grierson himself, writing in 1935, and before his conversion to the more socially purposive public information documentary which he advocated in the late-1930s, actually described *Pett and Pott* as "ingenious" and "effective":

> The coming of sound was something of a disaster for the silent comedians like Chaplin, Keaton, Langdon, Griffith and Lloyd. The realism of the spoken word destroyed the more distant atmosphere in which the silent art created them, and none of them has had the ingenuity to develop a use of sound which would preserve the ancient quality of their mask and ballet. Cavalcanti's film *Pett and Pott* shows how this could effectively be done by formalizing the sound and making it contribute to the mute (a) in comedy of music, (b) in comedy of sound image, and (c) in comedy of asynchronism.[10]

Forsyth Hardy finds Grierson's defence of *Pett and Pott* in 1935 "paradoxical",[11] but forgets that the film was originally conceived as an important project for the new GPO Film Unit – that is, the unit's first major experiment in sound film production. Hardy is also guilty of misrepresenting others' views of the film when he describes it as a "grotesque comedy" and "probably funnier in the making than in the end product".[12] Both descriptions originally appeared in Elizabeth Sussex's *The Rise and Fall of British Documentary* (1975), and Hardy appears to paraphrases these in his 1979 biography of Grierson. For example, in Sussex's book, Basil Wright's description of *Pett and Pott* as a "grotesque comedy" is, in a sense, a positive – or, at least, a non-judgmental – characterisation, whilst Wright also relates the film to Cavalcanti's *La P'tite Lilie* (1927) and *Le Petit chaperon rouge* (*Little Red Riding Hood*, 1929), describing it as a natural development from these earlier films.[13] Similarly, the full quotation from Legg states that:

> The old sort of reactionaries among us thought, 'Good God, what are we coming to – this lighthearted rubbish!' Others thought it was rather fun, and in fact it was very funny indeed – much funnier shooting it, of course, than the film when it was finished![14]

Although the full quotation retains the phrase "lighthearted rubbish", it also points to a division of opinion within the GPO Film Unit over the film, and it is not known, for example, what Humphrey Jennings, Len Lye or Norman McLaren thought about it. Nevertheless, others within the documentary film movement were clearly opposed to Cavalcanti's approach in *Pett and Pott*, and Wright's recollection that Grierson "made sure that nobody ever saw it" is probably accurate.[15]

The furore over *Pett and Pott* suggests that Cavalcanti's film marked a pivotal moment in the development of the documentary film movement, one in which Grierson's conception of a socially purposive public relations documentary filmmaking was fundamentally challenged. Far from being a minor or insignificant film, *Pett and Pott* was to establish the parodic style in which Cavalcanti's authorship would develop whilst he was working under Grierson's tutelage within the documentary film movement. *Pett and Pott* is also – with the possible exception of the collaboratively produced *Coal Face* (1935) – the most important film which Cavalcanti directed whilst at the GPO Film Unit, and remains one of the most interesting and watchable films produced by the documentary film movement between 1929 and 1939. It is, in effect, a film which deserves far more critical attention than it has received until now.

Coal Face and Granton Trawler (both 1935)

Granton Trawler is normally associated with Grierson, rather than Cavalcanti. According to Hardy, who draws on a 1976 interview with

Edgar Anstey for his information, Grierson directed and shot the film himself, whilst Anstey edited it.[16] However, it is more likely that Grierson merely shot the footage, and then handed it over to Anstey, who effectively shaped the final film.[17] In this sense, it could be argued that *Granton Trawler* was far more Anstey's film than Grierson's, and this view is also echoed by Richard Meran Barsam, who describes *Granton Trawler* as "Anstey's *Granton Trawler*".[18] In fact, Rachael Low queries whether Grierson even shot the footage for *Granton Trawler*, arguing that he was ill at the time. Low's view is that it is more likely that *Granton Trawler* was photographed by J D Davidson, a cameraman from the commercial industry who did occasional work for the documentary film movement.[19]

Granton Trawler was actually an EMB film which was shot and edited in 1933, prior to the establishment of the GPO Film Unit.[20] As such, it must have been one of the films for which, like *The Song of Ceylon* (1934), Cavalcanti would have been asked to develop a soundtrack when he joined the documentary film movement in 1934. In fact, Cavalcanti's work on the soundtrack of *Granton Trawler* may even have been his first for the documentary film movement, predating his involvement on *The Song of Ceylon*, *Pett and Pott* and *The Glorious Sixth of June: New Rates*.[21]

The impressionistic, atmospheric narrative of *Granton Trawler* is well summarised by Low:

> It begins with a dark screen and the sound of a mouth organ. We see the prow of a trawler, the *Isabella Grieg*, rising and falling gently. The changing rhythm of this rise and fall is felt throughout the film. We see the funnel, hear a couple of blasts, a shout, and the unobtrusive beat of the engine. Once at sea, on a gentle swell, men quietly get on with their work with mouth organ, rhythmic clatter and half heard voices, the creak of cleats and the rattle of chains, the cry of gulls in the background. There is some similarity to *Drifters*. The shots are lovely but not self-indulgently so, always justified by the accumulation of detail to build up the atmosphere of absorbed work. The seas get up, the wind blows, the gulls scream and wheel, and we are surrounded by the sounds of a violent sea. Finally, after getting the catch in, the men sit absorbed as they gut the fish. Evening falls, and with the darkening sea and sky comes peace again, and the mournful sound once more of the mouth organ.[22]

Granton Trawler contains some effective and well-edited photography, but its most important quality lies in the way in which the soundtrack of the film, which Low describes as having an "atmospheric power", is employed.[23] Writing about *Granton Trawler* in

1934, the art historian Herbert Read also focused on the use of sound in the film, and admired the way in which the "impressionistic character of the vocal sounds...combine with other sounds to produce an asynchronous reinforcement of the visual effect".[24]

The rhythmic character of the editing in *Granton Trawler* is complemented by that of the soundtrack, and a concern with the relationship between sound and image lies at the heart of the film. The soundtrack in *Granton Trawler* is also deliberately non-naturalistic, emphasising note, timbre and accent, rather than verisimilitude, and this approach imposes an overall ambience on the film. In this latter respect, *Granton Trawler* can be compared to Cavalcanti's *En rade* (*Stranded*, 1927) and *La P'tite Lilie* in its use of a compositional style which links all parts of the film into a unified aesthetic structure.

Given the importance of the soundtrack to *Granton Trawler*, it seems odd that the titles in the print of the film available at the National Film and Television Archive (NFTVA) make no reference to Cavalcanti's involvement, and even more perplexing that, speaking in the 1970s, Grierson should completely fail to mention Cavalcanti's contribution to the film.[25] However, there is no doubt that Cavalcanti's input was as crucial to the successful realisation of *Granton Trawler* as to that of *The Song of Ceylon*, and the fact that his role in the film was not properly acknowledged at the time indicates the presence of an incipient problem – one which was to become a more tangible issue in Cavalcanti's next film.

Coal Face (1935)

Although *Coal Face* was one of the most important films to be produced by the documentary film movement, it was also one of the most contentious, in that it brought to the fore disputes over the nature and ascription of authorship within the movement. As mentioned earlier, Grierson had always encouraged the practice of group filmmaking, whereby any one film would be assembled by a number of different filmmakers. Grierson advocated this approach to filmmaking because he wanted his inexperienced young filmmakers to be trained in all aspects of the production process, and so that the movement could expand as rapidly as possible. However, he also had an austere personal aversion to the idea of individual authorship, and championed the model of collaborative filmmaking as an end in itself. When, for example, he became first Film Commissioner of the National Film Board of Canada, he developed this model of team working into a systematic regime within which filmmakers were virtually unable to develop distinct, authorial personae.[26]

One consequence of this practice was that the designation of credits in the films made by the documentary film movement was frequently arbitrary and inaccurate. Writing in the 1970s, Grierson still seemed unconcerned about this:

The selflessness of some of the documentary people
was a very remarkable thing...They didn't put their
names on pictures...There were years when
Cavalcanti's name never went on a picture. It was
because we weren't concerned with names. We weren't
concerned with that aspect of things, with credits...one
of the aspects of the documentary movement, of its
difficulties over the thirties, and one of the signs and
symbols of its engagement with the larger purpose
was that it did not concern itself with personal
publicity.[27]

Nevertheless, this lack of concern over "personal publicity" did
cause problems at the time, notably over films such as *Coal Face* and
Night Mail (1936).[28] In addition, although Grierson claimed that "the
documentary people" were unconcerned with the issue of credits, Harry
Watt has pointed out that it was Grierson himself who decided what
credits were to be placed in particular films, and this substantial power
of jurisdiction provided him with the potential opportunity to attribute
credits both selectively and strategically.[29] The fact that, as Grierson
puts it, "[t]here were years when Cavalcanti's name never went on a
picture" does not necessarily mean that Cavalcanti approved of this
practice at the time, and the absence of his name from the credits of a
film as important as *Coal Face* has clearly angered him.
  This curious omission has been explained by Paul Rotha as
stemming from the fact that Cavalcanti did not wish to be identified
with such an avant-garde film because he feared such an association
would jeopardise his ultimate ambition, which was to enter the
commercial feature film industry:

> In an interview many years later, Cavalcanti was still
> complaining that his name had been suppressed by
> Grierson from credit titles and publicity on GPO films.
> He was especially sensitive about *Coal Face*, a film
> that had received greater recognition in post-war
> years than it had when it was made in 1935, for which
> he claimed he had not been given due credit...In
> afterthought, I think Grierson had a valid point in
> this one-sided argument when he recalled that
> Cavalcanti had asked for his name to be left off such
> films as *Coal Face, Granton Trawler* and *Night Mail*
> when they were made because he felt that association
> with such *avant-garde* work might jeopardize his
> chances of employment in British feature film
> production at that time.[30]

The interview to which Rotha refers was given by Cavalcanti
at the Leipzig Film Festival in 1967, but Cavalcanti was "still

complaining" in the 1970s, and was incensed by Rotha's claim that he had deliberately asked for his name to be kept from the credits of films such as *Coal Face*:

> I wasn't named three-quarters of the time, and then they say I was trying to grab a position in the fiction industry. I stayed for seven years at a wage of misery – I had to begin with £7 a week – because I was tired of fictional films in France. I was doing them, and I was very successful with the comedies I was doing, and I didn't want to go on. I wanted to experiment in sound.[31]

Although it is not clear why Cavalcanti did not complain about this issue at the time, there is no evidence to suggest that, only a year after joining the documentary film movement, he would have wanted his name kept off a film such as *Coal Face* because he wanted to join the British feature film industry, where he would precisely not have been allowed to "experiment in sound". Furthermore, Cavalcanti's critical reputation in Britain had been built around the avant-garde *Rien que les heures* (*Nothing But the Hours*, 1926), and it seems unlikely that he would wish to throw his reputation as a director of avant-garde films into question by disguising his involvement in the similarly avant-garde *Coal Face*. Grierson's aversion to what he referred to as "personal publicity" might have played a part in the suppression of Cavalcanti's titles, but Harry Watt argues that more was involved:

> He (Cavalcanti) had been, to my mind, tremendously exploited by Grierson. His contribution had never been sufficiently recognized in the way of credits, which is the most important thing in films.[32]

Whatever the truth of the matter, Cavalcanti is insistent that *Coal Face* was his film:

> I cut the film completely myself, the whole conception of the sound. It was library film. Harry shot one sequence, and Jennings shot one sequence. We used some of the old Flaherty tests...I faked – I did lots of shooting in the studios to be able to cut the Flaherty material in, and I wasn't given a credit. I didn't complain. After all, it was a small film. It was an experiment for *Night Mail*.[33]

Coal Face is a particularly interesting test case for notions of authorship in the cinema. As Cavalcanti suggests, it appears that sequences for the film were shot by Flaherty, Watt and Jennings.

However, it also appears, in another account, that additional sequences were shot by Legg and Wright.[34] Cavalcanti filmed all the studio-based sequences himself, but was not involved in location-shooting. The first version of the film appears to have been cut together by Stuart Legg, who had been asked by Grierson to make a two-reel film from the footage, either stock footage or newly-shot material provided by Jennings, Watt, Wright and himself.[35] This version of events is also supported by Hardy, who claims that Legg "edit[ed] the material which would become *Coal Face*".[36] However, the truth appears to be that Legg cut together the material initially, then handed it over to Cavalcanti, who recut it around the soundtrack and the studio sequences which he himself had shot. Cavalcanti also developed the soundtrack for *Coal Face* in conjunction with the poet W H Auden and the composer Benjamin Britten. The painter William Coldstream was also involved in editing the film at some stage, and it is his name, rather than that of Cavalcanti or Legg, which appears on the credits as editor.

Basil Wright has argued that *Coal Face* was "very much a question of teamwork. It's very difficult to pin anybody in particular down".[37] However, although the attribution of authorship is clearly difficult here, there is no doubt that the importance of *Coal Face* lies principally in Cavalcanti's treatment of sound and image relationships, and, whilst Auden, Britten and Coldstream also made important contributions to the film, those of Watt, Jennings, Wright and Legg were less significant. Certainly, the only contribution which Grierson seems to have made was to appoint Britten, taking him on when he was still a student at the Royal College of Music. Thereafter, however, both Britten and Auden worked under the overall guidance of Cavalcanti.

The Film Society programme for the première of *Coal Face* described the film as follows:

> This is presented as a new experiment in sound. A very simple visual band was taken and an attempt made to build up by the use of natural sound, music and chorus, a film oratorio. The usual method of speaking a commentary to a background of music was avoided and commentary and music were composed together...To this foreground of sound were added a recitative chorus of male voices and a choir of male and female voices. The recitative chorus was used to fill out, by suggestion, the direct statement of the commentary. The choir was used to create atmosphere. The poem was sung by the female voices on the return of the miners to the surface and was written by the poet W. H. Auden for the film.[38]

Coal Face begins with a commentary in the Griersonian manner which provides information about the structure of the coalmining industry in Britain. However, unlike a commentary in a conventional documentary, the words here are spoken in a harsh, abrupt voice, and the effect of this is that they become integrated into the compositional structure of the film, rather than function as a descriptive chronicle. Behind the commentary, discordant, dissonant music and sound effects also reinforce the jarring effect produced by the use of language. The editing in these sequences is similar to that used in *Granton Trawler*, in that it is rhythmic, and each shot is held for approximately five seconds. This first sequence ends with more details about the raw commodities and by-products of coalmining, and, as the names of these by-products are called out, the music track keeps time with the commentator, further reinforcing the overall compositional tempo of this part of the film.

The second part of *Coal Face* begins with a shot of a blank screen, upon which information about the distribution of coalfields across Britain gradually materialises. As the statistics gather pace, background choral music becomes increasingly evident, and a drum begins to beat time as the figures are called out. This is followed by shots of miners working underground, accompanied by a commentary which stresses the hardship and dangers of working conditions in the mine. Then, in one of the most well-known scenes from the film, two miners are seen breaking for lunch underground. As the men sit quietly eating, offscreen dialogue is heard against atonal background music. Although the imagery here is realist in style, it is nevertheless dominated by the modernist use of sound and music.

The commentary continues with information on accident and mortality rates within the coalmining industry. As the miners rise to the surface in the colliery escalator, the editing also speeds up, whilst the choral poem, written by Auden, reaches a crescendo as the escalator reaches the surface. After this, the jarring, dissonant tone of the film gives way to a more lyrical one, as we see miners returning home after work. The commentary also reinforces this more lyrical mood, solemnly proclaiming: "The miner's life is bound up with the pit, the miner's house is often owned by the pit, the life of the village is often dependent on the pit". The final shot in this sequence shows a tree, leaning into a strong wind, and set against a bleak flattened landscape: a desolate but poetic image of the impact of industrialisation on nature.

A more Griersonian section follows, containing sequences showing the distribution of coal by rail which are similar to the final sequences in Grierson's *Drifters* (1929). The modernist soundtrack also continues, with the use of discordant, non-synchronised sound effects and a disconcertingly jarring use of cymbals. The final sequences of the film return to the opening statement of the commentary, proclaiming that "coalmining is the basic industry of Britain", and, against a background of the mining village and pit head, a brief series of superimposed images of pit machinery lead on to a shot of a miner walking away from the camera. The choral music also returns to the opening refrain of the film here with "there are the miners, there is the mine", as a final pan up to a dark, ominous image of the pit wheel leads to the final credits.

Coal Face was designed as an uncompromisingly modernist experiment. However, and, as already mentioned, the only other film of Cavalcanti's with which it could be compared is *Nothing But the Hours*. In this sense, *Coal Face* should also be distinguished from *Stranded*, *Granton Trawler* and *Night Mail*, all of which are more typical of Cavalcanti's characteristic approach to filmmaking. The fact that *Coal Face* was devised as an experiment also means that, perhaps inevitably, it does not possess the sort of professional finish which can be found in a film such as *Night Mail*, and the ambitious collage of stylistic devices in the film also results in some sections working more effectively than others. Moreover, the most effective sequences in *Coal Face* are not the most modernist at all, but, on the contrary, the more lyrical and realist ones. Some of these are particularly moving, and may well have been shot by Humphrey Jennings. Some certainly reappear in *Spare Time* (1939).

Those in the documentary film movement who have commented on *Coal Face*, including Rotha, Wright, Hardy and Grierson, have all stressed the fact that it was intended to be a small-scale experimental film, and that it is characterised by unevenness and poor sound quality. Even Cavalcanti described it as a "small film".[39] Rotha also makes a distinction between Cavalcanti's work on *Coal Face* and that on *The Song of Ceylon*:

> [*Coal Face*] was a little avant-garde experiment. No more and no less. But through publicity it's been built up into something much more important than it ever was meant to be. But you get into a different level when you come to the sound-track in Basil Wright's film *Song of Ceylon*, the soundtrack of which Cavalcanti had a lot to do with is very important, it wasn't experimental.[40]

Other critics writing about *Coal Face* have tended to comment on either its modernism or its social purposiveness. For example, Erik Barnouw has argued that *Coal Face* sounds "a note of protest and of urgent need for reform",[41] whilst Barsam also regards the film as an important social exposé:

> Unique among early GPO films for its strong voice of social protest, Alberto Cavalcanti's *Coal Face* (1935) involved the collaboration of W. H. Auden and Benjamin Britten. Their attempts to integrate choral singing, chanting, narration, and music, while important as an experimental effort, result in a strident description of the processing and distribution of coal, rather than the successful symphonic fusion of

these elements that they achieved later in *Night Mail*. The chorus of miners conveys their oppression with a tone of bitterness and futility that is surpassed in intensity and effectiveness only by Henri Storck's *Les maisons de la misère* (1937).[42]

Unlike Rotha, Evelyn Gerstein thinks *Coal Face* a better film than *The Song of Ceylon*, and describes it as a "tour de force, a vigorous experiment in sound".[43] Similarly, John Corner also emphasises the experimental qualities of *Coal Face* when he describes it as "very much a film of Modernist enthusiasms".[44] Corner argues that modernism, rather than realism, is the dominant discourse within *Coal Face*, to the extent that, on those occasions when information about social conditions is given in the film, the dense articulation of sound, music, commentary, editing and photography which accompanies this information makes it difficult for even the most engaged viewer to assimilate it fully.[45]

It is difficult to disagree with Corner here. Although potentially recoverable as a social realist text, *Coal Face* is essentially concerned with aesthetic experimentation, and Cavalcanti himself never claimed realist credentials for it, regarding it as significant only in the sense that it experimented with sound, music and image relationships, and in that it provided the prototype for *Night Mail*. However, Corner's definition of *Coal Face* as a work of "modernist realism", although helpful, does require some modification.[46] If films such as *Stranded* and *Granton Trawler* are both modernist and realist, as I would argue, *Nothing But the Hours* and *Coal Face* belong to a different category of film, and require a different terminological denotation. Perhaps the term "high-modernist realism" would suffice.

The Swiss films

Following *Coal Face*, Cavalcanti directed a series of seven films set in Switzerland. These are: *Line to Tcherva Hut* (1936), *We Live in Two Worlds* (1937), *Who Writes to Switzerland?* (1937), *Message from Geneva* (1937), *Four Barriers* (1937), *Alice au pays romand* (*Alice in Switzerland*, 1938) and *Men of the Alps* (1939). With the exception of *Line to Tcherva Hut*, these films were made after Grierson's departure from the GPO Film Unit, and established a new pattern of production for the unit in the post-Grierson era.[47] Prior to 1937, films had generally been commissioned from external organisations on an individual basis. However, the Swiss series of films, which were made in collaboration with the Swiss Post Office, the Municipal Council of Lausanne, and the Swiss telephone company, Pro-Telephone Zürich, were commissioned as a group.[48]

Cavalcanti's Swiss films are quite different from the more parodic films which he produced with Lye, McLaren and others after 1936, and far more conventional in terms of their use of linear narrative structures and continuity editing. Unlike *Coal Face,* they also employ voice-over commentary in the traditional manner to provide information and explanation for the viewer. Rotha described the Swiss films as "technically mature", "model[s] of shooting, editing and imaginative use of sound", and as full of "subtle technique",[49] and it is certainly the case that in these films Cavalcanti returns, once again, to a more conventional realist tradition of filmmaking.

Message from Geneva describes the development, structure and organisation of the League of Nations, and the principal emphasis throughout the film is on the way in which communication technologies enable international communication and cooperation to prosper. Despite being made after both Mussolini's invasion of Ethiopia and the outbreak of the Spanish Civil War, the film avoids any reference to the international political context. Although considerable criticism was being levelled at the League's lack of effectiveness in combating the military expansionism of Italy and Germany at the time, no reference to such criticism appears in *Message from Geneva*. Instead, the general role of the League in working for peace is emphasised and summed up in the film's closing statement that "the world is turning to the League of Nations in its strivings for peace".

The general criticism that a reliance on sponsorship had limited the critical potential of many of the films produced by the documentary film movement could, in fact, be levelled at *Message from Geneva* even more so than at the usual target for such criticism, Anstey and Elton's *Housing Problems* (1935).[50] *Message from Geneva* also appears anodyne and shallow in comparison with other documentaries of the period, such as *Hell Unlimited* (Norman McLaren, 1936), *Crime Against Madrid* (Progressive Film Institute, 1937) and *Testimony of Non-Intervention* (Ivor Montagu, 1938), all of which forthrightly criticise the shortcomings of the League of Nations.

Of all the films in the Swiss series, Cavalcanti was most pleased with *Four Barriers* and *Line to Tcherva Hut,* both of which he preferred to the better-known *We Live in Two Worlds*:

> I am not at all like my colleagues. I think it is one of the many differences between us, that I am like certain mothers who prefer the ill-formed children to the strong and beautiful ones. So I, in general, prefer films of mine that haven't been as successful or haven't been well understood, perhaps...I don't like, for instance, something as well made as the Priestley film, *We Live in Two Worlds*. I prefer things like *Line to Tschierva [sic] Hut*.[51]

Line to Tcherva Hut and *Four Barriers* are both concerned with communications systems within Switzerland. *Four Barriers* begins with scenes of rural Swiss life, and a commentary which proclaims that "50 years ago the village was still the basis of life for the Swiss peasant".

However, these scenes of rural village life, set against a backdrop of mountain landscapes, are followed by an account of the building of the Saint Gothard tunnel, as the film emphasises the economic transformation of modern Switzerland. The "four barriers" which impede the development of modern communications systems within Switzerland, and, even more importantly, which obstruct the development of Switzerland's relationship with nearby countries are then named: (1) a shortage of raw materials; (2) Switzerland's geographical isolation, caused by its mountainous geography; (3) political isolation; and (4) economic isolation.

Like most of the films within the Swiss series, *Four Barriers* mobilises a rhetoric of internationalism which gestures towards the growing context of gathering European conflict outside the borders of Switzerland, without specifically referring to any particular political or military event. For example, the "third barrier", that of political isolation, is discussed against the context of the growth of political nationalism in Europe, whilst the "fourth barrier", that of economic isolation, is seen as the inevitable and ominous product of such nationalism. As with *Message from Geneva*, however, the international context of the gathering political crisis is referred to only indirectly in *Four Barriers*, and, like *Message from Geneva*, the film is more concerned with optimistically, if naïvely, urging the need for international communication. The final statement of the film, which echoes the concluding commentary in *Message from Geneva*, embodies this innocent political idealism in maintaining that "international co-operation will triumph over all barriers".

The subject-matter of *Line to Tcherva Hut* is the building of a telephone link to the "hut" in question, a climbing refuge set high in the mountains, and owned by the Swiss Alpine Club. In classic Griersonian style, the film shows the process of building the telephone link in some detail, depicting all the various stages of the process of construction. *Line to Tcherva Hut* can also be regarded as Griersonian in the way in which it creates dramatic development from within the process of labour activity itself, as the telephone engineers grapple with the problems caused by precipitous drops and sheer mountainsides. In fact, in its depiction of technical, labouring and professional skills, carried out against an imposing natural background, *Line to Tcherva Hut* is similar to early EMB Film Unit films such as Elton's *The Shadow on the Mountain* (1931) and Wright's *Windmill in Barbados* (1934).

Line to Tcherva Hut combines depictions of manual labour with a lyrically evocative representation of the mountainous Swiss countryside which emphasises the natural beauty of the landscape. There is far less emphasis on modernity and technology here than in *Four Barriers*, and a lyrical naturalism, reminiscent of the films of Baroncelli, pervades these scenes of high glaciers and precipitous chasms. This lyrical pastoralism is reinforced by showing the workmen who lay the telephone link as tiny, insignificant figures within this dramatic environment, and by the use of an evocative musical score composed by Benjamin Britten:

> The cinematography is excellent, especially the angle shots and the contrast between the bright snow and the darkly clad workmen. The music by Britten is very simple, but it augments and contributes to an imaginative film that is a model of subtle conception, shooting, and editing.[52]

Some of the sequences in *Line to Tcherva Hut* also resemble scenes from *Night Mail*, as, for example, when, in the latter film, the train is seen speeding through rolling landscapes of moorland and hill country. The same sense of atmosphere and imagery pervades both films, and it may be that, when Cavalcanti stated that he was particularly pleased with *Line to Tcherva Hut*, he was referring to the film's lyrical evocation of the natural environment.

The film most often referred to when the Swiss films are discussed is not *Line to Tcherva Hut*, however, but *We Live in Two Worlds* and, within the documentary film movement at least, this film is usually considered to be the most important of the group. For example, Rotha ranks it alongside Harry Watt's *The Saving of Bill Blewitt* as the most significant film to be produced at the GPO Film Unit in 1937,[53] whilst Forsyth Hardy describes it as an "ambitious" attempt to portray issues of international communications.[54] The origins of *We Live in Two Worlds* lay in Grierson's wish to utilise the footage left over from the making of *Line to Tcherva Hut*. In order to achieve this, Grierson asked the novelist J B Priestley to compose an appropriate "film talk", which could be illustrated by the left-over footage. Priestley then constructed his narrative around the existing footage:

> Most films are made by turning a narrative into a series of photographs. This film was made by turning a series of photographs into a narrative. In short, it was created backwards...John Grierson, then head of the GPO Film Unit and the great white chief of British documentary films, came to me and said that after doing a short film for the Swiss Post Office they had a mass of good stuff left over – lovely shots of Swiss peasants in the fields and so on – and perhaps I could see my way into turning this stuff into a good lecture film. They would add a certain amount of new material for me, but it would all have to be done very economically. So on the basis of the list of shots supplied to me, I concocted a little talk about nationalism and the new internationalism of transport and communications, blandly took Switzerland as an

example of both – for while it is ringed around with
heavily guarded frontiers, it is also an excellent
example of this new internationalism – and thanks to
a very able director, Alberto Cavalcanti, we ended
with an excellent little documentary film, which has,
I believe been quite popular.[55]

Priestley had been associated with the documentary film
movement for a few years before the making of *We Live in Two Worlds*.
His book *English Journey* (1934) had directly inspired Paul Rotha's *The
Face of Britain* (1935), and he had also published several articles in
World Film News, one of the house journals of the documentary film
movement.[56] In books such as *Angel Pavement* (1930) and *English
Journey*, Priestley focused on problems of corruption, unemployment
and poverty within Britain, and he was also active in the anti-Fascist
movements of the late-1930s.[57] All this made him sympathetic to the
general aims of the documentary film movement, and eager to
participate in the making of *We Live in Two Worlds*.

In *We Live in Two Worlds*, a distinction is made between the
two worlds which characterise modern society: the world of separate
nation states, and the "growing international world". The film begins
by depicting traditional Swiss folk traditions and labour practices. After
this, the focus of the film shifts to the theme of the modernisation of
Switzerland, and, in particular, to the role played by mass
communication in creating links with Switzerland's neighbours. In
contrast, the growth of nationalism and militarism in neighbouring
Germany is explicitly criticised, and contrasted with Swiss
internationalism. *We Live in Two Worlds* could be regarded as a
"Griersonian" documentary because of its emphasis on international
communications and the relationship between labour and institutional
structures; this, in turn, may explain why Griersonians such as Rotha
and Hardy thought so highly of it. The truth is, however, that *We Live
in Two Worlds* is a mediocre film, whilst Priestley's commentary, which
is full of pompous, vernacular Yorkshire *gravitas*, is often predictable
and rudimentary.

Cavalcanti's influence on *We Live in Two Worlds* can be found
mainly in the film's use of sound, and in the music track, which was
composed by Maurice Jaubert. That influence can be seen most clearly
in the final sequences of the film, in which Priestley's pedestrian
didacticism gives way to an idealistic proclamation concerning the way
in which the natural world transcends artificial nationalist
demarcations. These final sequences are almost abstract in quality, as,
for example, when superimposed images of ships at sea fade into a shot
of the Earth against Priestley's rhetorical claim that "rain and sea and
air serve all men". The final shots of the film re-create abstract
patterns of raindrops, and this leads to the appearance of the endtitles
of the film. These sequences, with their innovative and impressionistic
use of sound and image, can be clearly linked to Cavalcanti, and it is

these, rather than Priestley's commentary, which make *We Live in Two Worlds* worth watching.

The final two films directed by Cavalcanti to be discussed here are *A Midsummer Day's Work* (1939) and *Film and Reality* (1942). *A Midsummer Day's Work* is a routine documentary on the laying of an underground telephone cable in the Chilterns from Amersham to Aylesbury. Although credited to Cavalcanti by a number of sources, the film's titles do not specifically name him, nor anyone else for that matter, as director. R Q McNaughton is credited as editor, and J E N Cooper as music director, with Jonah Jones and James E (Jimmy) Rogers as cameramen, and sound by Ken Cameron. However, given that the content and style of *A Midsummer Day's Work* contain little obvious sign of Cavalcanti's input, one must seriously question whether his involvement in its making was anything more than marginal or routine. This, however, is certainly not the case with *Film and Reality*, an important film for both Cavalcanti and the documentary film movement. Although made after Cavalcanti had left the documentary film movement for Ealing Studios, it is more appropriately described here because it sums up Cavalcanti's views on the aesthetic achievement of the documentary.

Film and Reality (1942)

As the initial titles make clear, *Film and Reality* is an ambitiously comprehensive survey of the art of documentary and realist filmmaking, from its origins to the 1940s:

> The extracts in this film have been assembled to illustrate the development of the realist film from the earliest days of cinematography to the beginnings of World War Two...Their order is not strictly chronological. In many cases, works similar in style or subject are represented side by side, even when differing widely in date.

Film and Reality is divided into five main sections: (1) "Early Documentary"; (2) "The Newsreel Tradition"; (3) "The Romantic Documentary of Far-Off Places"; (4) "The Realistic Documentary of Life at Home"; and (5) "Realism in the Story Film". Each of these sections is, in addition, made up of a number of sub-sections, all introduced by captions and illustrated by sequences from documentary and other realist films.

"Early Documentary" begins with a sequence from Étienne-Jules Marey's photographic studies of animals in motion, which date from 1887. The physiologist Marey was, together with Eadweard Muybridge and Pierre Jules César Janssen, instrumental in developing means of recording a series of successive actions in static photographic images, and his work contributed to the later development of the cinema.[58] This sequence is followed by scenes taken from the Lumière brothers' *L'arrivée d'un train à La Ciotat* (France, 1895) and *L'Arrosseur arrosé* (*The Waterer Watered*, France, 1895). In making the leap from Marey in 1887 to the Lumières in 1895, Cavalcanti does, of course, miss out some of the key developments in the evolution of the Cinematograph, including Thomas Edison's invention of the Kinetoscope, and R W Paul's invention of the Animatographe. Rather than revealing an inherent francophone bias, however, Cavalcanti's approach here merely underlines the fact that his film is indeed an impressionistic, rather than systematic, account of the development of the realist film.

In addition to illustrating the development of actuality-filmmaking, the two sequences from the Lumière films in *Film and Reality* are comedic. This is particularly the case with *The Waterer Watered*, a short cameo about a small boy who causes an unfortunate gardener to be drenched by his garden hose. Cavalcanti's emphasis here is as much on the entertainment value of film as on its information content, and this stance is further reinforced when Cavalcanti moves on to the development of the entertainment film itself. Sequences from Walter Haggar's *The Life of Charles Peace* (GB, 1905), a dramatised reconstruction of the life of the eponymous criminal, are followed by scenes from Edwin S Porter's *The Great Train Robbery* (USA, 1903), a film which Rotha described as containing "surely...the first cabaret on the screen".[59] Cavalcanti describes the emergence of a melodramatic tradition here, illustrating this with a sequence from *Un Bouquet de violettes* (France, 1906), "a film on the lines of the cheap romantic novelettes", and *L'Assassinat du Duc de Guise* (France, Charles Le Bargy, 1908), "one of the first of the 'historic reconstruction' class of film that unhappily remains much in vogue amongst French directors".[60]

It is significant that, in this first section of his film, Cavalcanti dwells more on the emergence of the entertainment film than on that of the actuality film. Although he argues that the emergence of such "dramas" eventually led to a "loss of contact with reality", and that this loss, in turn, led to a renewed interest in "newsreels and interest films", he does not denounce the comedic entertainment film, but, on the contrary, celebrates its contribution to the new medium. Cavalcanti does, however, criticise *L'Assassinat du Duc de Guise* for its theatricality. From the 1920s onwards, Cavalcanti frequently voiced the opinion – one shared by the French Impressionists and Surrealists – that the development of the film medium would be inhibited by an over-reliance on theatrical conventions, and he takes the opportunity to reiterate this view in *Film and Reality*.[61]

Writing in 1936, Cavalcanti argued that the French cinema recovered from the set-back of films such as *L'Assassinat du Duc de Guise* through the development of the fantasy film and the "episodic comedy":

Cinematic art began with *L'Arrosseur Arrose* [sic] in
1900. Was the cinema aware of its possibilities? Was
it going to interpret human emotion, the comic life
itself? Also instead of catching its true voice in the
beginning indicated so clearly in this film, the year
lost itself in encumbrances with theatrical tradition...
The cinema reacts definitely against the double
influence of the theatre and of letters in the growth of
the episodic, the cultural and the comic film.[62]

Cavalcanti's equation of human emotion and "the comic life"
here is significant in the centrality which it places on the comedic, and
it is the melodramatic and comic realism of *The Waterer Watered*,
rather than its actuality content, which Cavalcanti emphasises.

The second part of *Film and Reality* turns from the
entertainment film back to newsreel and interest films. It begins with
sequences from the newsreel films *The Funeral of Queen Victoria* (GB,
1901), *The Launch of HMS Dreadnought by King Edward VII* (GB,
1906), *Suffragette Riots in Trafalgar Square* (GB, 1909) and
L'Assassinat du Roi Alexandre de Yougoslavie (France, 1904). These are
followed by sequences taken from scientific interest films such as *The
Electrolysis of Metals* (GB, Charles Urban, 1910), *Infant Welfare in the
Bird World* (GB, H Bruce Woolfe, 1920), *The Cultivation of Living
Tissues* (GB, 1924), *X-Ray Film in Medical Diagnosis* (GB, 1923) and
The Tough Un (GB, Mary Field and Percy Smith, 1938). This series of
extracts end with a sequence of shots taken from Jean Painlevé's
Crevettes (*Shrimps*, 1933), followed by a number of scenes taken from
travel and war films. Charles Urban's *Romance of the Railways* (GB,
1907) is described as "the grandfather of our present day British
documentary", and Urban's film is followed by sequences from *Pékin et
environs* (France, 1909), *With Scott in the Antarctic* (GB, Herbert
Ponting, 1913) and, finally, *The Battle of the Somme* (GB, Geoffrey H
Malins and J B McDowell, 1916).

Cavalcanti's inclination to focus more on the aesthetic and
poetic than on the factual qualities of these films is again evident in
this section of *Film and Reality*. Although Cavalcanti stresses the
enduring appeal of the newsreel in providing information on current
affairs, the film which is given most attention in this sequence of
extracts is Painlevé's *Shrimps*, which Cavalcanti describes as a "poetic
treatment of reality". Painlevé's film uses microscopic photography to
show the shrimps within their rather ethereal, watery environment,
and also emphasises the formal qualities of shape, form and movement.
In contrast, the most important British realist film of the pre-
documentary film movement period, *The Battle of the Somme*, is given
only passing attention. It is also possible that Cavalcanti's use of the
phrase the "poetic treatment of reality" was deliberately designed as a
mischievous reworking of Grierson's phase "the creative shaping of
[natural material]", which the latter had used as the basis of his theory

of documentary film.[63] Since Grierson had made it clear that he was opposed to the "poetic style" of documentaries such as Flaherty's *Man of Aran* (GB, 1934),[64] Cavalcanti's use of the term in a formulation so close to his own could do nothing but annoy and irritate him.

Unsurprisingly, Cavalcanti begins part 3, "The Romantic Documentary of Far-Off Places", with extracts from Flaherty, the greatest single influence on the Parisian documentary avant-garde when Cavalcanti was active in Paris during the 1920s. *Nanook of the North* (USA, Flaherty, 1922) is described as "the first realist drama — the first documentary film in the modern sense". The extracts from *Nanook of the North* are followed by a sequence from *Moana* (USA, Flaherty, 1926). These extracts are followed by shots from *Grass* (USA, Merian C Cooper and Ernest B Schoedsack, 1925), a film about the Bakhtiari tribesmen of central Iran, which has been described as "a dramatic document of the pastoral stage of man's struggle to live".[65] *Grass* is followed by extracts from the French ethnographic film *Ève africaine* (France, Léon Poirier, 1925), and then by two documentaries with which Cavalcanti had been involved: *Voyage au Congo* (*Voyage to the Congo*, France, André Gide and Marc Allégret, 1927) and *Au Pays du scalp* (*In the Country of the Scalp People*, France, Marquis de Wavrin, 1931). This section of *Film and Reality* closes with sequences from *Man of Aran* and *The Song of Ceylon*.

Although Cavalcanti links a wide variety of very different films together in this section, what unites them for him is their shared poetic stance towards the material they represent. All the extracts shown are concerned with the relationship between man and nature, and, in particular, with the cultural rituals which have developed within ethnic communities in response to their proximity to an often demanding natural environment. For example, *Voyage to the Congo* and *In the Country of the Scalp People* show ethnic South American tribes existing within a wild forest environment, whilst *Nanook of the North*, *Moana* and *Man of Aran* explore cultural activities formed through contact with forbidding natural environments in, respectively, the Arctic, the South Seas and the Irish Sea.

Cavalcanti describes *Man of Aran* here as characteristic of the "romantic style in documentary". More provocatively, however, he also ascribes to *The Song of Ceylon* "a poetic quality [which] sets it apart from the school of British documentary". It was precisely this kind of comment, which elevated the aesthetic dimension of the films made by the documentary film movement above their social and journalistic attributes, which so enraged Grierson and other members of the documentary film movement when they saw *Film and Reality*.[66] As with his use of the term "the poetic treatment of reality", it is difficult to believe that Cavalcanti was not aware of the impact such comments were bound to have on Grierson and the others.

Part 4 of *Film and Reality* is entitled "The Realistic Documentary of Life at Home". The section begins with a sequence from Cavalcanti's *Nothing But the Hours*, which is described as "an attempt to draw attention to the miseries of unemployment". This is followed by sequences from *Berlin – Symphony of a Great City* (Germany, Walter Ruttmann, 1927), described as "being conceived in the style of a piece of impressionistic music", and *Turksib* (USSR, Viktor Turin, 1930). Despite being apparently concerned with realism, it is, once again, the formal and aesthetic qualities of these films, rather than their social or political aims, which are emphasised. This is particularly the case with *Turksib*, a film which Grierson took as the model for his socially-purposive theory of documentary film.[67] However, Cavalcanti is less concerned here with *Turksib*'s "Griersonian" discourse about the growth of social unity across the wide expanses of the USSR, and more preoccupied with its artistic merit.

After this, Cavalcanti turns at last to the achievements of the Griersonian documentary. Here again, however, it is the aesthetic achievements of the documentary film movement which are emphasised, rather than its involvement in the production of civic propaganda. It is true that *Drifters* is described as starting "a powerful movement in civic education", and *Housing Problems* is briefly referred to. However, *Night Mail* is described as an "experiment in sound", and *North Sea* (GB, Watt, 1938) as "an exercise in the use of music and sound effects". In both cases, it is the visual style of these films, rather than their social message, which is highlighted.

In the conclusion to Part 4 of *Film and Reality*, Cavalcanti turns away from Britain and back towards Continental Europe. A sequence from Jean Benoit-Lévy's *Un grand potier* (*A Great Potter: Delaherche*, France, 1932), showing Delaherche at work, is followed by a sequence from Jean Vigo's *Taris* (France, 1931), a short sports film about a swimming champion. Once again, Cavalcanti concentrates on the poetic visual style of this film, commenting that, for Vigo, "realism was often scarcely to be distinguished from surrealism". This is followed by sequences from Jean Lods' *Le Mile* (France, 1934), a short experimental documentary in which the subjective experiences of a runner during a race are shown using slow-motion photography and other special effects techniques. This focus on the aesthetic attributes of the documentary continues with scenes from Robert Alexandre's *Un Monastère* (France, 1933) and Joris Ivens' *Zuyderzee* (The Netherlands, 1930). Ivens' film depicts the building of a dam in Holland, but the sequences selected by Cavalcanti emphasise the visual effects produced by moving water and other natural elements, rather than the overall process of development and construction. Part 4 of *Film and Reality* ends with sequences from Ivens' *Spanish Earth* (Spain, 1937) and Pare Lorentz's *The Plow That Broke the Plains* (USA, 1936). It is again significant that Cavalcanti should choose to end the part of *Film and Reality* which includes the British documentary film movement with sequences from such films.

The final part of *Film and Reality* is entitled "Realism in the Story Film", and consists of an eclectic and meandering combination of extracts, with little linking them together. A sequence from a film by

Mauritz Stiller is then followed by scenes from James Cruze's *The Covered Wagon* (USA, 1923) and *Stagecoach Man* (USA, Tom Mix, 1913). This is followed by sequences from *Bronenosets Potemkin* (*Battleship Potemkin*, USSR, Eisenstein, 1925), *The Life of Emile Zola* (USA, William Dieterle, 1937), *Love From a Stranger* (GB, Rowland Lee, 1937), *Kameradschaft* (Germany, Pabst, 1931), *La Grande illusion* (France, Renoir, 1937) and *Farewell Again* (GB, Erich Pommer, 1937). No commentary is used in this final section of *Film and Reality*, as Cavalcanti presents the viewer with a wide and somewhat unpredictable range of examples of the realistic story film. It is also significant that, in 1942, when he had already left the documentary film movement, Cavalcanti should end his study of film and reality not with documentary, but with the feature film, as though implying that one led on naturally to the other. In this sense, *Film and Reality* reaffirms Cavalcanti's own conviction that no fundamental distinctions should be made between the documentary and the feature film, and it also serves as a form of self-justification for his own move from documentary into feature filmmaking, a move which took place in 1940.

   Film and Reality was strongly criticised by members of the documentary film movement from the moment that it was first screened. Rotha argued that it was "muddled, chaotic and an insult to British documentary".[68] Later, he also argued that *Film and Reality* was responsible for bringing the underlying differences which existed within the documentary film movement, such as those concerning aesthetic form and social purposiveness, to an acrimonious head.[69] Writing in 1973, he was even more disparaging about *Film and Reality*, and accused Cavalcanti of making the film in order deliberately to foment divisions within the documentary film movement:

> Cavalcanti (presumably sent by the GPO) took the opportunity to create further tension between himself and Grierson, and those of the British documentary group who were associates with him, notably Wright and myself. This friction which obsessed Cavalcanti was crystallized in *Film and Reality*, a compilation film which the British Film Institute commissioned Cavalcanti to make in 1939-40.[70]

   Rotha went on to assert that, although "fascinating in parts", *Film and Reality* "did less than justice to the social aims of the British documentary group, whose work as shown, when at all, was inadequate and false".[71] In addition, Rotha accused Cavalcanti of deliberately removing references to his (Rotha's) work from the final version of *Film and Reality* because of the criticisms which he made of the film,[72] and also claimed that, in collaboration with the Associated Realist Film Producers group, he actually attempted to have *Film and Reality* withdrawn from circulation.[73]

Although Rotha published some of his criticisms of *Film and Reality* as soon as the film was premièred, Grierson himself did not criticise *Film and Reality* directly, but instead used its appearance to launch a stinging attack on Cavalcanti in one of his most vitriolic essays, "The Documentary Idea: 1942",[74] published in *Documentary Newsletter*. Here Grierson attempted both to re-establish his own conception of documentary as the dominant one within the documentary film movement, and to challenge Cavalcanti's approach to "film and reality".

As mentioned earlier, tensions between Grierson and Cavalcanti had existed almost from the beginning, and the appearance of *Pett and Pott* in 1934 made it immediately apparent that Cavalcanti did not share Grierson's view of the type of films which should be made by the documentary film movement. In addition, films such as *The Fairy of the Phone* (1936), *Trade Tattoo* (1937), *Mony a Pickle* (1938) and *Spare Time*, all of which were directly influenced by Cavalcanti, clearly indicate a quite different approach to filmmaking to that advocated by Grierson.

Initially, however, Grierson's views on documentary film were not that far removed from Cavalcanti's ideas on avant-garde realist filmmaking. Grierson's early theory of documentary film contained three principal features: a concern with the content and expressive richness of the actuality image; a preoccupation with the interpretive potential of editing; and a regard for the representation of social relationships.[75] All these features can be found in his early film theory, as well as in some of the films produced by the documentary film movement between 1929 and 1935. However, after 1935, and therefore shortly after Cavalcanti joined the documentary film movement, Grierson's earlier concern with philosophical aesthetics became gradually supplanted by a preoccupation with the need to mould the documentary film into an instrument of "civic education", whilst the poetic, montage style of films such as *Drifters* and *The Song of Ceylon* gradually gave way to the more didactic, journalistic style of films such as *Housing Problems*. This change of approach from the pre- to the post-1936 period can be explained in terms of a shift from a regard for a phenomenological naturalism of the image to a more directive style which was always implicit in Grierson's notion of the creative interpretation of reality. After 1936, this more directive approach became increasingly allied to the cardinal objective of representing social relationships, whilst the earlier aesthetic of the image was increasingly discarded.[76]

By 1942, Grierson had become completely converted to this later position, which he expressed most forcefully in "The Documentary Idea: 1942". Here Grierson talked about the need to "bang out one [film] a fortnight...with a minimum of dawdling", and argued that "the documentary idea was not basically a film idea at all...the medium happened to be the most convenient".[77] Grierson also argued that he "used" the aesthetes within the documentary film movement, describing

Flaherty and Cavalcanti as "fellow travellers", and implying that both were peripheral to the movement and motivated by self-interest.[78] Such acrimonious language indicates the extent of the division within the documentary film movement by 1942. Indeed, the furore over *Film and Reality* probably had little to do with the film itself, and was essentially an expression of that division, as well as a reflection of the conviction, held by Grierson, Rotha and others, that Cavalcanti had somehow betrayed or undermined the central principles on which the documentary film movement had been founded.

In retrospect, these criticisms of *Film and Reality* seem to verge almost on the hysterical, given that there is basically nothing wrong with the film other than that it does not contain the selection of extracts which either Grierson or Rotha would have chosen.[79] Nor does *Film and Reality* directly criticise the Griersonian documentary. On the contrary, both *Drifters* and *Housing Problems* are referred to positively, whilst a significant number of other films made by the documentary film movement, including *The Song of Ceylon, Industrial Britain* (1931), *Night Mail* and *North Sea*, are also mentioned. Cavalcanti also refers to key films within Grierson's canon of great realist works, including *Turksib, Nanook of the North, The Covered Wagon* and even *The March of Time*, the journalistic newsreel series which played such a pivotal role in converting Grierson to his post-1936 position on the documentary film.[80]

What is true, however, is that these films are often described in terms which Grierson himself would not have used in 1942, and that, in some cases, Cavalcanti has included some films which Grierson had previously criticised. For example, *Nanook of the North*, not *Drifters*, is described as "the first documentary film in the modern sense", whilst *Berlin – Symphony of a Great City* was often criticised by Grierson for its lack of social purpose and for its preoccupation with formalist aesthetics.[81]

Cavalcanti claimed that he deliberately tried to provoke Grierson by playing romantic music over the sequences from *Drifters* in *Film and Reality*:

> With my wrong sense of humour I did a bad turn to Grierson. I put Mendelssohn's 'Fingal's Cave' over *Drifters*, which was putting it back into romantic sort of films, and I don't think that pleased Grierson at all...But really you must realise that Grierson at the bottom was quite a demagogue.[82]

It may well have been the case that Cavalcanti was trying to provoke Grierson here. However, it may also have been that, at the time, he was actually attempting to reunite *Drifters* with the musical accompaniment originally proposed for it, but, afterwards, preferred to cultivate the idea that he had been making mischief at the demagogue's expense. As I have shown elsewhere, the original musical score for

Drifters did, in fact, contain extracts from Romantic composers such as Wagner, Rimsky-Korsakov, Liszt and Mendelssohn. Moreover, the music played at the première of *Drifters* at the Tivoli Palace, London, on 10 November 1929 was precisely Mendelssohn's "Fingal's Cave Overture".[83] Given this, there seems no reason why Grierson should be annoyed by Cavalcanti's "prank" and, in addition, there is no evidence that he actually was.

Although the account of the development of cinematic realism in *Film and Reality* was unacceptable to Grierson and his associates at the time, it proved indispensable to Michael Balcon, one of the key figures in the development of British film culture during the 1940s. Balcon based his influential 1944 essay "Realism or Tinsel" directly on the commentary within Cavalcanti's film, and in that essay argued that Cavalcanti "stands supreme" in his knowledge of the history of the documentary film[84] and ranks alongside Flaherty, Vertov and Ruttmann as "the first to realise...the social significance of the screen".[85]

Film and Reality is an ambitious, although unsystematic attempt to depict the development of the quality realist film tradition, and, although its survey of that tradition contains some extremely interesting extracts from rare films such as Vigo's *Taris*, it cannot be considered one of Cavalcanti's major achievements. The real significance of *Film and Reality*, however, lies firstly in its impact on the documentary film movement, and secondly in its influence on Balcon's ideas about cinematic realism.

Notes

[1]   Rachael Low, *The History of the British Film 1929-1939: Documentary and Educational Films of the 1930s* (London; Boston; Sydney: George Allen & Unwin, 1979): 77-78.

[2]   Ibid: 119.

[3]   Ibid: 78.

[4]   Paul Rotha, *Documentary Diary: An Informal History of the British Documentary Film, 1928-1939* (London: Secker and Warburg, 1973): 142.

[5]   Forsyth Hardy, *John Grierson: A Documentary Biography* (London; Boston: Faber and Faber, 1979): 74.

[6]   Elizabeth Sussex, *The Rise and Fall of British Documentary: The Story of the Film Movement Founded by John Grierson* (Berkeley; Los Angeles; London: University of California Press, 1975): 51.

[7]   Ibid.

[8]   Ibid.

[9]   Gavin Lambert, "Alberto Cavalcanti", *Screen* 13: 2 (summer 1972): 37.

[10]   John Grierson, "Summary and Survey: 1935", in Forsyth Hardy (ed), *Grierson on Documentary* (London; Boston: Faber and Faber, 1979): 60.

[11]   Hardy: 74.

[12]   Ibid: 74-75.

[13]   Sussex: 51.

[14]   Ibid.

[15]   Ibid.

[16]   Hardy: 69.

[17]   Sussex: 39-40.

[18]   Richard Meran Barsam, *Nonfiction Film: A Critical History*, revised and expanded edition (Bloomington; Indianapolis: Indiana University Press, 1992): 95.

[19]   Low: 59-60.

[20]   Ibid: 59.

[21]   Ibid.

[22]   Ibid.

[23]   Ibid: 60.

[24]   Herbert Read, "*Granton Trawler*", *Cinema Quarterly* 3: 1 (1934): 104.

[25]   Sussex: 39.

[26]   Ian Aitken, "The Films of the Documentary Film Movement", in Ian Aitken (ed), *The Documentary Film Movement: An Anthology* (Edinburgh: Edinburgh University Press, 1998): 28.

[27]   Sussex: 98.

[28]   Harry Watt, *Don't Look at the Camera* (London: Paul Elek, 1974): 89.

[29]   Sussex: 74.

[30]   Rotha: 232. Emphasis in original.

[31]   Elizabeth Sussex, "Cavalcanti in England", *Sight and Sound* 44: 4 (autumn 1975): 206, reprinted in Aitken (ed): 184.

[32]   Sussex, *The Rise and Fall of British Documentary: The Story of the Film Movement Founded by John Grierson*: 98-99.

[33]   Sussex, in Aitken (ed): 183.

[34]   Low: 79.

[35]   Sussex, *The Rise and Fall of British Documentary: The Story of the Film Movement Founded by John Grierson*: 29.

[36]   Hardy: 68.

[37]   Sussex, *The Rise and Fall of British Documentary: The Story of the Film Movement Founded by John Grierson*: 65.

[38]   Quoted in Rotha: 131.

[39]   Sussex, in Aitken (ed): 183.

[40]   Paul Rotha, in Eva Orbanz, *Journey to a Legend and Back: The British Realistic Film* (Berlin: Volker Spiess, 1977): 35.

[41]   Erik Barnouw, *Documentary: A History of the Non-Fiction Film*, second revised edition (New York; Oxford: Oxford University Press, 1993): 91.

[42]   Barsam: 106.

[43]   Evelyn Gerstein, "English Documentary Films", in Lewis Jacobs (ed), *The Documentary Tradition*, second edition (New York: W W Norton & Company, 1979): 114.

[44]   John Corner, "*Coalface* and *Housing Problems* (1935)", in *The Art of record: A critical introduction to documentary* (Manchester; New York: Manchester University Press, 1996): 60.

[45]   Ibid.

[46]   Ibid.

[47]   Hardy: 81.

[48]   Paul Swann, *The British Documentary Film Movement, 1926-1946* (Cambridge; New York; New Rochelle; Melbourne; Sydney: Cambridge University Press, 1989): 81

[49]   Paul Rotha, *Documentary Film: The use of the film medium to interpret creatively and in social terms the life of the people as it exists in reality*, second edition (London: Faber & Faber, 1939): 254.

[50]   Ian Aitken, *Film and Reform: John Grierson and the Documentary Film Movement* (London; New York: Routledge, 1990): 139.

[51]   Sussex, *The Rise and Fall of British Documentary: The Story of the Film Movement Founded by John Grierson*: 85.

[52]   Barsam: 102.

[53]   Rotha (1973): 134.

[54]   Hardy: 81.

[55]   Rotha (1973): 135.

[56]   Aitken (1990): 140.

[57]   Noreen Branson and Margot Heinemann, *Britain in the 1930s* (London: Panther, 1973): 299.

[58]   Barsam: 10.

[59]   Paul Rotha with Richard Griffith, *The Film Till Now: A Survey of World Cinema* (London: Vision Press, 1949): 70.

[60]   Alberto Cavalcanti, "The Evolution of Cinematography in France (1936)", in Aitken (ed): 202.

[61]   Ibid.

[62]   Ibid: 202-203.

[63]   John Grierson, "First Principles of Documentary (1932)", in ibid: 84.

[64]   Ibid: 84.

[65]   Jacobs (ed): 23.

[66]   Rotha (1973): 230-231.

[67]   Hardy (ed): 24.

[68]   Paul Rotha, letter of John Grierson, 10 April 1942, John Grierson Archive, Stirling University, G4.265.

[69]   Rotha (1973): 230.

[70]   Ibid.

[71]   Ibid: 231.

[72]   Ibid.

[73]   Ibid.

[74]   John Grierson, "The Documentary Idea: 1942", in Hardy (ed): 111-121.

[75]   Ian Aitken, "Grierson's Theory of Documentary Film", in Aitken (ed): 41.

[76]   Ibid.

[77]   Ibid: 41-42.

[78]   Ibid: 42.

[79]   Sussex, in Aitken (ed): 198.

[80]   Aitken (1990): 144.

[81]   Grierson, in Aitken (ed): 87.

[82]   Sussex, in Aitken (ed): 198.

[83]   Aitken (1990): 108.

[84]   Michael Balcon, "Introduction", *Realism or Tinsel* (Workers Film Association, 1944): n.p.

[85]   Ibid: 7.

5

Ealing Studios

> For my part, I am ever grateful to the Producer who
> enabled me to come back into the field of fictional film
> after my long and hard work in the documentary
> movement.[1]

> Cavalcanti had many qualities which I did not
> possess, but to balance this my long experience in the
> tougher world of commercial films served as a
> complement, and it was Cavalcanti's close association
> with me which provided the force from which emerged
> what are now thought of *en bloc* – though their
> variety was considerable – as the Ealing films.[2]

Given the way in which his filmmaking activities had evolved during
the late-1930s, Cavalcanti's relocation to Ealing Studios in 1940 can be
regarded as a logical and appropriate move. He himself believed that
there were clear continuities between Ealing and the documentary film
movement, and the move, when it finally came, felt more like a natural
progression than a radical change:

> I was as happy at Ealing as I had been at the GPO. It
> was a good atmosphere in part because of the boys I
> took in such as Watt and Hamer...Also the very good
> people who came later, particularly Alexander
> MacKendrick [sic], Charley Frend and Charley
> Crichton. The cooperation at Ealing was very similar
> to that at the GPO...Ealing was an absolute parallel
> to the GPO as far as I am concerned. We insisted on
> continuing our documentary work at Ealing which
> Mick [Balcon] accepted. I think we made films on the
> line of those we did for the GPO, such as *Yellow
> Caesar* (1941), *Greek Testament* (1943) and films like
> that.[3]

Cavalcanti's first indirect association with Michael Balcon, the film producer who enabled him to return to the feature film after his "long and hard work in the documentary movement", occurred when Balcon was overseeing the production of Flaherty's *Man of Aran* (1934) for the Gaumont-British Picture Corporation. Balcon's decision to invest in *Man of Aran* was widely regarded as a risky undertaking at the time, given Flaherty's capacity for disregarding budgets and production schedules in films such as *White Shadows in the South Seas* (1928) and *Tabu: A Story of the South Seas* (1931), both of which created difficulties for their respective Hollywood producers.[4] Even within the British documentary film movement, Flaherty's *Industrial Britain* (1931) ran so far over budget that responsibility for the film's final editing was removed from him and transferred to Edgar Anstey.[5] Later, Zoltan and Alexander Korda were to experience similar problems with Flaherty when producing *Elephant Boy* in 1937.[6]

Like Korda in the late-1930s, Balcon's decision to invest in *Man of Aran* during the mid-1930s was probably based on the belief that Flaherty's prestige would bring some critical distinction, as well as a modest profit, to Gaumont-British.[7] Nevertheless, prior to this, and under Balcon's guidance, Gaumont-British had already established a reputation for being willing to experiment – employing Alfred Hitchcock and Ivor Montagu during the early 1930s, and making controversial films such as Lothar Mendes' *Jew Süss* (1934).[8] Balcon's commitment to *Man of Aran* also seems to have been more genuine than Korda's later investment in *Elephant Boy*, and, in later years, he remained proud of the film which became known within the film trade as "Balcon's Folly".[9]

Balcon's involvement in such films, together with his support for the Film Society movement and the documentary film movement during the 1930s, made an impression on Cavalcanti.[10] However, it was not until the discussions which took place in 1939 over the possible transfer of the GPO Film Unit to Ealing Studios that their relationship became close. Cavalcanti's association with Balcon was also more familiar and long-standing than his earlier affiliation with John Grierson had been, and contained few of the tensions which had marred the earlier partnership. In later years, Cavalcanti sometimes spoke in ambivalent, and occasionally disapproving, terms about Grierson. Writing in 1952, for example, he claimed that Grierson was "basically a promoter. He had little impact as a director or producer".[11] However, in marked contrast, Cavalcanti's remarks about Balcon were generally characterised by a degree of warmth and affection which did not diminish with the passing of time. Writing as late as 1975, for example, he was still referring to Balcon as "the best producer I ever had".[12]

Nevertheless, although the relationship which developed between Cavalcanti and Balcon at Ealing was often a close and complementary one, considerable differences existed between the personality, outlook and background of the two men. Balcon came from a middle-class, Jewish background, and his conservative, provincial upbringing stood in marked contrast to Cavalcanti's more cosmopolitan, and particularly francophone, formative development. Balcon and Cavalcanti also shared radically different career trajectories within the film industry. Cavalcanti had largely been active in small-scale film production, within both the French avant-garde and the British documentary film movement, and his experiences in the commercial French film industry were a source of considerable unhappiness to him. Balcon, on the other hand, had largely worked within the corporate sector of the industry. In 1924, he established Gainsborough Studios, and, in the late-1920s, when Gainsborough was acquired by the Gaumont-British Picture Corporation, he also took charge of production at the Gaumont-British studios in Shepherd's Bush, whilst retaining production control of Gainsborough.[13] In 1936, following a recession within the British film industry, production at Shepherd's Bush was closed down, although Balcon had, by then, already accepted an offer from Metro-Goldwyn-Mayer to manage production at a new British branch of MGM.[14]

Balcon's background within the corporate sector initially led him to advocate a film production policy based on the production of big-budget films for the international market, and he firmly believed that this strategy represented the British film industry's best hope of achieving commercial success in the face of competition from Hollywood. However, the impact of the industry's collapse in 1936 caused him to revise his opinions on the merits of "internationalism", and instead to advocate the production of more "parochial" British films for the British market.[15] Balcon's involvement with MGM also proved to be an unrewarding experience and, in 1938, he left in order to take up a position as head of film production with Associated Talking Pictures at their studios in Ealing.[16]

Production of films at Ealing had begun in 1931 under the control of the studio's first head of production, Basil Dean. However, the films made under Dean were largely generic in nature, the most successful being comedy vehicles for Gracie Fields and George Formby, and, although Balcon carried on with the commercially successful Formby films when he was appointed Head of Production in 1938, they did not represent the type of films which he wanted Ealing to make. Balcon's preferred approach to filmmaking at that time is best illustrated by *The Gaunt Stranger* (Walter Forde, 1938), a moderately-budgeted thriller based on a detective story by Edgar Wallace entitled *The Ringer* (1926). Although containing a substantial amount of location-shooting, *The Gaunt Stranger* remains very much within the conventions of the thriller genre, and it is this combination of proto-realism and generic convention which best illustrates Balcon's approach to filmmaking at the time.

The films made at Ealing before Cavalcanti's arrival in late-1940 also included *The Ware Case* (1938), a film largely made as a vehicle for the actor Clive Brook. In addition, Ealing produced the George Formby vehicles *Come On George!* (Anthony Kimmins, 1939), *Let George Do It!* (Marcel Varnel, 1940) and *Spare a Copper* (John

Paddy Carstairs, 1940). Robert Stevenson, who had directed *The Ware Case*, directed *Young Man's Fancy* (1939), a romantic comedy, and *Return to Yesterday* (1940), which was set in the world of amateur theatricals. The most prolific director during this period was, however, Walter Forde, who directed *Let's Be Famous* (1939), a comedy embellished with songs by Noel Gay; *Cheer Boys Cheer* (1939), about the conflict between two brewery companies; *The Four Just Men* (1939), based on another Edgar Wallace story; *Saloon Bar* (1940), which starred the cockney comedian Gordon Harker; and *Sailors Three* (1940), a comedy vehicle for Tommy Trinder and Claude Hulbert. This group of films made up an uneven and transitional body of work which, with the possible exception of *Saloon Bar*, with its convincing emphasis on working-class characterisation and milieu, failed to establish a suitable foundation for the films which Balcon and Cavalcanti were later to produce during the war.

Three films which did help to establish such a foundation, however, were Penrose Tennyson's *There Ain't No Justice* (1939), *The Proud Valley* (1940) and *Convoy* (1940). By 1939, Balcon had become convinced of the need to make films which employed more positive representations of working-class experience if the cinema was to play a meaningful role in the cultural life of the nation, and *There Ain't No Justice* was designed as "[t]he first move in this direction".[17] *There Ain't No Justice* deals with match rigging and exploitation within the boxing world, and attempted, albeit with only limited success, to combine social realism and generic conventions, taking the positive representation of working-class communities several steps further than had been achieved in *Saloon Bar*. This was even more the case with Tennyson's second film, *The Proud Valley*. As in *There Ain't No Justice*, the focus of attention here is firmly on working-class characters, and considerable effort is put into evoking the experience of life within the south Wales mining communities. However, in contrast to these two films, Tennyson's third film, *Convoy*, although containing amounts of realistic location footage, is not principally concerned with working-class characterisation, but with the romantic exploits and heroics of the officer class.

Cavalcanti arrived at Ealing after these three films had been made, and his first production credits are for art direction on Marcel Varnel's *The Ghost of St Michael's* and *Turned Out Nice Again* (both 1941), on both of which he collaborated with the established Ealing scriptwriter Wilfrid Shingleton. Cavalcanti is described as a "consultant" in the credits for these films, a designation which probably reflects the fact that, as a recent appointee, it was not felt appropriate that he should be allocated specific production responsibilities. Neither of these films can be considered particularly significant as far as Cavalcanti's own personal career development is concerned, however, as they were both vehicles for Will Hay and George Formby, Ealing's most popular comedy stars of the period. Cavalcanti's credits for set design on these films are also the only such attributed to him during his time at Ealing, and, after that, his credits are for associate producer and director only.

Cavalcanti's first production credits as associate producer were for *Yellow Caesar*, *The Young Veteran* and *Mastery of the Sea*, three propaganda films which Ealing made for the MoI in 1941. Cavalcanti then worked as associate producer on Charles Frend's *The Big Blockade* (1942) and *The Foreman Went to France* (1942), before going on to produce Basil Dearden's *The Halfway House* (1944), and the short instructional film *Find, Fix and Strike* (1943). In addition, Cavalcanti claims to have been associate producer, together with Michael Relph, on Basil Dearden's *The Captive Heart* (1946).[18]

Yellow Caesar, *The Young Veteran* and *Mastery of the Sea* were made voluntarily by Ealing in addition to their quota requirement for propaganda films for 1941.[19] Balcon, who has described the films as being "right up Cavalcanti's street",[20] may well have commissioned them in order to allow Cavalcanti to cut his teeth at Ealing on the familiar ground of documentary, as much as to make a point to the MoI concerning Ealing's commitment to the war effort. All three films are targeted at American, as much as British public opinion, reflecting the then-current policy of encouraging US support for the British war effort. *Mastery of the Sea* and *The Young Veteran* also use the voice of the American journalist Michael Frank for their commentaries, further indicating the importance of the American orientation for these films, whilst *Yellow Caesar*, in drawing distinctions between Mussolini and "ordinary Italians", may have been targeting the Italian-American community.

The most important of these three films is undoubtedly *Yellow Caesar*. Produced by Cavalcanti, edited by Charles Crichton, and with dialogue by Adrian Brunel, the film contains no specific credits for direction, although the likelihood is that Cavalcanti played the leading role in this respect. *Yellow Caesar*'s parodic account of Mussolini's rise to power is deployed on two quite different levels. At one level, the film's commentary is often rhetorical and jingoistic, and its narrative about "the big bully of Rome" makes few concessions to historical accuracy or impartiality. However, on another level, *Yellow Caesar* seems to be concerned principally with pastiche and parody, and more interested in deploying film technique to parodic effect than in communicating propaganda about Mussolini. The resulting film is less crude jingoism than clever, comic caricature in which didactic ideological discourses are playfully undermined by the use of comedy, *mise en scène* and film technique. One can imagine Cavalcanti and his new colleagues enjoying making *Yellow Caesar*.

Mastery of the Sea and *The Young Veteran* are more routine than *Yellow Caesar*, and, at the level of propaganda address, embody the posture of stoic and dogged British resistance under fire which characterised better-known documentary films of the period such as *The First Days* (1939), *London Can Take It!* (1940) and *Christmas Under Fire* (1941). *Mastery of the Sea* shows a convoy of merchant and escorting warships setting out to sea, and uses a jingoistic and colloquial voice-over commentary which possesses none of the irony found in *Yellow Caesar*. Few of Cavalcanti's characteristic stylistic traits or thematic concerns are to be found here, with the possible exception of the rapid editing techniques used in the battle sequences.

Whilst no credits are available for *Mastery of the Sea*, making it difficult to know who was involved in the film apart from Cavalcanti – or even what Cavalcanti's precise role was – *The Young Veteran* is credited as being produced by Cavalcanti and edited by Charles Crichton, with Basil Dearden and Monja Danischewsky participating as assistant editors. Again, no specific credits are given for direction, suggesting that, like *Yellow Caesar*, the film was largely a collaborative effort, with Cavalcanti, by far the most experienced of this group, the dominant figure. *The Young Veteran* can also be distinguished from the other two films in this series in that it focuses on the experiences of one soldier, rather than on more general political or military circumstances. The message of the film is that, following British military defeats in Norway and Dunkirk, the young recruits drafted into the Army in 1940 had, through this baptism of fire, emerged as experienced, battle-hardened veterans. The film begins by showing the induction of a raw recruit, "young Bert". However, unlike later British wartime feature films such as *The Way Ahead* (1944), which is centrally concerned with the process of shaping new recruits into an effective fighting force, *The Young Veteran* quickly loses interest in young Bert, and becomes more expansive in its references to military events such as the evacuation at Dunkirk and the formation of the Home Guard.

These three wartime documentaries were routine propaganda vehicles in which Cavalcanti's authorial signature is exhibited much as it was in earlier films such as *The Fairy of the Phone* (1936) and *Pett and Pott* (1934), and the wartime documentaries are similarly most interesting when they use parody and film technique to undermine their own propaganda address. What is significant, however, is that, despite Cavalcanti's move from a government organisation to a commercial film studio, a move which seemingly should have provided him with a freer creative environment, a film such as *Yellow Caesar*, although interesting, does not approach the quality and complexity of GPO films such as *Spare Time* (1939) or *Men of the Lightship* (1940). Although Cavalcanti had managed to create conditions at the GPO Film Unit in which important and innovative films could be made, the question now was whether he could re-create such conditions at Ealing.

The Big Blockade and *The Foreman Went to France* (both 1942)

In 1942, Cavalcanti worked as associate producer on two films directed by Charles Frend: *The Big Blockade* and *The Foreman Went to France*. *The Big Blockade* was Ealing's third major production dealing with the war, after Penrose Tennyson's *Convoy* and Sergei Nolbandov's *Ships With Wings* (1941), neither of which had been particularly successful.[21]

However, although *The Big Blockade* was made in an attempt to produce a more viable model of film propaganda than had been achieved in either of the earlier films, it is unlikely that Balcon ever believed such a film could provide the model for future development at Ealing. *The Big Blockade* is too discursive, and contains few of the generic, romantic or melodramatic elements which Balcon believed were necessary features of any attempt to project Britain in the feature film. Although Balcon described *The Big Blockade* in his autobiography as being of "special significance", he also grouped it alongside three other films which provided "proof that feature films could be made to work for the war effort". However, Balcon clearly considered these three films – *Ships With Wings*, *The Foreman Went to France* and *The Next of Kin* (1942) – to be more important than *The Big Blockade*, which he almost certainly regarded as a relatively minor project.[22]

    The Big Blockade must also be understood within the context of a growing rift between Balcon and the MoI over the issue of film propaganda. During 1940, Balcon had publicly criticised the MoI Films Division for not doing enough to support commercial producers in making relevant war-orientated films, and for proposing projects which often proved unworkable.[23] Balcon also wanted greater autonomy in developing his own projects, and announced in December 1940 that Ealing was to go ahead with a programme of films without the assistance of the MoI, the first one of which would be *The Big Blockade*. Unlike *Ships With Wings* and *Convoy*, which were both made with MoI cooperation and approval, *The Big Blockade* was deliberately made outside MoI jurisdiction, a development about which the MoI was so concerned that it attempted to have the project halted.[24]

    The production context of *The Big Blockade* was, therefore, a complex one, and this complexity is reflected in the film itself. Although described as propagandistic and "bombastic",[25] *The Big Blockade* is, in fact, an underrated and innovative film. The opening scenes reveal an Expressionist or Impressionist influence in lighting and composition, whilst shots of clouds seen shortly after British aircraft have taken off in order to bomb Germany are reminiscent of similar images from the "Battle On the Ice" sequence in Eisenstein's *Alexander Nevsky* (1938). Cavalcanti was familiar with French Impressionism, German Expressionism and Eisenstein's film, and drew on these in designing the pictorial compositions within *The Big Blockade*.

    In addition to these aesthetic influences, *The Big Blockade* contains abundant and impressive comic caricature. One of the first characters introduced is a pompous German "sausage producer", Herr Schneider, who is first seen in Budapest, the "city of song and sausage". Later in the film, the management of a German ersatz rubber production factory are ordered to increase production by 100% under threat of transportation to Dachau, whilst, in a sequence which uses parodic musical and sound effects, Robert Morley, acting with megalomaniac gusto, plays the part of a demented Nazi official Von Gieselbrecht, who enjoys ridiculing his unfortunate Italian associates.

Cameo performances by Will Hay and Bernard Miles also follow, with Michael Redgrave playing the part of a sceptical Russian, travelling through an under-siege Germany during the period of the Nazi-Soviet non-aggression pact. Towards the end of the film, as the ersatz rubber factory is destroyed by British bombers, its director, saved from incarceration in Dachau, exclaims: "Thank God for the British air force".

The Big Blockade is a complex and sometimes awkward combination of documentary, comedy and didactic discourse, and develops the approach which Cavalcanti had first introduced in Yellow Caesar. As in that film, The Big Blockade assumes a tone of disinterested parody, and coaxes tongue-in-cheek acting performances from actors such as Robert Morley, Michael Redgrave, Will Hay and Bernard Miles. Although it has been argued that The Big Blockade is "overtly educational in purpose", and might not, therefore, have been appreciated by wartime audiences,[26] the film does, in fact, contain a considerable amount of entertainment value, and, whilst its ideological address may have succeeded in providing the audience with an "educational" sense of assurance about the activities of the Ministry of Economic Warfare, for whom it was made, its frequent use of comedy would also have been appreciated.

In many respects, The Big Blockade parallels Cavalcanti's earlier Pett and Pott. Like Pett and Pott, The Big Blockade was Cavalcanti's first major project after joining a new organisation. Moreover, both films were designed as experiments: Pett and Pott as a vehicle for exploring sound and image relationships, and The Big Blockade as an attempt to create a new and effective type of propaganda film. There are also other connections between The Big Blockade and the films which Cavalcanti made earlier for the documentary film movement, and, despite Frend's involvement in the film as its director, it is more appropriately associated with Cavalcanti. In its vigorous and experimental way, The Big Blockade offered an alternative to the more restrained realistic approach increasingly adopted by the British cinema during the war, and, although its flamboyant approach may have resulted in a film which was "by no means wholly successful", and was also "[c]rude, noisy and unrealistic",[27] it is nevertheless an invigorating work which looks forward to the gaudy intemperance of Champagne Charlie (1944).

One contribution which may have played a significant role in complementing Cavalcanti's approach in The Big Blockade was that of the film's scriptwriter, Angus MacPhail. Like Cavalcanti, MacPhail was fond of the music-hall. He had also studied French at university, and this may have helped his collaboration with the newly-arrived Cavalcanti.[28] MacPhail had worked for Balcon as a scriptwriter at both Gainsborough and Gaumont-British before joining Ealing, where he worked on the Will Hay vehicles The Ghost of St Michael's and Black Sheep of Whitehall (1942) immediately before, or at the same time as, working on The Big Blockade. His work on the Hay films, as well as his previous work with Fields and Formby, may have made him receptive to Cavalcanti's eccentric approach to the propaganda film, and, interestingly, *The Big Blockade* is also the only film on which MacPhail worked as sole scriptwriter in over twenty films with which he was involved at Ealing.

Cavalcanti's second feature film project as associate producer was *The Foreman Went to France*. The plot of this film concerns the Welsh foreman of an engineering firm who goes to occupied France in order to recover some important abandoned machinery. The film celebrates the self-sacrifice and sense of moral conduct exhibited by its English, Welsh, Scottish, French and American lower-class characters, but, in marked contrast, it denounces its English and French upper-class characters, who are depicted as either meddling bureaucrats or fifth-columnists.

Like *There Ain't No Justice*, *The Foreman Went to France* is an uneven and transitional work which attempts, often unsuccessfully, to combine realism with more conventional melodramatic and comedic narrative devices. Furthermore, Cavalcanti's influence on the film, although notable, was less tangible than it had been on *The Big Blockade*, which contains far more of the stylistic traits normally associated with his work. *The Foreman Went to France* was also the product of composite authorship. In addition to the contributions of Cavalcanti and Frend, the film was based on a short story written by J B Priestley, and the bluff, provincial common sense exhibited by the foreman in the film (for example, when asked if he can speak French, he replies that he can "make them understand plain English") echoes Priestley's own character and view of the world. Cavalcanti had worked with Priestley before on *We Live in Two Worlds* (1937) and, as in that film, the collaboration between the two on *The Foreman Went to France* was not entirely successful.

There are, however, some sequences in *The Foreman Went to France* which clearly reveal the presence of Cavalcanti. For example, a mildly satirical portrayal of French "types" is carried out with an authenticity which only someone familiar with French culture and comic traditions could achieve. But the film shows the influence of Cavalcanti most strongly during a sequence in which the foreman and his companions encounter a column of retreating refugees whilst driving through France in their captured lorry. The light-hearted banter which had characterised the film's dialogue to this point is replaced here by a more serious tone, as William Walton's sombre music plays over images of the harassed and victimised refugees. The individual shots in this sequence are carefully and formally composed, and are frequently shot from below in order to emphasise the dramatic qualities of the subject-matter. These sequences introduce a degree of emotional depth into a film which, prior to that, had laboured on under its Priestleyan discursive imperatives and rather forced attempt at undemanding comedy.

As these sequences continue, German planes attack the convoy of refugees, and a series of rapidly edited shots, a characteristic feature in Cavalcanti's films, raise dramatic tension to a climax. In one scene, shots of a German aircraft attacking the refugees are edited alongside shots of a child's face. As the aircraft's attack becomes increasingly violent, extreme close-ups of the attacking plane and the child's face are shot together, and a contrast is set up between the linear assault of the plane, and the child, who turns slowly in a circle, unable to escape. This impressive piece of editing was, in theory, the work of the film's editor, Robert Hamer. However, these editing structures correspond so closely to similar scenes in *Men of the Lightship*, which was edited by Cavalcanti and Stewart McAllister, that Cavalcanti must have been centrally involved in their realisation.

Unfortunately, after this impressive sequence, *The Foreman Went to France* quickly reverts to the tone of tiresome light-hearted quirkiness and commonsensical realism which had characterised it to this point. In the end, Cavalcanti's involvement in the film emerges most clearly in isolated sequences, and is highly mediated by generic conventions and ideological discourses which cannot be associated with him. Because of its concern with spies, fifth-columnists and the traitorous propensities of the upper-class Establishment, *The Foreman Went to France* has often been classed alongside Cavalcanti's *Went the Day Well?* (1942).[29] However, apart from their shared concern with "the enemy within", these two films have little in common.

The Halfway House (1944)

The third major Ealing film for which Cavalcanti received credits as associate producer was *The Halfway House*. *The Halfway House* is set in a Welsh inn run by Rhys (Mervyn Johns) and his daughter Gwyneth (Glynis Johns). During the course of the film, they are joined at the inn by a number of guests, all of whom are ill at ease, both with themselves and with the world around them. These include a French woman and her English husband, two black marketeers, a terminally ill musician, and a young married couple accompanied by their daughter. As the film progresses, the guests gradually realise that both they and the inn have been transported back in time by a year, and that Rhys and Gwyneth are, in fact, ghosts. The guests also come to understand that they have been transported into the past in order to be given a second chance to resolve their difficulties, and to make their peace with the outside world. As the film ends with the destruction of the inn by German bombers, the guests leave, renewed and with an enhanced sense of duty and their own social responsibilities.

The Halfway House differs from *The Foreman Went to France* both thematically and stylistically. The only continuities across the two films in terms of personnel are Cavalcanti, as associate producer, and Angus MacPhail, as co-scriptwriter. However, MacPhail's influence across the two films was mediated by the fact that he scripted the earlier film alongside John Dighton, Leslie Arliss and J B Priestley, and the latter alongside Diana Morgan, Roland Pertwee and T E B Clarke. *The Halfway House* also differs in that it is based on a play, rather than on a specially prepared literary treatment, as was the case with *The Foreman Went to France*. The two films also had different directors, art directors and editors. These two films also differ substantially in subject-matter and style. *The Foreman Went to France* has a war background, is set largely in France, and is concerned with issues of group solidarity in the face of the enemy. *The Halfway House*, on the other hand, is set in a rural Welsh inn, and is concerned with the moral regeneration of individuals who have no direct contact with the war, and who are obsessed with their own preoccupations and interests. Stylistically, *The Foreman Went to France* attempts to combine realist, comic and generic elements, whilst *The Halfway House* is far more concerned with psychological realism, and is also influenced by the theatrical conventions of the play from which it was derived.

As with *The Foreman Went to France*, Cavalcanti's influence on *The Halfway House* can be found in particular sections of the film, rather than in the film as a whole. For example, two characters, a black marketeering businessman and an ex-convict, are treated with a degree of likeable characterisation which is based around their avaricious, cynical view of the world. This world-view is convincingly rendered, and undercuts the dominant discourse of duty and responsibility which pervades other parts of the film in a way characteristic of Cavalcanti's films. In contrast to the egocentric rhetoric of these engaging villains, the patriotic outbursts of a Frenchwoman, Alice Meadows (Françoise Rosay), appear contrived and forced. Rosay's character seems ill-suited to *The Halfway House*, and her presence in the film is due to the fact that, as the film was being made, she wrote to Cavalcanti asking him to find her work. Cavalcanti then modified the plot of *The Halfway House* in order to accommodate her, but Rosay was less than happy with what she considered to be a minor role, and the tensions which emerged as a result of this may have contributed towards her somewhat laboured performance.[30]

At the end of *The Halfway House*, all the characters renounce their self-centred preoccupations, and embrace the clarion call of duty and responsibility. However, such narrative closure is often at odds with the more profligate portrait elaborated in other parts of the film. One can only assume Cavalcanti's influence on these more nonconformist aspects of the film, rather than prove it, but this kind of unorthodox iconoclasm is consistent with his films in general, and it is difficult to imagine him taking the film's overblown patriotism particularly seriously.

In terms of visual style, *The Halfway House* remains close to theatrical convention, and uses many static establishing shots in which dialogue takes place within sets clearly modelled on earlier stage sets. However, there are some shots and sequences in the film which depart from this theatrical style, and which can be associated with Cavalcanti. For example, the visual treatment of the landlord's daughter Gwyneth achieves an uncanny effect which is often unconvincingly represented in other, more theatrically-orientated parts of the film. This effect is achieved by the use of slightly out of focus close-ups of Gwyneth's face, and by her slow and measured speech and acting. Cavalcanti's understanding of how to frame the close-up for emotional effect, an understanding which he derived from the French avant-garde, probably influenced the visual treatment used here.

It is, however, the seance episode within *The Halfway House* which reveals Cavalcanti's influence most clearly. During the seance, which occurs towards the end of the film, a close-up of Françoise Rosay takes on the ethereal visual quality that had earlier characterised the Glynis Johns character. Over this image, a disembodied male voice is heard, apparently the voice of Alice's dead son speaking from beyond the grave. The construction of this scene, with its use of non-synchronised sound and image and sombre evocative complexity, resembles the final sequences of Cavalcanti's later *The Life and Adventures of Nicholas Nickleby* (1947), and can also be found in many of his other films. The seance scene also differs from the remainder of the film in the degree of attention given to pictorial composition within it, and, as with the refugee sequence in *The Foreman Went to France*, Cavalcanti appears to have shifted into a higher aesthetic gear here, elevating the film beyond its more routine formulaic aspirations.

Given the substantial degree of dissimilarity at all levels between *The Foreman Went to France* and *The Halfway House*, it is hardly surprising that Cavalcanti's authorial imprint cannot easily be discerned across the two films. His influence in *The Halfway House* can be found in particular stylistic effects, the treatment of acting performances, and the use of sound and image relationships, particularly during the seance scene. In general, *The Halfway House* can also be described as a more mature and successful film than *The Foreman Went to France*, because it is less clumsily generic. Much of the responsibility for this development must be put down to the intervention of Cavalcanti, who managed to inject a degree of dark ambiguity into what would otherwise have been a rather stage-bound film. Director Basil Dearden also made an important contribution to *The Halfway House*, but, without wishing to discount that, it should be borne in mind that his next and, in many ways, similar film, *They Came to a City* (1944), on which Cavalcanti did not work, lacks the complex characterisation and ambiguous visual symbolism of *The Halfway House*.

Although well over 30 feature films were made at Ealing Studios between 1940 and 1947, Cavalcanti received specific credits as associate producer for only three: *The Big Blockade*, *The Foreman Went to France* and *The Halfway House*. Cavalcanti's contract at Ealing stipulated that he would be expected to work alternately as an associate producer and director,[31] and the chronology of his work over this period is as follows: *The Big Blockade* and *The Foreman Went to France* – as associate producer; *Went the Day Well?* – as director; *The*

Halfway House – as associate producer; *Champagne Charlie* – as director; *Dead of Night* (1945) – as director; *The Captive Heart* – as associate producer; and *The Life and Adventures of Nicholas Nickleby* – as director. If Cavalcanti's short propaganda films are also taken into account, his output between 1940 and 1947 adds up to a total of fifteen films, averaging out at two per year. In addition, during this period he directed only three full-length feature films: *Went the Day Well?*, *Champagne Charlie* and *The Life and Adventures of Nicholas Nickleby*. This amounts to a creditable, although hardly towering, output over the eight years during which he was employed at Ealing.

If Cavalcanti's overall contribution as director and producer is compared with that of his colleagues at Ealing over the same period, his achievement also appears adequate, rather than outstanding. Of the major directors employed at Ealing between 1940 and 1947, Charles Frend directed five films, Basil Dearden six, Robert Hamer two, Harry Watt three, and Charles Crichton four. Seen in relation to these, Cavalcanti's output of three films is equivalent to that of Watt, but less than that of Frend, Crichton and Dearden. Of the associate producers working at Ealing over the same period, the most prolific was S C Balcon, who worked on nine films, whilst Hamer, Dearden, Michael Relph, Sidney Cole and Crichton worked on two or three projects each. Again, and seen in relation to this, Cavalcanti's work as associate producer places him alongside Dearden and Crichton in order of importance, but below that of S C Balcon.

However, Cavalcanti's position at Ealing was more important than these figures would suggest, and, in fact, his activities extended far beyond those normally associated with those of a director or associate producer. The reality of the situation was that Cavalcanti was probably the single most important influence on the development of filmmaking at Ealing during this period. In addition to his roles as director and producer, he had overall responsibility for Ealing's wartime production of documentaries and general artistic responsibility for its entire output of feature films.[32] His position at Ealing was therefore as central as it had been at the GPO Film Unit, and his contribution to Ealing's artistic development over this period was at least as great as, and possibly greater than, that of any other single individual.

Cavalcanti's greatest aptitude as a producer lay in his ability to bring out the best in the work of others by making suggestions which would invariably result in the resulting film becoming better, subtler and more complex:

> A picture was run and he'd call in to see it...and right away he would suggest a whole series of new ideas to put into it that would somehow make a real difference between a film being just rather ordinary or something special happening to it. It was astonishing.[33]

Cavalcanti's ability to augment the technical, aesthetic and entertainment value of the films which he produced made him invaluable to the organisations for which he worked. At the GPO, for example, the general manager of the Film Unit, Stanley Fletcher, argued that "Mr Cavalcanti is without doubt the best Producer in the country and it is vital that the Film Unit should continue to have use of his services".[34] At Ealing, Balcon was also well aware of Cavalcanti's abilities as a producer and facilitator, and of his impact on Ealing's apprentice filmmakers:

> Now, however talented they were – because take a man like Hamer, he was a minor poet, a brilliant mathematician and could have had a career anywhere – they were still short of experience in dealing with visual images on the screen. And this is what Cavalcanti could do for them. He was a vastly experienced man as to how to transfer images to the screen – a curious man, you know, in some respects, until he got going. By virtue of the fact that he didn't know English very well, he could sometimes be completely inarticulate, especially when he got excited. But somehow when he was on the floor, near the camera, talking to these people, just some little things he could do would make all the difference...Men like Charles Frend, good as they were, made better films with Cavalcanti by their side...Apart from anything else, he was a man of infinite taste. He knew about settings. He knew about music. He knew about European literature. He was a highly civilised man. They all were, but he was a particularly outstanding figure...All those things helped to make good films.[35]

Balcon has also claimed that, apart from himself, Cavalcanti was the most important person at Ealing during this period,[36] and that it was Cavalcanti's close association with him which "provided the force" from which emerged "the Ealing films".[37] Others involved with Ealing at the time have also expressed similar sentiments regarding Cavalcanti's importance. For example, Monja Danischewsky, Balcon's director of publicity, has claimed that "if Mick was the father figure, Cavalcanti was the Nanny who brought us up",[38] whilst Danischewsky's wife Brenda, who also worked at Ealing, has claimed that Cavalcanti] "produced *us*".[39]

The team which Balcon had assembled at Ealing was relatively inexperienced. Frend, Crichton, Hamer and Henry Cornelius had all worked as editors during the 1930s, but did not begin their directorial careers until Ealing. The same is largely true of Dearden and Nolbandov.[40] In addition, with the exception of Nolbandov, and the soon-to-depart Walter Forde, most were an average of between ten and fifteen years younger than Cavalcanti, and this age advantage endowed him with the kind of authority in relation to his new colleagues that he had earlier exercised within the documentary film movement. Beyond this, virtually all of Ealing's young filmmakers had served their apprenticeship within the British commercial film industry, and their respect for Cavalcanti was derived partly from their perception that he possessed a knowledge of European film culture and film technique which they, on the whole, did not.

One way in which Cavalcanti influenced filmmaking at Ealing was through his custom of suggesting detailed and subtle changes to the compositional or visual quality of specific scenes and sequences. For Ealing's filmmakers, who had been schooled in more straightforward commercial and conventional traditions of filmmaking, this encounter with a filmic sensitivity intent on making their films more intricate and ambiguous had a considerable impact:

> 'Did you ever hear anyone talk about Cav's murmur?' Brenda Danischewsky asked me. It was the few words that he might whisper into a director's ear that would provide the missing inspiration for a scene. 'Something magical happened in the studio,' the Ealing cameraman Douglas Slocombe remembered. 'Sometimes not by a direct idea, but somehow setting people off in a positive direction...Even a writer like Tibby Clarke often came out of a meeting with Cav and sometimes just one word from Cav would set him off on writing a whole script.'...'Cav would say in the rushes there was a shot where the camera fell over, but before the camera fell over there was something, something, something. Find me that...Cav had this fantastic memory. He could remember all the rushes long after the cameraman and the director had forgotten them.'[41]

It was this degree of attention to detail and close involvement with the immediate filmmaking process which had led to the emergence of such important films as *Spare Time* and *Men of the Lightship* during the last few years of the GPO Film Unit, and Cavalcanti employed the same intimate, informal approach to the supervision of film production when he moved to Ealing. More specifically, both at the GPO and at Ealing, Cavalcanti seems to have emphasised the need to consider the complexity and subtlety of pictorial relationships within the shot, scene or sequence, and particularly those involving sound and image relationships.

In addition to this emphasis on composition, Cavalcanti introduced a number of other features into filmmaking at Ealing. These included an emphasis on the importance of chance effects and the transitory as means of transcending or avoiding stereotyped or clichéd forms of representation, an emphasis on the representation of subjectivity, and a basic commitment to realism. These thematic and stylistic preoccupations were derived from Cavalcanti's experience of French realist, Impressionist and Surrealist cinema, and his application of that experience to filmmaking at Ealing played a considerable part in adding to Ealing's achievements in the period between 1940 and 1947.

Cavalcanti's abilities as a producer were so valuable to those such as Grierson and Balcon that his abilities as a director were often regarded as of secondary importance. Grierson effectively stopped Cavalcanti directing after the appearance of the decidedly un-Griersonian *Pett and Pott* in 1934, whilst Balcon was in no doubt that Cavalcanti was "better producer material than he was director material":

> Now that doesn't in any way denigrate him because, in the days that we were working, I thought the talents were equally important and probably the production talent rather more important. But everybody doesn't think that way, and most producers always want to be directors. Cavalcanti wanted to be a director, and of course he directed some films of some importance, but I still think his great work was and still could be if he were going on today, in production and the influences he brings to bear on other people.[42]

Balcon's claim that Cavalcanti "wanted to be a director" is correct, and the fact is that towards the end of his career at Ealing he was increasingly directing, as opposed to producing, films – making *Champagne Charlie*, *Dead of Night* and *The Life and Adventures of Nicholas Nickleby*. Furthermore, after Ealing, and up to the point at which he left Britain in 1949, he also directed three other films, *They Made Me a Fugitive* (1947), *The First Gentleman* (1947) and *For Them That Trespass* (1949), and produced precisely none. Writing in 1952, and defending himself against criticisms from Brazilian journalists who claimed that he had made too few feature films, it was his career as a director which Cavalcanti chose to emphasise:

> Here in Brazil, I am accused of never having been a director of fiction films, and of limiting my career in Europe to documentary. However, in reality, documentaries account for only a small proportion of the films I have made. Although I was the instigator of a certain form of novel-like documentary, with *Rien que les Heures*, in 1925, I have spent the greater part of my career directing commercial films, of which I have more than twenty to my credit.[43]

All of this suggests that Cavalcanti regarded himself primarily as a director, and Balcon's reasons for describing Cavalcanti as "better producer material than...director material" are ultimately unconvincing. For example, Balcon argued that Cavalcanti's foreignness made it difficult for him to direct English actors:

> [E]ven if he speaks many languages, there must be some difficulties in directing English actors for anybody who hasn't complete mastery of the language. From the visual side he'd always be all right. Whether he was equally good in the direction of actors is a matter for discussion.[44]

Cavalcanti's lack of proficiency in English, and his occasional tantrums on the set, when he would declaim in a colourful blend of French, English and Portuguese, may have given the impression to some that he experienced difficulty in communicating with, and directing, his actors. However, the fact that he was responsible for drawing fine performances from a number of English actors, most notably from Michael Redgrave in *Dead of Night*, Stanley Holloway in *Champagne Charlie*, and Griffith Jones in *They Made Me a Fugitive*, does not lend Balcon's charge much credibility. Richard Todd, who played another fine leading role in *For Them That Trespass* also recalls that Cavalcanti spent many hours talking to him about his acting technique. Far from being a weakness, Cavalcanti's difficulty with English actually led him to go to elaborate lengths in communicating his ideas to actors, as Todd recalls:

> I think I coped fairly well, thanks to Cavalcanti's quiet help. Everyday after filming finished he insisted that I sat with him at the rushes. At these sessions he would point out all my mistakes and weaknesses and lecture me on ways to eradicate them.[45]

Cavalcanti was also skilled at obtaining a particular type of performance from his actors, one characterised by a degree of emotional and sometimes hysterical excess. The best example of this is "The Ventriloquist's Dummy" sequence in *Dead of Night*, in which Michael Redgrave exchanges personalities with his malevolent mannequin, but such performances are common in Cavalcanti's other films, and Todd's performance in *For Them That Trespass* as Herb Logan, the wrongly convicted Irish labourer who is brought to the verge of a breakdown when confronting the lover who gave him up to the police, is a fine example of this aspect of Cavalcanti's work. Unfortunately for Cavalcanti, however, this type of acting did not conform to what Balcon regarded as suitable for Ealing, and Michael Redgrave's performance in *Dead of Night* is of a completely different order, for example, to the restrained, understated performances of actors such as Jack Hawkins and Donald Sinden in the very Balconian *The Cruel Sea* (1953).

In addition to compensating for his lack of fluency in English by spending considerable amounts of time with actors, Cavalcanti prepared painstakingly detailed plans of the sets on which he worked in order to ensure that his ideas were clearly understood during filming.[46] According to Monja Danischewsky, this attention to detail allowed him and others to "understand the curious and subtle processes of [Cavalcanti's] mind",[47] whilst, according to Sidney Cole, it enabled him and Cavalcanti to be "very much in tune as to how the film should be put together".[48] All of this contradicts Balcon's perception of Cavalcanti as a director whose abilities were limited by the fact that he was a foreigner, and reveals the underlying chauvinism which conditioned Balcon's view of Cavalcanti.

What is particularly illuminating about Balcon's remarks is the way in which they position Cavalcanti as a good producer, but only an average director. The statement "Cavalcanti wanted to be a director" implies that Cavalcanti wanted to direct more films than he was allowed to at Ealing, and the declaration that he "he directed *some* films of *some* importance" appears unnecessarily condescending – a remark made in retrospect, and whose purpose is to justify, to contemporary critics, Balcon's decision to channel Cavalcanti away from direction and into production. In fact, Balcon never regarded Cavalcanti as a top-rank director, and, as late as 1956, he was still arguing that "whilst he was working with me on the production of films, as distinct from direction, he made a wonderful contribution".[49]

One reason for Balcon's reluctance to allow Cavalcanti to direct more films – the perceived indispensability of Cavalcanti's work as a producer – has already been discussed. However, Balcon also had misgivings about the extent to which Cavalcanti shared his own convictions on the proper role of film within the national culture. Balcon's glowing assessment of his long-term associate Charles Frend gives an indication of the reservations which he harboured over Cavalcanti's ability to portray "traditional English values":

> His first film as a director was *The Big Blockade* and his second *The Foreman Went to France* and much as I praise Cavalcanti for his work on this film a great deal of the credit must go to Charles Frend. Later he followed up with two tremendous Ealing successes – *San Demetrio, London* and *The Cruel Sea*. Charles Frend, born in Kent, educated at King's School, Canterbury, an expert on Kentish beer when there were enough free houses in the county for him to indulge his hobby, a man with his roots firmly planted in the soil of this country, was, and is, the ideal man to deal with any subject concerning the traditional English values.[50]

Consider also Balcon's assessment of Hal Mason, one of Balcon's closest colleagues, and production controller at Ealing:

> He joined Ealing in the early war years and there he remained with me, progressively as first assistant director, production manager, studio manager and, ultimately, production controller and director of the company. His name appeared on every film we made and deservedly so as the whole organisation and physical control of the films came under his charge... In spite of being so well travelled, Hal has a remarkably conventional English outlook about 'abroad'. He is particularly conservative about food – he only likes roast beef or steak and he eats more steak and fried potatoes than any man I have ever met. He loathes the food on location or anywhere abroad.[51]

The inscription on the commemorative plaque which Balcon had installed at Ealing in 1955 when the studio was sold to the BBC declared: "Here during a quarter of a century were made many films projecting Britain and the British character". Balcon's favourite films, those which he believed projected Britain and the British character at their best were *The Captive Heart, Scott of the Antarctic* (Frend, 1948) and *The Cruel Sea.*[52] These films emphasise group solidarity, emotional restraint and understatement, and also reflect Balcon's view of an English national character which is characterised by a stolid seriousness, repressed sexuality, and more or less complete lack of irony. However, just as Cavalcanti's character was far removed from Balcon's assessment of those of Frend and Mason, the themes, subject-matter and forms of characterisation found in these films are also far removed from those discernible in Cavalcanti's work. Although other reasons also played their part, it was, to a significant extent, this degree of distance from the conception of Englishness which defined Balcon's vision, both of Ealing Studios and of the British cinema, which led to Cavalcanti's marginalisation as a director at Ealing.

Balcon's convictions concerning the role of the cinema within national life were premised on a belief that film should seek to project those traditional values and characteristics which, according to him, reflected and defined the common culture. This inevitably implied the need to proscribe or limit representations of the non-consensual and marginal:

> I have little patience with people who produce a certain kind of film and then shelter behind the argument that films must reflect the society in which we live. The flaw in this cliché is that it provides a hypocritical justification for sensationalism, squalor

and licence – usually sexual. The films I have in mind
do *not* reflect life in any wide sense but only some
aspects of the behaviour and point of view of a small
minority.[53]

This is essentially the same type of principled conservative
populism which Cavalcanti had earlier encountered whilst working
under Grierson, and, if Balcon's view that film should not represent
minorities is correlated with his claim that "the producer's greatest
responsibility is towards the State",[54] and these claims are then
compared with Grierson's assertion that filmmakers should work within
the "degree of general sanction" legitimated by the institutions of
state,[55] a clear parallel emerges – one grounded in a moral
conservatism lying at the heart of British "quality" film culture.
However, contrary to the consensualist inclinations of Balcon and
Grierson, Cavalcanti's films frequently display a concern with marginal
or minority figures and groups. This is true of early films such as *Rien
que les heures* (*Nothing But the Hours*, 1926) and *En rade* (*Stranded*,
1927), as well as post-Ealing films such as *They Made Me a Fugitive*,
For Them That Trespass, *O Canto do Mar* (*Song of the Sea*, 1953) and
Die Windrose (1956). In addition, as will be seen, Cavalcanti's Ealing
films display a similar preoccupation with marginal or atypical
characters, and it was this which put Cavalcanti at odds with Balcon
at Ealing, and which determined that the number and types of film he
would be allowed to direct there would be closely circumscribed.

Balcon and others who worked at Ealing during the 1940s have
described the process of discussion and development of ideas which took
place there as one characterised by animated and gregarious decision-
making, based around heated discussions at the local pub, and at the
"round table" where the Ealing directors, scriptwriters and associate
producers met in order to discuss proposals for future projects.
However, although the degree of cooperative activity which Balcon
fostered at Ealing may have been considerable, that activity was also
managed and directed by him, and the consensus which emerged from
this process also reflected his own ideas and predispositions.

The chief means through which the maintenance of a culture
of consensus at Ealing was managed was via the careful initial
selection and appointment of people whom, Balcon felt, shared his own
convictions.[56] According to Balcon, this strategy ensured that the films
produced at Ealing were the product of a genuine accord between
himself and those assigned to particular projects, so that "rarely is a
subject put forward in our studios on which an associate producer and
a director are tremendously keen, which I find I cannot support".[57]
Balcon also reinforced the control which this recruitment policy gave
him by ensuring that, although his filmmakers might enjoy a degree of
autonomy during the actual production process, he was the final arbiter
on the choice of subject-matter:

It is no use a director coming to me and saying he is
tremendously enthusiastic about making a film
dealing with the life of, say, Neville Chamberlain, if
he and I do not share the same point of view about
Neville Chamberlain. We may agree that his life
would make an admirable film subject, but obviously
we cannot work together if he happens to be a great
admirer of Neville Chamberlain and plans to make a
film which would redeem or embellish that
statesman's reputation, while I may happen to feel
strongly the other way about Chamberlain and would
therefore wish to make a film exposing his failure or
weaknesses as a statesman.[58]

Although expressed in language which appears to state the
obvious – that two people who disagree should not collaborate on the
same project – these remarks also imply that, if a director's views did
not match those of Balcon, the film would not be made. The phrase
"obviously we cannot work together" does not mean that an Ealing
director could work for someone else within Ealing (that was
impossible), but that he or she would have to leave. This meant that
Ealing's output was essentially representative of Balcon's views on the
"projection of Britain", and that his values and tastes were "written all
over the output".[59]

Despite his recollections to the contrary, Balcon's insistence on
maintaining an absolute jurisdiction over the choice of themes and
subject-matter in the films produced at Ealing did lead to tensions
amongst those who formed the creative core of the Ealing staff. Charles
Barr has described the meetings in the pub after the round-table
discussions as opportunities for directors and scriptwriters to "let off
steam" about Balcon,[60] and Danischewsky has also argued that these
drinking sessions played an important, if peculiar, role in maintaining
the status quo. According to Danischewsky, "The Red Lion" was often:

[L]oud with the psychologically therapeutic cries of
those of us who had had a rough passage at the round
table meeting earlier: 'I'm going to tell Mick tomorrow
– straight to his face – if *that's* what he wants, he can
find himself another boy!' Thus we let off steam and
exorcised the complaining devils within us.[61]

The actress Googie Withers, reflecting on her years at Ealing,
found it incongruous that Balcon appeared to condone the fact that his
staff consumed so much alcohol. According to Withers, Balcon may have
been "a moralist – didn't like any hanky-panky", but he also "had all
these men around him getting terribly tight all over the place...there
was always the evening at the pub over the way. They all went there
and most of them got very, very drunk".[62] However, Balcon tolerated

these frequent heavy drinking sessions because they functioned as a pressure valve, allowing discontent, which might otherwise have developed into more serious challenges to his authority, to be defused.

Balcon liked to characterise Ealing as his "academy of young gentlemen", and others have described it as an "exclusive school" or club, with Balcon as the paternalistic headmaster or director of the club.[63] However, Ealing culture was far more idiosyncratic than these analogies might suggest. Writing in 1955, in an article entitled "Ealing's Way of Life", the critic Kenneth Tynan described Ealing as "a home for erratic adolescents who need a patriarchal atmosphere to give them security", and quoted Balcon declaring, rather curiously, that "[q]uite frankly...I like to impose myself on young people".[64] There is an odd contradiction here between Balcon's general endorsement of traditional values and the fact that he presided over an alcohol-fuelled, eccentric and seemingly regressive environment at Ealing. The "Ealing way of life" may have been deliberately fostered as a strategy for nourishing creativity, but that strategy also had its negative aspect, and led to the "boyishness" and "repressions" which Barr finds in so many of the films made there.[65]

A distinction must also be made between those closest to Balcon, including T E B Clarke, Angus MacPhail, Charles Frend, Charles Crichton and Basil Dearden, and others such as Harry Watt, Robert Hamer, Alexander Mackendrick and Cavalcanti, all of whom experienced difficulty in conforming to the "Ealing way of life". The often truculent and testy Watt, for example, never really fitted into Balcon's "academy of young gentlemen", and, shortly after making *Fiddlers Three* (1944), was despatched abroad, making *The Overlanders* (1946), *Eureka Stockade* (1949), *Where No Vultures Fly* (1951), *West of Zanzibar* (1954) and *The Siege of Pinchgut* (1959) in Africa and Australia.

Cavalcanti, Mackendrick and Hamer have been described as "the three outcasts, the rebels and troublemakers of Ealing",[66] and, whilst Cavalcanti's relationship with Watt was often as strained as Balcon's was, he had a much closer relationship with Hamer. The problems which Hamer experienced at Ealing also illustrate the type of difficulties which Cavalcanti encountered whilst he was there. Like Cavalcanti, Hamer was familiar with French literary culture. His attraction to the darker aspects of the human condition was influenced by the same French naturalist tradition which had influenced Cavalcanti, and *It Always Rains on Sunday* (1947) is clearly informed by a knowledge of the French poetic realist cinema of the 1930s, revealing the influence of Carné's *Quai des brumes* (1938) and Renoir's *La Bête humaine* (1938) in particular. Hamer worked closely with Cavalcanti at Ealing, and his first credit as a director is for "The Haunted Mirror" episode in the joint Cavalcanti, Hamer, Crichton and Dearden venture, *Dead of Night*. *Pink String and Sealing Wax* (1945) and *Kind Hearts and Coronets* (1949) also reveal the dark, ironic humour and, in the former film, naturalist sensibility, which can be found in Cavalcanti's work, but which is missing from other Ealing films of the period.

Hamer, whom Cavalcanti brought with him to Ealing from the GPO Film unit, found his wish to make "difficult" films at Ealing constrained by what he called "the unshaded characterization which convention tends to enforce on scripts".[67] He had a number of film projects turned down because they were regarded as too controversial or pessimistic in tone, and he was eventually forced to make films such as the disappointing and over-theatrical *His Excellency* (1952), for which he had little enthusiasm. His close friend and colleague at Ealing, the screenwriter Diana Morgan, has characterised his career at Ealing as a "thwarted" one,[68] and there seems little doubt that, had he enjoyed more freedom to realise the projects to which he was committed than he was allowed, he would have produced work to rival, or even surpass, *It Always Rains on Sunday* and *Kind Hearts and Coronets*.

Just as Balcon intervened in Hamer's projects if he thought them too sombre or contentious, he also interfered in those of Cavalcanti if he believed them to be too obscure or equivocal. During the development of *Went the Day Well?*, for example, Balcon wrote to the film's associate producer and editor (S C Balcon and Sidney Cole, respectively) complaining that the sequences which he had seen were too "vague", the action "not urgent enough", and the "performances too leisurely".[69] Balcon also wrote to Cavalcanti during the production of *The Halfway House*, insisting that the question of whether two of the principal characters in the film were undergoing a legal separation, or a divorce, should be thoroughly clarified.[70] Balcon also felt that the relationship between these two characters and their daughter should be elucidated so that the final reconciliation between the three is unambiguously confirmed: "the idea that they should start quarrelling even more violently once they are outside the Inn [and after their reconciliation] is very high art, and not likely to be understood".[71]

Balcon's interventions during the production of *Went the Day Well?* and *The Halfway House* were motivated by his desire to ensure that the final version of each film would be clear and unambiguous, and that all evidence of cryptic "unshaded characterization" and ambivalent, ironic imagery was removed. This prosaic and uninspiring tutelage caused problems for both Hamer and Cavalcanti, although it was Hamer who reacted the most strongly of the two to Balcon's moralising reproofs. In contrast, Cavalcanti seems to have kept his head down and quietly tolerated Balcon's governance. Ultimately, that exploitable strain in his character, which enabled him to become embroiled in the minutiae of work whilst tolerating the manipulation of others, led him to put up with the paternalistic Balcon, just as it had earlier led him to tolerate the megalomaniac Grierson.

The experiences of Alexander Mackendrick, Ealing's third "outcast, rebel and troublemaker", also illuminate one key strategy which Cavalcanti employed in order to deal with Balcon's censorious interventions. Mackendrick, who arrived at Ealing shortly before

Cavalcanti left, argued that one way of circumventing Balcon's supervision of a film's theme and subject-matter was through the making of comedies. Balcon did not regard comedy as an important genre, and consequently did not scrutinise comedies as carefully as he did more "elevated" genres. Mackendrick has argued that this relative freedom from surveillance allowed him to include material in *Whisky Galore!* (1949) and *The Man in the White Suit* (1951) which would, in more "serious" films, have led to conflicts with Balcon.[72]

Cavalcanti was also aware of the ability of comedy both to undercut the normative inclinations of those who employed him, and to express important ideas. Writing in 1938 about the films of the Marx Brothers, he argued that "the deliberate cruelty of their work carries it near to the spirit of revolution...theirs is the most practical of all joking. It is in revolt against the established order".[73] Cavalcanti went on to argue that "comedy can deal with the bitterest realities, the most cruel facts, it can tackle the most vital problems [and] can fight against injustice and elude the censor".[74] As will be seen later, *Champagne Charlie*, a comedy which Balcon did not rate highly, and which effectively caricatures many of the values which the latter promoted in other Ealing films, is a good example of this kind of subversive humour, and, therefore; in its modest way, is also a kind of "revolt against the established order".

Cavalcanti's experiences at Ealing must also be situated within the larger context of the relationship between producer and director which existed within the British cinema during the 1930s and 1940s. Like other producers of the period, Balcon was influenced by the model of filmmaking developed in Hollywood, whereby a clear distinction was made between the mental labour of subject and script development, and the actual shooting process on the studio floor. Under the system of production developed by producers such as Irving Thalberg at MGM, a detailed shooting script was prepared and then handed over to a director who was expected to carry out instructions more or less to the letter. This was a system dominated by producers, editors and scriptwriters, and one in which the director was regarded as little more than a talented craftsman.

This was also the model which Balcon operated at Gaumont-British and Ealing, and, although Balcon allowed his directors more autonomy during the production process than had generally been the case in Hollywood, he also ensured that "the most important work on the film is done before and after it goes on the studio floor".[75] Ealing was a producer's, rather than a director's, studio, and Balcon believed that producers were simply more important than directors.[76] What Balcon wanted from his directors was the ability to imprint an individual, although not necessarily "personal", articulation on the general Ealing style and approach to subject-matter, so that Ealing films remained consistent in tone yet individually different.[77]

The French filmmaker Bertrand Tavernier has argued that Balcon thought of the director as little more than "a good craftsman you bring in to film a script. Not someone who...brings to the film a vision of his or her own".[78] Tavernier is partly right, but fails to appreciate that Balcon was more than happy for a director to bring his own vision to a film, as long as that vision reflected his own. Hence Balcon's previously quoted tributes to Frend's understanding of, and ability to express, "traditional English values".[79] The system of film production established by Balcon at Ealing was therefore one in which directorial autonomy was encouraged, but also kept within specific stylistic and ideological parameters, and this is one reason why Cavalcanti did not thrive there as a director. The system which Balcon operated at Ealing also made it difficult for outstanding films to emerge, and those which did came from the "outcasts, rebels and troublemakers": *It Always Rains on Sunday, Dead of Night* and *Kind Hearts and Coronets* from Hamer, *The Man in the White Suit* and *The Ladykillers* (1955) from Mackendrick, and *Went the Day Well?, Dead of Night* and *Champagne Charlie* from Cavalcanti.

Cavalcanti resigned from his position at Ealing around March 1947. He left for a number of different reasons, one of which was his desire to earn a higher salary than could be obtained under the terms of his contract with Ealing. Cavalcanti had always been dissatisfied with the salary which Balcon paid him, and, whilst the close companionship and promise of permanent employment he had enjoyed at Ealing during the war had compensated for his relatively low level of income, this was no longer the case after 1945. However, Cavalcanti's ambition to achieve monetary advantage was hardly the consequence of a suspect avaricious nature. It should be remembered that he had been living off relatively low wages uncomplainingly since 1934, and Balcon did, as the Ealing actor John McCallum recalled, pay "a pittance".[80]

Cavalcanti also had financial problems. In October 1946, he asked Balcon if he could be allowed to direct what eventually became *They Made Me a Fugitive* for Warner-Alliance. Although Balcon thought the film would not "add to Cav's prestige from the directorial point of view", he reluctantly agreed to the request because of "Cav's urgent desire to accept the project for financial reasons".[81]

At the beginning of 1947, Cavalcanti opened negotiations with Balcon over a new contract. However, he broke new ground by doing so through an agent. Balcon was not amused, and interpreted Cavalcanti's action as a betrayal of trust:

> [Q]uite frankly, the relationship between you and me is so personal that I do not want to negotiate with agents. In fact I shall feel very embarrassed indeed if I have to discuss your arrangements, or those of any of the other Associate Producers or Directors, with outside people...personally, I am sorry if any of you think this necessary because we have operated for so many years in a rather different way, and quite happily.[82]

Cavalcanti's action in employing an agent clearly upset Balcon, but he insisted that he would retain the agent, Kenneth Harper, and then went on to request that he be allowed to make some films outside Ealing on a regular basis:

> The ideal arrangement for me would be to complete this year's work at Ealing as agreed between us, by the making of 'Toilers' and afterwards give you the yearly film that the space in Ealing allows me to make and try to do one, or possibly more films outside. Would it be a sensible suggestion if, after 'Toilers', I could guarantee a yearly film for you at a salary and at a date that only somebody like Kenneth Harper, who is definitely going from now on to try and manage my work, would fix with you in the most friendly manner?[83]

However, Balcon rejected Cavalcanti's request, and made it clear that under no circumstances [would he] enter into non-exclusive contracts with either directors or associate producers.[84] Balcon believed that it was essential for Ealing's continued success that the directors and associate producers he employed worked only for him, and it was because of this that he refused to allow his staff to work for others.[85] Balcon also believed, in particular, that, if he acceded to Cavalcanti's request, other filmmakers at Ealing would soon follow suit:

> I know somebody made the comment about Soviet Russia that 'all men are equal but some are more equal than others'. I am afraid this cannot apply to Ealing Studios because if I arranged a non-exclusive contract with you it would mean similar contracts with others, and under no circumstances will I be a party to this. It could only result in complete chaos and undermine everything we have built up for years.[86]

Balcon reluctantly waived this policy when Cavalcanti pleaded with him to be allowed to make *They Made Me a Fugitive* whilst he was also making *The Life and Adventures of Nicholas Nickleby* at Ealing. However, as far as Balcon was concerned, this was the exception to the rule.

The truth is that Cavalcanti did not leave Ealing simply because he wanted more money, as Balcon rather uncharitably suggests. Cavalcanti did not, in fact, want to leave Ealing at all: had Balcon allowed him to direct more than one film a year, he would probably have stayed, despite the fact that he could have earned much more elsewhere. Financial considerations played a part in Cavalcanti's decision to leave Ealing, but his principal consideration was his wish to direct more films. As he himself put it, "[t]he prospect of making two pictures a year does appeal to me, as opposed to the one picture yearly that I could make under the arrangement with you".[87] Significantly, however, whilst Balcon refused to allow Cavalcanti the opportunity to make films outside Ealing, he also declined to offer him the prospect of directing more than one film a year within Ealing. Consequently, Cavalcanti had no alternative but to resign. Even after announcing his resignation, however, he still expressed the hope that his departure "would not preclude me from working for you [Balcon] again in the future, should the occasion arise".[88] In this, however, he was to be disappointed, for Balcon would never allow him to work for Ealing again.

One final reason for Cavalcanti's departure from Ealing was the general sense of change which pervaded the studio immediately after the war. Balcon refers to a "change of mood" at Ealing, in which the ideas which held the studio together during the war "began to disintegrate".[89] Cavalcanti was always a semi-detached member of Balcon's "academy", and the postwar period provided him with the possibility of breaking free from his producer's authority. He was, however, one of the few who did so, and the Ealing team remained remarkably stable: Frend, Watt, Relph, Crichton, Hamer, Mackendrick and Dearden stayed well into the 1950s, whilst only Cavalcanti and Henry Cornelius left the studio for good during the 1940s.

Notes

[1]   A de A Cavalcanti, "A Film Director Contributes...", in M Danischewsky (ed), *Michael Balcon's 25 Years in Films* (London: World Film Publications, 1947): 48.

[2]   Michael Balcon, *Michael Balcon presents... A Lifetime of Films* (London: Hutchinson, 1969): 131.

[3]   Gavin Lambert, "Alberto Cavalcanti", *Screen* 13: 2 (summer 1972): 45-46.

[4]   Richard Barsam, *The Vision of Robert Flaherty: The Artist as Myth and Filmmaker* (Bloomington; Indianapolis: Indiana University Press, 1988): 47-50.

[5]   Forsyth Hardy, *John Grierson: A Documentary Biography* (London; Boston: Faber and Faber, 1979): 65.

[6]   Barsam: 73-74.

[7]   Ibid: 59.

[8]   Tom Ryall, "A British Studio System: The Associated British Picture Corporation and the Gaumont-British Picture Corporation in the 1930s", in Robert Murphy (ed), *The British Cinema Book* (London: British Film Institute, 1997): 32.

9   Charles Drazin, *The Finest Years: British Cinema of the 1940s* (London: André Deutsch, 1998): 103.

10   Danischewsky (ed): 48.

11   Alberto Cavalcanti, "The British Contribution (1952)", in Ian Aitken (ed), *The Documentary Film Movement: An Anthology* (Edinburgh: Edinburgh University Press, 1998): 205.

12   Elizabeth Sussex, "Cavalcanti in England", *Sight and Sound* 44: 4 (autumn 1975): 209, reprinted in Aitken (ed): 192.

13   George Perry, *Forever Ealing: A Celebration of the Great British Film Studio* (London: Pavilion/Michael Joseph, 1981): 35.

14   Drazin: 101.

15   Margaret Dickinson and Sarah Street, *Cinema and State: The Film Industry and the Government 1927-84* (London: British Film Institute, 1985): 77.

16   Balcon: 120.

17   Ibid: 123.

18   Drazin: 131.

19   *Michael Balcon: The Pursuit of British Cinema*, essays by Geoff Brown and Laurence Kardish (New York: Museum of Modern Art, 1984): 55.

20   Sussex, in Aitken (ed): 196.

21   Perry: 61.

22   Balcon (1969): 132.

23   James Chapman, *The British At War: Cinema, State and Propaganda, 1939-1945* (London; New York: I B Tauris, 1998): 75.

24   Ibid: 76.

25   Charles Barr, *Ealing Studios*, second edition (London: Studio Vista, 1993):27.

26   Perry: 66.

27   Robert Murphy, *Realism and Tinsel: Cinema and society in Britain 1939-48* (London: Routledge, 1989): 36.

28   Drazin: 91.

29   Barr: 33.

30   Hermilo Borba Filho, "Une vie (1953)", in Lorenzo Pellizzari and Claudio M Valentinetti (eds), *Alberto Cavalcanti* (Locarno: Éditions du Festival international du film de Locarno, 1988): 158.

31   Ibid: 157.

32   Drazin: 123.

[33]   Ibid: 124.

[34]   Quoted in Chapman: 121.

[35]   Sussex, in Aitken (ed): 193-194.

[36]   Ibid.

[37]   Balcon (1969): 131.

[38]   Monja Danischewsky, *White Russian – Red Face* (London: Victor Gollancz, 1966): 134.

[39]   Drazin: 117. Emphasis in original.

[40]   Murphy (1989): 35.

[41]   Drazin: 124.

[42]   Sussex, in Aitken (ed): 194.

[43]   Cavalcanti, in ibid: 210.

[44]   Sussex, in ibid: 194.

[45]   Richard Todd, *Caught in the Act: The Story of My Life* (London; Melbourne; Auckland; Johannesburg: Hutchinson, 1986): 226.

[46]   T E B Clarke, *This is where I came in* (London: Michael Joseph, 1974): 143.

[47]   Danischewsky: 134.

[48]   Brian McFarlane (ed), *Sixty Voices: Celebrities Recall the Golden Age of British Cinema* (London: British Film Institute, with the assistance of Monash University, 1992): 65.

[49]   Balcon, letter to Christopher Mann, 23 January 1956. Ivor Montagu Collection, Special Collections, British Film Institute: F/43.

[50]   Balcon (1969): 138.

[51]   Ibid: 139-140.

[52]   Barr: 77.

[53]   Balcon (1969): 138. Emphasis in original.

[54]   Michael Balcon, *The Producer: Being a lecture given to the British Film Institute's 1945 Summer School of Film Appreciation* (London: British Film Institute, 1945): 5.

[55]   Ian Aitken, *Film and Reform: John Grierson and the Documentary Film Movement* (London; New York: Routledge, 1990): 190.

[56]   Vincent Porter, "The Context of Creativity: Ealing Studios and Hammer Films", in James Curran and Vincent Porter (eds), *British Cinema History* (London: Weidenfeld & Nicolson, 1983): 185.

57   Ibid.

58   Ibid: 184.

59   JC [John Caughie], "Balcon, (Sir) Michael", in John Caughie, with Kevin Rockett, *The Companion to British and Irish Cinema* (London: Cassell/ British Film Institute, 1996): 25.

60   Barr: 44.

61   Danischewsky: 136. Emphasis in original.

62   McFarlane (ed): 234.

63   Clarke: 141.

64   Kenneth Tynan, "Ealing's Way of Life", *Films and Filming* 2: 3 (December 1955): 10.

65   Barr: 79.

66   Bertrand Tavernier, "Tavernier on Mackendrick", *Sight and Sound* 4: 8 (August 1994): 16.

67   Drazin: 74-75.

68   Ibid: 82.

69   Balcon, letter to S C Balcon and Sidney Cole, 10 August 1942. Aileen and Michael Balcon Collection, Special Collections, British Film Institute [hereafter AMBC]: F/7.

70   Balcon, letter to Cavalcanti, 21 June 1943. AMBC: F/40.

71   Ibid.

72   Porter: 189.

73   Alberto Cavalcanti, "Comedies and Cartoons", in Charles Davy (ed), *Footnotes to the Film* (London: Lovat Dickson and Reader's Union, 1938): 83.

74   Ibid: 86.

75   Porter: 186.

76   Sussex, in Aitken (ed): 194.

77   Porter: 182.

78   Tavernier: 16.

79   Balcon (1969): 138.

80   McFarlane (ed): 234.

81   "Notes re Cavalcanti", 24 March 1947. AMBC [notes collated by Balcon from meetings with Cavalcanti; this dated 1 October 1946].

82   Balcon, letter to Cavalcanti, 22 January 1947. AMBC: F/17.

83   Cavalcanti, letter to Balcon, 23 January 1947. AMBC: F/17.

84   Balcon, letter to Cavalcanti, 28 January 1947. AMBC [no reference number].

85   Clarke: 141.

86   Balcon, letter to Cavalcanti, 28 January 1947. AMBC [no reference number].

87   Cavalcanti, letter to Balcon, 12 February 1947. AMBC [no reference number].

88   Ibid.

89   Sussex, in Aitken (ed): 199.

6

Went the Day Well? to The Life and Adventures of Nicholas Nickleby

Went the Day Well? (1942)

The plot of *Went the Day Well?* concerns the occupation of the fictional village of Bramley End by a platoon of German paratroopers. The film begins with a framing narrative in which the verger of Bramley End's church recounts the events of the incursion. The narrative proper begins before the verger (Mervyn Johns) has finished speaking, with a flashback to the events which took place in the village a year ago, on 21 May 1942. A party of 60 German soldiers, disguised as Royal Engineers, arrive in the village demanding billets. At first, the villagers believe that the Germans are the visiting platoon of British soldiers that they claim to be, and they are actively encouraged to believe this by Wilsford (Leslie Banks), a resident of the village, who is also a German spy.

The Germans' true identity is eventually discovered by the vicar's daughter Nora (Valerie Taylor), and, following this, Wilsford and the German commanding officer, Ortler (Basil Sydney), put "plan B" into action. The village is then cordonned off from the outside world and the villagers are imprisoned in the church. As the assembled villagers are told about the situation by Ortler, the vicar (C V France) attempts to ring the church bells in order to raise the alarm, but is shot and killed by Ortler. The villagers then make a number of failed attempts to escape, until two of them: the local poacher, Purves (Edward Rigby), and a young evacuee (Harry Fowler) engineer a successful breakout. Purves dies in the attempt, but the boy escapes to raise the alarm. The British Army then arrives and, after a protracted battle, the Germans are defeated. Near the end of the film, Wilsford is shot by Nora, after which the narrative returns to the framing story with which the film began.

The origins of *Went the Day Well?* lie in "The Lieutenant Died Last", a short story written by the author and film critic Graham Greene in the spring of 1940. Greene, who had been recruited into the propaganda service early in 1940, worked in a branch of the MoI charged with the commission of books and pamphlets for propaganda purposes, and "The Lieutenant Died Last" was contracted as part of the policy objective of influencing opinion in the United States about "the value of the British character". Greene's story was eventually published in the American periodical *Collier's Weekly* on 29 June 1940, although its impact on the American public's appreciation of the British character remains unclear.[1] "The Lieutenant Died Last" concerns the fictional incursion of a group of German paratroopers into the small English village of Potter. Greene's Potter is, however, far removed from the traditional stereotype of a cosy rural English village, and is, on the contrary, a drab, introverted place cut off from the modern world and peopled by eccentric and backward villagers.[2] Potter's insular lethargy is brutally shattered when the Germans, who are intent on destroying the nearby main railway line to Scotland, arrive on the scene. The Germans first imprison the villagers and then set about their plans. However, they are eventually foiled by the ingenuity of the local poacher, Bill Purves, who, although hardly cutting a heroic figure, still possesses the necessary native guile and determination to vanquish the Germans.

It has been argued that Greene's unflattering depiction of the villagers in "The Lieutenant Died Last" might well have proved counter-productive, given the policy objective at that time of seeking to reinforce American support for the British war effort by raising the profile of "the British character".[3] However, Greene's story did correspond, at least to some extent, with the then-current MoI strategy of presenting an understated account of Britain and the British.[4] This low-key approach, which must have influenced Greene as he worked on the story, can also be seen in some of the early wartime productions of the GPO and Crown Film Units, such as *The First Days* (1939), *Christmas Under Fire* (1941) and *London Can Take It!* (1940). Like "The Lieutenant Died Last", these films also emphasise the ordinary and the everyday, and even the insular and the eccentric, rather than the extraordinary and the heroic.

However, although Greene's dolorous story more or less conformed to the MoI's preferred approach to propaganda at that time, "The Lieutenant Died Last" was more than simply a piece of commissioned propaganda, and, although it can be related to the context of official sanction for an understated approach to propaganda, it also contains material which "works intentionally against the propaganda grain".[5] "The Lieutenant Died Last" was originally conceived by Greene as a work of literature, in which some of the insular and regressive aspects of English rural life would be critically explored for their own sake, rather than for propaganda purposes. It was only when it was later taken up by the MoI that Greene's story was given more discursive content.[6] The story which eventually became the source for *Went the Day Well?* was therefore the product of both instrumental and critical aspirations, and both sets of objectives are incorporated within the final, complex and inevitably contradictory text.

Greene's association with the documentary film movement began during the mid-1930s. He was particularly impressed by Basil

Wright's *The Song of Ceylon* when it appeared in 1934, and regarded it as a landmark of the British cinema. He was also aware of the significant contribution which Cavalcanti had made to the soundtrack of the film. Greene appears to have met Cavalcanti for the first time in mid-1939, although he had admired Cavalcanti's work since the late-1920s. In a review of *Rien que les heures* (*Nothing But the Hours*, 1926) for *The Times* in January 1929, for example, Greene argued that Cavalcanti's film was superior to Walter Ruttmann's far better known *Berlin – Symphony of a Great City* (1927).[7] Greene's praise of Cavalcanti is also evident in a review of *Men in Danger* (1938), a documentary directed by Pat Jackson and produced by Cavalcanti, in which Greene argued that Cavalcanti had succeeded in showing the "horror" which underlies the treatment of the worker in modern mass production.[8] Writing elsewhere, Greene was less enthusiastic about Cavalcanti's *The First Days*. He regretted the film's use of "highflown clichés", but regarded *The First Days* as a hopeless project to begin with anyway, by virtue of the fact that it was produced as a work of propaganda, and he excused Cavalcanti on the grounds that "I am not sure that anyone, who, like Mr Cavalcanti, has a concern for truth could have succeeded [with it]".[9] Cavalcanti and Greene became close friends in 1939, and, shortly after he moved to Ealing in 1940, Cavalcanti approached Greene with a proposition that they should collaborate together on a film project. It is highly probable, although not absolutely certain, that this project was to be an adaptation of "The Lieutenant Died Last". However, before Cavalcanti and Greene could get very far on this assignment, they were both moved on to other briefs. Greene went abroad as part of his work for the MoI, whilst Cavalcanti was transferred to another Ealing production, possibly *The Big Blockade* (1942), on which work commenced at the end of 1940.[10] At that time, the story treatment for the Greene-Cavalcanti project was shelved, and lay dormant for almost two years, before a variety of circumstances, including both the external military context, and internal matters at Ealing, caused it to be revived.

By early 1942, successive military set-backs, most notably the fall of Singapore on 15 February, had led to an increase in public concern over the likelihood of a German invasion of Britain. The Home Office Intelligence Report for February found that "many people were now taking the possibility of invasion seriously", and, in response, the MoI began to address the issue of "the role of the civilian in the event of invasion".[11] *Went the Day Well?* went into production under its initial title of *They Came in Khaki* within a month of the publication of the Home Office Report. Studio work began on 26 March 1942, and location-shooting on 18 May. The urgency with which the project was developed, from its initial instigation in March 1942 to the première of the completed film in October, suggests that its production was actively encouraged by the MoI. However, there is no evidence to suggest any direct involvement in the film by the MoI or by any other government agency.[12] Shortly before shooting commenced on the film, Angus

MacPhail and John Dighton, Ealing's chief scriptwriters, began work on the treatment of "The Lieutenant Died Last" which had been developed by Greene and Cavalcanti. However, in this process, MacPhail and Dighton changed Greene's initial story significantly. Many of the less appealing aspects of Potter now disappeared, to be replaced by more virtuous representations of traditional English village life. The rather curt title of Potter was dropped in favour of the more wholesome Bramley End, and Greene's lowly, tin-roofed village church was transformed into a noble 13th-century stone-built church complete with vicarage and verger. The central character of "The Lieutenant Died Last", the dissolute poacher, Purves, was also transformed from a semi-senile degenerate into an engaging and idiosyncratic old rogue with a pronounced affection for his faithful dog.

MacPhail and Dighton worked on the script of *They Came in Khaki* for a while, but must have found it difficult to integrate Greene and Cavalcanti's darker vision into the more positive and uplifting tale of stout English yeomanry which they had been called upon to deliver. At some point, both abandoned the task, no doubt with some relief, in order to deal with more tractable projects, and responsibility for the further development of the script was then handed over to a third scriptwriter, Diana Morgan, who was somewhat dismayed by what she found:

> I went over and found this script which was almost ready to be done...And it was unplayable. I think that's the word. They knew it was, and that's why they sent for me. It was all a fearful muddle. The story was there, the action was there, but the people weren't. They were just names. And what I really did was make them into parts for the actors and make them actable scenes.[13]

One feature of Cavalcanti's filmmaking that has already been referred to here is his tendency to use a number of equally weighted characters, rather than one or two central characters in his films. This is true of his early French films, and is also the case with *Went the Day Well?*, *The Life and Adventures of Nicholas Nickleby* (1947), *They Made Me a Fugitive* (1947), *For Them That Trespass* (1949) and, to a lesser extent, *Champagne Charlie* (1944). The origins of this aspect of Cavalcanti's work lie in the French naturalist tradition, with its focus on the intimate relationship between character and environment, but Cavalcanti's sense of himself as a foreigner in England, observing what was, to him, a peculiar and unfamiliar culture, also reinforced the tendency towards multiple characterisation in his work.

Ironically, one of the outcomes of MacPhail and Dighton's normative reworking of the script of *They Came in Khaki* was precisely to provide Cavalcanti with the basis for the kind of ensemble effect which he liked. As the script was developed, MacPhail and Dighton were forced to dilute the central importance of the problematic Purves by reducing his role within the script, and by building up those of more acceptable characters. Although this meant that the script which was eventually handed to Morgan was filled with a collection of half-developed character profiles, it provided Cavalcanti with the opportunity to pursue his inclination to disseminate characterisation more widely across the canvas of the finished film.

There is evidence to suggest that quite a number of people within Ealing, including Morgan, Balcon and the production supervisor John Croydon believed that *Went the Day Well?* was too slow, prolonged and equivocal. For example, Balcon found the film "too vague, not urgent enough...The performances far too casual and the film too leisurely, particularly at the beginning".[14] What Balcon and others found particularly difficult to understand about *Went the Day Well?* was why so much time was spent on incidental aspects of characterisation and background, and why it took so long to arrive at the decisive point in the plot where the German presence in the village is finally discovered. Much of the work done by the scriptwriters was aimed at eliminating these *longueurs*, and at making the build-up of dramatic action in the film more urgent and more easily understood.

Much of the written documentation on the production of *Went the Day Well?* has been lost, and consequently there is no conclusive evidence that Cavalcanti ever objected to these prescriptive interventions by Balcon and his scriptwriters. However, given Cavalcanti's reaction to Balcon's interference on the making of *The Halfway House* (1944), where he *did* complain about Balcon's attempts to have the film simplified, it is highly probable that he was also unhappy about the various attempts to turn *Went the Day Well?* into a more forthright and conventional film.[15] Evidence of this unhappiness surely lies in the fact that Cavalcanti simply left out many of the changes which Morgan and MacPhail had introduced to the script in order to make it clearer. One of the most significant of these reverses occurs near the end of the film, and involves the crucial sequence in which Nora shoots Wilsford. Morgan has Wilsford attempting desperately to explain himself, both to Nora and the audience, but Cavalcanti excludes this, allowing Wilsford only to call out her name as he is shot. In filming the scene in this way, Cavalcanti maximises the impact of its sudden and emotional violence, and also rendered its finale more ambivalent and disturbing.

Cavalcanti's influence on *Went the Day Well?* can be discerned in the long, slow build-up to the scenes in which the presence of the Germans is finally determined. Here characters are drawn in relation to their environment with a degree of detail which goes far beyond the demands of the plot. The insular and highly local world of Potter is retained, and, although the inhabitants of the village are not exactly the sullen grumblers of Greene's original story, they remain idiosyncratic and insular. These opening sequences appear to work on two different levels. On the one hand, they establish character in a fairly conventional manner in order to develop plot. On the other hand, however, as already mentioned, they dwell on the peculiarities of the culture and lifestyle of the inhabitants of Bramley End, giving that culture and lifestyle a peculiar and, at times, surreal colouring.

Another aspect of *Went the Day Well?* which can be ascribed to Cavalcanti is the unsettling atmosphere which pervades much of this opening section of the film. What makes these sequences so unsettling is the fact that the Germans are both like, yet also fundamentally unlike, the villagers, and this intimate proximity between the commonplace and its extreme opposite gives the film a particularly disconcerting edge. The ease with which deception takes place here is disquieting. The conspirators are confident and determined, their confidence such that they can even afford to play games with the villagers – as, for example, when Ostrer, the German commander, tricks the leader of the Home Guard into divulging the layout of the village defences. The Home Guarder, believing that he is talking to a British officer, is happy to help, and Ostrer thanks him for "making my job a good deal easier". At the time, critics found this aspect of *Went the Day Well?* difficult to stomach, and reacted defensively to it by protesting that they found the relationship between the Germans and the villagers "implausible".[16]

The opposition between premeditated calculating reason and insular preoccupation with the everyday and trivial is central to these opening sections of the film. The English villagers are depicted as eccentrics, locked into village life, and unable to comprehend what is about to be unleashed upon them. This is equally as true of the vicar, the Lady of the Manor, the scatterbrained postmistresses, and Purves. It is as though the film is attempting to develop a series of cameos of an English society which is fatally flawed in its indifference to, and lack of awareness of, present danger, and it is the extent to which this is rendered which is, in part, responsible for the ambivalent complexity which pervades much of *Went the Day Well?*

Other scenes in the film which reveal the influence of Cavalcanti all centre around acts of sudden, intense violence, mainly perpetrated by, or witnessed by, women. One such scene is when Mrs Collins (Muriel George), the postmistress, kills the German soldier billeted with her. This scene occurs shortly after the Germans have taken over the village. The post office is the only means of contact with the outside world because all telephones calls are routed through there, and, as a consequence, Mrs Collins is guarded there by a German soldier, instead of being interned in the church with the other villagers.

Up to this point, Mrs Collins has been depicted as a scatterbrained but kindly figure, and it is her transformation from this into a determined killer which is partly responsible for the dramatic impact of this particular scene. Mrs Collins hands the German soldier a pepper-pot, knowing that he will be unable to open it. They talk about the soldier's children: he is unmarried, but has "two fine sons who will soon be old enough to fight". She replies that she is "broad-minded" and that "accidents will happen", after which she throws the pepper in the German's face. The temper of the camerawork then changes. A series of close-ups focus on the German as he falls. A moving camera shot then shows Mrs Collins striding towards her victim, axe in hand, and the blow she strikes is particularly fierce. After the killing, an extreme close-up of Mrs Collins' face shows her to be in the grip of strong, near hysterical emotion, and it is the degree of emotion shown here, in combination with the emphasis on Mrs Collins' intensified subjectivity, which marks out this scene both as unusual in a British film of the period, and as bearing Cavalcanti's characteristic authorial signature.

After this, there are other violent incidents, and the overall tone of the film becomes progressively darker. Wilsford kills an escapee; Purves is shot by a German soldier; Nora and Mrs Frazer (Marie Lohr) discover that Wilsford is a traitor; and Mrs Frazer is later killed by a hand-grenade in an act of self-sacrifice. Two other scenes also show women in the grip of intense emotion following acts of violence. In the first of these, Tom Sturry (Frank Lawton), a sailor home on leave, kills a German by clubbing him to death. As the fatal blow is struck, Cavalcanti cuts to a close-up of two women gazing at the scene with excited fascination. In a later scene, Daisy, Mrs Collins' assistant at the post office, is shown in extreme close-up, her face contorted with near hysterical emotion, as her German captor is killed in front of her. Elsewhere, the threatening proximity of female emotion also causes Ostrer, the German commander, to insist that the wife of a murdered member of the Home Guard be removed from the church in which the villagers are held captive because she might become hysterical. It is, in fact, this hysteria, and the ruthless violence which accompanies it, which seem to provide a greater threat to the Germans than the more rational offensive strategies adopted by the men of the village.

The second scene involving women and intensified emotion in the presence of sudden violence is that in which Nora shoots Wilsford. In many respects, this scene parallels the earlier one in which Mrs Collins kills the German soldier. There is, for example, the same play with language and double meanings as in the first incident. In that sequence, Mrs Collins states that "accidents will happen", whilst her intention is clearly to cause such an accident. Similarly, in the later incident, Nora picks up a pistol, intending to confront Wilsford. She asks if it is loaded, and, when informed that it is, is asked if she thinks she "can handle it". She replies "well enough", but it is clear that it is Wilsford, not the pistol, that she intends to handle.

As Nora walks down the stairs to confront Wilsford, a moving camera shot follows her, again paralleling Mrs Collins' approach to her victim. Wilsford is taking down the barricades from a window, and is framed in a highly composed, Expressionistic lighting set-up. As Nora shoots him, there is a shot/reverse-shot of him looking down at her, and her up at him. As he falls, slow-motion camerawork is used, and Nora shoots him twice more, after which, distraught and quivering with emotion, she covers her face with her hands. As with the scene in which Mrs Collins kills the German soldier, it is the intensity of this scene, together with the unusual use of slow-motion, which marks it out from much of the rest of this and other films of the period.

Went the Day Well? received a generally negative critical reception. Some found the violence and "display of hate" in the film offensive, whilst others were affronted by what they took to be a "frivolous" treatment of the film's highly topical subject-matter.[17] Critics were also offended by what they perceived to be the film's overly simplistic and jingoistic tone. *Documentary Newsletter*, for example, commented that the film had "all the appearance of having been made with one eye on the clock and the other on a copy of the *Boys' Own Paper*". In similar vein, *Kinematograph Weekly* described it as "[f]air average thick-ear fiction for the unsophisticated masses", whilst the *Motion Picture Herald* condemned it as a "[c]andidate only for the most transparent and fantastic type of penny dreadful fiction...Scarcely good foreign propaganda for British films".[18] The most trenchant review of *Went the Day Well?* was, however, penned by the film critic of *The Observer*, Caroline Lejeune:

> After *Went the Day Well?* went I home rather sadly, turning over some reflections on war films in general. One is that a film praising the British spirit, as most British films at this time should and will, is obviously the more effective if it presents our enemies with a fair measure of continence. It is a dangerous thing to show your opponents as clowns or bullies, who only got results by treachery, brute force, or the long arm of coincidence. A director who does this merely cheapens his own countrymen, since victory over such people seems empty and meagre. Another is that any display of hate, except in the hands of an expert director and artists, is to be avoided, since high passions without high performance are less likely to lead to conviction than laughter. A third is that the nearer a plot sticks to life at this tense moment of our fortunes, the nearer it gets to drama. And the fourth is simply that the most patriotic film can lose nothing by the exercise of a little talent and taste.[19]

It is clear from the above that what particularly offended Lejeune was her belief that *Went the Day Well?* appeared to have rejected the model of understated psychological and narrative realism which, by the mid-1940s, had more or less developed into a critical consensus within the British film Establishment. Lejeune's criticisms of *Went the Day Well?* are also similar to some of the views she had expressed elsewhere on the work of Powell and Pressburger, two filmmakers who, like Cavalcanti, were also criticised at the time for casting off the realist paradigm in films such as *The Life and Death of Colonel Blimp* (1943), *A Canterbury Tale* (1944) and *A Matter of Life and Death* (1946). Writing about *A Canterbury Tale*, for example, Lejeune argued that "to my mind, nothing will make it [the film's theme of a glue-throwing magistrate determined to uphold traditional English values] a pleasant one".[20] The critical reaction to *Went the Day Well?* and Lejeune's reaction in particular must, therefore, be understood in relation to the context of a dominant realist aesthetics, and to a situation in which critics were unsympathetic to films which did not conform to the central principles of that aesthetic.

It has been argued that Michael Powell was "[u]ndoubtedly one of the major victims of the realist aesthetic",[21] but so also was Cavalcanti, and the critical furore over *Went the Day Well?* provides an important insight into why Balcon did not consider him to be a trustworthy or dependable director. Balcon would not have appreciated an Ealing film described as "thick-ear fiction for the unsophisticated masses". He must also have been surprised and bewildered by the film itself, as he had expected it to be very different from what eventually emerged:

> He [Balcon] clearly expected an adventure story, with all the ingredients of suspense that his old protégé Hitchcock would have exploited so expertly...Really Cav and Balcon wanted to make two different kinds of film. Whether or not Balcon had any sense of such a conflict of principle, or just thought that Cav wasn't quite up to it, I think this was the root of his prejudice against him as a director.[22]

In his biography, Balcon hardly mentions *Went the Day Well?*; when he does, it is to imply that its qualities stem more from the original Greene script than from Cavalcanti's direction.[23] Balcon's response to *Went the Day Well?* may also have strengthened his already existing misgivings about Cavalcanti, and persuaded him that the latter should not be given the opportunity of directing any more controversial or topical films at Ealing.

Postwar accounts of *Went the Day Well?* have tended to focus on the film's critique of the English class system, and on its depiction of violence. Charles Barr, for example, has argued that *Went the Day Well?* contains a critical assessment of middle and upper-class leadership,[24] and this view is also adopted by Raymond Durgnat, who argues that the film expresses "distrust and dissatisfaction with our paternalist betters".[25] However, Anthony Aldgate and Jeffrey Richards feel that Barr and Durgnat overstate this issue, arguing that *Went the Day Well?* also affirms "traditional class structure and social hierarchy",[26] (although elsewhere Richards has argued that "there is [in the film] radicalism in the suggestion of the unsoundness of the old ruling class").[27] All those who have discussed *Went the Day Well?* have commented on its portrayal of brutal violence. Robert Murphy calls it "a remarkably savage film", and also describes Cavalcanti's view of war as "uncomfortably bleak",[28] whilst Richards refers to the film as a "powerful and at times chilling account".[29] More recent accounts of *Went the Day Well?* have tended to focus on the film's equivocal surreality. Penelope Houston has argued that the film was "the wild card, the joker in the British war-time cinema pack", and that what makes it so different from other British war films of the period, and therefore so significant, is the very unusual world-view which it contains. According to Houston, the world of Bramley End is characterised by rapid changes of mood and sudden alterations from quirky comedy to hysterical violence.[30] Charles Drazin also comments on these surrealistic or irrational aspects of the film, as well as on its Darwinian-naturalist view of the human condition, arguing that *Went the Day Well?* is "shot through with the inexplicable" and that "[b]eneath the village's appearance of civilization there lies a barbarity – the villagers who, in repelling their attackers, find that killing can be fun".[31] It has been argued that *Went the Day Well?* should be regarded as more of a collaborative venture than an authored work, and that Cavalcanti's influence upon the film as director should not be overstated.[32] In some respects this is clearly the case, and *Went the Day Well?* could legitimately be regarded as a product of the Ealing studio system, in that Balcon, various associate producers, editors and trusted scriptwriters all participated in bringing the film to fruition. *Went the Day Well?* also contains many sequences which appear to be unconvincingly and carelessly executed. The characterisation of Wilsford might, for example, be considered intriguingly enigmatic, but it is also very schematic. Similarly, although some of the rapid changes of mood in the film do appear genuinely sardonic and intentionally inexplicable, others appear merely careless and underdeveloped, possessing, as *Documentary Newsletter* bluntly put it, "all the appearance of having been made with one eye on the clock and the other on a copy of the *Boys' Own Paper*".[33]

Nevertheless, what is most arresting about *Went the Day Well?* is the extent to which it contains passages which are radically different from the standard Ealing film or, for that matter, from other British films of the period. Traces of the darker vision of the original Cavalcanti/Greene treatment remain within the film, and levels of emotional intensity are reached which mark the film out as unique in many respects. Although it is true that the collaborative authorship of *Went the Day Well?* resulted in the finished film possessing a degree of inconsistency and discrepancy which made the final version something of a muddle, these inconsistencies also contribute towards making *Went the Day Well?* a complex and perplexing work which considers, however obliquely, questions of heightened subjectivity, the banal brutalism inherent in the naturalist vision of the human condition, and the irrational contingency which characterises much human experience.

Champagne Charlie (1944)

Cavalcanti's second directed film for Ealing differed in many respects from *Went the Day Well?*. *Champagne Charlie* is a musical comedy set in 1860s London, and it was designed as a vehicle for its two principal stars, the comedians Stanley Holloway and Tommy Trinder. *Champagne Charlie* opens as two miners, George and Fred Sanders (Tommy Trinder and Leslie Clarke), forsake their mining village of Leybourne for London, where they hope to launch Fred on a career as a boxer. At the "Elephant and Castle" inn, the brothers seek out a well-known fighter called Tom Sayers (Eddie Philips), who agrees to spar with Fred in order to assess his potential. However, it soon becomes clear that Fred no longer possesses the stamina and lung capacity necessary to become a boxer. Fred then returns to Leybourne, but George remains, having proved a great success at the inn when invited to sing.

The opening titles of *Champagne Charlie* proclaim: "In the year of grace 1862, two brothers set off from the village of Leybourne for London Town". Fred and George are then seen leaving Leybourne on their journey towards London, and then approaching the Elephant and Castle. Up to this point, the film has been almost entirely silent, and the photography, which principally consists of high-angle long-shots of the narrow confining streets adjoining the Elephant and Castle, is reminiscent of scenes from both *Nothing But the Hours* and *For Them That Trespass*. These opening scenes also have a sombre, pensive tone and a documentary character in keeping with the seriousness of the brothers' urgent need to find employment.

However, the atmosphere of the film changes noticeably as the brothers enter the "Elephant and Castle", and as the more formal and composed documentary style of the opening sequences is abandoned in favour of one which echoes the informality and bustle within the tavern. As Fred and George enter the "Elephant and Castle", a fragment of song is heard whose lyrics, "a vagabond I'll always want to be", seem to allude to the brothers' own predicament, and this close interaction between characterisation and musical commentary permeates these opening sequences of the film. The world of the "Elephant and Castle" is a relaxed and pleasurable one, dominated by music and song, and the film represents this milieu in intimate detail as the camera moves amongst the customers of the inn as they talk, drink and sing.

In many respects, the opening scenes of *Champagne Charlie* fulfil the same function as those of *Went the Day Well?* in that they portray the commonplace relationships which exist between character and environment. As in *Went the Day Well?*, these opening scenes focus on the detailed depiction of milieu, rather than on the development of plot or character, and it is the tapestry of incidental moments which the film displays which are significant: characters crossing or appearing at the perimeters of the screen, bursts of song intermingling with each other, and fragments of conversation materialising, then disappearing, as the camera moves on. The impressionistic, naturalistic montage style employed here is also similar to that used in *Nothing But the Hours* and *Spare Time* (1939), and is, in fact, far more equivocal than that found in the opening sequences of *Went the Day Well?*, which remain guided and channelled by the exigencies of plot.

After spending some time at the "Elephant and Castle", Joe's ability as a singer comes to the attention of Miss Bessie Bellwood (Betty Warren), the principal star and manageress of The Mogador music hall and, according to Tom Sayers, "the best artist in the halls". Bessie invites George to audition at the Mogador, and, when he arrives there, George finds Bessie onstage singing "Give Us Another One, Do", a song with obvious sexual connotations about a girl who "always wants more". Despite witnessing the audience's enthusiastic response to Bessie's raunchy song, Sanders perversely decides to sing a temperance song entitled "Don't Bring Shame on the Old Folk", about the worries visited upon the elderly when their progeny turn to drink. This, predictably, goes down badly, as the Mogador's customers disdainfully turn their backs on Sanders, and enjoy a drink or two. However, despite this lapse into unwelcome puritanism, Sanders is eventually hired by Bellwood, changes his name to Leybourne, and goes on to enjoy a successful career at the Mogador. The next song he is seen singing there is entitled "Hit Him on the Boko". Largely consisting of verses of cockney rhyming slang taken from the world of boxing, it contrasts starkly with the dolorous sentimentalism of "Don't Bring Shame on the Old Folk".

Leybourne and Bellwood then enter into rivalry with The Great Vance (Stanley Holloway), who performs at an even more up-market hall called the Oxford. This marks the beginning of the contest between the two which culminates in the drinking song duel between Vance and Leybourne, in which the two entertainers attempt to outdo each other by performing songs which extol the virtues and pleasures of alcohol. The film first cuts from Leybourne singing "Ale, Old Ale" to Vance's "I Do Like a Little Drop of Gin". As the contest heats up, the songs refer to drinks increasingly higher up the social scale. Leybourne performs "Burgundy, Claret and Port" dressed as a French waiter and sporting a comic French accent, whilst Vance retaliates with "Rum, Rum Rum". Leybourne then responds to this with "The Brandy and Saltzer Boys", and Vance with "A Glass of Sherry Wine". The climax of the duel is reached when Leybourne finally gets the better of The Great Vance by singing "Champagne Charlie", the song which establishes him as the dominant "lion comique".

This whole sequence, like much of *Champagne Charlie*, is a paean to the pleasures of intoxication. In *Champagne Charlie*, alcohol is seen as a liberating agent, which both stimulates pleasure and releases debilitating inhibitions. Bessie Bellwood expects George to get drunk and to have hangovers, and worries about him when he appears too frequently sober. Similarly, the chairman of the Mogador always needs a few drinks before he is able to compose George Leybourne's songs, whilst the music-hall's clientele are seen constantly drinking, and suffering no apparent ill effects as a consequence. On the other hand, however, those opposed to alcohol are regarded as prudish, and seeking to impose a normative order upon the culture which is flourishing under the influence of "the fruit of the vine".

 Champagne Charlie affirms the value of pleasurable diversion, and alcohol, like music and song, is seen as a central ingredient in this. This view of the fruitful effect of prolific alcohol consumption may have been influenced by the culture of drinking which existed at Ealing. Cavalcanti patronised "The Red Lion" alongside Hamer, MacPhail and the others,[34] but he was also a frequent visitor to Le Petit Club Français, the dining and drinking place established by the film enthusiast Olwen Vaughn at the beginning of the war. Cavalcanti, a close friend of Vaughn's, had first visited Le Petit Club Français when he was still at the GPO Film Unit, and, when he joined Ealing, he introduced the studio's already hardened drinkers to the club's convivial, Francophile and often-inebriated atmosphere. Dedicated to French culture and the cinema, Le Petit Club Français was a place where Cavalcanti felt at home, and Drazin's account of it as a place where "beds [were] on hand to put up people who had had too much to drink or had nowhere to go", and where, on Bastille Day, revellers spilled out of the bar onto the street, dancing to the tune of an accordion, may indicate one source for the congenial world of *Champagne Charlie*.[35] Yet another source was The Players, a cabaret which re-created the experience of the Victorian music-hall, and where "the audience sat at beer tables and sang along to the choruses, just like the patrons of the Mogador".[36] Like Le Petit Club Français, Cavalcanti was also a patron of The Players.

 The emphasis which *Champagne Charlie* places on intoxication and pleasure is closely related to another important theme within the film, that of community. The accent placed on the bonds which bind a specific community together is, of course, a characteristic feature of many Ealing films. However, in most of the other films such links are established through a moral discourse based on values such as integrity, decency and obligation. This is the case, for example, with such classically Balconian films as *The Blue Lamp* (Dearden, 1950) and *Scott of the Antarctic* (Frend, 1948). In *Champagne Charlie*, however, it is the pursuit of guileless pleasurable gratification, rather than social standing and self-sacrifice, which appears to bond this particular community together, and such a celebration of hedonist intemperance clearly distinguishes *Champagne Charlie* from most other Ealing films of the period.

 The dominant moral discourse in *Champagne Charlie* can be characterised as one in which acceptance of others is deemed to be of the highest value. This basically humanist orientation means that the differences of social class, gender, age and geographical region which appear in the film are all subsumed within its overall portrayal of the polyglot community of music-hall goers. However, the humanist orientation found in *Champagne Charlie* is far from insipid or bland. *Champagne Charlie* mobilises a vigorous humanism, shot through with sardonic irony, which nevertheless indirectly allows issues of class and gender difference to be voiced. Nor is the community depicted in *Champagne Charlie* licentious or morally lax, as some at the time may have thought.[37] On the contrary, the community of people depicted could be described as hedonist, if that term is taken to stand for a belief that the pursuit of happiness is the proper aim of human action. More contentiously, perhaps, the world of *Champagne Charlie* could be described as "epicurean", in its emphasis on the importance of communal friendship, and in its evocation of a community set apart from the everyday realities of its wartime context.[38]

Alongside its primary concern with the rivalry between Leybourne and The Great Vance, and its overriding concern with issues of individual expression and communal pleasure-seeking, *Champagne Charlie* also contains a number of minor and unconvincing sub-plots. One of these concerns the romance between Bessie Bellwood's daughter Dolly (Jean Kent) and Lord Petersfield (Peter de Greeff), a young and plummy member of the aristocracy. However, this sub-plot is very much a routine narrative device introduced in order to inject some romantic interest into a film which otherwise would have none. The sub-plot touches superficially on the difficulties faced by love in surmounting the class divide, and is reminiscent of similar situations in earlier Ealing films starring Gracie Fields and George Formby. However, the issue is not treated seriously here, and the acting performances by de Greeff and Austin Trevor (Petersfield's father, the Duke) are unconvincing, whilst Jean Kent's performance as Dolly could only be described as rudimentary.

The inevitable irrelevance of this sub-plot to *Champagne Charlie* as a whole is determined by the fact that the theme of love, or of intimate relationship, does not arise at any other point in the film, as all the principal characters enjoy convivial and peer, rather than romantic, relationships with each other, and appear to be satisfied with that. This reflects the innocent epicureanism which pervades the film as a whole, but it may also reflect Cavalcanti's own sexual orientation. In general, and with the notable exception of *For Them That Trespass*, heterosexual romance is not a prevalent theme within his films.

The other major sub-plot in *Champagne Charlie* concerns the attempt by those described in the film as the "theatre people" to close the music-halls down. Towards the end of the film, this issue becomes increasingly prominent, and also provides the rationale for the film's cathartic finale, in which Leybourne and Vance present a united defence of the music-halls. A "committee of enquiry" has been established in order to decide the fate of the music-halls, and Leybourne, Vance and Bellwood attend the hearings of the committee in order to put their case. In an impassioned speech, Leybourne accuses the "theatre people" of being behind the attempt to close the halls:

These theatre people think they'll get Parliament to back them up, and why, because there are a whole lot of busybodies in this country who are set on stopping the ordinary folks enjoying themselves. They used to call it merry England, but if these nosy parkers get their way it will be about as cheerful as Christmas day in the workhouse.

This issue of the attempt to regulate and control working-class culture is present as a continuous background theme within *Champagne Charlie*. However, like the romantic sub-plot involving Dolly and Lord Petersfield, this is largely peripheral to the film's central thematic concerns, and *Champagne Charlie* ultimately fails to address it in any meaningful way. Instead, the conflict between the music-halls and the theatres is presented as an attempt by "improvers" and special-interest groups to abolish an organic form of popular culture. The theatre people are defined as unscrupulous entrepreneurs, at odds with both the people and a basically benevolent Establishment, and this opposition between a cohesive society and a parasitic group acting to further their own interests may reflect contemporaneous notions of the "people's war".

At the time, the idea of a people's war, in which all classes worked together for the common good, was accompanied by the demonisation of groups such as criminals, black marketeers, and other antisocial elements who were perceived as benefitting from the sacrifices made by the majority. In *Champagne Charlie*, the real historical conflict between the music-halls and the theatres during the 1860s loses its historical specificity, and becomes transformed into a more general opposition between the community and those who threaten it. This type of use and adaptation of historical events in order to meet the ideological exigencies of the war was by no means uncommon in the films of the period, and the celebration of Victorian values in *Champagne Charlie* can be regarded as performing the same kind of ideological task as, for example, Olivier's version of *Henry V* (1945) did in respect to Elizabethan values.

In the end, the attempt to close down the music-halls in *Champagne Charlie* fails, due to a strengthening of the bond between the people and the Establishment, and the film ends in a satisfying conclusion, with the assured survival of the halls, the newly-formed friendship between Leybourne and Vance, and, inevitably, the engagement of Dolly and Lord Petersfield. As with most other films of the period, *Champagne Charlie* concludes by endorsing a notion of Britain as a unified community, although this is by no means the principal concern of the film.

Stylistically, *Champagne Charlie* is grounded in a naturalistic style. One critic has argued that the film shows "minimal attention...to the aesthetics of composition".[39] However, one feature of Cavalcanti's work which should be noted in this respect is his tendency to employ a neutral visual style influenced by the French realist and naturalist traditions. Therefore, it is less that *Champagne Charlie* fails to address the "aesthetics of composition" than that Cavalcanti has deliberately chosen to adopt a more neutral, realist approach here, involving the frequent use of static, deep-focus long shots, in which movement largely takes place within the frame. It is only in the opening scenes of the film, with their carefully composed noirish photography, and in the climax to Leybourne's performance of the song "Champagne Charlie", that a more formal aesthetic style emerges, and the film departs from the neutral naturalism which otherwise pervades it.

Critical responses to *Champagne Charlie* have varied considerably. One recent critic has described it as "one of the most important films in the British cinema",[40] and another as "one of the most vibrant and unusual narratives in British cinema".[41] However, *Champagne Charlie* has not, in general, been considered an important film. At the time of its release, it was regarded as a successful, although minor, work. For example, the *Monthly Film Bulletin* thought that its direction was "vivid", and argued that it was an "amusing and invigorating comedy",[42] whilst *To-day's Cinema* thought it "rumbustious", and its direction "fast and sure".[43] The American *Motion Picture Herald* also thought *Champagne Charlie* had great "gusto", and admired the quality of its acting, whilst arguing that it was a "good antidote to the so-called British school of documentaries".[44]

However, although trade reviews for *Champagne Charlie* were generally appreciative, critics, both then and now, have often taken a different view. In an article published in 1950, in which he reflected on important British film comedies, Michael Balcon did not even mention *Champagne Charlie*.[45] Most critical studies of the British cinema written since then have usually slighted *Champagne Charlie*. Durgnat feels that the film is "well-washed, cheerful, determinedly innocent", and that "a sense of rugged life is far more present in the tavern sing-songs of *Oliver Twist*".[46] Murphy describes *Champagne Charlie* merely as "a celebration of the good old days of the English music hall",[47] although elsewhere he provides a more positive assessment of the film, describing Cavalcanti's direction as "sure-footed", and the film as "a glitteringly attractive view of the old music hall".[48] However, Murphy also supports Andy Medhurst's contention that *Champagne Charlie* fails to achieve the "breathtaking iconographic power" of films such as *Millions Like Us* (1943) or *I Thank You* (1941).[49]

Sue Harper has probably written the most negative account of *Champagne Charlie*, describing the film as "too episodic to engage the audience's imagination", lacking "visual pleasure", and displaying "minimal attention...to the aesthetics of composition".[50] What is also surprising is that many critical studies of British cinema have completely ignored the film.[51] In this sense, and as Drazin has argued, *Champagne Charlie* could be described as a "forgotten" film.[52]

One possible explanation for the lack of critical attention given to *Champagne Charlie* is that Cavalcanti's quirky, surreal and dissident inclinations, embedded, as they so often are, in an often purposeless playfulness, are difficult for English film critics to understand. It is strange, for example, that the odd surreality of *The Big Blockade* has been largely missed by such critics, and it is surprising that it is only now that some are pointing to the extent to which *Champagne Charlie* mischievously caricatures and subverts the normative ideology of Balcon/Ealing. Made during a period of moral and alcoholic abstinence, *Champagne Charlie* actively celebrates intoxication, sexual licence ("Give Us Another One, Do", "Strolling in the Park" and "Hunting After Dark"), and appetite in general. Whilst some Gainsborough films of the period also covertly address these issues, *Champagne Charlie* does so overtly, and may well be unique in that respect. It is also a mistake to compare *Champagne Charlie* too closely with other British films which appeared at the time, and which also used the Victorian music-hall as a background. *Champagne Charlie* is a far more complex and subversive film than more conventional works such as *Trottie True* (1949), *I'll Be Your Sweetheart* (1945) or *Gaiety George* (1946). In fact, the film to which *Champagne Charlie* can be most closely compared is not a contemporaneous British film at all, but a later French one. Jean Renoir's three theatrical films of the 1950s, *Le Carrosse d'Or* (*The Golden Coach*, 1953), *French Cancan* (1955) and *Eléna et les hommes* (1956) are all musical comedies, and all re-create enclosed, circumscribed worlds in the same way in which *Champagne Charlie* does. Of the three, the closest to *Champagne Charlie* is undoubtedly *French Cancan*, in which, as in *Champagne Charlie*, "[t]he outside world of politics impinges comically and cryptically".[53]

   Champagne Charlie is not a work of critical realism, and therefore does not comment consequentially on issues of class inequality. For example, the hedonistic milieu of the music-hall evacuates class difference, and binds its working-class and middle-class pleasure-seekers into a closely linked community. Issues of class difference or exploitation are rarely broached within Cavalcanti's films, which generally have a social and humanist, rather than class, focus, and *Champagne Charlie* is no exception. The central figure in the film is George Leybourne, and in the original draft scripts for the film more was made of Leybourne's mining background, whilst his songs contain more critical material about class inequality. However, this material was largely removed from the final version of the film. This may have been done under Balcon's auspices, but it is more likely to have been the work of the film's scriptwriters, Austin Melford, John Dighton and Angus MacPhail. In later films, when he was free of the overbearing presence of producers such as Grierson and Balcon, Cavalcanti would prove that he was more than willing to engage with social realism in a critical way. This is particularly the case, for example, with films such as *O Canto do Mar* (*Song of the Sea*, 1953) and *Die Windrose* (1956), but I would argue that *For Them That Trespass* can also be placed within this category. It must be remembered, however, that, under Balcon's tutelage, a subversive, rather than critical, posture was all that was available to Cavalcanti – hence the approach in *Champagne Charlie*.

It is also a mistake to argue that Leybourne is an "innocent" and "insecure" working-class figure learning to "imitate the codes of [his] superiors".[54] George and Fred are vulnerable and damaged outsiders, driven from their mining village of Leybourne by unemployment and poverty, and drawn into the bosom of a confident working-class culture, at home and secure within the city. George's rite of passage can therefore be interpreted as a metaphor for a vulnerable working class, moving from a position of fragmented insecurity towards one of communal strength, and repudiating the culture of constraint imposed upon it.

Champagne Charlie caricatures and undermines the "poverty of desire" which was characteristic of Ealing, and of the quality realist British cinema during this period. It is at this level, and not that of radical engagement, that it played a productive role in contesting normative orthodoxy. To complain that it is not sufficiently critical or radical, as some have, is to misunderstand its purpose, quality and contribution. *Champagne Charlie* may not overtly critique dominant ideologies, but it played a modest part in undermining them.

The Life and Adventures of Nicholas Nickleby (1947)

By 1944, when *Champagne Charlie* was made, it had already become clear that the public demand for war films was beginning to wane, and Ealing responded to this by initiating a programme of production within which a variety of different types of film were made. Between 1944 and 1947, when *The Life and Adventures of Nicholas Nickleby* was produced, the studio produced a musical comedy, *Fiddlers Three* (Watt, 1944); the futuristic *The Halfway House* and *They Came to a City*; (Dearden, 1944), a portmanteau ghost film, *Dead of Night* (1945); a period costume drama, *Pink String and Sealing Wax* (Hamer, 1945); and an Australian-based adventure film, *The Overlanders* (Watt, 1946). Like these films, *The Life and Adventures of Nicholas Nickleby* was a product of this context of experimentation with a range of different categories of film, and was also Ealing's first and only attempt to adapt a work of classic literature.

Ealing began to develop the *Nicholas Nickleby* project around May 1944. At that time, Cavalcanti was probably involved in the project as a producer, rather than as a director. However, sometime in early 1945, the project was shelved because its principal actor, Derek Bond, was conscripted into the Army.[55] Cavalcanti then went on to direct *Champagne Charlie* and *Dead of Night*, and also carried out other production duties at Ealing. Sometime after the completion of *Dead of Night*, he also travelled to Germany to supervise location-shooting for *The Captive Heart* (Dearden, 1946). Production work on *The Life and Adventures of Nicholas Nickleby* recommenced in summer 1946, with Cavalcanti now established as the film's director, and, after a prolonged and much-delayed period of development, the finished film was finally premièred in March 1947.

The plot of *The Life and Adventures of Nicholas Nickleby* largely follows that of the novel. Ralph Nickleby (Cedric Hardwicke) is informed of his brother's death, and that his brother's wife, son and daughter will shortly approach him seeking assistance. He agrees to help, establishing the son, Nicholas (Derek Bond), as a schoolmaster at Dotheboys Hall, a decrepit school in Yorkshire run by the vulgar Wackford Squeers, and the daughter Kate (Sally Ann Howes), as a seamstress working in the sweatshop run by the exploitative Mantalinis. However, it soon becomes clear to Nicholas and Kate that Ralph is more interested in exploiting them than in helping them.

After confronting Squeers (Alfred Drayton) over his abuse of the children at Dotheboys Hall, Nicholas flees with the brutalised Smike (Aubrey Woods) and tries to find work elsewhere. The family's fortune suffers a further decline when Nicholas, attempting to defend Kate against her uncle's attempt to exploit her for his own purposes, foils an important business deal organised by Ralph. Eventually, however, Nicholas finds employment with the benevolent Cheeryble twins (both played by James Hayter), and the family move to an idyllic cottage at Bow. Meanwhile, Ralph discovers that Smike is actually his illegitimate and abandoned son. When Smike dies, Ralph is betrayed to the police by his manservant, Newman Noggs (Bernard Miles), and, when he finds that he cannot escape, commits suicide by hanging himself.

In contrast to *Champagne Charlie*, contemporary reviews of *The Life and Adventures of Nicholas Nickleby* were not, on the whole, particularly favourable. The *Motion Picture Herald* found the film "long-winded", and other trade papers adopted a similar point of view.[56] *The Life and Adventures of Nicholas Nickleby* also suffered through comparison at the time with two more successful Dickens adaptations: *Great Expectations* (David Lean, 1946) and *Oliver Twist* (1948). Since then, most critical commentators have taken a generally negative view of *The Life and Adventures of Nicholas Nickleby*. Barr has argued that it did not "come off",[57] whilst George Perry has claimed that it "presents a bewildering parade of minor characters throughout its meandering length".[58] As with *Champagne Charlie*, *The Life and Adventures of Nicholas Nickleby* has also been accused of lacking critical substance. Harper, for example, argues that the film erases many of those aspects of the novel which emphasise class distinction and inequality, and that, in doing so, it ushers in a "celebration of a middle class".[59]

Such criticisms appear more justified in relation to *The Life and Adventures of Nicholas Nickleby* than to *Champagne Charlie*, and the former film rarely, if ever, takes up the subversive stance which is characteristic of the latter. The claim that *The Life and Adventures of Nicholas Nickleby* lacks much critical depth is also borne out by Cavalcanti's own recollections that he and his colleagues at Ealing felt the film should "come out of the tawdry and poor atmosphere of the general book as a relief to the public".[60]

As has already been argued, an important feature of Cavalcanti's work, and one successfully realised in the opening sections of both *Went the Day Well?* and *Champagne Charlie*, is the way in which his films explore the relationship between character and environment. However, Cavalcanti was unable to achieve similar success in *The Life and Adventures of Nicholas Nickleby*, and was ultimately unable fruitfully to combine his own naturalist inclinations with Dickens' emphasis on sentiment and picaresque caricature. In addition, although Cavalcanti attempted to inject a realist dimension into the film by, for example, modelling the set of Dotheboys Hall on the Yorkshire school which Dickens had originally used as the model for his novel, and by taking considerable care to guarantee the period authenticity of the costumes worn in the film, these attempts at realism are ultimately frustrated by the film's reliance on somewhat one-dimensional characterisation.

Nicholas Nickleby also contains few of the characteristic visual and stylistic features commonly found in Cavalcanti's films. One scene in the film which does reveal such concerns, however, and which deserves particular attention here is the penultimate one, in which Ralph Nickleby commits suicide. The sequence begins when Ralph returns home after witnessing the death of his son Smike, and after being reported to the police by his manservant Noggs. As Nickleby returns home, a storm breaks, with thunder and lightning. The lighting effects emphasise encroaching shadow, with Nickleby framed by darkness. As the police arrive and Nickleby realises he cannot escape, the disembodied voice of Noggs is heard, repeating an earlier denunciation of Nickleby: "I've seen the boy, Smike, the very image of his mother, of your wife. Ha, ha, ha. They'll transport you for that. Ha Ha ha. It doesn't matter what you do, you can't save yourself. You're too late". As the police enter the house, Nickleby slowly mounts the stairs, still pursued by Noggs' denunciations. Finally, he locks himself into a room near the top of the house, and hangs himself. As the policemen break into the death chamber, the camera pans across the room, fixing on the twitching hanging rope, before panning out through a window. Nickleby's body remains unseen, and the final images of the scene are of grey, stormy skies.

Cavalcanti claimed that, in adapting *The Life and Adventures of Nicholas Nickleby*, he was chiefly concerned "to give the style and to try to grasp what the author wanted".[61] However, those parts of the film which work best – those scenes set in Dotheboys Hall, and the suicide of Ralph – can be distinguished from the remainder of the film in that they do, in fact, draw on, and engage with, Cavalcanti's own characteristic authorial concerns. For example, the execution of the suicide scene is considerably different from the approach adopted by Dickens in the novel. In the novel, Ralph Nickleby rails theatrically against his approaching fate, shaking his fist defiantly at the "dark and threatening" sky and cursing the world around him: "No bell or book for me; throw me on a dunghill, and let me rot there to infect the air!". The novel then cuts to a group of men gathered on the pavement outside Nickleby's house. They enter the house and find the body, and the scene finishes with a final melodramatic flourish:

> He had torn a rope from one of the old trunks and hanged himself on an iron hook immediately below the trap-door in the ceiling – in the very place to which the eyes of his son, a lonely, desolate, little creature, had so often been directed in childish terror, fourteen years before.[62]

Cavalcanti dispenses with the more verbose and melodramatic aspects of these scenes, and replaces them with an Expressionist and, to some degree, reflexive use of sound, music, language and imagery, which both evoke an atmosphere of brooding menace, and are substantially different from the style and spirit of the original novel. The suicide scene in Cavalcanti's film is a *tour de force* of filmmaking, and any denunciation of the film as a whole must take into account the fact that it is only really here, in a sequence of considerable aesthetic quality, that Cavalcanti's authorial presence emerges from what is, otherwise, an unremarkable film. Furthermore, Cavalcanti should not be held too culpable for the fact that *The Life and Adventures of Nicholas Nickleby* was ultimately so disappointing. Cavalcanti made it clear that he did not particularly want to direct the film, and that he also disliked Dickens' work in general:

> [F]urthermore I personally don't have the admiration that you English-speaking people have toward Dickens. I think of another writer of his century who was born almost at the same time, with about ten years difference; Balzac is a far greater writer than Dickens, much more human and much more socially important, because Balzac's work covers all strata of society in France from the workers to the aristocracy, and it is a much more complete work. I object in Dickens to many things, especially the sentimentality. That perhaps was a help to me, because I had great detachment in trying to capture what I thought was his style and the atmosphere of his books.[63]

As has already been mentioned, Cavalcanti was strongly influenced by the French realist tradition founded on the work of writers such as Balzac, Flaubert and Zola, and it is not surprising that he should compare Dickens unfavourably to Balzac. It is also significant that Cavalcanti should point to that feature which was central to Balzac's writing: his attempt to cover "all strata of society in France from the workers to the aristocracy".

However, Cavalcanti's enthusiastic endorsement of Balzacian realism is at odds with the fact that he himself never made what could be described as a Balzacian film, one which attempted to cover "all strata of society". The realism found in Cavalcanti's films is far more impressionistic, and far less systematic, than that found in the novels of Balzac, and, in this respect, Cavalcanti can also be differentiated from a filmmaker such as Jean Renoir who, although influenced by the same French realist tradition, did make filmic versions of the Balzacian *chronique*, with works such as *Le Crime du Monsieur Lange* (*The Crime of Monsieur Lange*, 1935), *La Grande illusion* (1937) and *La Règle du jeu* (*The Rules of the Game*, 1939). Cavalcanti's endorsement of Balzacian realism must therefore be seen more as a reflection of his lack of sympathy with Dickens than as a positive endorsement of this approach to filmmaking, and he himself is more closely related to the naturalist, rather than realist, tradition.

When he was eventually offered the responsibility of directing *The Life and Adventures of Nicholas Nickleby*, Cavalcanti accepted because he was desperate to direct, and wanted to get behind a camera.[64] However, rather than merely accept the project which he had first worked on in 1944, he suggested that radical modifications should now be made to it. In effect, Cavalcanti proposed that *The Life and Adventures of Nicholas Nickleby* project be abandoned and replaced by another Dickens project to be called *The Green Chair*, a portmanteau film which would be modelled on *Dead of Night*, the episodic film which he had part-directed in 1945:

> I wanted to replace *Nicholas Nickleby* with another Dickens subject. I wanted to make a film called *The Green Chair* which would be played by any old important actor easy to find, because there are lots of old actors in England playing Dickens, with his chair, doing these lectures he did at the end of his life, reading dramatic scenes from *David Copperfield*, and other novels. I wanted to do a film like *Dead of Night* (with little sections) having Dickens in his chair doing a commentary and introducing each piece, but Mick of course wouldn't spend that money. He had the film [ready to be] made; he insisted as my producer that I did it.[65]

Although *The Green Chair* never saw the light of day, one can imagine what it might have been like. Following on from the generally dark obsessions of *Dead of Night*, one can imagine a film quite unlike the "sunny" *The Life and Adventures of Nicholas Nickleby*,[66] which would contain an interpretation of Dickens which shared the same degree of careful compositional attention and visual and dramatic potency as the Ralph Nickleby suicide scene. The episodic nature of *The*

Green Chair would also have suited Cavalcanti's preferred indeterminate and episodic approach to narrative and plot construction far more than the digressive linearity of *The Life and Adventures of Nicholas Nickleby*, and the stress on heightened, hysterical states of subjectivity in "The Ventriloquist's Dummy" sequence in *Dead of Night* also suggests that Cavalcanti might have adopted a similar emphasis in *The Green Chair*. Unfortunately, Cavalcanti's aspirations were – and not for the first time at Ealing – to be frustrated, and *The Life and Adventures of Nicholas Nickleby* was the less than satisfying outcome.

Dead of Night (1945)

The origins of *Dead of Night* lie within the same context of a need to experiment with different film forms which led to the production of the later *The Life and Adventures of Nicholas Nickleby* at Ealing. The initial idea for the film was developed by Sidney Cole and Charles Frend, who conceived it as "an anthology film on the works of writer MR James, ghost stories which were very chilling and frightening".[67] Frend and Cole worked on the James stories for a while, but eventually decided that they could not be used because they were not sufficiently "visual".[68] Shortly after this, Frend left the project to direct *Johnny Frenchman* (1945) and responsibility for its further development passed into the hands of two associate producers, Cole and John Croydon. After this, the project was then discussed in depth at Ealing, and Cole recalls that it "involved practically the entire studio".[69] He also recalls that the film was made by two parallel teams, and that there was "a kind of friendly rivalry between the two units".[70] The constitution of these two teams can be deduced from information available on those involved in making the film.[71] One consisted of Basil Dearden, Charles Crichton, and the actors Basil Radford, Naunton Wayne, Antony Baird and Judy Kelly; the other consisted of Cavalcanti, Hamer, and the actors Googie Withers, Ralph Michael, Sally Ann Howes and Michael Redgrave. Friendly rivalry there may have been, but, given the superiority of talent in the latter team, this was a contest which could only ever have had one winner.

    Dead of Night consists of five relatively autonomous episodes, all of which are connected by a linking narrative. The linking story was directed by Basil Dearden, who also directed the first episode, "The Hearse Driver". The second episode, "The Christmas Party", was directed by Cavalcanti, and the third, "The Haunted Mirror", by Robert Hamer. The fourth episode, "The Golfing Story", was directed by Charles Crichton, and the final episode, "The Ventriloquist's Dummy", by Cavalcanti. Each of the episodes features one major actor or actress, aided by a relatively small number of supporting players. The principal actor in the linking narrative is Mervyn Johns, who plays the role of the architect Walter Craig. In "The Hearse Driver", Antony Baird plays the role of the injured racing car driver Hugh, and Sally Ann Howes plays the leading role of Sally O'Hara in "The Christmas Party". Googie

Withers plays the leading role of Joan in "The Haunted Mirror", and Michael Redgrave that of Maxwell Frere in "The Ventriloquist's Dummy".

The narrative structure of *Dead of Night* is elliptical in nature, and probably the most convoluted of any Ealing film. The film begins as the architect Walter Craig arrives at Pilgrim's Farm, having been commissioned by the farm's owner, Eliot Foley, to draw up plans for some building work there. For some time previous to this, Craig had been troubled by a recurring dream, and, as he enters the farmhouse, he is shocked to discover that both the house and its occupants correspond exactly with the contents of his dream. Craig explains this to the other characters in the house: Mr and Mrs Foley, Hugh, Joan, Sally and Dr Van Straaten, and all (with the exception of Van Straaten) are inclined to believe his story to be true. Van Straaten, a psychologist, attempts to provide a rational refutation of Craig's experience, but the others insist on its credibility, and go on to recount their own experience of inexplicable and mysterious events. At this point, the linking narrative is left behind as the first episode, "The Hearse Driver", opens.

The first to speak is the racing car driver, Hugh. In his dream, Hugh has had a motoring accident, and is recovering in hospital. One night, he becomes aware that the time registered on his bedside clock has inexplicably changed from ten o'clock in the evening to 4.15 in the afternoon. He rises from the bed and, on opening the curtains in his room, discovers that it is broad daylight. Parked on the road immediately outside his room is a horse-drawn hearse, whose driver then addresses him, informing him that there is "just room for one inside, sir". Sometime later, when Hugh has left the hospital, and is waiting for a bus, he is asked if he knows what the time is. Hugh replies that it is 4.15. When the bus arrives, Hugh notices that the conductor is the same person as the driver of the hearse. As the conductor informs him that there is "just room for one inside, sir", Hugh steps back in shock. The bus pulls away, but is soon involved in a horrific accident.

After Hugh's story, the film briefly returns to the linking narrative, where Van Straaten attempts to explain Hugh's uncanny experience of premonition. Sally then recounts her own experience of encountering the uncanny. During a Christmas party at a friend's house, she takes part in a game of hide and seek. She hides in the attic, where she encounters a small boy who is weeping. He tells her that his half-sister has been bullying him. She comforts him, then returns downstairs. Earlier, she had been told that, in 1860, a young boy had been murdered in the house by his sister. Later, she realises that the boy she had encountered was, in fact, the murdered child.

The film then returns briefly to the linking narrative, where Van Straaten again attempts to explain Sally's account of encountering the supernatural. Joan then tells her story and the film moves from the linking narrative into "The Haunted Mirror" episode. Joan has bought her fiancé Peter an ornate Victorian mirror which, unknown to her, was once owned by a man who murdered his wife in a fit of jealous rage before committing suicide. Peter begins to see the room of the killer reflected in the mirror and becomes gradually unhinged by this experience. He confides in Joan, but she cannot understand. Eventually she discovers the truth about the mirror and, when Peter tries to strangle her in a fit of jealousy, she destroys the mirror and breaks its hold over him.

The film then returns once again to the linking narrative, in which, following Joan's story, the mood has become much more sombre. Craig tells the others that he believes his dream was given to him as a warning that "something horrible" was about to happen. As he attempts to leave, he is dissuaded by Eliot Foley, who then recounts his own whimsical encounter with the supernatural. The film then enters the episode of "The Golfing Story", in which two golfing enthusiasts come into conflict over a girl with whom they are both in love. They agree to play a game of golf to decide who should get the girl, but one of them cheats, and the loser then commits suicide by drowning himself. Afterwards the dead man returns to haunt his unscrupulous rival.

As the film returns to the linking narrative, Dr Van Straaten describes his own encounter with the occult. His experience concerns a ventriloquist called Maxwell Frere, whose mind was gradually unhinged by his malevolent dummy, Hugo. In a fit of paranoid jealousy, Frere shoots a fellow ventriloquist, Sylvester Kee, whom he believes is trying to entice Hugo away from him. Frere is imprisoned for his crime, and lapses into a severely introverted state. Hugo is then returned to Frere in prison, in an attempt to cure him. However, Frere destroys the dummy, believing that it/he intends to desert him for Kee. Finally, in the hope that he might be able to draw Frere out of his now near-catatonic condition, the prison authorities convey Kee to the prison. When Kee eventually addresses the sick man, however, Frere responds using the dummy's voice, rather than his own. He has apparently become possessed by the mannequin.

When the film returns to the linking narrative, Craig realises that the dream is about to turn into a nightmare. He becomes compelled to kill Van Straaten, and eventually does so. At this point, the linking narrative becomes increasingly connected to the previous episodes within the film. Craig is seen attacking Sally in the world of "The Christmas Party", then asking Peter, from "The Haunted Mirror" episode, if he can hide in the "room in the mirror". Craig then finds himself alongside Sylvester and Hugo in the nightclub from "The Ventriloquist's Dummy". Panicking, he runs to the centre of the stage, where the guests at the nightclub surround him and throw him into a prison cell, where a now clearly animate Hugo attempts to strangle him. The nightmare ends when, in the next scene, we see Craig waking up, and this suggests that everything in the film up to that point has merely been the content of a dream, although this is not entirely clear.

One way of interpreting *Dead of Night* is, in fact, to regard the entire film as an account of a dream. For, although we see Craig apparently waking from a dream near the end of the film, the fact that the final scenes of the film – of him approaching Pilgrim's Farm in his car – are identical to those near the beginning of the film, when the dream has already begun, suggests that both he and the entire film remain firmly within the parameters of the dream. In addition, the only way of making sense of the fact that the five autonomous episodes in the film become integrated within the linking narrative at the end of it, when it changes from a dream to a nightmare, is by interpreting the film's narrative logic as based on the incorporating, irrational logic of a dream. If this is the case, the film can best be understood as depicting Craig's recurrent dream through one of its cycles, and as ending as the next cycle is about to begin.

Another interpretation of *Dead of Night* is that the film is a dream up to the point at which Craig wakes up near the end of the film, and that, when he arrives at Pilgrim's Farm, he encounters a "real" situation which the dream has warned him is about to occur. This would echo the emphasis on foreknowledge of the future in "The Hearse Driver" episode, and is also supported by the fact that, in the linking narrative, Craig makes frequent reference to his belief that his dream has granted him forewarning of terrible events to come. However, the problem with this interpretation is that, if the dream does conclude near the end of the film, Craig must already be part of the dream at the point at which he expresses these earlier convictions. In other words, Craig's conviction that he has had a dream granting him foreknowledge of future events is actually part of another dream: that constituted by the film's overall diegetic logic. The fact that, unlike Hugh, Craig is unable to change the course of events, as though he were trapped within a nightmare which he was unable to control, also reinforces the interpretation of the film as a whole being the account of a dream.

If *Dead of Night* is structured like a dream, Cavalcanti's knowledge of Surrealism must have played a significant role in its conception and execution. Cavalcanti may have had his differences with the Surrealist movement in the 1920s, but he was also influenced by one of the central tenets of Surrealist filmmaking: that the relationship between films and dreams was a close one. He was, for example, aware of the debate over whether or not Germaine Dulac's *La Coquille et le Clergyman* (*The Seashell and the Clergyman*, 1927) had successfully reproduced the structure of dream-work, and he was also influenced by Luis Buñuel's *Un Chien andalou* (1928), which attempted to incorporate the logic of the dream into its narrative structure. In later films such as *Simão, O Caolho* (*One-Eyed Simon*, Cavalcanti, 1952) and *Song of the Sea*, Cavalcanti also employed sequences based on the structure of the dream, in which the boundaries between the real world and the dream world merge into each other.

It has been argued that the use of an episodic narrative

structure in *Dead of Night* was influenced by the appearance of similar compositional arrangements in a number of other films produced during the 1940s. These films often used multiple narrative structures to show how individuals from different walks of life became integrated into the national community during the war. The most well-known example of such a film is probably *In Which We Serve* (Noël Coward/David Lean, 1942), which tracks the separate, but parallel, exploits of individuals from working-, lower-middle and middle-class backgrounds within relatively autonomous narrative strands.[72] However, although *Dead of Night* was undoubtedly influenced by this type of multiple narrative film, it can also be distinguished from most, if not all, of the other films which can be placed within this category. Compared to these other films, *Dead of Night* is exceptionally episodic, and, unlike a film such as *In Which We Serve*, its multiple-narratives are not, in the end, subsumed within a single, clearly understandable and unified finale.

In addition to the influence of this British tradition of multiple-narrative filmmaking, the episodic nature of *Dead of Night* was influenced by Cavalcanti's knowledge of the French Impressionist tradition. Filmmakers such as Marcel L'Herbier, Abel Gance and Germaine Dulac all advocated the use of the episodic impressionistic film, and Cavalcanti's own *Nothing But the Hours* embodies such an approach.[73] The episodic nature of *Dead of Night* might have originated in developments within British filmmaking, and in what Barr has called a "communal Ealing enterprise",[74] but it was also influenced by a European avant-garde tradition of episodic filmmaking upon which Cavalcanti was able to draw here, as in many of his other films.

Unfortunately, no categorical evidence exists of the kind which "would convince a judge and jury" (as Craig complains when referring to Van Straaten's obstinate refusal to accept the veracity of his experience), which could demonstrate the precise extent of Cavalcanti's influence on the overall narrative structure of *Dead of Night*. However, it seems reasonable to assume that that influence was considerable. The plot of *Dead of Night* may have emerged as the result of collaborative discussion, but no other Ealing film matches it in its elliptical complexity, and the only other episodic film made at Ealing, *Train of Events* (Cole, 1949), was made after Cavalcanti had left, and is far less sophisticated. All of this suggests, although does not conclusively prove, that Cavalcanti's influence on this film was decisive.

"The Ventriloquist's Dummy"

"The Ventriloquist's Dummy" is probably the piece of filmmaking for which Cavalcanti is best known, and Emir Rodriguez Monegal, for one, regards it as his "masterpiece".[75] Whether or not this is the case, "The Ventriloquist's Dummy" has had a considerable influence on both film critics and filmmakers. If, as one critic has claimed, *Dead of Night* is "the most famous ghost story ever produced within British cinema",[76] "The Ventriloquist's Dummy" is, as Barr admits, "the most celebrated of the sections" in the film.[77]

Whilst the central concern of both the linking narrative and "The Hearse Driver" episode in *Dead of Night* is foreknowledge of the future, the principal consideration of "The Haunted Mirror" and "The Ventriloquist's Dummy" episodes is that of identity. Barr places far greater emphasis on "The Haunted Mirror" than on "The Ventriloquist's Dummy". According to Barr, the significance of "The Haunted Mirror" lies in the way in which it depicts aspects of experience, such as sexuality and violent emotion, which are normally expurgated from the Ealing account of the human condition. However, according to Barr, although "The Haunted Mirror" initially raises the possibility that the darker forces which exist beneath the veneer of civilised constraint may break out, and with devastating consequences, by the end of the film these darker forces are once again contained, and the status quo is restored:

> But Ealing shuts the door on them, smashes the mirror. It will not enter the dark world, the Lawrentian 'otherness', again; it accepts instead, to use the terms articulated within the film itself, *constraint* on *energy*, meaning sexuality and violence.[78]

For Barr, the importance of "The Haunted Mirror" lies in the fact that it is, in the end, a typical Ealing film, because, although it acknowledges the darker energies which cannot be accommodated within Ealing's emotionally restricted conception of human experience, it also turns away from them. In contrast, Barr regards "The Ventriloquist's Dummy" as "overrated", probably because it is not a typical Ealing film in the above sense.[79] Nevertheless, although it may be the case that "The Haunted Mirror" is important because of the extent to which it ultimately conforms to, and exemplifies, Ealing's view of the world, the importance of "The Ventriloquist's Dummy" lies in the fact that it does not. "The Ventriloquist's Dummy" enters "the dark world", and remains there.

As a whole, *Dead of Night* characteristically blurs distinctions between the normal/natural and the abnormal/supernatural, but "The Ventriloquist's Dummy" takes this tendency to an extreme, leaving these distinctions fundamentally unresolved. For example, the question of whether Hugo is an inanimate wooden dummy or a sentient animate being is never finally determined. Van Straaten tells us that Frere is "the most complete case of dual identity in the history of medical science", and that the "Hugo half of his personality" is malevolent. But the extent to which Hugo appears "to have a will of his own" makes it difficult to believe that his apparent sentience is solely the product of Frere's disturbed mind.

For example, Kee, the professional ventriloquist, cannot understand how Frere is able to make Hugo behave as though he possessed an autonomous will, and the point in the film where Hugo leaves teeth marks in Frere's hand, and then somehow manages to get into Kee's room "under his own steam", are never fully explained. At certain points in the film, Hugo comes close to explaining the nature of the relationship between himself and Frere to Kee, but Frere always prevents him, apparently terrified of the consequences should this information be divulged. As a consequence, Hugo's real nature remains a mystery, both to Kee and to the spectator.

This ambivalence over the question of Hugo's autonomous and "real" nature also extends to that of Frere's indeterminate sense of his own identity, and it is never made clear whether he is a schizophrenic, or actually possessed by Hugo in some way. Whether or not Hugo is autonomously sentient, Frere's own identity is clearly not an autonomously self-directed or self-sufficient one. On the contrary, his is a determined identity, and one whose precarious hold on sanity is contingent upon its umbilical link to Hugo. Nor, for that matter, is Frere in any sense a worthy figure. On the contrary, he is a self-obsessed neurotic who is masochistically dependent on Hugo. Hugo has the more confident and assertive personality of the two, but Hugo is also manipulative and totally bereft of moral rectitude. In terms of typical Ealing conceptions of masculinity, therefore, both Frere and Hugo are, perhaps more than any characters in any other Ealing film, fundamentally perverse figures.

What makes the relationship between Frere and Hugo particularly perverse in Balconian terms is that it is, in one sense, a sado-masochistic one. A number of critics have also suggested that it is a metaphorically homosexual relationship. For example, Monegal finds, somewhat politically incorrectly, that the film possesses "horrible overtones of homosexuality".[80] In *Um Homem e o Cinema* (*One Man and the Cinema* Cavalcanti, 1976), Cavalcanti also describes the relationship between Frere and Hugo as "a love story", and Frere does appear at times to fuss over Hugo like a possessive lover.

The relationship between Frere, Hugo and Kee could also be construed as a macabre version of the eternal triangle, complete with object of desire and competing rivals, and the film contains a number of scenes in which Kee and Frere are seen in bedrooms together, as well as one in which Kee puts both Frere and Hugo to bed. There is also a peculiar rationale built into the film which provides an explanation for Hugo's motives, and for his desire to form a new relationship with Kee. Hugo's relationship with the neurotic Frere is regressive, and, in some sense, his attempt to abandon Frere and establish a more mature relationship with the self-confident Kee seems, within the perverse logic of the film, to be almost a progressive development.

When all of this is taken into account, it becomes clear that "The Ventriloquist's Dummy", with its emphasis on mental illness, self-obsession, and implicit sado-masochism and homosexuality, is deeply subversive of Balconian mores. Furthermore, if *Champagne Charlie* could be said to undermine normal Ealing through parody, and the endorsement of a hedonistic or epicurean lifestyle, "The Ventriloquist's Dummy" could be said to undermine Balconian discourse in perhaps a more threatening way, through the representation of aspects of the human condition which simply cannot be accommodated within the world-view of "normal" Ealing.

Dead of Night has always been regarded as a film which raises important questions concerning sexual and psychological identity. For example, it has been argued that the film questions the viability of heterosexual relationships, and that it frequently places its male characters within passive or typically "feminine" roles.[81] There is much in the film to support this argument. In "The Hearse Driver" episode, for example, Hugh is rendered physically incapable by his accident, and is looked after by his nurse. Similarly, in "The Christmas Party" and "The Golfing Story" episodes, it is women, rather than men, who play a decisive role in the outcome of events, whilst the male characters appear weak or vacillating. Most strikingly, however, in both "The Haunted Mirror" and "The Ventriloquist's Dummy" episodes, male characters are depicted as weak, passive and effeminate, whilst strong female characters are prominent. In "The Haunted Mirror", the Googie Withers character appears to be far more self-confident than the Michael Relph character, whilst, in "The Ventriloquist's Dummy", where admittedly there are hardly any female characters, we do at least see one successful professional black woman.

It has been argued that these representations of "strong women and weak men"[82] in Dead of Night, together with the film's emphasis on male characters who have pronounced feminine traits, reflect "fears, anxieties and uncertainties about the role of the male in a post-war British society".[83] However, whilst this may be the case – and it is not an easy case to prove – such representations must surely also reflect the influence and inclinations of those who authored this film. The two most important episodes in Dead of Night are "The Haunted Mirror" and "The Ventriloquist's Dummy", and the fact that demasculinised men appear in both must, at least to some extent, be linked to the fact that both Hamer and Cavalcanti were homosexual. It could also be argued, given that Cavalcanti's influence on Dead of Night was so fundamental, that it would be a mistake to interpret the film entirely in terms of ideological discourses concerning "the role of the male in a post-war British society", and, consequently, that it would be a mistake to ignore the context of Cavalcanti's authorship.

Nor can Dead of Night be compared too closely with other films of the period which explore the impact of the war on understandings of masculinity. Many films made during the war period are set in all-male communities, usually within one or other of the armed services. As a result, these films inevitably, and frequently, depict relationships of activity and passivity, dominance and submission, within the intra-male relationships which they portray. There are "passive" male roles in films as diverse as In Which We Serve, San Demetrio London (Frend,

1943), *The Bells Go Down* (Dearden, 1943), *Fires Were Started* (Jennings, 1943), *Nine Men* (Watt, 1943), *The Captive Heart* and other films of the period, precisely because such films depict groups of men who are forced, through circumstance, to participate in activities normally delegated to the domestic sphere.

Dead of Night can be compared to these films to some extent, but it is also quite different from them in the extent and degree to which both it, and "The Ventriloquist's Dummy" in particular, implicitly questions heterosexual norms. It is also debatable whether *Dead of Night* can legitimately be regarded as "Ealing's attempted reconstruction of the male as a sexualised individual".[84] In fact, *Dead of Night* works against the grain of normal Ealing, and is more appropriately regarded as Cavalcanti's (and, to a lesser extent, Hamer's) reconstruction of sexualised male identity.

Charles Barr has argued that *Dead of Night* can also be grouped alongside a number of other British films which appeared around the mid-1940s which displayed "a spectacular shift...from the public sphere to the private, with a stress on vision and fantasy", and, in this respect, he compares *Dead of Night* with films such as *A Matter of Life and Death* and *Brief Encounter* (Lean, 1945).[85] However, although there are some resemblances between the three films, *Dead of Night* can also be distinguished from the other two in that the disavowal of reason which it mobilises is far more fundamental. Both the other films which Barr mentions depend on the articulation of reasoned discourses to balance their mobilisation of "vision and fantasy". However, *Dead of Night* undermines the rule of reason itself, and remains fundamentally inexplicable.

Barr is correct in identifying the presence of a critique of rationality in *Dead of Night*[86] but does not adequately address the authorial source of that critique. The irrationality at the heart of *Dead of Night* may stem from the process of social reflection in the aftermath of the war, and which, following the discovery of the Nazi death camps, led to a reappraisal of the profits and liabilities of reason. However, once again, this is a difficult argument to prove. Without discounting that argument entirely, it should nevertheless be remembered that Cavalcanti was schooled in a tradition of filmmaking which was essentially anti-rationalist, and this seems a more likely source for the irrationality which lies at the heart of *Dead of Night*, and particularly "The Ventriloquist's Dummy", than speculations concerning widespread social reaction to the "rational male control" of the imaginative life of the postwar subject.[87]

Finally, in terms of visual style, "The Ventriloquist's Dummy" broadly uses a neutral, realist style of visual composition, although some Expressionistic lighting is occasionally employed to emphasise the oddity of Hugo and Frere. Some of Cavalcanti's characteristic editing techniques can also be found in the film. As in most of his films, there is, for example, a scene in which, during a sudden act of violence – in this case when Frere slaps Hugo in the Chez Beulah nightclub – the editing becomes dramatically rapid and abrupt. The scene in which Frere shoots Kee also provides Cavalcanti with the opportunity to use special effects techniques in order to represent Kee's experience of being shot. A close-up of Kee's horrified face, eyes gaping, slowly fades into a blurred empty screen as Frere shoots. As Frere shoots again, the room around him turns darker, and the next shot, of Kee lying on the floor, slowly goes out of focus, indicating Kee's gradual loss of consciousness. This is followed by a shot of the hysterically laughing Frere spinning around in space. All this is designed to emphasise Kee's subjective experience of being shot, but it also provided Cavalcanti with the opportunity to experiment, playfully and parodically, with some special effect techniques.

Notes

1   Penelope Houston, *Went the Day Well?* (London: British Film Institute, 1992): 13.

2   Anthony Aldgate and Jeffrey Richards, *Britain Can Take It: The British Cinema in the Second World War*, second edition (Edinburgh: Edinburgh University Press, 1994): 117.

3   Houston: 16.

4   Aldgate and Richards: 117.

5   Ibid.

6   Houston: 16.

7   David Parkinson (ed), *The Graham Greene Film Reader: Mornings in the Dark* (Manchester: Carcanet, 1993): 4.

8   Ibid: 294.

9   Ibid: 344.

10   Aileen and Michael Balcon Collection, Special Collections, British Film Institute [hereafter AMBC]: F/3.

11   Houston: 24.

12   Ibid: 26.

13   Ibid: 18.

14   Michael Balcon, letter to Sidney Cole and S C Balcon, 10 August 1942. AMBC: F/7.

15   Alberto Cavalcanti, letter to Michael Balcon, 1 July 1943. AMBC: F/40.

16   Houston: 58.

17   Ibid: 53-54.

18   Ibid: 54-55.

19   Aldgate and Richards: 134-135.

20   Robert Murphy, "The Heart of Britain", in Robert Murphy (ed), *The British Cinema Book* (London: British Film Institute, 1997): 77.

21   Julian Petley, "The Lost Continent", in Charles Barr (ed), *All Our Yesterdays: 90 Years of British Cinema* (London: British Film Institute, 1986): 106.

22   Charles Drazin, *The Finest Years: British Cinema of the 1940s* (London: André Deutsch, 1998): 126.

23   Michael Balcon, *Michael Balcon presents... A Lifetime of Films* (London: Hutchinson, 1969): 140.

24   Charles Barr, *Ealing Studios*, second edition (London: Studio Vista, 1993): 31.

25   Raymond Durgnat, *A Mirror For England: British Movies from Austerity to Affluence* (London: Faber and Faber, 1970): 16.

26   Aldgate and Richards: 131.

27   Jeffrey Richards, "National Identity in British Wartime Films", in Philip M Taylor (ed), *Britain and the Cinema in the Second World War* (London: Macmillan Press, 1988): 48.

28   Robert Murphy, *Realism and Tinsel: Cinema and society in Britain 1939-48* (London: Routledge, 1989): 38.

29   Jeffrey Richards, *Films and British national identity: From Dickens to Dad's Army* (Manchester; New York: Manchester University Press, 1997): 100.

30   Houston: 35-36.

31   Drazin: 126.

32   Aldgate and Richards: 131.

33   Quoted in Houston: 54.

34   Charles Drazin, interview with Norma Boddle, London, November 1998.

35   Drazin, *The Finest Years*: 238.

36   Ibid: 129.

37   Stanley Holloway, *Wiv a Little Bit O'Luck: The Life Story of Stanley Holloway (as told to Dick Richards)* (London: Leslie Frewin, 1967): 263.

38   Anthony Flew (ed), *A Dictionary of Philosophy* (London: Pan Books in association with The Macmillan Press, 1984): 108-109.

39   Sue Harper, *Picturing the Past: The Rise and Fall of the British Costume Film* (London: British Film Institute, 1994): 111.

[40]   Drazin, *The Finest Years*: 130.

[41]   Anonymous review of Charles Drazin, *The Finest Years*, *The Guardian* 25 April 1998.

[42]   "Champagne Charlie", *Monthly Film Bulletin* 11: 129 (30 September 1944): 99.

[43]   *To-day's Cinema* 87: 7634 (22 October 1956).

[44]   *Motion Picture Herald* 19 September 1944: 2091.

[45]   Michael Balcon, "Film Comedy", in Peter Noble (ed), *British Film Yearbook 1949-50* (London: Skelton Robinson, 1950): 25.

[46]   Durgnat: 172.

[47]   Robert Murphy, "The British Film Industry: Audiences and Producers", in Taylor (ed): 40.

[48]   Murphy (1989): 202.

[49]   Ibid.

[50]   Harper: 111.

[51]   See Basil Wright, *The Long View* (London: Secker and Warburg, 1974); James Curran and Vincent Porter (eds), *British Cinema History* (London: Weidenfeld & Nicolson, 1983); Aldgate and Richards; Andrew Higson, *Waving the Flag: Constructing a National Cinema in Britain* (Oxford: Clarendon Press, 1995); Andrew Higson (ed), *Dissolving Views: Key Writings on British Cinema* (London: Cassell, 1996); Sarah Street, *British national cinema* (London; New York: Routledge, 1997); Murphy (ed).

[52]   Drazin, *The Finest Years*: 130.

[53]   Leo Braudy, *Jean Renoir: The World of His Films* (London: Robson Books, 1977): 97.

[54]   Harper: 111.

[55]   John Harrington and David Paroissien, "Alberto Cavalcanti on *Nicholas Nickleby*", *Literature/Film Quarterly* 6: 1 (winter 1978): 50.

[56]   *Motion Picture Herald* 169: 7 (15 November 1947): 3930.

[57]   Barr (1993): 66.

[58]   George Perry, *Forever Ealing: A Celebration of the Great British Film Studio* (London: Pavilion/Michael Joseph, 1981): 97.

[59]   Harper: 113.

[60]   Harrington and Paroissien: 53.

[61]   Ibid: 48.

[62]   Charles Dickens, *The Life and Adventures of Nicholas Nickleby* (Harmondsworth: Penguin Books, 1978): 906-907.

[63]   Harrington and Paroissien: 49.

[64]   Drazin, *The Finest Years*: 131.

[65]   Harrington and Paroissien: 50.

[66]   Murphy (1989): 135.

[67]   Brian McFarlane, *An Autobiography of British Cinema: as told by the filmmakers and actors who made it* (London: Methuen, 1997): 137.

[68]   Ibid.

[69]   Brian McFarlane (ed), *Sixty Voices: Celebrities Recall the Golden Age of British Cinema* (London: British Film Institute, with the assistance of Monash University, 1992): 64.

[70]   Ibid.

[71]   Charles Barr, *Ealing Studios* (London: Cameron & Tayleur, in association with David & Charles, 1977): 186-187.

[72]   Andrew Higson, "Addressing the Nation: Five Films", in Geoff Hurd (ed), *National Fictions: World War Two in British Films and Television* (London: British Film Institute, 1984): 25.

[73]   Ian Aitken, "Distraction and redemption: Kracauer, surrealism and phenomenology", *Screen* 39: 2 (summer 1998): 129.

[74]   Barr (1993): 196.

[75]   Emir Rodriguez Monegal, "Alberto Cavalcanti", *The Quarterly of Film, Radio and Television* 9: 4 (summer 1955): 350.

[76]   Peter Hutchings, *Hammer and beyond: the British horror film* (Manchester; New York: Manchester University Press, 1993): 26.

[77]   Barr (1977): 187.

[78]   Barr (1993): 57. Emphases in original.

[79]   Barr (1977): 187.

[80]   Monegal: 351.

[81]   Hutchings: 31.

[82]   Ibid.

[83]   Ibid: 34.

[84]   Ibid: 36.

[85]   Charles Barr, "Introduction: Amnesia and Schizophrenia", in Barr (ed): 16.

[86]   Ibid: 18.

[87]   Ibid.

7

They Made Me a Fugitive to *For Them That Trespass*

Michael Balcon allowed Cavalcanti to direct *They Made Me a Fugitive* (1947) in tandem with *The Life and Adventures of Nicholas Nickleby* (1947), even though he was unhappy with the arrangement and with Cavalcanti's choice of material in particular:

> Although M.E.B. [Balcon] did not consider this subject could add to Cav's prestige from the directorial point of view, he consented in view of Cav's urgent desire to accept the assignment for financial reasons.[1]

Given the critical concerns expressed over both *Went the Day Well?* (1942) and "The Ventriloquist's Dummy", Balcon may have been concerned that, with *They Made Me a Fugitive*, Cavalcanti was about to embark on yet another exercise which would reflect badly on Ealing, even though *They Made Me a Fugitive* would not actually be produced at Ealing. Balcon may also have been worried that Cavalcanti was now, and for the first time, in a position to indulge his own – and, as far as Balcon was concerned, suspect – authorial ambitions.

However, although *They Made Me a Fugitive* was produced outside Ealing and, therefore, outside the normative constraints over subject-matter which Balcon normally exercised there, it was affected by a number of other mediating factors. *They Made Me a Fugitive* was produced at the Riverside Studios in Hammersmith. Riverside, like other British film studios, experienced an unsettled history during the 1930s and 1940s. In 1935, the studios were purchased by the cinema entrepreneur Julius Hagen, who intended to use them to produce low-budget quota quickies. Hagen sold the studios to the film and stage star Jack Buchanan in January 1937, and Buchanan then presided over a regime of low-cost small-scale film production there until 1947.

Riverside Studios experienced something of a renaissance during the immediate postwar period, and a number of successful films, including Compton Bennett's award-winning *The Seventh Veil* (1945), were produced there. In addition, a number of well-known actors and actresses, including Michael Redgrave, James Mason, Ann Todd, Patricia Roc, Valerie Hobson and Flora Robson worked at Riverside during this period.[2] Although it remains unclear as to how or why Cavalcanti came to make *They Made Me a Fugitive* at Riverside Studios, he may well have been attracted by the revival of fortunes at the studio, and by its growing reputation as a centre for quality, small-budget filmmaking.

They Made Me a Fugitive was initially to have been both produced and directed by Cavalcanti, in association with the scriptwriter Noel Langley and the regular Riverside director James Carter.[3] However, in 1947, Jack Buchanan sold Riverside to Alliance Film Studios, a company with a background in quota quickie film production.[4] One consequence of this was that Cavalcanti's role as producer on *They Made Me a Fugitive* was handed over to the Managing Director of Alliance Film Studios, Nat Bronsten, "a man I hardly knew, who had been a financial agent of sorts".[5] The credits on *They Made Me a Fugitive* name Cavalcanti as director only, with Noel Langley as associate producer and screenwriter, and James Carter as executive producer. An Alliance regular, Fraser Foulsham, was credited as production manager, with Bronsten in overall charge as producer.

They Made Me a Fugitive can be grouped alongside a number of other gangster or "spiv" films produced in Britain during the late-1940s, all of which, to varying degrees, were modelled on Hollywood "hardboiled" conventions of acting, characterisation and dialogue. Films within this group included *Dancing With Crime* (John Paddy Carstairs, 1947) *It Always Rains on Sunday* (Robert Hamer, 1947), *Good-Time Girl* (David Macdonald, 1948), *Brighton Rock* (John Boulting, 1948) and *They Made Me a Fugitive*. *Dancing With Crime*, like *They Made Me a Fugitive*, was also produced by Alliance Films. Many of these films were designed with the American market in mind, and most received American distribution. *Brighton Rock*, for example, was distributed in the United States under the title of *Young Scarface*, whilst *They Made Me a Fugitive* was distributed by Warner Bros as *I Became a Criminal*.

Cavalcanti claimed that he and others working on *They Made Me a Fugitive* were unhappy about Alliance Films' take-over of Riverside: "we protested but it was in vain".[6] However, it is not entirely clear what Cavalcanti and his colleagues feared, or what, if any, impact the new management had on the progress and development of *They Made Me a Fugitive*. However, it seems highly likely, given that *Dancing With Crime* – a film deliberately designed in the "hardboiled" style – was already under production at Alliance, that Bronsten would have insisted that *They Made Me a Fugitive* adopt the same approach.

It is, unfortunately, only possible to speculate on whether the final version of *They Made Me a Fugitive* was what Cavalcanti and Langley had originally intended it to be. However, it seems unlikely that Cavalcanti would have been enthusiastically committed to the hardboiled approach, given that such an approach was so far removed from his usual stylistic and thematic concerns. The fact is, however, that *They Made Me a Fugitive* does indeed contain many "hardboiled" features and one must therefore conclude that, like *Went the Day Well?*, that film was also the product of a number of contributing and mediating factors, one of which was Alliance's commitment to make films in the style of American films such as *The Lady in the Lake* (1946). All of this throws Raymond Durgnat's contention that *They Made Me a Fugitive* is Cavalcanti's "most personal British film" into considerable question.[7]

The plot of *They Made Me a Fugitive* is centred on the relationship between Clem (Trevor Howard), a demobilised and disillusioned ex-RAF pilot, and Narcissus (Narcy) (Griffith Jones), the leader of a criminal gang dealing in stolen goods, who use the Valhalla Funeral Parlour as a front for their activities. Narcy invites Clem to join his gang because he believes that Clem's middle-class background might prove useful: "He's got class, has Clem. Not that I ain't. But Clem was born into it." Clem agrees to join the gang, but then attempts to leave when he discovers that Narcy is dealing in drugs. After a verbal confrontation with Narcy, Clem decides to stay on, even though he also suspects that his girlfriend Ellen (Eve Ashley) has begun an affair with Narcy.

Having decided that Clem can no longer be trusted, and must be disposed of, Narcy sets out to frame him. One night, whilst Clem, Narcy and Soapy (Jack McNaughton – another of the gang members) are raiding a warehouse, Narcy deliberately sets off an alarm. Then, whilst Narcy, Clem and Soapy flee the scene of the crime in a car, Narcy deliberately knocks down and kills a policeman, and then knocks Clem unconscious. Narcy and Soapy escape, but Clem is captured by the police, tried for the murder of the policeman, and sent to Dartmoor Prison for fifteen years. Whilst at Dartmoor, he is visited by Narcy's ex-girlfriend Sally (Sally Gray), who asks him for help in getting Narcy back from Ellen, with whom Narcy has started an affair. However, Clem refuses, mistrusting Sally's motives. Later, Clem escapes from Dartmoor Prison and returns to London in order to clear his name.

Back in London, Narcy, who suspects that Sally knows that he was responsible for the murder of the policeman, violently beats her up. She is then comforted by Cora (René Ray), the girlfriend of Soapy. However, Cora also has her own concerns: she is worried that Narcy might attempt to have Soapy killed because he knows the truth about the murder. Later, Soapy is pursued and killed by Narcy's associates, after Cora, having been tortured by Narcy, reveals his whereabouts. Clem is then picked up by the police, but immediately released, so that he can act as bait to trap Narcy.

The climactic scenes of the film take place on the roof of the Valhalla Funeral Parlour, and are framed against the Valhalla's towering "RIP" sign. Narcy and Clem fight on the roof until Narcy, in attempting to flee, slips and falls to his death. As he lies dying, Sally and Clem entreat him to confess, in order to clear Clem's name and save him from prison. However, Narcy refuses, telling the other two that they can "rot in hell". As the film ends, Clem prepares to go back to prison, and Sally tells him that she will wait for him. The final shot in the film is of Sally, alone, in the rainswept street.

Themes of manipulation, confinement and entrapment thread through Cavalcanti's work across films as diverse as *Rien que les heures* (*Nothing But the Hours*, 1926), *En rade* (*Stranded*, 1927), *Went the Day Well?*, "The Ventriloquist's Dummy" episode of *Dead of Night*, *They Made Me a Fugitive*, *For Them That Trespass* (1949) and *Song of the Sea*. In *Stranded*, "the son" is incapable of escaping either the cramped streets of Marseilles, or his own possessive mother. In "The Ventriloquist's Dummy", Maxwell Frere is unable to free himself from the hold which the demonic Hugo exercises over him, whilst in both *They Made Me a Fugitive* and *For Them That Trespass* the central characters are both figuratively and literally "imprisoned".

In *They Made Me a Fugitive*, Clem is first snared by his own inability to survive in an alien, peacetime environment, and then incarcerated on Dartmoor. Even after his escape, he remains bound by the need to prove his innocence, and, at the end of the film, he once again returns to prison. Cavalcanti deliberately emphasises the sense of claustrophobia which accompanies representations of entrapment in *They Made Me a Fugitive* through the construction of close, stifling sets, and through shooting from acutely low angles. For example, in the long scene set in Sally's apartment, where Sally removes lead pellets from Clem's back, Cavalcanti shoots his characters from below, and frames them against objects whose physicality appears oppressive. Clem is on the run at this point, whilst both Narcy and the police are in close proximity, and Cavalcanti's use of *mise en scène* and editing within these scenes mirrors this threatening context.

Alongside these themes of entrapment and manipulation, another thematic preoccupation found in *They Made Me a Fugitive* is that of the aberrant. For example, death and the rituals of internment, normally subjects treated with sober reverence in the British cinema of the period, are treated with distinct irreverence here. The Valhalla Funeral Parlour, within which Narcy and his gang run their illicit business, is a sham, and a cover for the buying and selling of stolen goods, including proscribed drugs. One coffin brought into the Valhalla turns out to be full of nylons and heroin, and, towards the end of the film, when Clem confronts Narcy and his gang inside the Valhalla, members of the gang hide in coffins which they refer to as "chocolate boxes".

Many of the characters in *They Made Me a Fugitive* also behave in ways which parody conventional mores. Aggie (Mary Merrall) keeps referring to her "boyfriend", even though she appears to be well into late middle age, and is described by one of the gang members as "mutton dressed as lamb". It is not simply that Aggie is an eccentric older woman here, but that the conventional order of things has, to some extent, been inverted within the world she inhabits with Narcy and the others. For example, Narcy claims that he is "helping an ex-service man" when he offers Clem a job in his gang, and defines the gang's criminal activities as "free enterprise". Narcy also appears to be able to socialise openly with other racketeers in an underworld which parallels, but is fundamentally different from, conventional society.

Personal relationships in *They Made Me a Fugitive* are also unorthodox, brittle and contingent. Ellen drops Clem for Narcy without hesitation because Narcy is more charismatic and successful. Similarly, Narcy drops Sally for Ellen when he becomes bored with her. He also beats Sally up viciously when the need arises, and has no scruples about murdering Soapy and the policeman or torturing Cora. With a few notable exceptions, the view of the human condition expressed in *They Made Me a Fugitive* is uncomfortably bleak, in which self-interest and survival of the fittest, both of which are personified in the character and behaviour of Narcy, are the dominant social and individual imperatives.

Writing about *They Made Me a Fugitive* at the time, the critic Arthur Vesselo argued that these aspects of the film amounted to "an inversion and disordering of moral values".[8] What precisely is disordered and inverted in this film is a wartime, middle-class, ideological consensus grounded in notions of duty, respectability, constraint and decency. Most gangster films construct diegetic "underworlds" which are, of necessity, the inverse of the normal world of law, order and morality which exists outside them. Nevertheless, these criminal communities are usually shown to possess their own ethical canons and codes of honour, however eccentric or subversive those might be. However, it is difficult to find any moral code in *They Made Me a Fugitive* other than perhaps that which determines the loyalty shown to Clem by Sally, and to Soapy by Cora. However, even these expressions of faithfulness are ultimately seen to be masochistic, as Soapy is doomed, and Clem jail-bound.

The most aberrant character in *They Made Me a Fugitive* is, unquestionably, Narcy. Narcy is one of the hate figures of the war period: the parasitic gangster and black marketeer who has grown rich dishonestly whilst others sacrificed their lives for their country. Cora refers to him derisively as "cheap after-the-war trash", and Inspector Rockliffe (Ballard Berkeley), the policeman charged with bringing him to justice, regards him with complete disdain. Narcy is a "spiv" – a type who began to appear in a number of films made shortly after the war – and is vain, arrogant, unscrupulous and vicious. Like other spivs, Narcy distinguishes himself from those around him through his exotic tastes in clothes and women, and, even though he comes from humble beginnings, he acknowledges nobody as his superior. Although he may not have been "born into class", he thinks he knows what it is, and is determined to be part of it.

It could be argued, however, that, in his sheer unpleasantness, Narcy can be distinguished from spivs found in similar films of the period. Scheming spivs such as Ted Purvis (Stewart Granger) in *Waterloo Road* (Sidney Gilliat, 1944), paranoid, frightened spivs such as Tommy Swann (John McCallum) in *It Always Rains on Sunday*, and neurotic, adolescent spivs such as Pinky (Richard Attenborough) in

Brighton Rock are depicted as antisocial and deviant, but they also possess some compensating, albeit highly equivocal, characteristics.

However, Narcy is unremittingly unpleasant. More than merely a "truly rotten working-class hero",[9] he is a grotesque figure. It is this which distinguishes Narcy from the typical generic spiv character of the period, and, just as, in *They Made Me a Fugitive*, Cavalcanti went further in "inverting and disordering" dominant moral values than other British "hardboiled" films of the period had done, in creating Narcy he also succeeded in transforming the generic British spiv into something much more sinister and European in origin. If Narcy cannot be associated with other British fictional figures, he can, it could be argued, be associated with characters from the French naturalist tradition, who are impelled to satisfy their will for power at all costs.

One important leitmotif which recurs in Cavalcanti's films is that of the relationship between principal male characters. In *Went the Day Well?*, it is between Wilsford and Ottler, in *Champagne Charlie* (1944) between Leybourne and Vance, and, in *The Life and Adventures of Nicholas Nickleby*, between Ralph Nickleby and his manservant Noggs. The pivotal relationship in *They Made Me a Fugitive* is between Clem and Narcy, and, whilst the female characters in the film are important, it is this relationship, rather than, for example, the more clichéd or conventional heterosexual romance between Clem and Sally, which provides the impetus for narrative and plot development. This focus on a central male-to-male relationship in Cavalcanti's films often means that his principal male characters both complement, and are in competition with, each other. Narcy, with his confidence and sense of self-preservation, embodies precisely those characteristics which the confused and increasingly drunken Clem lacks. Narcy could also be regarded as the "active" partner in this relationship, and Clem the passive, echoing the active-passive relationship between Ottler and Wilsford in *Went the Day Well?* and Kee and Frere in "The Ventriloquist's Dummy".

Whilst the centrality of male-to-male relationships is a recurrent feature in Cavalcanti's films, another common theme is that of women in the grip of, or subject to, violence and violent emotion. In some respects, the implicit sado-masochistic relationships of *Dead of Night* (1945) reappear in more overt fashion in *They Made Me a Fugitive*. For example, Sally and Cora seem resigned to humiliation and abuse. When Sally is beaten up by Narcy, Cora takes her home and cares for her. However, there is little sense that anything particularly untoward has occurred, or, for that matter, that anything can be done about it. As in a number of other films, Cavalcanti appears to be concerned here with female characters who, although they may be more moral than their male counterparts, and less obsessed with their own self-interest, also suffer as a consequence.

One scene in *They Made Me a Fugitive* which is most suffused by a covert, libidinous masochism, and the one which created most disapproval amongst critics at the time, is that in which Cora is threatened with a beating by Narcy. Sally and Cora have been abducted by Narcy, and taken to the gang's new hide-out. In a downstairs cellar, Sally stands in the background, as Jim, Narcy's brutish henchman, prepares to beat Cora with his belt. Cora's hair is dishevelled and she cowers fearfully on the stairway, her bare shoulders exposed. When she finally breaks down and reveals Soapy's whereabouts to Narcy, she becomes distraught, knowing that she has condemned her lover to death. Afterwards, when Soapy has been killed as a result of her information, she becomes hysterical, and Narcy slaps her, telling her to "shut your trap, there's a draft".

This sequence is centred on Cora's degradation, and on her submissive, but also correspondingly sexually alluring, demeanour. Indeed, Cora is made to look more beautiful here than in any other part of the film. Towards the end of this scene, Cora and Sally embrace protectively, united in their shared experience as victims of humiliation, and also in a mutual recognition that, unlike the men in the room, they alone understand the value of moral action and purpose. Given the implicit representations of sadism, masochism, power and submission in this scene, it is hardly surprising that it caused such a critical reaction at the time.

Stylistically, *They Made Me a Fugitive* makes frequent use of noirish or Expressionistic lighting and photography, but contains few of the special effect sequences which Cavalcanti normally employs in his films. One exception to this, however, occurs in the scene in which Narcy beats up Sally. The scene begins with one of Cavalcanti's recurring motifs, that of the mirror. In Cavalcanti's films, mirrors enable characters both to see themselves "as they really are", and to communicate with each other when direct exchange is inadmissible. So, for example, in this scene, Sally and Narcy address each other through their reflections in the mirror of Sally's room, rather than confront each other directly. At first, Narcy's reflection appears normal, but, after he has slapped her for the first time, it becomes inexplicably distorted, as though disclosing the underlying brutality normally masked by his handsome appearance. This shot, achieved through the use of lighting effects, is one of the most literal representations of the naturalist "inner beast" in all of Cavalcanti's films. As Narcy continues to beat Sally, Cavalcanti uses more special effect techniques. As the editing gathers pace, it builds to a crescendo in which Cavalcanti uses a shot of Narcy spinning like a top in order to emphasise the violence of his assault. It is the same type of shot used in "The Ventriloquist's Dummy", when Frere shoots Kee.

As in *The Life and Adventures of Nicholas Nickleby*, the final sequences of *They Made Me a Fugitive*, in which Clem confronts Narcy for the last time, are particularly arresting. The sequence begins by emphasising the dark, rainswept streets near the Valhalla Funeral Parlour. A series of fades and moving camerawork then drive the action on into the interior of the funeral parlour. Inside, in typical Cavalcanti fashion, the mood alternates between the deadly serious and surreal slapstick. For example, the crooks hide in empty coffins as Narcy anachronistically whistles the tune of "Silent Night". The camera also lingers teasingly on signs which contain portentous warning, such as "Death Can Come Suddenly", "Insure Against Accidents" and "Keep Death of the Road". As Clem breaks in and fights with Narcy and his gang, the film alternates between emphasising the gravity of the struggle and depicting it as a knockabout farce. The tone only becomes fully serious when Clem and Narcy fight each other on the roof of the Valhalla, and when Narcy falls to his death.

The uneven and quirky combination of surreality, psychological realism, reflexivity and generic convention in this final sequence of the film is typical of Cavalcanti's eclectic and iconoclastic approach to filmmaking. In Cavalcanti's films, parody is never far away from realism, and *They Made Me a Fugitive* embodies this dialectic between dark humour and tragedy throughout the course of its narrative. Paradoxically, this also makes the film's use of generic "hardboiled" features appear even odder and more difficult to interpret. As with *Champagne Charlie*, critical reaction to *They Made Me a Fugitive* within the trade press was generally positive. The trade considered *They Made Me a Fugitive* to have been largely successful in mimicking the Hollywood hardboiled style, whilst periodicals such as *The Cinema* acclaimed Cavalcanti's film as "full-blooded fare".[10] In adopting this attitude, the press may have been responding to the popular success of this and other similar films that year, as *They Made Me a Fugitive* was one of the top box-office successes of 1947, alongside the similarly "full-blooded" *It Always Rains on Sunday* and *Brighton Rock*.[11]

Despite this success, however, *They Made Me a Fugitive* was harshly criticised for what was seen at the time as a dubious engagement with squalid subject-matter. For example, the *Monthly Film Bulletin*, reflecting the voice of the liberal film Establishment, criticised the film for trying to "out-Hollywood Hollywood" and also objected to its "sordid sensationalism".[12] *Monthly Film Bulletin* was particularly offended by those scenes within the film which showed women being beaten up, and did not find this "enjoyable entertainment".[13] Similar sentiments were expressed by the critic Arthur Vesselo, writing in that other voice of the British film Establishment, *Sight and Sound*:

> *They Made Me a Fugitive* might have come straight out of a German studio of the 'twenties. Half-a-dozen other recent British films, superficially perhaps not quite so obviously in this class, have nevertheless an unpleasant undertone, a parade of frustrating violence, an inversion and disordering of moral values, a groping into the grimier recesses of the mind, which are unhealthy symptoms of the same kind of illness... Cavalcanti's *They Made Me a Fugitive*, a tale of sordidness, corruption and violence almost unrelieved.

> It is too easy to claim that this film is merely a copy of the American gangster-model, or that it is defectively put together. In fact, the atmosphere of London's underworld is all too plausibly conveyed (let us hope it is no more than imagination); and as for technique, the film is horrifyingly well-made.[14]

Although such criticisms of *They Made Me a Fugitive* were voiced in relation to what was then regarded in some quarters as a worrying trend within the British cinema, they were also similar to the accusations of bad taste previously levelled at both *Went the Day Well?* and "The Ventriloquist's Dummy". However, these criticisms appear to go beyond the charge of bad taste itself, and to raise the greater charge that, in films such as *They Made Me a Fugitive*, Cavalcanti had betrayed both the cause of realism, and the crusade for the quality film.

Many within the film industry, including Balcon and some within the documentary film movement, had expected Cavalcanti, with his politically correct documentary credentials, to play a major role in the attempt to build a socially responsible, realist, quality cinema in Britain. This was, in effect, why Balcon had brought him to Ealing in the first place. These critics must have felt bewildered, and even a little betrayed, by films such as *Went the Day Well?*, with its graphic descriptions of violence; *Champagne Charlie*, with its celebration of intoxication; "The Ventriloquist's Dummy", with its covert homoerotic overtones; and *They Made Me a Fugitive*, with its sadistic treatment of women and portrayal of a world on the margins of acceptable morality.

The bewilderment felt at Cavalcanti's transformation from saint to sinner appears to have come to a head over *They Made Me a Fugitive*, and was expressed at the time by, amongst others, the critic of *The Sunday Chronicle*, Paul Dehn, who protested that "Cavalcanti, one of our best directors of documentary [has] turned suddenly bacteriologist – hauling muck to the surface and smearing it, for our minute inspection, under glass".[15] *They Made Me a Fugitive* clearly bemused critics such as Dehn and Vesselo, and may also have surprised many of Cavalcanti's past and present colleagues. However, Cavalcanti himself regarded the film as one of his most important, bracketing it alongside *Went the Day Well?* as one of the films with which he was most pleased. As late as 1970, he was still trying to track down a complete copy of the negative:

> It turns up now and again on American TV. They cut out all the violence and also destroyed the negative. There's a collector somewhere who is said to have a complete copy and I'm trying to get in touch with him.[16]

Since its première *They Made Me a Fugitive* has largely been neglected by critics. One exception to this is Raymond Durgnat, who has commented on the "strange poetry distilled by its strange blend of humour, brutality and seedy studio realism",[17] and has compared the film favourably to Jules Dassin's noirish classic *Night and the City* (1950), arguing that Cavalcanti's knowledge of French poetic realism "a tradition more sensitively melancholy than American deadpan Expressionism" makes *They Made Me a Fugitive* the better film of the two:

> Faces and voices are limned with a disabused sensuality (Sally Gray's sulky lips, hurt angry eyes and husky voice) or disgust (Griffith Jones's cruel, witty, irrational malice). Trevor Howard, as a cynic fallen amongst racketeers, is caustic, explosive, reflexive as Bogart. This sleazy brew of meanness and sadism is Cavalcanti's most poetic, gloomy mood piece since his avant-garde years.[18]

Alongside its noirish qualities, most discussion of *They Made Me a Fugitive* has centred on the figure of Narcy. For example, Robert Murphy describes Narcy as "a character whose handsome, jovial exterior conceals a soul as black as soot".[19] Elsewhere, Murphy describes Narcy as one of the great villains of British cinema, and "a truly rotten working-class hero".[20]

They Made Me a Fugitive may well have suffered as a consequence of its production context, and particularly as a result of the change of ownership which took place at Riverside Studios whilst the film was in production. This may also have led to the imposition of a "hardboiled" style over what, otherwise, might have been an English work of poetic realism in the French style. This was certainly the direction which Cavalcanti took after *They Made Me a Fugitive*, with films such as *For Them That Trespass* and *O Canto do Mar* (*Song of the Sea*, 1953). Unfortunately, one can only speculate on this, as there is little evidence to clarify the situation, and scrutiny of the only available draft script fails to illuminate the matter any further. However, the draft script does reveal that, as with *Went the Day Well?*, Cavalcanti was intent on making the final version of *They Made Me a Fugitive* more ambiguous than the script had originally envisaged. One of the most surreal scenes in *They Made Me a Fugitive*, and one worthy of Buñuel, occurs when Clem stumbles into the house of a woman who asks him to kill her alcoholic husband. Clem refuses and leaves, but the woman then kills her husband herself, and pins the blame on Clem. In the script, the film ends by returning to the woman, Mrs Fenshaw (Vida Hope), and forcing her to confess to the murder, thus freeing Clem from his prison sentence. However, in the final version of the film, this conventional form of closure is avoided, as Clem returns to prison and Sally walks alone into the night.

For Them That Trespass (1949)

Unlike *They Made Me a Fugitive*, *For Them That Trespass* was made after Cavalcanti had completely severed his ties with Ealing Studios, and was produced by the Associated British Picture Corporation (ABPC) at Elstree Studios. At one level, Ealing and ABPC could hardly have been more different, and, in contrast to the "studio with the team spirit",[21] ABPC was, together with the Rank Organisation, then one of the two largest filmmaking corporations in Britain. ABPC and Elstree were also largely taken over by Warner Bros in 1946, and, from then onwards, the company developed a policy of making relatively large-budget mid-Atlantic films for both the British and American markets.[22]

Despite being produced within what eventually became known as "Britain's Hollywood", however, *For Them That Trespass* does not give the impression of being the product of an industrial studio system. In fact, Cavalcanti's choice (if that is what it was) of ABPC to make his next film turned out to be a fortunate one. When postwar film production at ABPC recommenced in 1946, the company initially concentrated on making relatively low-budget films for the home market, partly because the reconstruction of Elstree had not yet been fully completed. ABPC's first postwar film at Elstree was a routine crime film called *Man on the Run* (1949), and *For Them That Trespass*, produced the following year, was designed in much the same vein.

These modest low-budget films were designed to kick-start ABPC's and Elstree's operations back into life, and prepare the ground for more expensive productions later. As a consequence, Cavalcanti was to enjoy a degree of autonomy and licence in the making of *For Them That Trespass* that most later ABPC directors did not. For example, only a year after *For Them That Trespass* was made, ABPC embarked on its policy of making larger-budget "mid-Atlantic" films with Hollywood stars, the first of which was *The Hasty Heart* (1949), which starred Patricia Neal and Ronald Reagan.

It would appear, therefore, that Cavalcanti benefitted from making *For Them That Trespass* during the relatively brief period before ABPC's principal production strategy had been fully implemented. As a consequence, Cavalcanti may have experienced less interference in the making of this film than he had with *They Made Me a Fugitive*, and this suggests that it is *For Them That Trespass*, rather than, as Durgnat claims, *They Made Me a Fugitive*, which should be considered Cavalcanti's "most personal British film".[23] Whether or not this is the case, the fact is that *For Them That Trespass* points much more clearly towards the films which Cavalcanti would soon make in Brazil than does *They Made Me a Fugitive*.

The plot of *For Them That Trespass* is centred on three principal characters: an aspiring middle-class writer, Christopher Drew (Stephen Murray), a working class labourer, Herb Logan (Richard Todd), and Herb's girlfriend Rosie (Patricia Plunkett). Drew seeks greater experience of the life around him to provide inspiration for his writing, and, to find such inspiration, visits a poor part of London called Lenten Town, where he meets, and becomes captivated by, the effervescent Frankie (Rosalyn Boulter). However, Frankie also lives with the brutish and jealous Jim Heal (Fredrick Lawrence). One night, Jim returns home to find Drew leaving Frankie's room, and, in a fit of rage, murders Frankie. Herb, who has also been seeing Frankie, is then accused of committing the crime. Although Drew knows that Herb is innocent, he keeps this knowledge to himself because he does not want his family and friends to know that he has been associating with Frankie, and secretly visiting Lenten Town.

Herb goes on the run, but is given up to the police by Rosie, who is convinced that there is no alternative but to do so. Herb is then convicted of the murder and condemned to death. Later, his sentenced is commuted and he is sent to prison, whilst Drew goes on to establish a successful literary career which draws on his experiences in Lenten Town. When Herb is eventually released from prison after serving his time, he returns to Rosie. He then discovers Drew's identity and tries to persuade him to confess to the police. However, Drew refuses. Sometime later, Herb learns that Jim Heal is Rosie's murderer. The two men then confront each other in a railway tunnel, and, after a fight, Heal is killed by a passing train. Finally, Herb manages to trick Drew into revealing the truth about Frankie's death to the police, and the film ends with Drew facing possible imprisonment himself, whilst Herb is, at last, free to live a normal life with Rosie.

It has been argued that *For Them That Trespass* is chiefly concerned with the moral cowardice and guilt of the Drew character.[24] However, Drew is, in fact, peripheral to the central preoccupations of the film: his role as the clergyman's secretary who aspires to be a poet, and who benefits from the misfortunes of the working-class inhabitants of Lenten Town, has, to a considerable extent, the feel of a routine plot device. *For Them That Trespass* is far more concerned with the characters in Lenten Town than with Drew, and, in particular, with the relationship between Herb and Rosie. Their predicament is wholly unjust, but they bear it with loyalty to each other, and determination to persevere in the face of injustice.

As in many of his other films, Cavalcanti's interest in characters affected by powerful emotion is again apparent in *For Them That Trespass*, but here the obsessive and paranoid obsessions of "The Ventriloquist's Dummy" give way to more affirmative representations of virtues such as loyalty, love and the quest for justice. A sea change seems to have occurred here, in which *For Them That Trespass* can be distinguished from Cavalcanti's Ealing films and *They Made Me a Fugitive*, and situated alongside his later Brazilian films. It is as though Cavalcanti has voluntarily given up the role of the parodic subversive, surreptitiously undermining Balconian mores in films such as *Champagne Charlie* and *Dead of Night*, and has decided to express a more positive vision of the human condition.

One of the most striking scenes in *For Them That Trespass*

occurs when Rosie visits Herb in prison. In many ways, this scene echoes that in *They Made Me a Fugitive*, when Sally visits Clem in prison. However, the hardboiled dialogue and affected heroics which characterise the earlier film are completely abandoned here. It was Rosie who, convinced by her friends that it would be in Herb's best interests, handed him over to the police. The two meet in a park, where Herb tells Rosie how he intends to lie low until he has proved his innocence. But Rosie has already passed information about their whereabouts to the police, and, as they talk, the police arrive. When Herb realises that Rosie has betrayed him, he is overcome by feelings of anger and bitterness.

Herb uses this anger to sustain himself in prison, and when Rosie visits him there he is, at first, openly hostile to her. What happens next, however, makes it clear how different *For Them That Trespass* is from *They Made Me a Fugitive*. When Rosie tells Herb that she is sorry, and will wait for him, his defences crumble and he breaks down completely. During this extremely moving scene Cavalcanti shoots Herb and Rosie talking to each other through the mesh barrier which divides them from each other. It is the same technique as that used in *They Made Me a Fugitive*, but the effect here is far more powerful, emphasising the substantial nature of the barrier which society has placed between two individuals who are determined to remain committed to each other.

It would be tempting to argue that the theme of heterosexual romance was virtually absent from Cavalcanti's films, were it not for the persuasive portrayal of the relationship between Herb and Rosie in *For Them That Trespass*. Like Cora and Sally in *They Made Me a Fugitive*, Herb and Rosie are damaged innocents, who cling to each other in order to protect themselves against predatory outside forces. However, whereas elements of melodrama and reflexive, generic noir permeate the personal relationships in *They Made Me a Fugitive*, the relationship between Herb and Rosie in *For Them That Trespass* cannot be characterised as melodramatic. Instead, it is more properly explained by reference to notions of transcendent love and poetic innocence which can be found within the French poetic realist and Surrealist traditions.

For Them That Trespass is also characterised by a fine use of noirish cinematography and pictorial composition. In addition, although the overall style of the film is one of expressive realism, Cavalcanti introduces a number of more formally edited sequences at strategic points in the film, most of which serve to depict different forms of subjective experience. For example, near the beginning of the film, Frankie fires off a soda syphon into the face of a female rival. However, rather than show the soda hitting the woman's face, Cavalcanti shows it striking the camera lens. This is done in order to evoke, rather than merely describe, the experience of being struck in the face. Similarly, during the scene in which Rosie's friends convince her to give Herb up to the police, Cavalcanti has each of them address the camera, rather than Rosie, forcing the spectator to identify with Rosie's subject position and her turbulent emotional state.

One of the most elaborate depictions of subjective experience in *For Them That Trespass* occurs in the passage in which Jim Heal kills Frankie. As Jim begins to strangle Frankie, his image becomes increasingly blurred, and then begins to spin around. It is the same technique as that used in both *Dead of Night* and *They Made Me a Fugitive*, and, as in those other films, represents the gradual loss of consciousness. The scene ends with Jim's face superimposed over shots of railway tracks, as a train enters a tunnel, and the screen goes completely dark.

In *For Them That Trespass*, the spivvery and Americana of *They Made Me a Fugitive* have been completely abandoned, and instead replaced by a touching tale of moral courage and commitment amongst the poor. Cavalcanti returns to the French poetic naturalist tradition here, and Durgnat is correct in comparing it to the films of Marcel Carné when he argues that "[t]he film remains notable for its mood of diffuse guilt and for Cavalcanti's sense, quite worthy of Carné, of the sad poetry of squalid, smoky streets".[25] *For Them That Trespass* is a rarely seen film, and deserves to be far better known.

Unfortunately, the same cannot be said of *The First Gentleman* (1947), which Cavalcanti made between *They Made Me a Fugitive* and *For Them That Trespass*. The plot of *The First Gentleman* concerns the activities of the Prince Regent, the future George IV. However, there is little in this film which bears any relation to Cavalcanti's other films. It was adapted from a successful West End play, and is largely a vehicle for its principal stars, Cecil Parker and Jean-Pierre Aumont. Large parts of the film are taken up showing Parker, who plays the Regent, and Aumont, who plays Prince Leopold of Saxe-Coburg, cavorting around within various stately homes with other members of the aristocracy.

Despite its general lack of quality, however, *The First Gentleman* does possess some qualifying characteristics. For example, it has been argued that the film's depiction of the Regent is "pointedly irreverent",[26] and it is true that Cecil Parker plays the Regent as a conceited, arrogant oaf. The film was rather surprisingly (given that it was a Cavalcanti film) selected for a Royal Command Film Performance in 1947, when Parker's portrayal of the Regent apparently caused some offence.[27] The film also rises above its general tone of light-hearted whimsy when the much-abused Regent's wife is introduced. Disgusted by her husband's debauchery and infidelity, she designs a wax effigy of him, into which she enthusiastically sticks pins whilst cursing him: "My debauched and voluptuous swine of a husband. I bequeath you to the Jezebels that line up in Mayfair, may you burn, may you burn in the everlasting fire". She then throws the effigy into the fire, and the Regent's laughing face can be seen gradually consumed by the flames. Strong stuff for a Royal Command audience perhaps, but hardly "The Ventriloquist's Dummy", and, although such moments provide some relief from the generally vacuous tone of *The First Gentleman*, they are few and far between.

Unsurprisingly, contemporary reviews of *The First Gentleman* were mixed. For example, *To-day's Cinema* found the film to be a "first-rate production. Excellent popular entertainment", and also praised the "brilliant versatile performance" of Cecil Parker, and Cavalcanti's "fluent direction".[28] The *Monthly Film Bulletin*, which had so slated *They Made Me a Fugitive*, had no such problems with the far more innocuous *The First Gentleman*, emphasising the film's "brilliant" "reconstruction of the period", and adding that "Cavalcanti's direction makes of this film almost a window into the past".[29] However, the American *Motion Picture Herald* was less pleased with the film, finding it "slow paced, often dull, with little to recommend it to American audiences".[30] Few, if any, of the themes and stylistic characteristics common within Cavalcanti's films can be found in *The First Gentleman*, and, although it is as rarely screened as *For Them That Trespass*, it cannot be compared with that fine film.

Notes

[1]   "Notes re Cavalcanti", 24 March 1947. Aileen and Michael Balcon Collection, Special Collections, British Film Institute: F/3.

[2]   Patricia Warren, *British Film Studios: An Illustrated History* (London: B T Batsford, 1995): 95.

[3]   Alberto Cavalcanti, "O Produtor", in *Filme e Realidade* third edition (Rio de Janeiro: Editora Artenova, in collaboration with Empresa Brasileira de Filmes – Embrafilme, 1977): 85.

[4]   Warren: 95.

[5]   Cavalcanti: 85.

[6]   Ibid.

[7]   Raymond Durgnat, *A Mirror For England: British Movies from Austerity to Affluence* (London: Faber and Faber, 1970):217.

[8]   Arthur Vesselo, "The Quarter in Britain", *Sight and Sound* 16: 63 (autumn 1947): 120.

[9]   Ibid: 153.

[10]   *The Cinema* 25 June 1947.

[11]   Robert Murphy, "Riff-Raff: British Cinema and the Underworld", in Charles Barr (ed), *All Our Yesterdays: 90 Years of British Cinema* (London: British Film Institute, 1986): 298.

[12]   "They Made Me a Fugitive", *Monthly Film Bulletin* 14: 163 (31 July 1947): 95.

[13]   Ibid.

[14]   Vesselo: 120.

[15]   Robert Murphy, *Realism and Tinsel: Cinema and society in Britain 1939-48* (London: Routledge, 1989): 155.

[16]   Geoffrey Minish, "Cavalcanti in Paris", *Sight and Sound* 39: 3 (summer 1970): 135.

[17]   Durgnat: 217.

[18]   Raymond Durgnat, "Some Lines of Inquiry into Post-war British Crimes", in Robert Murphy (ed), *The British Cinema Book* (London: British Film Institute, 1997): 100.

[19]   Murphy (1986): 296-297.

[20]   Murphy (1989): 153.

[21]   Charles Barr, *Ealing Studios* (London: Cameron & Tayleur, in association with David & Charles, 1977): 6.

[22]   Warren: 74.

[23]   Durgnat (1970): 217.

[24]   Ibid: 23-24.

[25]   Ibid: 24.

[26]   Ibid: 108.

[27]   Ibid.

[28]   *To-day's Cinema* 70: 5627 (30 March 1948): 8.

[29]   "First Gentleman, The", *Monthly Film Bulletin* 15: 172 (30 April 1948): 46.

[30]   *Motion Picture Herald* 174: 8 (19 February 1949): 4506.

8

Brazil

It will only be from the base of documentary that our cinema will fulfil its role in the life of Brazil. To limit film to theatre and romance is to betray the largest of all the means of expression that we possess today for, without the cinema, a great nation cannot really exist today.[1]

But it is necessary to mention at least the manner in which a man of the cinema like Cavalcanti was treated, by a group of non-entities from a capital in the north, and which resembled the blind and gratuitous hatred found meted out to animals who are punished.[2]

The period between summer 1948 and summer 1949 was a depressing one for Cavalcanti. The problems which he had experienced over *The First Gentleman* (1947) and *For Them That Trespass* (1949) had left him uncertain about his future within the British film industry, and that sense of anxiety was further increased when, in 1949, the Rank Organisation withdrew abruptly from a project to develop a film version of Charles Morgan's novel *Sparkenbroke* (1936), which Cavalcanti had been contracted to direct.[3] Cavalcanti had already prepared the shooting script and chosen the leading actor when Rank revoked the agreement, a week before shooting was due to commence, on the grounds that the film would be "above the understanding of the public".[4]

According to Cavalcanti, "a very commercial type" within Rank, possibly the Managing Director John Davis, vetoed the project, and paid Cavalcanti off for his work on the scenario.[5] Cavalcanti was particularly upset by this because he had invested a great deal of time and energy in the project, and because he felt that the resulting film would have been one of his most important.[6] However, had he known more about John Davis' predilection for withdrawing precipitously from projects which he felt would not be commercially viable, he might not have taken the set-back as badly, or as personally, as he did.[7] Coming so soon after the problems over *The First Gentleman* and *For Them That Trespass*, however, the experience with Rank merely confirmed Cavalcanti's growing conviction that, away from the security of Ealing, life in the British film industry would, as Charles Crichton had put it, be "very much colder".[8]

In addition to these problems, the death of Cavalcanti's mother after the end of the war appears to have seriously distressed him. He had been extremely close to his mother, and had lived with her for almost all his life. After her death, and in a spirit of retreat or reclusion, he moved back to the area of Blackheath in London where he had first lived when he joined the GPO Film Unit in 1934. There he lived alone in a large Georgian house, with a parrot and a cat for company.[9] Little is known about Cavalcanti's private life during this period. He certainly travelled to Paris at one point, as Charles Hassé recalls, and Hassé also remembers him not being "very well" – whether physically or psychologically is not made clear.[10] Although evidence about his private life during this period is scarce, it seems reasonable to conclude that Cavalcanti, whose occasionally flamboyant lifestyle, volatile temper and, at that time, illegal sexuality had to a considerable extent been tempered by his mother's proximity, and that he must have felt disorientated after her death. Certainly, his homosexuality and fits of temper were soon to become an issue in Brazil in a way in which they had never been in England.

In the late summer of 1949, the Brazilian Ambassador to Britain, Francisco de Assis Chateaubriand, visited Cavalcanti at Blackheath and invited him to give a series of ten lectures on film at the Museu de Arte Contemporânea (Museum of Modern Art) in São Paulo.[11] Chateaubriand, whom Cavalcanti described as a "Charles Foster Kane" type,[12] was a high-profile cultural dignitary and entrepreneur who owned a chain of newspapers and a television station in Brazil. In addition, Chateaubriand was a philanthropist and sponsor of the arts, and was associated with the Museum of Modern Art in São Paulo. It was as a result of this connection, and the Museum's wish to develop its support for the art of cinema, that Chateaubriand sought out Cavalcanti, who was, at that time, the only Brazilian filmmaker with an international reputation.

Although at first reluctant to embark on such a long and demanding trip abroad, the failure of the *Sparkenbroke* project and absence of any suitable offers of work in England led Cavalcanti to accept Chateaubriand's invitation.[13] In addition, just before she died, his mother had expressed the wish that after her death Alberto should return to Brazil, which was, after all, "his own country".[14] In addition to providing some much-needed capital, therefore, the offer from Chateaubriand allowed Cavalcanti to respect his mother's final wishes.

Cavalcanti arrived in Brazil on 4 September 1949, and duly delivered his lectures at the Museum of Modern Art. However, just before he was due to return to England he was approached by a group of four São Paulo businessmen and theatre people, who, although possessing no knowledge or experience of film production themselves, wished to establish a film company, to be called Companhia Cinematográfica Vera Cruz. The leader of the group, Francisco Matarazzo Sobrinho, was an important figure in São Paulo, and head of Matarazzo Metalúrgica, the leading steel production company in Brazil. The three others were Franco Zampari, Adolfo Celi and Ruggero Jacobi, all of whom were associated with the Brazilian Comedy Theatre, also based in São Paulo.[15]

Sobrinho and the others wanted Cavalcanti to produce Vera Cruz's first film, which was to be directed by Celi, and then to direct another film himself. However, Cavalcanti did not feel that this commission was substantial enough to justify delaying his return to England, and suggested instead that he be appointed as overall head of film production at Vera Cruz, arguing that his expertise would be needed at that level, given the Italians' lack of background within the film industry. Sobrinho and the others may have accepted this argument, but it is more likely that they simply believed it to be in their interest to have someone with Cavalcanti's unique status, as the only internationally renowned Brazilian film director, associated with Vera Cruz. Whatever the reason, Sobrinho accepted Cavalcanti's proposal and offered him a four-year contract, to begin in January 1950. He would be Head of Production, answering only to Sobrinho, and would have a house built for him at the company's studios at São Bernardo dos Campos on the outskirts of São Paulo.[16]

Cavalcanti returned to Europe on 9 November 1949 in order to secure his affairs, sell his house in Blackheath, and close up his property in Capri. Before he left Brazil, he had drawn up a set of instructions on how he wished Vera Cruz's new studios to be equipped, and had asked Zampari and Celi to order the necessary equipment, and to organise a distribution arrangement for the company's films with Columbia Pictures. Celi had also been instructed to develop the company's first film, *Caiçara* (Adolfo Celi, 1950), on which Cavalcanti had already begun working before he left in November.[17] Whilst he was in England, Cavalcanti also recruited a number of film workers and technicians for Vera Cruz drawn from England, Denmark, Germany, France and central Europe, and, when he returned to Brazil on 4 January 1950, he brought this highly experienced and cosmopolitan team with him.

When Cavalcanti returned to Brazil at the beginning of a new decade, his hopes were high. In theory, he was in a marvellous position, able to play a principal role in the development of a revitalised Brazilian cinema, one which would be genuinely popular, but which would also attempt to depict the experience of ordinary Brazilians in a valuable and progressive way. Cavalcanti, the covert parodic subversive under Grierson and Balcon, was, for the first time in his career, and at the age of 53, now in charge of a substantial venture, with the kind of responsibilities which he had never shouldered before. Although it is true that he had substantial responsibilities at both the GPO Film Unit and Ealing, his activities at these two organisations were always circumscribed and managed, first by Grierson, then by the constraints of working within a government department, and then, finally, by Balcon. Cavalcanti's typical response to this at the time was to adopt an ironic, semi-detached posture in relation to the priorities of the organisations within which he worked. However, such a posture would not be appropriate in Brazil, now that he had accepted the mantle of leadership at Vera Cruz, and the responsibility for building a new Brazilian cinema.

This change of attitude on Cavalcanti's part also had an impact on his approach to his own filmmaking. The sexually ambivalent, parodic and sado-masochistic overtones of films such as *Dead of Night* (1945) were no longer suitable or relevant to the more socially responsible position he now held, and this led him to adopt a more realistic and socially-orientated style of filmmaking. This move towards social realism had to some extent already begun in his last British film, *For Them That Trespass*, and had always existed as an important current within his films, from *Rien que les heures* (*Nothing But the Hours*, 1926) onwards. However, it appears that Cavalcanti's adoption of a more social realist and less parodic style from 1947 to 1954 was significantly influenced by the fact that, during that period, he enjoyed a greater degree of control and authority over the films which he made than had previously been the case. It was the relative independence which Cavalcanti experienced during this period, and the increased sense of personal development which stemmed from that which led him away from parody, and towards social realism. However, despite Cavalcanti's initial aspirations for the success of Vera Cruz, the development of his own filmmaking, and the rebirth of Brazilian cinema, what appeared to be a promising situation in January 1950 soon turned out to be the reverse. As a consequence, Cavalcanti resigned from his post within the year, and Vera Cruz eventually went bankrupt.

The reasons for the rise and fall of Vera Cruz, and for Cavalcanti's failure to achieve his objectives, can be traced back to earlier developments within the Brazilian film industry. By as early as 1911, the industry was already dominated by Hollywood, and had become a "tropical appendage" of the North American market.[18] During the 1930s, the industry expanded under the influence of the sound film, which, as in other countries, stimulated the growth of indigenous genres based on pre-existing traditions of popular theatre and song. The most successful of the indigenous groups of films to emerge in Brazil during the 1930s were the *chanchada*, a genre of films modelled on American musicals and Brazilian popular and carnival songs.[19] These films were extremely popular, partly because they were genuinely entertaining, and rooted in popular culture, and partly because of the irreverent attitude which they frequently displayed towards the Brazilian Establishment. However, and partly as a consequence of the latter, the *chanchada*, which could be regarded as the first genuinely national form of Brazilian cinema to emerge from under the hegemonic sway of Hollywood, were also critically reviled by bourgeois opinion-leaders, and deemed an unsuitable foundation upon which to build a new Brazilian national cinema.[20]

During the late-1940s, a number of debates took place within Brazil concerning the future character and development of Brazilian cinema. These debates eventually crystallised around the endorsement of a model which was the exact opposite of the "vulgar" working-class *chanchada*: that of the classical Hollywood film and studio mode of production. Although this endorsement later turned out to be spectacularly misguided, it was, in many respects, an understandable position for film producers and critics in Brazil to adopt at the time. Hollywood films saturated Brazilian cinemas during the 1940s, and the native product, particularly the *chanchada*, looked markedly inferior in quality in comparison to the glossy, high-budget spectacles produced by studios such as Metro-Goldwyn-Mayer.

It was this first world model of filmmaking, together with the Hollywood studio mode of production, which Sobrinho, Zampari and the others wished to develop at Vera Cruz. However, Vera Cruz was not unique in this respect, and must be seen within the context of a number of related attempts by other Latin American countries to create national cinemas based on the Hollywood model. For example, Mexico attempted to develop a system of industrial film production in the 1930s which reached a peak in 1938 with the production of some 50 films, whilst Argentinian film production at the Sono Films Studios in Buenos Aires also reached a peak of 56 films by 1942. Prior to the founding of Vera Cruz, several attempts had also been made to establish filmmaking on the Hollywood model in Brazil, with the founding of Cinédia in 1930, Brasil Vita Filmes in 1933, and Atlântida in 1943.[21] However, what has been described as the "last and most spectacular attempt at industrialization on the Hollywood model" in Latin America was undoubtedly Vera Cruz.[22]

The expansion of the Brazilian film industry after 1945 was influenced by events which took place during the war. As in other countries involved in the conflict, Brazilian government intervention in the economy increased during this period. During the postwar period, this intervention persisted and was motivated by the perceived need to modernise Brazilian industry and society. This, in turn, established the economic and political context for the expansion and modernisation of the Brazilian film industry.[23] The endorsement of the Hollywood model in Brazil during the 1950s was, therefore, closely linked to the attempt to forge a new sense of nationhood after the Second World War, one premised upon a belief in the urgent need to modernise and industrialise the country on the American model.

The issue of "underdevelopment" was particularly important in Brazil during this period, and this was also linked to the aspirations of the Brazilian Establishment – that Brazil should become not only a major economic world power, but also an important military one.[24] One consequence of these aspirations was that, in the national elections held in 1950, President Getúlio Vargas was returned to power on a campaign supported by the military, which promoted a programme of rapid industrialisation and modernisation as the solution for the widespread poverty and unemployment which afflicted Brazil.[25]

Such views were particularly influential in São Paulo, which was then at the leading edge of this drive towards economic and industrial development. By 1940, industrial and commercial development in São Paulo was amongst the fastest in Latin America,[26] and this rapid growth led to the creation of new centres of wealth and power within the city, as well as to the rapid expansion of the professional middle classes there.[27] This, in turn, led to the appearance of new cultural institutions, such as museums, theatres and art galleries, which came into being in order to meet the needs of this expanding public. Between 1945 and 1950, for example, the city witnessed the establishment of two art museums, a prestigious theatre company, a film library, a biennial exhibition of plastic arts, and myriad concerts, lectures and expositions. Many of these new cultural initiatives were financed by Sobrinho's group, and it was Sobrinho who founded São Paulo's Museum of Modern Art, where Cavalcanti lectured in 1949. Sobrinho and Franco Zampari were also influential in founding the Brazilian Comedy Theatre, which provided many of the personnel for Vera Cruz,[28] and Vera Cruz itself was founded in 1949 in order to repeat the success of the Brazilian Comedy Theatre in the far more potentially lucrative domain of the cinema.

Vera Cruz must therefore be understood as having been fashioned in order to realise two interconnected objectives. The first of these was to establish a modern, industrial form of film production in São Paulo, whilst the second was to embody the bourgeois cultural aspirations of the Brazilian Comedy Theatre. This had three major implications for the types of film which Vera Cruz would eventually make. Firstly, in order both to cover their costs and attract the kind of bourgeois audiences which the Brazilian Comedy Theatre attracted, the films would have to be aimed at an international, rather than a Brazilian, audience. Secondly, these films would have to be made to international levels of technical quality, and would inevitably be expensive to produce. Thirdly, in order to appeal to an international audience, the films of Vera Cruz would have to present images of Brazil which would be readily understood abroad. One ironic consequence of this latter factor was that, although Vera Cruz was founded in order to "modernise" Brazilian cinema, its marketing strategy forced it to produce films which emphasised rural and traditional themes, because foreign audiences perceived Brazil as an underdeveloped country, and were more likely to respond to such representations.

It has been claimed that Cavalcanti's intention when accepting the Vera Cruz post was, in the first instance, to attempt to build a small-scale vertically integrated system of film production and distribution in Brazil. The first films were to be shot on location to save costs, and a modest amount of capital was to be invested in a stage, sound department and cutting rooms. At the same time, it is claimed, Cavalcanti envisaged that a small cinema circuit, with a cinema in each major Brazilian city, would be either purchased or built. To begin with, these cinemas would have to show a number of Hollywood films to remain solvent, but it was hoped that they would eventually be able to show an increasing number of European and Vera Cruz films. Then, as more capital became available, the company would build its own studio and establish its own distribution company.

According to this account of the situation, Cavalcanti's careful and cautious plans for Vera Cruz were then sabotaged, when, at some point, the Vera Cruz executives were persuaded by Hollywood to begin big-budget film production immediately, and to build a large, Hollywood-style studio.[29] According to this account, these events effectively undermined Cavalcanti's position at Vera Cruz and led to the company's eventual decline.

However, there are considerable problems with this account of events. As has already been argued, Vera Cruz had, from the beginning, been founded on the premise that it would engage in large-scale, not small-scale, film production, and the plans and investment for the company's studio near São Paulo were well in place before Cavalcanti arrived. The decision to make expensive films for the international market was agreed between Sobrinho, Cavalcanti and Zampari from the outset, and was based on the belief that, although those films would be too expensive for the Brazilian market, they would be cheaper to make than most European films, and therefore could carve out a reasonable share of the international market.[30] Similarly, although it is true that early Vera Cruz films such as *Caiçara* contained extensive and relatively low-cost location footage, they also contained a considerable quantity of expensively produced studio-based work, carried out to what was, in Brazilian terms, previously unknown standards of technical excellence. In addition, the decision that *Caiçara* should be the first film to be made at Vera Cruz was taken before Cavalcanti was appointed.[31]

In fact, there is no record of Cavalcanti ever claiming that the dispute which developed between him and Zampari at Vera Cruz was over the general direction of film policy. On the contrary, the problems which occurred were principally related to Cavalcanti's perception that his authority was being undermined by Zampari, and to the power struggle which then ensued between the two men. This struggle largely took place over relatively prosaic, rather than fundamental, issues. For example, Zampari refused Cavalcanti's request that Ruggero Jacobi should direct *Caiçara* because he wanted Jacobi to direct at the Brazilian Comedy Theatre instead.[32] Similarly, after *Caiçara*, Cavalcanti planned to adapt a biography of Noel Rosa, to be called *O Escravo da noite*, but this project was again frustrated by the actions of the Italians. Initially, and without consulting Cavalcanti, Zampari insisted that Adolfo Celi direct the film. However, when Cavalcanti then asked Celi to commence work, Celi refused, preferring, instead, to direct a play at the Brazilian Comedy Theatre. When Cavalcanti complained about this, his criticisms were ignored by Zampari, and the film was abandoned.[33] Cavalcanti also claimed that Zampari would routinely enter the studio when shooting was taking place in order to provoke arguments with him.[34] All of this led him to believe that those he described disparagingly as "the Italians" were deliberately trying to create a "climate of hostility" against him.[35]

It is clear therefore that, at least initially, the schism which developed between Zampari and Cavalcanti had little to do with general questions of film policy. Both agreed from the outset that Vera Cruz should make quality films for the international market. Both also probably agreed that, whilst these films would engage to some extent with critical portrayals of contemporary Brazilian society, they would also present internationally accepted, well-understood and, therefore, inevitably stereotypical depictions of Brazil. It may be that Cavalcanti would eventually have come into conflict with the executives of Vera Cruz over the issue of the critical content of the films made there, and the long drawn-out and difficult production history of *Caiçara* might indicate the early emergence of such conflicts.[36] However, Cavalcanti was dismissed before *Caiçara* was even finished.

The relationship between Cavalcanti and Zampari began to deteriorate sharply when the company itself began its slow process of gradual disintegration. Vera Cruz collapsed because its strategy for breaking into the international market was an unrealistic one, and because it made investments which it could not recover. In addition, far from encouraging Vera Cruz to succeed, as has been suggested,[37] Hollywood ensured that its demise would be inevitable by refusing to sell it film stock, and by cutting off distribution for Vera Cruz films.[38] As the crisis escalated at Vera Cruz during 1950, Zampari began to intervene more frequently in Cavalcanti's affairs. Cavalcanti interpreted this as an attack on his own authority within the company, but the increasingly frantic Zampari was probably more concerned with saving a fast-deteriorating situation.

Eventually, a complete change of policy at Vera Cruz was adopted, in which big-budget international filmmaking was abandoned, and the company instead turned to the domestic market. From that point onwards, Vera Cruz made more commercial productions, and its most successful films, such as the comedy *Esquina da Ilusão* (Ruggero Jacobi, 1952), even began to resemble the *chanchada* to which Vera Cruz films had originally been designed as an alternative.[39] It was also at this point that Zampari and Sobrinho decided to remove Cavalcanti from his post of Head of Production, and to replace him with a commercial producer, Fernando de Barros:

> They announced that my policy of production of international films was too expensive and that M. Fernando de Barros...had been engaged with the title

of Head of Production.[40]

It was essential for Vera Cruz to appoint someone able to produce films within the new policy of making cheaper production orientated towards the home market, as Cavalcanti was clearly unsuited to such a task. Fernando de Barros on the other hand, a producer of low-budget popular commercial films, fitted the bill exactly. Initially, Cavalcanti tried to work alongside de Barros, in the hope that some prestige productions could be retained. However, as Vera Cruz's economic problems worsened, the company was forced to commit itself entirely to the commercial productions which were de Barros' forte.[41]

Zampari now decided to get rid of Cavalcanti, but did not want to court controversy by publicly dismissing him, and so offered to pay the remainder of his salary over the next three years if he would agree to leave the studio and live quietly in his apartment in Rio de Janeiro.[42] However, regarding such an offer as an insult to his professional pride, Cavalcanti refused and threatened to go public over the affair. It was at this point that the relationship between Cavalcanti and Vera Cruz finally broke down, in considerable acrimony.

The bitterness which developed over the Vera Cruz affair pursued Cavalcanti from that point until he finally left Brazil in 1954. Filho claims that a "ferocious campaign" was mounted against him,[43] whilst Cavalcanti himself has spoken of individuals who pursued him with "an incredible virulence [in] a campaign of defamation".[44] One source of that campaign was the belief, held by those within Vera Cruz, that Cavalcanti intended publicly to discredit the organisation which had dismissed him. Cavalcanti denied this, claiming that he signed a document, which was also co-signed by Zampari and Sobrinho, in which all three promised to exercise discretion over the affair.[45] However, Carlos Augusto Calil has argued that it was Cavalcanti who was first to go public over the matter, and that it was only after this that Vera Cruz retaliated.[46] Cavalcanti also admitted that, as a response to what he considered to be Zampari's ongoing attempts to discredit him, he frequently took the opportunity to talk about "the affair Vera Cruz".[47] Such indiscretions, however warranted, were, when targeted at a collapsing organisation facing large financial losses, bound to raise the temperature.

The animosity between Zampari and Cavalcanti reached a peak when Zampari employed Gustavo Nonenberg, whom Cavalcanti had earlier sacked as Head of Publicity at Vera Cruz, to coordinate what Cavalcanti described as "a campaign of defamation" against him.[48] As part of this campaign, Zampari attempted to blame Cavalcanti for Vera Cruz's plight, and, although this was clearly absurd, the accusation had the extremely damaging effect of associating Cavalcanti, in the eyes of many Brazilian critics and intellectuals, with Vera Cruz's industrial failure, and with the stereotypical and superficial representations of contemporary Brazil found in some of the studio's films. This association was later to lead to strong criticism of Cavalcanti by

Glauber Rocha and other filmmakers associated with Cinema Novo.[49]

During this period, Cavalcanti's homosexuality was also used to discredit him. He had apparently been less than discreet at Vera Cruz, and Gini Brentani, the wife of Jacques Deheinzelin, the cameraman on *Terra é sempre Terra* (*The Earth Is Always the Earth*, 1951), has spoken of him having "numerous contacts with pederasts" in, or near, the studio.[50] This behaviour was later to be used against Cavalcanti in a series of extremely personal attacks, probably coordinated by Zampari and Nonenberg, some of which originated from the Brazilian political right, and some from the Catholic Church. Cavalcanti's homosexuality had rarely been an issue in England. There is evidence to suggest that it caused Grierson some alarm at the GPO Film Unit,[51] although one of Grierson's closest associates, Basil Wright, was also gay. However, there is no evidence to suggest that problems emerging around Cavalcanti's sexuality ever became an issue at Ealing. It was to be a different matter in Brazil.

In addition to criticisms levelled at his sexuality, Cavalcanti was accused of being a Communist by some within Vera Cruz, and he also claims that the "American companies" (presumably Hollywood film distribution companies) mounted a campaign against him on the same basis.[52] In addition, the charge of abandoning his country for the good life in Europe was laid against Cavalcanti. All these criticisms, when combined with those of films such as *Caiçara*, which was accused of being too lightweight and superficial,[53] seem to have built up to the point at which, according to Filho, Cavalcanti became the object of "blind and gratuitous hatred".[54]

Cavalcanti also claimed that official forces in São Paulo then made it impossible for him to find work.[55] Although it is not entirely clear to which "forces" Cavalcanti was referring here, some speculative hypotheses can be drawn which would substantiate his case. As already mentioned, São Paulo was at the forefront of industrial development in Brazil during the early 1950s. Much of this expansion was accompanied by a disregard for legal niceties, and the city was largely run by a corrupt administration under the leadership of Adhemar de Barros, who was widely regarded as a crook.[56] In addition, the Italian immigrant community played an extremely important role within the *Paulista* Establishment.[57] Given the links which Italians such as Zampari, through Sobrinho, would have had with de Barros and the ruling São Paulo élite, it is not difficult to understand how Zampari could have effectively succeeded in having Cavalcanti blacklisted within São Paulo.

Whilst this campaign of criticism against him was continuing, Cavalcanti was unexpectedly approached by the President of the Republic, Getúlio Vargas, and asked to provide recommendations for the establishment of a new Brazilian national film institute, the Instituto Nacional do Cinema (INC).[58] According to Monegal, Cavalcanti had four fundamental objectives in drawing up plans for the INC: (1) to plan the organisation of all official film activity and centralise its production; (2) to develop policy guidelines for improving Brazilian film production, distribution and exhibition; (3) to establish a national film library and future film school; and (4) to establish procedures for the official censorship of films.[59]

Unfortunately, Cavalcanti's decision to accept Vargas' commission actually led to an intensification of the campaign mounted against him. Vargas had introduced the first series of protectionist measures designed to support the Brazilian cinema in the 1930s.[60] However, these measures were highly controversial, given the extent of the dependence of the Brazilian film industry on Hollywood. Opposition to government intervention in the Brazilian film industry ran along similar lines as in England, with distributors and exhibitors opposed to the measures on the grounds that such intervention constituted unacceptable government interference in the free market. The fact that Cavalcanti had proposed such interventions in his recommendations to Vargas only increased the perception, in the eyes of some, that he harboured Communist sympathies. However, Cavalcanti's recommendations came under criticism not only from the film trade and the political Right. Ironically, some on the Left also criticised his proposals for being insufficiently radical, and for endorsing the need for a national system of censorship.

Beyond this, Cavalcanti's association with Vargas was bound to cause him problems. The Vargas regime of 1951-54 advocated the creation of centralised corporate institutions such as, for example, Petrobrás, the national petroleum company.[61] The foundation of the Brazilian national film institute was, therefore, yet another example of the regime's centralising tendencies. However, Vargas was opposed by many entrenched conservative forces in Brazil, who resented his centralising and populist approach.[62] The Vargas regime was particularly opposed to the Brazilian mayoral system, where strong, independent mayors such as de Barros ruled cities such as São Paulo. In becoming involved with the Vargas regime, therefore, Cavalcanti was unsuspectingly stepping into a powder-keg of conflicting interests, and was bound to be damaged as a result.

The problems which Cavalcanti experienced during his period in Brazil stemmed from a number of interconnected factors, the principal one of which was a misconceived attempt by a group of cultural entrepreneurs to establish an untenable system of industrial First World film production in a Third World country. As with previous attempts to develop national systems of film production in Latin America, the major Hollywood studios sought to wreck the Vera Cruz project from the outset by cutting off access to distribution outlets and by starving the company of necessary raw materials. By the time that Vera Cruz changed its production policy to one of making smaller-budget films for the home market it was already too late. In 1953, the State Bank of São Paulo suspended finance for the company, and bankruptcy followed a year later.[63]

It could be argued that Cavalcanti should not be blamed too

much for failing to realise that the strategy of international filmmaking on which he had embarked at Vera Cruz was incompatible with the prevailing economic reality. He was, after all, a film director first, producer second, and executive last. Nevertheless, it could also be argued that his responsibilities as Head of Production at Vera Cruz should have led him to become more aware than he apparently was of the serious problems which the company faced. In effect, Cavalcanti interpreted his role as Head of Production in the same terms as the duties which he had earlier carried out at the GPO Film Unit and Ealing. There, he had been mainly engaged in helping to make films, rather than in coping with strategic financial and administrative matters. At the GPO Film Unit, for example, such matters had been deliberately removed from his remit during the reorganisation of the Unit which took place during 1936, on the grounds that they were beyond him.[64] Similarly, at Ealing, it was Michael Balcon, not Cavalcanti, who took strategic decisions regarding production policy, and the fact that Cavalcanti did not have an official title of "Head of Film Production" at Ealing reflected Balcon's opinion that he did not possess the strategic skills necessary to carry out such a post.

However, Cavalcanti's position and scale of responsibilities at Vera Cruz were quite different from those with which he had coped successfully at the GPO Film Unit and Ealing. Although it could be argued that it was Zampari's, rather than Cavalcanti's, responsibility to grasp the potential problems inherent in the project which Vera Cruz had set itself, it could also be claimed that, as Head of Production, Cavalcanti also shared responsibility for the well-being and vitality of the company. Where Cavalcanti can be said to have failed substantially was in his apparent inability to manage the developing crisis at Vera Cruz, and in his failure to associate himself closely with the company's attempt to save itself. Such failure is not surprising, however, given the fact that Cavalcanti possessed neither the knowledge nor the experience necessary successfully to develop a complex industrial institution such as Vera Cruz.

Some commentators, including Cavalcanti himself, have attempted to account for the problems which Cavalcanti experienced at Vera Cruz by blaming the difficulties which arose on the malicious interference of Zampari and the other Italians.[65] The story which emerges here is one of a principled filmmaker, thwarted and frustrated by the forces of entrenched commercial philistinism. Such an account has familiar correspondences with other testimonies forwarded by members of the documentary film movement to explain the reasons for the movement's eventual decline during the 1940s.[66] However, as with these other "heroic" accounts of the documentary film movement, Cavalcanti's story is also only half of the true picture. One critic, writing about Grierson and his filmmakers during the 1930s, has described them as a set of well-meaning but bungling amateurs, unable to adapt to quickly changing circumstances, and responsible for undermining attempts made by others to establish effective systems of film production.[67] Whether or not this was the case, it was probably Zampari's view of Cavalcanti, and, whereas Cavalcanti did not seek deliberately to undermine the attempts being made to save Vera Cruz, he certainly did little which would have helped to resolve the company's problems.

One question which remains unclear is the extent to which Cavalcanti was ever genuinely committed to, or persuaded by, the Vera Cruz policy of industrial film production. At one level, it seems unlikely that he ever was. Vera Cruz was quite unlike anything he had ever experienced before, and was far more grandiose in its aspirations than Ealing Studios had ever been. Yet, Cavalcanti appears to have been persuaded by Sobrinho and Zampari's ambitious plans for Vera Cruz, claiming, for example, when talking about the need to develop a film industry in Brazil, that "it is well known that you cannot create an industry without first having factories".[68] Such claims indicate that Cavalcanti was, at least for a while, fully behind what Maria Rita Galvão has called the attempt to create a "Brazilian Hollywood" in São Paulo.[69]

The collapse of Vera Cruz was by no means inevitable. Had the company decided from the outset to build on the tradition of the *chanchada*, and to produce the kind of low-budget generic films for the home market which they began to make after 1951, with period dramas such as *Sinhá Moça* (Tom Payne, 1952) and *Nadando em Dinheiro* (Abílio Pereira de Almeida, 1953), the company's fortunes may well have been different. However, as Cavalcanti himself admitted, it was Zampari, not he, who decided on abandoning what Cavalcanti called his "policy of production of international films".[70] Cavalcanti may well have been content simply to carry on, whilst all collapsed around him.

Cavalcanti's return to Brazil turned out to be what he himself described as an "unhappy adventure".[71] In many ways, it could hardly have been otherwise. Vera Cruz was a totally impracticable operation, and the power relationships which existed within São Paulo at the time must have been a complete mystery to him. At the same time, Cavalcanti was also insufficiently aware of the cultural context developing around the cinema in Brazil at the time. He was a fish out of water, who, unfortunately for him, happened to encounter some extremely carnivorous and determined opponents.

Filme e Realidade (1952)

During 1951, and after he had been dismissed from Vera Cruz, Cavalcanti gathered together many of the papers on the cinema which he had written during his career, and began to develop them into a book, *Filme e Realidade*, which was published in 1952. The book is divided into eleven main sections, the first three of which, "Filme e Realidade", "Panorama do Cinema Brasileiro" and "O Filme Documentário", are concerned with the development of the silent cinema, the cinema in Brazil, and the documentary, respectively.

The first section of *Filme e Realidade* examines the silent cinema and the evolution of the sound film. In many respects, Cavalcanti followed the narrative structure of his 1942 *Film and Reality* here, starting with the evolution of cinematography, and going on to chart the contributions of the Lumière brothers, William Friese-Greene and Edwin S Porter. Cavalcanti's central argument in this section of the book is that film's original affinity with reality, as exemplified in the films of the Lumière brothers, and in films such as Walter Haggar's *The Life of Charles Peace* (1905), was quickly replaced by a dependency upon theatrical convention and artifice, and that "[t]he contact with reality, lost in the drama film, was [then] preserved by the documentary and the newsreel".[72] The German Expressionist cinema is criticised here because of its reliance on special effects and heightened composition, and is contrasted unfavourably with the re-emergence of realism in the Scandinavian films of Victor Sjöström, Benjamin Christensen and Gustaf Molander.

Cavalcanti goes on to claim that the importance of the Parisian avant-garde lay in its rejection of the theatrical heritage within French cinema, although he argues that, in fact, little other than this bound the avant-garde together. Turning to the emergence of the sound film, he criticises the way in which the sound film augmented the hegemony of dialogue, and the legacy of the theatre within the cinema. However, he then argues that true cinematic qualities continue to be practised within the field of documentary, and praises film such as Basil Wright's *The Song of Ceylon* (1934), Joris Ivens' *Spanish Earth* (1937) and Leni Riefenstahl's *Olympia* (1938) and *Triumph des Willens* (*Triumph of the Will*, 1934).[73] In a sub-section of "O Filme Documentário" entitled "A Contribuição Britânica", Cavalcanti discusses the role played by the British documentary film movement in the development of cinematic realism. He describes the word "documentary" as having "a taste of dust and boredom", and claims to have told Grierson that the documentary film movement should have been called the "neo-realist" school long before the postwar Italian neo-realist movement came into existence.[74] Controversially, Cavalcanti describes Grierson here as "basically a promoter [with] little impact as a director or producer", and he also describes *Drifters* (1929) as "a disappointing work when we review it today, characterised by innumerable montage fusions and undiscriminating camerawork".[75] In contrast to his depiction of Grierson, however, Cavalcanti describes the GPO Film Unit in glowing terms as "the first to show the British Isles, and the rest of the world, the landscape, people and work of this country".[76]

Cavalcanti ends his chapter on documentary by returning to the advice he gave to "young Danish directors" in 1948. He argues that "three fundamental elements" coexist within documentary: the social, the poetic, and the technical, and that these must be kept in balance in any particular film. Cavalcanti also argues that the filmmaker has a duty to experiment, and that "[w]ithout experiments, the documentary loses its value...[and]..ceases to exist".[77]

Cavalcanti sets out a realist, rather than an avant-garde, programme for filmmaking in *Filme e Realidade*. He argues that particular, rather than general, subjects should be tackled ("you can write an article about the post, but you should make a film about a letter)"; that images and sound, rather than commentary, should "tell the story"; that a narrative should be told "with clarity and simplicity"; and that "gratuitous angles", an overuse of "rapid 'montage'", "too many special effects", "excessive use of music" and "[overcharged] synchronised sound effects" should be avoided.[78] This set of guidelines matches the overall tone of *Filme e Realidade*, which is firmly located within the documentary realist tradition.

Sections 4 to 11 of *Filme e Realidade* all explore different aspects of the craft of filmmaking. In "O Produtor", Cavalcanti describes the various responsibilities of the producer, but what he recounts here is the type of intimate contact with the filmmaking project which he had experienced at Ealing, rather than the broader production responsibilities he bore at Vera Cruz. Similarly, the examples he gives of his own activities as a producer are also drawn from his experiences at Ealing, rather than at Vera Cruz. In one respect, Cavalcanti's comments here, which all refer to his British, rather than Brazilian experiences, reinforce the point made earlier in this chapter, that he did not succeed in adapting his production activities sufficiently well, or appropriately, to the new and very different environment of Vera Cruz.

Particularly significant in this section of the book is also Cavalcanti's claim that he disliked being both producer and director on the same film, as was the case, he argues, with filmmakers such as John Huston and Joseph L Mankiewicz, both of whom enjoyed a considerable degree of autonomy in the development of their own projects. In contrast to these more "modern" directors, Cavalcanti admits to "always needing a producer when I directed".[79] These comments reinforce the perception that Cavalcanti never saw himself as an "auteur" in the full, art-cinema sense of that term, and also indicates the extent to which he had been influenced by his period in the British cinema: a cinema dominated by producers such as Balcon, Korda, Rank and Filippo del Giudice. Cavalcanti's remarks also position him as, in Louis Marcorelles' words, an "old-fashioned" ("guindé")[80] filmmaker by 1952. In declaring such convictions as he does in *Filme e Realidade*, Cavalcanti was standing against the current of change which was sweeping through international cinema in the early 1950s, and which eventually brought an auteurist cinema into existence within Europe, with films such as Robert Bresson's *Journal d'un curé de campagne* (*Diary of a Country Priest*, 1950), Jean-Pierre Melville's *Les Enfants terribles* (1950) and Ingmar Bergman's *Sommaren med Monika* (*Summer with Monika*, 1953).

Cavalcanti then turns to the impact of sound on the cinema, and, as elsewhere in his writings, he again stresses the importance of non-synchronised sound, arguing that the "non-synchronised word should add ideas to the image", as in films such as *Night Mail* (1936), and not simply describe or interpret the image.[81] Commentary should also be lyrical and subjective, rather than factual, and should attempt to reproduce "the metaphoric and allusive style of the silent film",[82] whilst sound should have a degree of autonomy from the visual narrative and should "represent its own role".[83]

Although the overall position of *Filme e Realidade* is a realist one, Cavalcanti also adopts a modernist stance when discussing the relationship between sound and image. Much of the music written for the cinema is dismissed by him as "stuck in the final period of the romantics" and as "already outdated in 1895".[84] Cavalcanti relies heavily here on the ideas of his French colleague Maurice Jaubert, who worked with him on *Le Petit chaperon rouge* (*Little Red Riding Hood*, 1929) and *Au Pays du scalp* (*In the Country of the Scalp People*, 1931), who is quoted as arguing that "the musician should know the precise moment in which images escape realism and need poetic extension".[85]

Throughout this section of *Filme e Realidade*, Cavalcanti continues to stress the point that sound and music must retain their own autonomy within the overall work of the film, and this is also true of what he calls "surrounding sounds". Cavalcanti argues that surrounding sounds can be orchestrated in three ways: by creating a "perspective", by creating "dominant notes", and by using "punctuation", and he goes on to give a detailed example of this in *Night Mail*, a film which he describes as dominated by surrounding sounds:

> First of all the sound was selected for each sequence. After this the accompanying sound was constructed with the dominant notes, which are different in each section. The film begins with a spoken scene about the departure of the train, followed, as a transition, by signals, with synchronised sound. This was followed by a number of scenes which follow the train, filmed from an aeroplane, and after, scenes from the control tower, with all the characteristic sounds, seeing, at various times, the train from outside. The whistle of the train would become, many times, the dominant note in the sound track. In the scenes which we labelled 'Crew After Midnight' we used all the shouts of the porters, all the characteristic noises of the station. Following this, the sound of the train passes into our second plan, and an orchestra of surrounding sounds, punctuated by shouts, suggests the industrial regions which the train passes through. The scenes of the countryside are accompanied by the simplified rhythms of the train, this time almost imperceptible. We arrive at the climax of the film: the train receiving and unloading sacks of mail with great swiftness.

Some of the earlier whistles are repeated here,
together with the first turnings of the locomotive
wheel. Finally, after a short musical interlude, used as
an anti-climax, the train is on its way to Scotland, and
finishes with a lyrical sequence, in which the verses of
W. H. Auden follow the rhythms of the train,
producing a great dramatic effect.[86]

Filme e Realidade is an uneven book which cannot be regarded
as a major text on film history and style. Compiled and written
hurriedly, whilst Cavalcanti was waiting for film projects to emerge, it
is often rambling and repetitive. Whilst not, in itself, amounting to a
significant work on the cinema, however, it does contain within its
pages a considerable amount of information which enables a better
understanding of Cavalcanti's later filmmaking aesthetic to be reached.

The films

In addition to his first film, *Caiçara*, Cavalcanti produced three short
documentaries at Vera Cruz: *Painel* (*Painting*, Lima Barreto, 1951), a
film about the painting of a mural entitled "Tiradentes" by the
Brazilian artist Cândido Portinari; *Santuário* (*Sanctuary*, Lima Barreto,
1951), which concerns the plight of the poor in rural Brazil; and *Volta
Redonda* (John Waterhouse, 1952), about the Brazilian steel industry.
In addition to these documentaries, Cavalcanti produced *The Earth Is
Always the Earth*, and began work on a third feature, *Ângela* (Eros
Martim Gonçalves, 1951), before being dismissed from his post before
the film was completed.

During the 1950s, a number of small, independent film
production companies emerged in Brazil. These included Companhia
Maristela, Multifilmes, Kino-Films and others,[87] and Cavalcanti's first
film project after leaving Vera Cruz, *Simão, O Caolho* (*One-Eyed
Simon*, 1952), was produced by Companhia Maristela. Although *One-
Eyed Simon* was a considerable commercial success, Cavalcanti always
regarded it as a relatively unimportant work[88] and was, in fact, initially
reluctant to undertake the project at all because he was offered "the
lowest salary he had ever received in his career" to direct it.[89] However,
despite his reservations, Cavalcanti's precarious financial position left
him little choice but to accept the commission. Nevertheless, despite
Cavalcanti's negative assessment of the film, *One-Eyed Simon* is a
complex and convincing work, which Glauber Rocha even thought
superior to *O Canto do Mar* (*Song of the Sea*, 1953).[90] Although it is
difficult to agree with Rocha on this point, *One-Eyed Simon* does
deserve closer critical attention than Cavalcanti evidently felt that it
warranted.

The central character in *One-Eyed Simon* is the eponymous
Simão himself, played by the lugubrious one-eyed Mesquitinha.
Mesquitinha's performance in the film is subtle and sardonic, and it is

not difficult to understand why this accomplished comic actor was so popular at the time. His persona is that of the good natured, Chaplinesque little man, who is constantly harassed by friends, family and officials, but who nevertheless perseveres, despite suffering a succession of minor indignities. The characterisation elsewhere in the film is also sharp and effective, and draws successfully on a variety of character types taken from the tradition of the *chanchada*.

One aspect of *One-Eyed Simon* which may have impressed Rocha was the emphasis on realism within the film. Simão lives in a run-down inner-city area, and the film's cinematography, which lingers on images of shanty-like housing and children playing in the streets, is reminiscent of that found in Italian neo-realist films such as *Ladri di biciclette* (*Bicycle Thieves*, 1948). During the course of the film, issues relating to political and industrial corruption are also broached, and the impact of modernisation is depicted ambivalently and sardonically, as the film establishes an opposition between the cosy familiarity and comradeship of Simão's shanty-like neighbourhood, and the vulgar pretensions of politicians, businessmen and the bourgeoisie.

In many respects, *One-Eyed Simon*, with its anarchic comic approach, locus within the working-class community, and tendency to satirise the Brazilian Establishment, can be regarded as carrying on the *chanchada* tradition. The apparently effortless assurance which characterises the acting performances in the film indicates that all the actors, including Mesquitinha, were thoroughly comfortable and familiar with their roles, and this raises the further question of the nature and extent of Cavalcanti's contribution to this aspect of the film. *One-Eyed Simon* may well be another example, together with films such as *Dead of Night*, *Champagne Charlie* (1944) and *For Them That Trespass*, of Cavalcanti's ability to extract fine acting performances from his actors. On the other hand, it may be the case that these actors were so securely grounded in the tradition of the *chanchada* that they needed only moderate guidance from Cavalcanti in order to perform well.

One of the most impressive sequences within *One-Eyed Simon* is an extended fantasy sequence, which may also have served as a prototype for a similar, and crucial, sequence in Cavalcanti's next film, *Song of the Sea*. In this sequence, Simão falls asleep in his chicken shack, and dreams that his lost eye has suddenly materialised in order to inform him that modern science is now capable of reinstalling it back in his head. Simão then visits a rather unconvincing surgeon, one of his "amigos" in real life, who specialises in reattaching body parts. The surgeon manages to reinstall Simão's eye and provides him with a magic formula which enables him to transport himself instantaneously through space, and which also has the power to render him invisible. Armed with these powers, Simão sets out on a crusade to highlight the corruption of big business, and, after his success in this arena, he successfully challenges for the presidency of Brazil. Shortly after becoming President – and employing a bevy of beautiful models wearing swimming costumes as his Cabinet – he wakes up to find himself back in the chicken shack, resigned to his impecunious, one-eyed but comfortable existence.

As with the *chanchada* in general, the overall tone of *One-Eyed Simon* is frequently parodic and irreverent. The film also employs techniques which appear almost Brechtian in character, and Cavalcanti may have drawn on Mesquitinha's performance here when developing the later role of Puntila in his adaptation of Brecht's *Herr Puntila und sein Knecht Matti* (*Mr Puntila and His Hired Man Matti*, 1955). It is unlikely, however, that Cavalcanti consciously drew on the work of Brecht in making *One-Eyed Simon*, and the disjunctive "foregrounding" techniques which the film deploys are more properly related to the influence of Brazilian popular cultural forms, and Cavalcanti's own characteristically "jarring" approach to filmmaking. In this sense, *One-Eyed Simon* can be compared with films such as *The Big Blockade* (1942) and *Went the Day Well?* (1942), as all three films share the same lively, fractured and sometimes irrational narrative style, characterised by abrupt transitions of tone and mood.

Despite Cavalcanti's opinion to the contrary, therefore, *One-Eyed Simon* is an effective and convincing film. Cavalcanti's involvement with Maristela was also to be a far more rewarding experience than his extremely stressful involvement with Vera Cruz. The owner of Maristela, Mário Audra, was to become a lifelong friend of Cavalcanti's, and also defended him against the attacks mounted against him by Zampari and "the Italians". Writing later, in his autobiography, Audra was to compliment Cavalcanti on his "excellent work" on *One-Eyed Simon*.[91]

Whilst he was working on *One-Eyed Simon*, Cavalcanti was approached by representatives of Kino-Films, another of the companies which had emerged during the gradual collapse of Vera Cruz, and was invited to direct a film which would launch the new company. Cavalcanti accepted the commission and began work on the adaptation of a scenario which he had first begun at Vera Cruz in 1950. The resulting film, *Song of the Sea*, the first to be produced by Kino-Films, was directed and produced by Cavalcanti, who also developed the film's scenario in collaboration with the writer José Mauro Vasconcelos, and the dialogue in conjunction with the playwright Hermilo Borba Filho.

Like the earlier *Caiçara*, Cavalcanti wanted to make *Song of the Sea* in a neo-realist style, and, in order to achieve this, much of the film was shot on location in Recife, the picturesque regional capital of the north-eastern state of Pernambuco, where Cavalcanti's family originated from. This part of Brazil is dry and drinking water is scarce, and Cavalcanti drew on these features in order to emphasise the hardship experienced by the local fishermen and their families. In addition to its proximity to a poor rural hinterland, however, Recife is a coastal city, with a deep-water harbour and a major shipping port, and, as in *En rade* (*Stranded*, 1927), Cavalcanti drew on the imagery and atmosphere of the docks when making *Song of the Sea*. In order to ensure that *Song of the Sea* would have an appropriately authentic texture, Cavalcanti employed local actors, fishermen and townspeople, and was also able to obtain the services of the then-well-known Brazilian documentary cinematographer, Cyril Arapoff.[92] *Song of the Sea* is undoubtedly one of Cavalcanti's most important films, and probably the first since *Nothing But the Hours* and *Stranded* in which he was able fully to realise his intentions, unconstrained by the qualifying mediations of producers or other factors. However, in addition to its status as an authored text, *Song of the Sea* is notable because, more than any of Cavalcanti's other Brazilian works, it represented the kind of film which he hoped would form the basis of a new Brazilian film culture.

Cavalcanti based the plot of *Song of the Sea* on the plot structure of *Stranded*. In *Stranded*, a young man seeks freedom from the oppressive influence of his mother by forming a relationship with a waitress in a nearby café, and then attempting to go to sea with her. This basic scenario is retained in *Song of the Sea*. At the beginning of the film, we are introduced to the central characters: the mother Maria, and her three children, Raimundo, Ponina and Siluimo. However, whilst in *Stranded* it was only the son who sought escape from the influence of his mother, here it is both the son and daughter who seek flight. However, their quest is for deliverance not only from their mother's hold on them, but also from the searing poverty which afflicts their community.

Towards the end of the film, Raimundo attempts to leave Recife with his girlfriend Aurora on board a ship bound for the south. Maria, who is alerted by Ponina, finds the third-class passage tickets which Raimundo had purchased, and destroys them, making his and Aurora's departure impossible. In the end, however, Maria's actions prove to be unnecessary as, just prior to this, Raimundo has discovered that Aurora has already left Recife with his rival, a charismatic older man with his own financial resources. This discovery breaks Raimundo's resolve to leave, and the film ends with him walking disconsolately along the waterfront, whilst the day draws to a close.

As in *Stranded*, the son in *Song of the Sea* is also befriended by a vagabond character, who is merely described as "the idiot" in *Stranded*. However, in *Song of the Sea*, the vagabond character is José-Luiz, Raimundo's alcoholic and mentally-disturbed father. José-Luiz does not live with his family, but sleeps rough along the waterfront, having apparently been thrown out of the house by Maria. In the past, José-Luiz was the successful owner of a splendid sailing ship, the *Maria do Mar*, named after his wife. However, after a fierce storm eight years ago, in which the *Maria do Mar* was lost and José-Luiz suffered a blow to the head, he gradually declined into his present state of alcoholic regression. Towards the end of the film (and as in *Stranded*), Maria confronts José-Luiz over his involvement in Raimundo's attempted departure. In desperation, José-Luiz tries to reach the ship which he thinks his son is leaving on by rowing out to meet it in a small boat. However, as with the idiot figure in *Stranded*, he is drowned at sea.

Although *Song of the Sea* is grounded in the same plot structure and naturalist milieu as *Stranded*, it would be a mistake to regard the latter film as a "version" of the earlier, as some critics have argued,[93] and, in fact, *Song of the Sea* is very different from Cavalcanti's French film. For example, in *Song of the Sea*, it is a family, rather than a triangle of central characters, which lies at the heart of the film's concerns. In addition, that family is positioned in relation to other families within the community in which it exists, and, whilst these forms of social realist representation are important features within *Song of the Sea*, they are virtually non-existent in *Stranded*. The depiction of old Marseilles in *Stranded* also contains little information about the social context of the place, whereas, in *Song of the Sea*, Cavalcanti addresses issues such as poverty, class inequality, prostitution and infant mortality, and locates these firmly within the specific environment of Recife. In this sense, *Song of the Sea* can be defined as a work of poetic realism, whereas *Stranded* is more appropriately defined as a work of avant-garde poetic naturalism.

The relationship between mother and daughter in *Song of the Sea* also introduces a psychological dimension which is missing from *Stranded*, and which is based upon Ponina's desire for emotional and sexual independence. The first shots of Ponina show her sitting languidly on her bed, her thighs exposed, as she protests about the hardship of her life, and the effect of this on her appearance. She displays her hands to her mother, saying that they "are beautiful", and that she does not want them to become wrinkled and dry, like her mother's have become. Ponina then asks Maria if she can take some clothes she has washed to the owner, a prostitute who lives in the red-light district of Recife. Maria refuses, and warns Ponina that she is in danger of becoming "lost" – that is, falling into prostitution herself.

Later, Maria agrees to allow Ponina to take the clothes to the prostitute. In the prostitute's apartment, Ponina tries on an article of the prostitute's clothing, a black semi-transparent item of lingerie. There follows one of Cavalcanti's characteristic stylistic devices: the use of a mirror, whose principal function here is to show Ponina "as she really is". As Ponina looks at herself in the mirror, she sees a beautiful young woman, rather than a bedraggled workhorse, and the prostitute remarks that she has "a good shape". The implication here is that Ponina should make the most of her looks, and that prostitution provides a possible way out of her predicament. Ponina then breaks down in tears, complaining about the frustrations and limitations of her life at home. Later, at Ponina's request, the prostitute visits the family home, and tries to persuade Maria to allow Ponina to move in with her. Maria refuses, but Ponina's descent into prostitution continues unabated and with a sense of inevitability. Later in the film, she sells herself to a jeweller in order to obtain a necklace which she covets, and, towards the end of the film, Maria sees her at the harbour side, openly soliciting the local sailors.

The scene in which the prostitute visits Ponina's house also contains one of Cavalcanti's most recurrent stylistic characteristics: the use of rapid montage to represent acts of violence. After the prostitute has left the house, an argument ensues, and Maria slaps Ponina repeatedly, whilst rapid editing is used to reinforce the violence of the act. The scene is identical in many respects to similar scenes in *Went the Day Well?*, *Dead of Night*, *They Made Me a Fugitive* (1947) and other films in which Cavalcanti uses special effects techniques in order to raise levels of emotional intensity. What differentiates this scene from any in Cavalcanti's other films, however, is that, here, violence is meted out by one woman to another.

Unlike many of Cavalcanti's other films, female characters play a pivotal role in *Song of the Sea*, and the central character in the film is, in many respects, the mother, who is played superbly by Margarida Cardoso. Maria is a complex and ambivalent character. Carefree and vivacious in her youth, the decline in her family's fortunes and estrangement from her husband have embittered and hardened her, and Cavalcanti portrays her as both cruel and a victim of circumstances, equivocally seeking to sustain her family in the face of poverty, illness and bereavement, whilst also determinedly resisting her children's attempts to better themselves.

Maria's ambivalent character is most clearly illustrated by her relationship to her husband José-Luiz. Raimundo still loves and respects José-Luiz, and regularly brings him the alcohol he craves. However, Maria is jealous of this relationship, and seeks to replace José-Luiz in Raimundo's affections. In one scene, Maria takes José-Luiz to the local asylum, and seeks to have him incarcerated there. José-Luiz panics as the gates are closed behind him, but is overpowered by the hospital attendants and led inside. Later, Maria is called to the hospital and told that the care of José Luiz is her responsibility, and not the hospital's. Reluctantly, she leaves the hospital with José-Luiz, and outside the hospital gates tells him to return home to eat. However, her tone is harsh, and she eventually walks away from the frightened José-Luiz, leaving him alone once again.

Maria may also be indirectly responsible for the death of her husband. When she confronts José-Luiz on the harbourside over his role in Raimundo's attempted departure, Maria appears to tell José-Luiz that Raimundo is leaving on a ship sailing out of the harbour, even though she knows this not to be the case. She gestures forcibly towards the ship, shouting, "Raimundo is leaving on that ship". At this point, Maria believes that the two tickets she has found in Raimundo's belongings were for Raimundo and José-Luiz, not Raimundo and Aurora. In a fit of rage, she tears up what she thinks is José-Luiz's ticket in front of him, and throws it into the sea. It is Maria's assertion, one that she knows to be untrue, that Raimundo is on board the ship, which leads José-Luiz to attempt to catch up with the ship in a small boat, an attempt which eventually ends in his death.

Cavalcanti's treatment of Maria's character in *Song of the Sea* can be understood if reference is made to the French poetic naturalist tradition. Here, characters are moulded by the oppressive environment within which they find themselves, and this can also lead them to take on the attributes of that environment. In *Song of the Sea*, Maria's cruelty is a reflex of the severity inherent in the environment around her, rather than something which stems from within her own nature, and, in Maria, Cavalcanti has created another of those harsh, ambiguous figures which people his films. Like Narcy in *They Made Me a Fugitive*, Wilsford in *Went the Day Well?*, Ralph Nickleby in *The Life and Adventures of Nicholas Nickleby* (1947), and, to a lesser extent, Hugo/Frere in *Dead of Night*, Maria is not fully explainable in terms of models of psychological realism, but is an embodiment, and product, of a perverse, fractured or brutish social context.

One of the most significant episodes in *Song of the Sea* concerns the death of the youngest child, Siluimo, and the degree of pathos generated by this event marks *Song of the Sea* as quite distinct from the more disinterested avant-garde naturalism of *Stranded*, and from the majority of Cavalcanti's British films. Siluimo becomes ill and dies within a very short space of time. Later, as the body of the dead child is laid out on the table and ritually washed, the room fills with neighbours who have brought lamps to illuminate his journey to the afterlife. As the rituals of purification and farewell are performed, the mother looks on quietly and unemotionally, although it is clear that she is deeply affected by the degree of tragedy with which she and the other women present are only too familiar. This scene is striking not only for its classically-composed photography, but also for its effective social and psychological realism, and for the images of Maria's lined face, twisted in grief and anguish. As Maria dictates the letter which will accompany Siluimo's spirit beyond the grave, she also writes, in total seriousness, that she "hopes he is happier with you [God] than he ever was with me".

Despite the psychological realism contained in these scenes, however, the overall diegesis of *Song of the Sea* is based not on the pictorial and narrative conventions of psychological realism, but on those of poetic naturalism. Cavalcanti describes a predestined world here, in which providence does not exist, and in which an often ethically dubious self-interested search for freedom is continuously thwarted by ill luck and misfortune. One example of this is José-Luiz's death, which comes about as a result of something as banal as Maria's misunderstanding over whom Raimundo had bought the boat tickets for. Raimundo's need for personal fulfilment also appears to transcend any sense of filial loyalty he might possess. Not only is he prepared to deceive, and leave, his mother, but he is also prepared to abandon the father who is both devoted to him, and attendant on him.

In the same way, Aurora's decision to desert Raimundo also appears callous. However, Aurora has been hardened by the abuse and innuendo she has had to suffer from the men who frequent her stepfather's bar where she works, and she has also been badly affected by her mother's second marriage to her overbearing stepfather. Her decision to accept the overtures of the truck driver, who offers her the prospect of a new life, is consequently borne out of necessity rather than impulse. Like Maria, Aurora has been shaped by her environment, and is similarly depicted as exploited and exploitative. To compensate for her own sense of entrapment, she keeps a room full of caged birds. When she leaves, she opens the cages and lets the birds go free, and, when her mother discovers her departure, she asserts that, in giving the birds their freedom, "she [Aurora] has done one good thing at last".

Song of the Sea is shot in an imposing realist manner, and uses imagery which is frequently highly composed. The impressive aesthetic quality of the photography and editing in the film is also reinforced by its pace and atmosphere, which is generally slow and lyrical in tempo and tone. In addition, little real plot development or action takes place throughout the course of the film, which dwells in considerable depth on the relationship between characters and environment. Cavalcanti also uses the soundtrack in *Song of the Sea* to counterpoint what is occurring within the image track. For example, in the sequence which portrays the funeral of Siluimo, the attitude of the characters and timbre of the *mise en scène* express a mood of resigned acceptance. However, Cavalcanti uses the music track within this sequence in order to counterpoint what is occurring within the film visually, and, in contrast to the composed lyricism which pervades these scenes, the musical score is resonant with emotion. Although music and sound are used elsewhere in *Song of the Sea* to complement the image track, in this and other scenes Cavalcanti puts into practice the convictions on the relative autonomy of sound and image which he had earlier expressed in *Filme e Realidade*.

In addition to its deployment of psychological and social realism, *Song of the Sea* contains performative aspects which draw on Brazilian carnivalesque traditions, and which depict popular carnival acts, songs, dances, choral singing and religious ceremonies. The most overtly performative scene in the film is that in which the song "Maria do Mar" is performed. This takes place within the context of a narrative flashback, in which Maria reflects on her youth when her husband sang the song to her on board their ship, the *Maria do Mar*. A similar scene also occurs later in the film when Aurora's suitor sings the song "O Canto do Mar". In these sequences, melodramatic and performative discourses can be clearly distinguished from the psychological realism which pervades other scenes within the film.

In addition to the use of realistic and performative styles, another important feature of *Song of the Sea* is the employment of a more formalist or modernist approach associated with the representation of memory and dreams. Subjective point-of-view camerawork was one of the principal stylistic features of Cavalcanti's work within the French avant-garde of the 1920s, and is also a recurrent feature in *Song of the Sea*. In the scenes referred to above,

Cavalcanti uses subjective point of view within a framework of remembered events. However, elsewhere in the film, formative elements are displayed within the context of the visualisation of a dream, or in sequences which depict the hysteria and rapture emanating from religious ceremonies. This approach allows Cavalcanti to develop a number of sequences in which film technique is used in a formative manner in *Song of the Sea*.

The most complex formative sequence in *Song of the Sea* attempts to express the surreal, narrative and visual character of the dream. Here the realism of the narrative gives way to a pronounced surreality, and to a succession of highly complex editing structures. The dream illustrates Raimundo's sense of his own entrapment, and is rich in allegorical and religious symbolism associated with the themes of pursuit and punishment. Rapid spatial and temporal transitions are employed here, and Cavalcanti marks the transitions between the different phases of the dream with a motif of swirling water. Like the final sequences of *The Life and Adventures of Nicholas Nickleby*, in which Ralph Nickleby commits suicide, this dream sequence is a visual and cinematic *tour de force*, in which Cavalcanti's predisposition to portray a dark surreality in his films comes strikingly to the fore. *Song of the Sea* received a generally negative reception from the Brazilian film trade when it was premièred, a reception based on hostility towards the film's depiction of Brazil as an underdeveloped and impoverished country. One of the criticisms of earlier Vera Cruz films such as *Caiçara* and *Sanctuary* had been that they presented Brazil in this way, and much of the press criticism of *Song of the Sea* was based on a similar perception within the industry that Cavalcanti's film perpetuated this impression.

Another criticism of *Song of the Sea*, this time stemming from film critics and filmmakers, rather than from the industry and the trade press, was that the film departed too radically from the style of Italian neo-realism. At the time, the type of low-budget, naturalistic and socially-committed filmmaking found in films such as Vittorio De Sica's *Bicycle Thieves* seemed to offer Brazilian filmmakers a model for the future development of a revitalised Brazilian film culture. Cavalcanti had drawn on neo-realist techniques in making *Caiçara*, and parts of *Song of the Sea* also bear a strong resemblance to *La Terra trema* (*The Earth Trembles*, 1948), Luchino Visconti's melancholic tale of impoverished Italian fishermen. However, *Song of the Sea* cannot be too closely identified with a typical neo-realist approach to filmmaking, and is, in many respects, closer in style and spirit to some of Luis Buñuel's Mexican films of the 1950s, such as *Los olvidados* (*The Forgotten Ones*, 1950), *El bruto* (*The Brute*, 1952) and *Abismos de pasión* (*Wuthering Heights*, 1953). However, it was neo-realism, and not the more idiosyncratic films of Buñuel, which influenced Brazilian critics of the period, and the critical reception to *Song of the Sea* reflected this. For example, the radical independent filmmaker Glauber Rocha criticised *Song of the Sea* for abandoning the neo-realist tradition, and compared its portrayal of Recife unfavourably to that produced by a school of documentary realist writers based in north-east Brazil. Rocha specifically criticised Cavalcanti's choice of scriptwriter on *Song of the Sea*, José Mauro Vasconcelos, whom he dismissively described as a "man of São Paulo with a poor knowledge of the north-east".[94]

Another criticism made against *Song of the Sea* was that it attempted to mobilise the same "exotic" image of Brazilian culture which Vera Cruz had attempted to deploy in films such as *Caiçara*. Rocha, for example, described *Song of the Sea* as "wallowing in exoticism".[95] This was an important issue for Rocha, who regarded such a use of the exotic as a form of cultural colonialism, a way in which the "European observer...cultivates the taste of that misery...as an esthetic object within his field of interest".[96] Cavalcanti may well have cultivated such descriptions of social hardship as an aesthetic objective in *Song of the Sea*, but Rocha's accusation that the film "wallow[s] in exoticism" is unfounded and unfair. Although *Song of the Sea* utilises images of traditional Brazilian culture, it does so only within an overall framework which attempts to integrate these into its predominantly dark and fatalistic concerns. These concerns should be identified not with cultural colonialism, but with the tradition of French naturalism and poetic realism.

Rocha's strongest criticism of *Song of the Sea* is that it is steeped in a poetic realist style inappropriate for contemporary Brazilian cinema. As a consequence, Rocha argues, *Song of the Sea* is guilty of "social aestheticisation", and is "old-fashioned, escapist and anti-social".[97] The charge of aestheticising or romanticising the condition of the poor was one of the strongest criticisms which Rocha and others within Cinema Novo could have made about a film. For example, Carlos Estevam, another figure associated with Cinema Novo, argued that:

> For this reason we repudiate the romantic conception held by many Brazilian artists...For such groups the people are like a bird or a flower, an esthetic object whose potential for beauty, primitive strength, and Biblical virtue has not yet been duly explored by erudite art; we, in contrast, see the people above all in their heroic quality as future combatants in the army of national popular liberation.[98]

Given such statements, it is not surprising that *Song of the Sea* was received so negatively by some critics.

Rocha's criticisms of the way in which *Song of the Sea* poeticised its subject-matter were also echoed by others writing about the film during the 1950s. For example, Catherine de la Roche, writing in 1955, claimed that *Song of the Sea* used an inappropriate poetic realist style:

But what Cavalcanti, who wrote the original story as well, intended as realism, is regarded by his critics as unjustified gloom and futility. Above all, he has been reproached for using an idiom that belongs to the 1930s.[99]

The criticisms of poetic realism voiced by Roche, Rocha and others must be viewed against the context of the emergence of a radical and politically-committed cinema in Brazil during the mid-1950s. The criticisms of *Song of the Sea* expressed in the above quotations are also strikingly similar to those levelled against Jean Renoir's 1938 poetic realist film, *La Bête humaine*. In both cases, the films concerned were condemned for being unjustifiably pessimistic, and for disregarding the political struggles going on around them. It appears that French poetic realism had acquired a negative reputation in Brazil by the 1950s, and that films such as Marcel Carné's *Quai des brumes* and *Hôtel du nord* (both 1938) were seen as examples of an "aestheticised" cinema which had turned its back on the political struggle against European Fascism. In view of this, the deliberate adoption of a poetic realist style in *Song of the Sea* was bound to lead to an adverse critical reaction.

Rocha's abrasive criticism of *Song of the Sea* must also be seen for what it is: a reiteration of the basic tenets of Cinema Novo; a movement with a strong, and explicitly political, commitment to revolutionary change. However, Cavalcanti never was a political filmmaker in this sense, and his view of the human condition is generally a dark and ironic one, in which redemption is rarely, if ever, achieved through the medium of political activism. Like other filmmakers within the poetic realist tradition, such as Robert Hamer, Marcel Carné and Jean Renoir, Cavalcanti is inclined to represent fatalistic situations within his films, without including the "positive" redeeming elements demanded by more politically-committed filmmakers. Writing in 1970, Cavalcanti also criticised Rocha's *Antônio das Mortes* (1969) for its representation of the people of north-eastern Brazil as latent revolutionaries, arguing that "they're not like that at all. It's a country of defeatedness and despair, not melodrama".[100]

Rocha was correct to identify *Song of the Sea* as a work of poetic realist cinema. However, he made no real attempt to understand or appreciate the film, and appears oblivious to what Roche has described as its "masterly pictorial style...sombre, poetic symbolism... moments of poetic vision...[and] beautiful imagery".[101] *Song of the Sea* is a complex mixture of Italian neo-realism, French poetic realism and Buñuelesque Surrealism. It also, in many respects, marks the flowering of a mature aesthetics, and one which Cavalcanti had been developing from the late-1940s.

If considerable exception is taken here to Rocha's negative appraisal of *Song of the Sea*, his description of *Mulher de Verdade* (*The Real Woman*, 1954) as "a very mediocre comedy" is borne out by a viewing of the film.[102] Cavalcanti's second and final film for Kino-Films is a superficial bourgeois comedy of manners which is as far removed from *Song of the Sea* as it could possibly be. Shot largely in São Paulo, it concerns two parallel relationships between two sets of couples. One couple live in a run-down apartment block, and the other in a more expensive location. However, the film has no statement to make about class difference or inequality, and often merely acts as a showcase for interior designs and fashion.

Very little, if any, of Cavalcanti's characteristic concerns can be found in this film, and his reasons for making it immediately after *Song of the Sea* can only be speculated upon. It may have been that Kino-Films, worried about the negative publicity which followed *Song of the Sea*, felt that their second film should be lighter in tone in order to stand a better chance of making a profit. Hence the decision to opt for a safe, commercial formula in *The Real Woman*. However, a commercial failure when it was released, *The Real Woman* sealed the fate of Kino-Films, which went out of business shortly after the film's première.

Notes

[1]   Alberto Cavalcanti, "The British Contribution (1952)", in Ian Aitken (ed), *The Documentary Film Movement: An Anthology* (Edinburgh: Edinburgh University Press, 1998): 212.

[2]   Translated from the French: "Mais il faut dire au moins que la manière dont fut traité un homme de cinéma comme Cavalcanti, par un groupe d'inconnus d'une capitale du nord, ressemble à la haine aveugle et gratuite qu'éprouvent les animaux quand ils sont punis". Hermilo Borba Filho, "Une vie (1953)", in Lorenzo Pellizzari and Claudio M Valentinetti (eds), *Alberto Cavalcanti* (Locarno: Éditions du Festival international du film de Locarno, 1988): 169.

[3]   Ibid: 356.

[4]   Elizabeth Sussex, "Cavalcanti in England", *Sight and Sound* 44: 4 (autumn 1975): 211, reprinted in Aitken (ed): 201.

[5]   Translated from the French: "un type très commercial". Fabiano Canosa, "Conversation avec Alberto Cavalcanti (New York, 1972)", in Pellizzari and Valentinetti (eds): 356.

[6]   Filho, in ibid: 165.

[7]   Geoffrey Macnab, *J. Arthur Rank and the British Film Industry* (London; New York: Routledge, 1993): 199.

[8]   Brian McFarlane, *An Autobiography of British Cinema: as told by the filmmakers and actors who made it* (London: Methuen, 1997): 153.

[9]   Charles Drazin, *The Finest Years: British Cinema of the 1940s* (London: André Deutsch, 1998): 133.

[10]   Charles Drazin, transcript of an interview with Charles Hassé and

Judy Hassé, 29 September 1996.

11   Emir Rodriguez Monegal, "Alberto Cavalcanti", *The Quarterly of Film, Radio and Television* 9: 4 (summer 1955): 352.

12   Claudio M Valentinetti, "La période brésilienne (1950-1954)", in Pellizzari and Valentinetti (eds): 43.

13   Filho, in ibid: 165.

14   Drazin (1998): 134.

15 .   Carlos Augusto Calil, "A Vera Cruz e o mito do cinema industrial", in Carlos Augusto Calil (ed), *Memória Vera Cruz* (São Paulo: Secretaria da Cultura/Mis, 1987): 10-11.

16   Filho, in Pellizzari and Valentinetti (eds): 172.

17   Calil: 13.

18   Randal Johnson and Robert Stam (eds), *Brazilian Cinema*, expanded edition (New York: Columbia University Press, 1995): 22.

19   Ibid: 27.

20   João Luiz Vieira, "From *High Noon* to *Jaws*: Carnival and Parody in Brazilian Cinema", in Johnson and Stam (eds): 262.

21   Roy Armes, *Third World Film Making and the West* (Berkeley; Los Angeles; London: University of California Press, 1987): 173.

22   Julianne Burton-Carvajal, "South American Cinema", in John Hill and Pamela Church Gibson (eds), *The Oxford Guide to Film Studies* (Oxford: Oxford University Press, 1998): 586.

23   Armes: 169.

24   E Bradford-Burns, *A History of Brazil* (New York: Columbia University Press, 1980): 427.

25   Peter Flynn, *Brazil: A Political Analysis* (London: Ernest Benn, 1978): 145.

26   E Bradford-Burns, *Nationalism in Brazil: A Historical Survey* (New York; Washington; London: Frederick A Praeger, 1968): 80.

27   Ibid: 81.

28   Maria Rita Galvão, "Vera Cruz: A Brazilian Hollywood", in Johnson and Stam (eds): 273.

29   Drazin (1996).

30   Galvão, in Johnson and Stam (eds): 274-275.

31   Calil: 13.

32   Filho, in Pellizzari and Valentinetti (eds): 175.

[33]   Ibid: 180.

[34]   Ibid.

[35]   Ibid: 181.

[36]   Calil: 15.

[37]   Drazin (1996).

[38]   Valentinetti, in Pellizzari and Valentinetti (eds): 355.

[39]   Galvão, in Johnson and Stam (eds): 276.

[40]   Translated from the French: "Ils m'annoncèrent que ma politique de production de films internationaux était trop coûteuse et que M. Fernando de Barros...avait été engagé comme producteur de la Compagnie". Alberto Cavalcanti, "Le projet Vera Cruz (1955)", in Pellizzari and Valentinetti (eds): 181.

[41]   Calil: 16.

[42]   Cavalcanti, in Pellizzari and Valentinetti (eds): 182.

[43]   Translated from the French: "campagne féroce". Filho, in Pellizzari and Valentinetti (eds): 169.

[44]   Translated from the French: "une incroyable virulence sa campagne de diffamation". Valentinetti, in Pellizzari and Valentinetti (eds): 49.

[45]   Cavalcanti, in ibid: 183.

[46]   Calil: 16.

[47]   Cavalcanti, in Pellizzari and Valentinetti (eds): 183.

[48]   Translated from the French: "une campagne de diffamation". Ibid: 184.

[49]   Glauber Rocha, "Cavalcanti et la Vera Cruz (1962)", in ibid: 372.

[50]   Translated from the French: "il y avait les pédérastes, naturellement, et comme ils étaient en contact avec Cavalcanti on peut imaginer s'ils étaient nombreux". Valentinetti, in ibid: 48-49.

[51]   Ian Aitken, interview with Forsyth Hardy, Edinburgh, 8 May 1986.

[52]   Felix Martialay, "'J'étais surréaliste, avec une tendance au réalisme'", *Film Ideal* (December 1960), reprinted in Pellizzari and Valentinetti (eds): 335.

[53]   Calil: 15.

[54]   Translated from the French: "la haine aveugle et gratuite". Filho, in Pellizzari and Valentinetti (eds): 169.

[55]   Ibid: 187.

[56]   Flynn: 144.

[57]   Calil: 10.

58   Monegal: 352.

59   Ibid: 353-354.

60   Randal Johnson, "The Rise and Fall of Brazilian Cinema, 1960-1990", in Johnson and Stam (eds): 367.

61   Bradford-Burns (1968): 83.

62   Flynn: 151.

63   Galvão, in Johnson and Stam (eds): 276.

64   Ian Aitken, *Film and Reform: John Grierson and the Documentary Film Movement* (London; New York: Routledge, 1990): 141.

65   Drazin (1998): 134.

66   Ian Aitken, "Introduction", in Aitken (ed): 1.

67   Ibid: 1-2.

68   Galvão, in Johnson and Stam (eds): 271.

69   Ibid: 270.

70   Translated from the French: "politique de production de films internationaux". Cavalcanti, in Pellizzari and Valentinetti (eds): 181.

71   Sussex, reprinted in Aitken (ed): 200.

72   Translated from the Portuguese: "O contacto com a realidade, perdido nos filmes dramáticos, foi sendo mantido pelo filme documentário e pelos jornais de atualidades". Alberto Cavalcanti, "O Filme Silencioso", in Alberto Cavalcanti, *Filme e Realidade* third edition (Rio de Janeiro: Editora Artenova, in collaboration with Empresa Brasileira de Filmes – Embrafilme, 1977): 38.

73   Cavalcanti, "O Filme Sonoro", in ibid: 42.

74   Alberto Cavalcanti, "A Contribuição Britânica", reproduced as "The British Contribution (1952)", in Aitken (ed): 205.

75   Ibid.

76   Ibid: 211.

77   Ibid: 214.

78   Ibid: 213-214.

79   Translated from the Portuguese: "Confesso que desde o momento em que comecei a alternar as funções de diretor e de produtor, não me adaptei a este sistema, necessitando sempre de um produtor quando dirigia". Cavalcanti (1977): 89.

80   Louis Marcorelles, "L'impossible gageure", *Cahiers du Cinéma* 13: 77 (December 1957): 54.

81   Translated from the Portuguese: "não sincronizada deveria acrescentar

idéias à imagem". Cavalcanti (1977): 142.

[82]   Translated from the Portuguese: "o estilo metafórico e alusivo do filme mudo". Ibid: 144.

[83]   Ibid.

[84]   Translated from the Portuguese: "calcado no período final do romantismo" and "tornara rançoso em 1895". Ibid: 147, 148.

[85]   Translated from the Portuguese: "O músico deve saber o momento preciso em que as imagens escapam ao realismo e solicitam a extensão poética da música". Ibid: 150.

[86]   Translated from the Portuguese: "Primeiro foram os ruídos selecionados para cada sequência. Depois construiu-se o acompanhamento sonoro com as 'notas dominantes', que são diferentes em cada secção. Começa o filme com uma breve cena falada sobre a partida do trem, sucedida, como transição, por sinais, com o som sincronizado; segue-se uma série de vistas que acompanham o trem, tomadas de avião e, após, cenas na torre de controle, com todos os ruídos característicos, vendo-se depois, várias vezes, o trem filmado de fora, com seu ritmo real e seus apitos como 'notas dominantes'. Neste trecho suprimimos todas as paradas em estações, que foram condensadas na sequência seguinte, 'Crew, depois de meia-noite'. Nas plataformas de Crew usamos todos os gritos, todos os barulhos de vagonetas, das locomotivas chegando e saindo e outros efeitos de uma estação. Deixando Crew, o ritmo do trem passa para segundo plano e uma orquestração de ruídos, pontuada por explicações quase gritadas, sugere as regiões industriais que o trem atravessa. As cenas do interior são acompanhadas, de novo, pelo ritmo simplificado do trem, desta vez quase imperceptível, e que, se bem me recordo, era feito pela bateria; os operários falam em sincronismo, com grande naturalidade. Estamos no patamar que prepara o clímax do filme; o trem apanhando e descarregando sacos de cartas, a grande velocidade. Aqui se repetem alguns apitos não sincronizados sobre primeiros planos das rodas da locomotiva, servindo novamente de pontuação. E finalmente, depois de um pequeno interlúdio musical – usado como anti-clímax mostrando a alvorada – a subida para a Escócia, que termina com a sequência lírica, em que os versos de W. H. Auden seguem o ritmo do trem e produzem um grande efeito dramático." Ibid: 153.

[87]   Galvão, in Johnson and Stam (eds): 271.

[88]   Monegal: 353.

[89]   Translated from the French: "un contrat...le plus bas qu'il eût jamais signé dans sa carrière". Filho, in Pellizzari and Valentinetti (eds): 169.

[90]   Glauber Rocha, "Cavalcanti et la Vera Cruz (1962)", in Pellizzari and Valentinetti (eds): 372.

[91]   Mário Audra Jr, *Cinematográfica Maristela: Memórias de um Produtor* (São Paulo: Silver Hawk, 1997): 76.

[92]   Monegal: 354.

[93]   Rocha, in Pellizzari and Valentinetti (eds): 373.

[94]   Translated from the French: "un homme de São Paulo bénéficiant

d'une connaissance fort hypothétique du Nord-Est". Ibid.

[95]   Translated from the French: "Cavalcanti se complut dans l'exotisme". Ibid.

[96]   Glauber Rocha, "An Esthetic of Hunger", in Johnson and Stam (eds): 69.

[97]   Translated from the French: "l'esthétisation du social...Film vieillot, escapiste, anti-social". Rocha, in Pellizzari and Valentinetti (eds): 373.

[98]   Carlos Estevam, "For a Popular Revolutionary Art", in Johnson and Stam (eds): 62.

[99]   Catherine de la Roche, "Cavalcanti in Brazil", *Sight and Sound* 24: 3 (January-March 1955): 119.

[100]   Geoffrey Minish, "Cavalcanti in Paris", *Sight and Sound* 39: 3 (summer 1970): 135.

[101]   de la Roche: 119.

[102]   Translated from the French: "une très médiocre comédie". Rocha, in Pellizzari and Valentinetti (eds): 372.

9

East Germany

By 1954, Cavalcanti had come to accept that his attempt to re-establish himself in Brazil had failed. However, although he was eager to leave the country as soon as he could, he was not in a financial position to do so. Despite the official opposition he had encountered in São Paulo, he had somehow managed to obtain modest employment in TV Tupi, the São Paulo television company owned by Francisco de Assis Chateaubriand, the "Charles Foster Kane" type,[1] who had first brought him to Brazil. Although no evidence exists to indicate what work Cavalcanti actually did for TV Tupi, he was probably employed as a producer, rather than as a director, and, although the income which he derived from this fairly routine television work was modest, it earned him the income he needed in order to subsist relatively comfortably.

It has already been argued elsewhere in this book that Cavalcanti's sense of *Realpolitik* was by no means his strongest attribute, and this lack of political acumen was again demonstrated in 1954 when he accepted an invitation from cinema officials in the Soviet Union to visit the country and meet Russian filmmakers. Cavalcanti was eager to leave Brazil, even if only for a short period of time, and, in addition, he was too much of a gentleman to refuse such a respectful invitation from a major filmmaking nation. However, had he reflected more thoughtfully on the wisdom of undertaking such a trip at that particular time, he might well have decided against accepting the Russian invitation.

By 1954, Cavalcanti had already been accused of being a Communist by some in Brazil, and by others serving the interests of American distribution companies.[2] Cavalcanti would also have been regarded as a Communist fellow traveller in the United States because of his earlier association with John Grierson, who had been refused a visa by the State Department in February 1947 on the grounds that he was a Communist sympathiser.[3] By 1954, the Cold War was at its height, the Warsaw Pact Treaty was about to be ratified, and, in Hollywood, the proceedings of the House Un-American Activities Committee (HUAC) had only just ended, with the black-listing of some 324 people.[4] In the Soviet Union, a significant number of explicitly anti-American films had been made since 1949, and continued to be produced after Stalin's death in 1953, whilst, in the United States, a group of virulently anti-Communist films appeared throughout the 1950s.[5] It was against this decidedly inauspicious background that Cavalcanti undertook his controversial trip to the Soviet Union.

Although Brazilian and American claims that Cavalcanti was a Communist sympathiser may have influenced the Soviet decision to invite him to Russia, the Soviet film Establishment would also have been impressed by Cavalcanti's filmmaking activities in Brazil. Vera Cruz did, in many respects, represent the same kind of attempt to build a national cinema which the Soviet Union had established long before, with the foundation of Mosfilm and other state cinema institutions. Of course, parallels cannot be drawn too closely here, as Vera Cruz was a commercial organisation which operated in the open market, whilst Mosfilm was a publicly-controlled state institution. Nevertheless, the attempt to establish Vera Cruz in a Third World country whose film industry was dominated by Hollywood would have interested Soviet cinema officials, given the context of debate at the time in Russia over the issues of cultural imperialism and the Third World. During the period immediately following the death of Stalin, the competitive confrontation between the Soviet Union and the United States became more intense, and Soviet policy responded to this by emphasising the affinity which existed between the Soviet Union and Third World countries, and by claiming that the Second and Third Worlds were involved in a similar struggle against American hegemony.[6] Cavalcanti's invitation to visit the Soviet Union in 1954 must therefore be associated with, and was undoubtedly part of, this larger context of Soviet policy, although he himself was probably completely unaware of this.

The films which Cavalcanti made at Vera Cruz, particularly *O Canto do Mar* (*Song of the Sea*, 1953), also corresponded in a number of ways to the official Soviet aesthetic style of Socialist Realism. After Stalin's death, and during the so-called "thaw" period from 1953 to 1958, the doctrine of Socialist Realism lost some of its monolithic hold within the Soviet Union, and Russian filmmakers began to explore other models of filmmaking which, nevertheless, remained grounded within a realistic style.[7] One of the most significant of these new approaches was a form of humanist realism which can be seen in films such as Mihail Kalatozov's *Letjat žuravli* (*The Cranes Are Flying*, 1957) and Grigorij Čuhraj's *Ballada o soldate* (*Ballad of a Soldier*, 1959). The term "humanist realism" was used at the time to characterise these and other films which appeared within the Communist bloc during the thaw period. Although not necessarily explicitly Marxist, these films were deemed to be both stylistically and politically progressive, and were promoted and praised on those grounds. In many respects, Cavalcanti's *Song of the Sea* could be regarded as a precursor to such films, and was, in fact, described in the East German press at the time as an example of "humanist realism".[8]

Cavalcanti's trip to the Soviet Union turned out to be highly advantageous for him. However, when he returned to Brazil, his enemies quickly pounced on the issue, believing that this vindicated their claim that Cavalcanti harboured Communist sympathies. Although it was inevitable that Cavalcanti would be severely criticised for going to the Soviet Union, he also made matters worse by publishing an article entitled "Diario de São Paulo"),[9] in which he was highly critical of the São Paulo film Establishment. On his return to Brazil, he discovered, perhaps unsurprisingly, that his contract with TV Tupi, which had provided him with his only source of income, had been revoked, and, once again, he found himself in an extremely precarious financial situation. It was fortunate, therefore, that, during his trip to Russia, which had also included visits to East Germany and Czechoslovakia, he had managed to obtain commissions for what were to become his next two films: *Herr Puntila und sein Knecht Matti* (*Mr Puntila and His Hired Man Matti*, 1955) and *Die Windrose* (1956).

One positive event which occurred in 1954 was the warm reception which *Song of the Sea* received at the Cannes Film Festival. Sadly, Cavalcanti was unable to attend the festival because of the problems he was experiencing in Brazil. However, during his visit to Russia and East Germany he had been able to attend a Communist-controlled film festival in Czechoslovakia, the Karlovy Vary Film Festival, where a screening of *Song of the Sea* also received a warm welcome. In fact, *Song of the Sea* was awarded the festival's Grand Prize for *mise en scène*, and also received acclaim for the "politically sound way" in which it treated its subject-matter of social disadvantage and inequality amongst the Brazilian poor.[10]

Whilst he was in Eastern Europe, Cavalcanti also took the opportunity to renew contact with some of his old friends, one of whom was the Dutch filmmaker Joris Ivens. In late-1954, after Cavalcanti had returned to Brazil, Ivens contacted Cavalcanti and informed him that he had succeeded in persuading Bertolt Brecht to engage Cavalcanti to direct a film version of one of his plays. Given his situation in Brazil, Cavalcanti was only too eager to accept the commission, although he did have a number of misgivings about the project. He was concerned, in particular, that Brecht was known to have disliked the two previous attempts to adapt his plays into films, and that he was regarded as a difficult and temperamental collaborator.[11]

The first film adaptation of a play by Brecht was G W Pabst's *Die Dreigroschenoper* (*The Threepenny Opera*, 1931). The original play, written in 1928, was so satirical and abrasive that it was criticised by the German Communist Party as being too cynical.[12] In addition to its abrasive edge, Brecht's play employed frequent alienation effects, or "Verfremdungseffekte", whose principal function was to unsettle the spectator, and to engage his or her critical faculties.[13] One of the central characteristics of Brecht's aesthetic was the belief that a progressive theatre should strive to make the spectator aware of his or her own conditioning by dominant ideologies by making those ideologies appear "strange".[14] One way in which Brecht attempted to achieve this was by disrupting the naturalistic continuity of his dramas through the use of Verfremdungseffekte.[15] The end result was plays such as *The Threepenny Opera*, which were often jarring, demanding and difficult to watch. However, in his adaptation of the play, Pabst introduced elements of melodrama, and a more naturalistic style, which Brecht believed undermined the ideological and stylistic substance of the play. In fact, Brecht was so unhappy with Pabst's film that he began legal proceedings to have it banned.

Whilst he was fighting this court case, Brecht also began work on *Kuhle Wampe, oder wem gehört die Welt?* (*Kuhle Wampe, or Who Does the World Belong To?*, 1932). Brecht developed the scenario for the film in conjunction with the writer Ernst Ottwald, who practised a form of montage-based writing similar to Brecht's own episodic approach to narrative development.[16] The musical score for the film was also composed by Hanns Eisler, who had first collaborated with Brecht on the didactic play, *Die Massnahme* (*The Measures Taken*, 1930), and who later provided the score for Cavalcanti's film version of *Puntila*. *Kuhle Wampe* was a far more didactic and episodic film than *The Threepenny Opera*, and consequently was much closer to Brecht's own aesthetic convictions. Brecht's next involvement with the cinema was in Hollywood. There he worked on *Hangmen Also Die* (1943) with Fritz Lang, but found it difficult to reconcile his ideas with the requirements of classical Hollywood realism.[17]

After this, Brecht's attitude towards working with film became increasingly negative, and it is not surprising that, back in East Germany, and installed as one of the most important cultural luminaries within the new DDR, he should initially react with apprehension to the suggestion that a filmmaker he did not know should be commissioned to make a version of *Puntila*. *Puntila* was originally written by Brecht in Finland, in collaboration with the Finnish writer Hella Wuolijoki.[18] Premièred in Zürich in 1948, the play was the first production of the newly-established Berliner Ensemble, and was first performed in the DDR in 1949.[19] In an article written at the same time, entitled "Notes on the Folk Play", Brecht described the type of approach which he intended to adopt in *Puntila*:

> The 'Volksstück' or folk play is normally a crude and humble kind of theatre which academic critics pass over in silence or treat with condescension...It is a mixture of earthy humour and sentimentality, homespun morality and cheap sex.[20]

Brecht went on to argue that a "new folk play" of this kind would avoid "any unified and continuous story" and would revive "the 'Pranks and Adventures' of the old popular epics", whilst also inflecting the genre with "high ideals". *Puntila* is, therefore, in some respects a relatively undemanding play, and has even been described as "lowbrow".[21] The overall tone of the play is set by the "Prologue", when a milkmaid proclaims that, because "the times are sad...we present a comic play tonight".[22] However, alongside this use of comic forms, *Puntila* also employs the Verfremdungseffekte and episodic, discontinuous narrative structures which are central to Brecht's conception of Epic Theatre.

The central character in Brecht's play is Puntila, a Finnish landlord, "a monster from a prehistoric age – Estatium possessor – the owner of big estates".[23] Puntila is humane and decent whilst drunk, but self-centred and unpleasant when sober. During the course of the play, he attempts to marry his daughter Eva to a vacuous upper-class character known as the Attaché. However, Puntila eventually sees the error of this, and instead encourages her to marry his chauffeur Matti. Eva eventually agrees, but Matti argues that two people from such different class backgrounds could not be compatible, and she eventually comes to accept his point of view. At the end of the play, concerned that his employer, when sober, might accuse him of attempting to worm his way into the family fortune, and reflecting on the irreconcilable differences between the classes, Matti leaves Puntila Hall, and looks forward to a time when he, and other working-class people, will become the new masters:

> Sad as I am to find out in the end...That oil and water
> cannot ever blend...It's not much help, there's nothing
> I can do: so – time your servants turned their backs
> on you. They'll find a decent master pretty fast...Once
> they've become the masters here at last.[24]

Although, as Louis Marcorelles has argued, *Puntila* is, in Brecht's own words, "a play without a message",[25] a central theme within the play is that of the exploitative behaviour of a ruling class too powerful and disinterested to care about the consequences which its actions have on ordinary people. However, although Puntila causes chaos all around him, his aberrant social position is also represented as an affliction which causes him distress, and the alcoholism in which he indulges allows him temporary escape from the contradictions of his privileged life, and an opportunity to express what remains of his humanity. For example, he describes the moments in which he is sober as periods in which he suffers "attacks of total senseless sobriety...I sink to the level of the beasts",[26] whereas he regards his bouts of intoxication as beneficial for both himself and those around him.

Cavalcanti claimed that his principal objective when adapting *The Life and Adventures of Nicholas Nickleby* in 1947 was to remain faithful to the spirit of Dickens' original novel, and, when adapting *Puntila*, he expressed a similar wish to remain close to Brecht's intentions. However, whilst he claimed to have disliked Dickens novels, he acclaimed Brecht's theatre as "the most popular in the world, after Shakespeare's",[27] and this degree of esteem for Brecht's work played a substantial role in ensuring that his adaptation of *Puntila* turned out to be a far more satisfactory experience for him than his work on *The Life and Adventures of Nicholas Nickleby* had been. Cavalcanti also attributed the good relations which he enjoyed with Brecht during the shooting of *Puntila* to the fact that, according to Cavalcanti, Brecht understood that he would not try to impose his own vision on the work.[28] Any attempt at such an imposition would, of course, have led to a disastrous breakdown in his relations with Brecht anyway, given the latter's well-known predisposition for rejecting projects with which he disagreed, but it was Cavalcanti's beliefs about adaptation, rather than any capitulation to Brecht's authority, which led him to adopt the approach that he did in *Puntila*.

Nevertheless, although remaining close to what he perceived to be the essential spirit of Brecht's play, the film also departs from the original in a number of ways. In the play, verses from "The Puntila Song" are sung immediately after the Prologue, and between the different acts of the play, by the actress playing the part of Liana the cook. However, in the film, Cavalcanti, perhaps drawing on his experience with *The Halfway House* (1944) and *Dead of Night* (1945), dispenses with both the milkmaid's Prologue and Liana's musical interventions, and replaces both with a framing device, in which a group of working-class sewing-women recall the story of Puntila and Matti. It is one of these women who sings the verses of "The Puntila Song". As each verse is sung, the film leaves the main action and turns to this framing scenario, before returning again to the main action.

Other changes to the original play involve the various characters in the film. For example, in the play, Puntila insults the Attaché after refusing to allow him to marry his daughter, and the Attaché then disappears from the scene altogether. However, in the film, Cavalcanti turns this confrontation into a comic chase sequence, with Puntila chasing the Attaché around the house and gardens, and finally dunking him in a pool of water. Cavalcanti also introduces a love affair between Matti and Fina (the maid) which does not exist in the play. At the end of the play, for example, Matti leaves Puntila Hall alone and in an embittered, angry mood, whereas, in the film, Matti and Fina leave Puntila hall together, happily embracing each other in the back of a farm cart.

These modifications have the effect of qualifying the more austere, word-centred and theatrical aspects of Brecht's play, whilst also making it more accessible to a popular cinema audience. However, it could also be argued that they dilute the critical content of the play in the same way in which Pabst's adaptation of *The Threepenny Opera* had. Marcorelles, for example, has described the scene in which Puntila chases the Attaché as played "in a pseudo-Marx Brothers style which is terribly old-fashioned".[29]

Brecht opposed these changes, and initially rejected the scenario which Cavalcanti and Vladimir Pozner had prepared, insisting that Cavalcanti conform strictly to the outlines of the play. However,

Cavalcanti, apparently with the help of the film's other scenarist, Ruth Wieden, was able to persuade him that the changes proposed were necessary in order that a "work of cinema" would emerge, rather than a mere piece of filmed theatre.[30]

In order to effect some of the changes which he wished to make to Brecht's play, Cavalcanti was also forced to adopt a strategy which was later to have unforseen, and unwelcome, consequences. The songs and music in the original play had all been composed by Paul Dessau, a colleague of Brecht's and a long-established member of the Berliner Ensemble. However, Cavalcanti felt that Dessau's music, although effective on the stage, would be far less so on film, and invited Hanns Eisler, who had earlier written the music for *Kuhle Wampe*, to compose a new music track for *Puntila*. Brecht eventually agreed to this, but, according to Cavalcanti, some members of the Berliner Ensemble took exception to what they regarded as the demotion of Dessau, and this resentment later re-emerged in a number of negative reviews of the film.[31] However, notwithstanding these problems, Cavalcanti was in no doubt, either then or later, that his work with Eisler on *Puntila* had led to the production of the best musical score in any of his films.[32]

As in Brecht's original conception of the play, the acting in Cavalcanti's *Puntila* is deliberately exaggerated and parodic, and this is particularly the case with the central performance by Kurt Bois in the role of Puntila. However, Cavalcanti felt that Bois, who had also played Puntila for the Berliner Ensemble's production of the play in 1949, lacked effective screen presence, and looked more like a "travelling salesman" in front of the camera than a great landowner.[33] Cavalcanti also held similar reservations concerning the actors Heinz Engelmann and Maria Emo, who played the parts of Matti and Eva, and who, he felt, were unable to achieve the levels of parodic liveliness necessary for his film. Cavalcanti was ultimately unable to resolve these problems, and, consequently, the performance of all three central actors failed to capture the sardonic eccentricity of the characters in Brecht's original play.

The exaggerated acting style in *Puntila* is also reflected in the manner in which the film is edited, and particularly by Cavalcanti's use of moving camera shots and abrupt jump cuts, all of which serve to emphasise the film's formal construction, and provide a whimsical cinematic equivalent of Brecht's theatrical alienation effects. The set designs within the film, designed by the Danish designer Erik Aaes, are also similarly stylised, and employ a pronounced, and rather shrill, yellow and blue colour scheme. According to Cavalcanti, these ornamental decorative effects were modelled on what he called the "Chinese theatre", and were made deliberately garish in order to contrast with the more sombre surroundings of the women in the chorus, surroundings which are represented using a colour scheme of sepia-based brown tones.[34]

Although it is not completely clear what Cavalcanti meant when he used the phrase "Chinese theatre" here, in an article written in 1936 entitled "Verfremdungseffekte in der chinesischen Schauspielkunst" ("Alienation Effects in Chinese Acting"), Brecht himself drew on the Chinese theatre as a basis for his ideas on Verfremdungseffekte.[35] However, although it seems likely that Brecht and Cavalcanti would have discussed how the use of stylistic features derived from the Chinese theatre might generate Verfremdungseffekte in *Puntila*, there is no recorded evidence of such a discussion having taken place, and, consequently, it remains unclear exactly how Cavalcanti used the Chinese theatre in *Puntila*.

Although Cavalcanti claimed that Brecht approved of his set designs for *Puntila*, other members of the Berliner Ensemble clearly did not. The characteristic set designs for plays mounted at the Deutsches Theater during this period employed generally neutral, or even just black-and-white, colour schemes, and Cavalcanti's *Puntila*, with its ebullient and ornamental decorative style, was regarded as having departed too radically from this tradition. These criticisms also echoed Brecht's own earlier criticisms of Pabst's adaptation of *The Threepenny Opera*, in which he complained that his original "austere mathematical sets" had been replaced by "something closer to baroque ornamentalism".[36] Nevertheless, despite this, there is no evidence to suggest that Brecht disapproved of Cavalcanti's similarly baroque and ornamental *Puntila*.

Cavalcanti's Puntila received a mixed critical reception in the East German press. Unsurprisingly, given the extent to which the media in the DDR were controlled by the ruling Communist Party, some commentators complained about the film's lack of apparent engagement with the ideals of Communism.[37] However, the greatest criticism of the film was that it lacked any real social content, or concern with the issue of class struggle.[38] Closely related to this was the charge that Cavalcanti had failed to understand Brecht's intentions in writing the original play,[39] and that, in particular, his film had failed to accommodate the sense of aggression and anger which had been an important aspect of the play.[40] Closely associated with this criticism was the complaint that *Puntila* was too lightweight and too much of a farce.[41] Paradoxically, given Cavalcanti's views on the matter, one of the few aspects of *Puntila* which received favourable reviews was the performance of Kurt Bois, and one commentator even went as far as to argue that, without Bois' performance, the film would have "sunk without trace".[42]

One of the key issues to arise amongst critics in East Germany regarding *Puntila* was the extent to which the film illuminated the more general problem of how to transfer Brechtian theatre to the cinema. Some reviewers argued that *Puntila* replaced Brechtian distanciation devices with slapstick,[43] whilst others questioned whether the "failure" of *Puntila* revealed the presence of a more fundamental contradiction between a Brechtian approach and cinematic realism.[44] This issue would also be returned to in later reviews of *Puntila* written outside the DDR, in France and Italy.

Because it was produced in East Germany at the height of the Cold War, *Puntila* received little distribution in the West, although it was shown at the Locarno Film Festival in 1956. However, those critics in the West who did see the film were largely unenthusiastic. For example, the influential French critic Bernard Dort considered it be a "failure", arguing that it amounted to an unsuccessful attempt to integrate slapstick comedy, Brechtian techniques and cinematic realism.[45] Dort also compared *Puntila* unfavourably to films such as Michelangelo Antonioni's *Il Grido* (*The Cry*, 1957) and *L'Avventura* (1960), Claude Chabrol's *Les Bonnes femmes* and Louis Malle's *Zazie dans le Métro* (both 1960), all of which, he believed, employed Brechtian alienation techniques more successfully than *Puntila* did.[46] Restating the earlier criticisms made by reviewers of the film within the DDR, Dort also argued that there may be an intrinsic incompatibility between Brechtian theatre and the cinema, and that this may account for the fact that all the attempts to adapt Brecht for the screen, including *Puntila*, have been failures. According to Dort, this explains why *Puntila* was a "failure" ("échec") and *The Threepenny Opera* a "betrayal" ("trahison").[47]

The French critic Louis Marcorelles echoes Dort's belief that there is an inherent incompatibility between Brechtian theatre and the cinema by describing Cavalcanti's *Puntila* as a "mission impossible". Marcorelles also argues even more strongly that *Puntila* is "without doubt a failure",[48] and that it displays a lack of understanding on Cavalcanti's part of the proper relationship between theatre and cinema. Marcorelles concludes an extremely critical review by describing *Puntila* as "jarring" and "intellectually flashy" in its unsuccessful attempt to integrate Brechtian formalism and cinematic realism, and accuses Cavalcanti of trying to be more Brechtian than Brecht by "accenting the schematicism of the subject".[49]

At the heart of Marcorelles' criticism of *Puntila* is the view, also expressed by Dort, that cinema's inherent affinity for representing reality clashes with Brecht's "schematisation" ("schématisme") – that is, with Brecht's use of schematic characterisation and *mise en scène* to represent social types and ideological positions.[50] Marcorelles' fundamental criticism of *Puntila* is that it is unable to resolve how cinematic realism and Brechtian distanciation could be successfully combined, and the result, for him, is that *Puntila* is a "grating" ("grincer") film, which actually, and ultimately counter-productively, accentuates the schematic treatment of characterisation in the play.[51]

Marcorelles also complains that, whilst Brecht's *Puntila* is a synthesis of the ancient *commedia dell'arte* and the modern realist comedy of manners, Cavalcanti has – wrongly in Marcorelles' view – based his version of *Puntila* on examples of the Brechtian epic theatre such as *Mutter Courage und ihre Kinder* (*Mother Courage and Her Children*, 1941) and *Der kaukasische Kreidekreis* (*The Caucasian Chalk Circle*, 1949), plays which are very different from *Puntila*. Marcorelles argues that the confusion which has resulted from this leads to an uncertainty within Puntila over how to integrate epic and parodic elements. Marcorelles also protests that Cavalcanti has interpreted the *commedia dell'arte* in terms of pantomime, rather than "wild improvisation", and that this has led to the film appearing like a second-rate and old-fashioned version of a Marx Brothers film.[52]

Many of these criticisms of *Puntila* appear justified on viewing the film. Cavalcanti admitted that the central acting performances were weak, and it is true that both Matti and Eva are stiff rather than stoic, whilst Puntila just appears extremely odd. Although Cavalcanti had, in the past, drawn fine performances from his actors, this was not the case here. The pantomimic aspects in the film which Marcorelles highlights also appear misconceived, and Marcorelles' central point that the film displays an unsuccessful attempt to combine cinematic realism with Brechtian "schematisation" and distanciation also appears valid. One major problem with *Puntila*, as with *The Life and Adventures of Nicholas Nickleby*, is that it contains a large number of characters, few of whom are sufficiently or adequately developed. This would not have been a problem for the play, which was delivered in a demonstrative and rhetorical manner by the Berliner Ensemble in 1949. However, it is difficult for the film, grounded – as all films are – in realism, to depict such a range of characters convincingly.

The biggest problem with Cavalcanti's *Puntila*, however, and what marks the film out above all else as seriously flawed, is Cavalcanti's failure to understand the character of Matti. One of the strongest influences on Brecht in developing Matti was Jaroslav Hašek's comic novel *Dobrý voják Švejk (The Good Soldier Švejk)*. In this novel, Schweik routinely rebuffs those who seek to exert authority over him by calculatingly exposing their stupidity:

> Schweik is more than a mere character: he represents a basic human attitude. Schweik defeats the powers that be, the whole universe in all its absurdity, not by opposing but by complying with them. He is so servile, so eager to please and to carry out the letter of any regulation or command that in the end the stupidity of the authorities, the idiocy of the law is ruthlessly exposed. Brecht not only entered into the ways of thought of Hašek's immortal character so completely that twenty years later he could reproduce the authentic accents of the little soldier in his own play on *Schweik in the Second World War*; he also made the Schweikian attitude his own. Many of the characters in his later plays show features of this ironic servility: the hired man Matti in *Puntila*, the rascally judge Azdak in *The Caucasian Chalk Circle*, the great Galileo himself.[53]

Unfortunately, the character of Matti in Cavalcanti's *Puntila* fails to display this calculating and ironic Schweikian servility, and instead is represented much more straightforwardly, as a put-upon worker, who is largely resigned to his own condition and place within the scheme of things. This more straightforward characterisation is also reinforced towards the end of the film, where Cavalcanti leaves out Matti's final speech with its prediction of the coming revolution. Although Heinz Engelmann's performance certainly did not help Cavalcanti to bring Matti to life, as it were, it may be that this kind of representation of the Schweikian character was simply beyond Cavalcanti's capabilities. Paradoxically, although many of his films possess an ironic dimension, Cavalcanti almost always produced fine acting performances within the context of a serious, rather than parodic, attempt to represent character: Maxwell Frere in *Dead of Night*, Narcy in *They Made Me a Fugitive* (1947), Herb in *For Them That Trespass* (1949) and Margarida Cardoso in *Song of the Sea* are obvious examples.

Cavalcanti's *Puntila* succeeds best in the sections of the film which are the least Brechtian and the most realist. The scenes set in the room of the sewing women, for example, are delivered with particular conviction, as are those set in the "worker's market", where labourers display themselves to prospective employers. Furthermore, it could be argued that *Puntila*'s strengths lie less in Cavalcanti's direction than in Erik Aaes' set designs, and Hanns Eisler's musical compositions. However, in defence of Cavalcanti, it must have been difficult for him to shift so radically from the social realism of *Song of the Sea* to the Brechtian antirealism of *Puntila*, and, in this sense, *Puntila* can be seen as standing in opposition to the move towards social realism upon which Cavalcanti had embarked with *They Made Me a Fugitive* and *For Them That Trespass*, and which reached a culmination with *Song of the Sea*.

Cavalcanti claimed that Brecht approved of *Puntila*, and, if so, this may have been because of the distanciation effects within the film, which, although significantly responsible for the film's aesthetic failure, did correspond to Brecht's own ideas on how his work should be adapted for the screen. However, there is no evidence, apart from Cavalcanti's own testimony, that Brecht actually did like the film. In addition, *Puntila* has always been regarded as a minor work of the Brechtian cinema, hardly mentioned in critical commentaries, and virtually never screened or broadcast. When compared with the other major Brechtian adaptations – Pabst's *The Threepenny Opera*, Dudow's *Kuhle Wampe* and Peter Palitzsch and Manfred Wekworth's *Mother Courage* – Cavalcanti's film is usually regarded as by far the weakest.[54]

Cavalcanti also claimed that, after Brecht's death in August 1956, criticisms were levelled at both himself and *Puntila* by members of the Berliner Ensemble.[55] One of the reasons why members of the Berliner Ensemble disapproved of Cavalcanti's film was that they considered it to be apart from, or irrelevant to, debates on the development of a committed art practice then current in the DDR.

Although Cavalcanti had been associated with committed filmmaking in France during the 1920s, and in England during the 1930s, he did not associate himself with, or become involved in, debates on the development of a Marxist artistic practice then taking place in East Berlin, debates in which Brecht and the Berliner Ensemble were fully involved.

Cavalcanti's "disinterested" position in this respect can be contrasted with that of his friend and colleague Joris Ivens. Just before making *Die Windrose* with Cavalcanti in 1956, Ivens had made *Das Lied der Ströme (Song of the Rivers* (1954), a co-production between the East German DEFA-Documentarfilm and the Communist-controlled World Federation of Trade Unions. The film, which won the prize dedicated to "the struggle for a better life" at the Karlovy Vary Film Festival in 1954, explores the relationship between ordinary people and seven rivers around the world, the seventh "river" being the international working-class movement, which was then meeting in Vienna.[56] In contrast to the highly committed Ivens, Cavalcanti's knowledge of, and interest in, Marxism was superficial and marginal, and this was bound to cause problems for him in what was at that time one of the most highly politicised countries in the world. It was ultimately because of this lack of engagement that Cavalcanti eventually became identified by members of the Berliner Ensemble and others within the DDR as peripheral to the development of a progressive film culture there.

This lack of involvement also lay behind a number of other criticisms of Cavalcanti, and Marcorelles claimed that he was an "old-fashioned" filmmaker, and out of touch with both his critical contemporaries and current requirements. Marcorelles argued that Cavalcanti appeared doomed to displease[57] because of this, and it is certainly the case that his films have been the object of remarkably wide-ranging critical disparagement, from English critics such as Lejeune, Balcon, Wright, Rotha and Grierson to French critics such as Dort and Marcorelles, Brazilian critics such as Rocha, and various Italian and East German critics. In each case, the basis of criticism was that Cavalcanti, a prominent figure, had chosen to distance himself from the important issues or movements of the day, and this perception of Cavalcanti as a disinterested fellow traveller, and someone who would not toe the Party line, is what has annoyed critics from the 1920s onwards.

Typically, Cavalcanti's response to such criticisms was not to address the issues which they raised, but to claim that he was misunderstood by others who made no attempt to appreciate his contribution to international cinema. His sense of hurt at being the object of such sustained criticism must have been considerable. The fiasco of Vera Cruz had been quickly followed by the criticisms of the Berliner Ensemble, and it had been some time, perhaps as far back as *Champagne Charlie* (1944), that he had received significant praise for a film for which he did not, at the same time, also suffer substantial criticism.

One final reason for the criticisms of *Puntila* which appeared in East Germany during this period was that Cavalcanti's film did not correspond to either the official doctrine of Soviet Socialist Realism, or the model of modernist social realism then being developed by the Berliner Ensemble. Writing in 1954, around the same time that he was working with Cavalcanti, Brecht argued that a modernised Socialist Realism should explore the "dialectical laws of movement", show events as alterable and contradictory, and appeal to the working class.[58] However, this aesthetic model did not conform to the official doctrine of Soviet Socialist Realism, and this led Brecht and the Berliner Ensemble to come into occasional conflict with the East German and Russian authorities. The problem as far as Cavalcanti was concerned was that *Puntila* did not correspond to either the official Socialist Realist model or that proposed by Brecht, and this, in turn, led to criticisms of the film appearing from both the advocates of orthodox Socialist Realism, and Communist modernists such as those associated with the Berliner Ensemble.

Cavalcanti's next, and final, East German project, *Die Windrose*, was a joint venture. *Die Windrose* consists of a prologue and five sections, each of which was directed by a different filmmaker. The prologue was directed by Cavalcanti; the Brazilian episode by Alex Viany; the Russian by Sergej Gerasimov; the French by Yannick Bellon; the Italian by Gillo Pontecorvo; and the Chinese by Wu Kuo-yin. Cavalcanti also supervised the overall filming of the project alongside Joris Ivens. Both Ivens' and Cavalcanti's roles seem to have been poorly defined during the making of this film, and their contact with the various filmmakers involved appears to have been marginal in some cases. For example, Pontecorvo claims never to have met Cavalcanti during the production of the film.[59] The end result is a film which is more a number of autonomous sections than a unified work.

The central theme of *Die Windrose* is the condition of women around the world, and each of the sections of the film deals with the plight of women in a number of different countries. In this respect, the film can be compared with a number of other films emerging from East Germany in the 1950s, such as *Frauenschicksale* (*Women's Fate*, 1952), which depict family and personal problems from a woman's point of view.[60] The DDR had some of the world's most progressive policies over women's rights during the 1950s, and East German women enjoyed particularly high levels of child care provision, maternity leave and equal rights legislation.[61] Nevertheless, the advocacy of women's rights in the DDR was closely connected to the policy objectives and interests of the Communist Party, and this dictated the way in which feminist discourses developed. In the same way, the "feminist" discourses in *Die Windrose* were also guided and informed by official propaganda policies.

Cavalcanti also suffered from the fact that, unlike *Puntila*, which was filmed in Austria, *Die Windrose* was made in East Germany, under the close scrutiny of officials within the state film organisation DEFA (the Deutsche Film Aktiengesellschaft), and Cavalcanti claims

to have experienced interference during the making of the film.[62]
Nevertheless, although *Die Windrose* clearly bears the mark of official
Party policy in its representation of the plight of working-class women,
it is also a striking film, shot in a documentary realist style influenced
by Italian neo-realism, and pulls few punches in its representation of
exploited and abused women.

One of the most powerful episodes in this respect is the
Brazilian one. As the episode opens, we see migrant women workers
boarding a truck. Later, as the truck travels through the countryside,
it is forced to halt, and a young, heavily pregnant woman is helped out.
The woman gives birth on the ground, but, as soon as the child is born,
the male drivers force the woman back onto the truck. The scene
emphasises class and female solidarity, and the assertion that women's
exploitation is linked to the existence of capitalism and middle-class
privilege. As in the other episodes, the central character in the
Brazilian episode of *Die Windrose* is a young woman, Anna, who takes
a leading role in protecting the other workers from exploitation.

Although the Brazilian episode is convincingly acted, and shot
using a documentary style whose effective realism manages to
transcend the propagandistic intent and tone of the film's commentary,
large parts of *Die Windrose* are over-didactic and pedantic, and the
voice-over commentary is extremely pedantic. The Russian episode, in
particular, is shot in an "official" Soviet Socialist Realist style, and is
extremely stage-bound and heavy on dialogue. The Italian episode is
again highly didactic, but it does have the advantage over the Russian
episode of having been shot in a freer and more documentary-based
Italian neo-realist style. It is also the only episode with an industrial
setting. The East German media were most impressed at the time with
the Chinese episode in *Die Windrose*. However, this was largely because
this episode deals with issues of gender equality, clearly a topical
subject for International Women's Day. Like the Russian episode, the
Chinese episode is extremely didactic and ponderous. Perhaps the most
curious episode in *Die Windrose* is the French episode, not because it
is particularly striking in itself, but because it rather unexpectedly
stars Simone Signoret and Yves Montand. Signoret plays the part of a
schoolteacher who also happens to be a Communist activist, whilst
Montand plays the part of a radically-inclined window-cleaner. The
involvement of Signoret and Montand here seems to have slipped
entirely from the annals of film history, but there they are, putting
their political ideals into practice in *Die Windrose*.

A far more obscure film than even *Puntila*, *Die Windrose*
remains almost unknown in the West. Although he never explicitly
disowned the film, Cavalcanti never referred to *Die Windrose* in any of
his writings, and this suggests that he did not regard it as important
or worthwhile. Nevertheless, in contrast to *Puntila*, *Die Windrose* was
well-reviewed in the East German press. Commissioned in order
celebrate International Women's Day, most reviewers found the film
be both authentic and moving.[63] Attention was particularly focuse

the film's humanism, in a way which reflected the earlier celebration of the humanist characteristics of *Song of the Sea* in the East German press.[64]

In addition to making *Puntila* and *Die Windrose* in the 1950s, Cavalcanti played another significant role within East Germany during the 1960s. Since its inception, the DDR had struggled to assert its own autonomous identity, and, in pursuit of this, regularly attempted to raise the international profile of the new state by mounting international sporting and cultural events. One of these was the annual Leipzig International Documentary and Short Film Festival. The fifth festival, held in 1962, happened to coincide with Cavalcanti's 65th birthday, and this provided the opportunity for the festival organisers to mount an international retrospective of his work. Cavalcanti was then invited to the DDR, where the state film archive duly mounted the retrospective, and also published the first book-length study of his work: Wolfgang Klaue's *Alberto Cavalcanti*.[65] The appearance of the book and the retrospective itself – the first major retrospective mounted by the Festival – clearly mark an attempt by the East German film authorities to identify Cavalcanti's achievements with those of the Republic.

The critical commentaries on Cavalcanti which appeared during the Festival attempted to position him as an important Socialist filmmaker, and one with close links to the DDR. For example, he was described as a name "not unknown to the German people"[66] and as a "loyal guest over many years of the Leipzig Documentary Film Week".[67] Alongside the claim that Cavalcanti was close to the DDR, the reviews also seek to position him as one of the world's most important international documentary filmmakers.[68] Elsewhere, Cavalcanti is described as a "pioneer" of documentary,[69] as "a man whom the art of film has much to thank",[70] as "one of the leading personalities in film",[71] and as "immensely influential in the area of documentary film".[72]

These critical reviews also attempted to position Cavalcanti as a committed anti-Fascist. Cavalcanti's career at Ealing is described as a "positive contribution to the anti-Fascist struggle". *Yellow Caesar* (1941), Cavalcanti's minor parodic film about Mussolini, is described as "without doubt one of his best films",[73] whilst *The Big Blockade* (1942) and *The Foreman Went to France* (1942) are described as "anti-Fascist films",[74] and as contributing to the "mobilisation of the British people".[75] Other writers went even further, describing Cavalcanti as "contributing to the strengthening of the struggle against German and Italian Fascism with powerful films",[76] and as dedicating "all his powers to the fight against Fascism".[77] Alongside the celebration of Cavalcanti's anti-Fascist credentials, these reviews also celebrate his internationalism. For example, the relatively minor *We Live in Two Worlds* (1937) is described as "a work of understanding between nations".[78]

These reviews also attempted to position Cavalcanti as a social realist filmmaker opposed to formalism. Cavalcanti's relationship to the French avant-garde in the 1920s is seen as a problem, as, within the official cultural policy of the DDR, formalism and the avant-garde were regarded as decadent manifestations of bourgeois capitalist culture. Consequently, much is made of the fact that Cavalcanti left the avant-garde in order to join the British documentary film movement, an organisation whose realist credentials were far more acceptable to these Communist critics.[79] Cavalcanti is also described as "one of the first people in Western Europe to take up social issues in film and attend to humanistic matters of concern",[80] and as "venturing into life with his camera, film[ing] the people of his environment in a realistic manner".[81] Finally, much is made of Cavalcanti's attempt to establish a new, socially-purposive national cinema in Brazil, and *Song of the Sea* is seen as particularly important in this respect. The failure of Cavalcanti's Brazilian venture at Vera Cruz on the other hand is ascribed to capitalist interference, particularly from Hollywood which is accused of "throttling" the Brazilian cinema.[82]

Much of the approach taken towards Cavalcanti here reflects the Party line at the time. Anti-Fascism, humanism, social realism and a concern with creating a national cinema opposed to Hollywood are all read into Cavalcanti's films, with the intention of establishing him as a figurehead whom the East German authorities can hold up as a friend and cultural icon of the DDR. Cavalcanti may not have been fully conscious of the extent to which his reputation was being used by the DDR in this way, but he clearly went along with what was taking place. Pleased to be well thought of, for once, Cavalcanti decided to play his part, knowing full well that he was not the committed Socialist, anti-Fascist and pro-Communist filmmaker which the reviewers claimed him to be.

As with his Brazilian period, Cavalcanti's East German sojourn was marked by dissent and disagreement, and, having fled from one set of problems in São Paulo, he soon found himself immersed in another set in Berlin. Cavalcanti's association with East Germany also had one other deleterious effect on his career. Unhappy with his experiences at DEFA, he wrote to Michael Balcon, asking about the possibility of employment at Ealing Studios.[83] However, the suspicions which Balcon harboured about Cavalcanti in the 1940s were now reinforced by the latter's new and, for Balcon, unacceptable association with the DDR. The result was that Cavalcanti did not return to Ealing.[84]

Notes

[1]   Claudio M Valentinetti, "La période brésilienne (1950-1954)", in Lorenzo Pellizzari and Claudio M Valentinetti (eds), *Alberto Cavalcanti* (Locarno: Éditions du Festival international du film de Locarno, 1988): 43.

[2]   Claude Beylie, Didier Lemarchand and Christian Michaud, "Entreti avec Alberto Cavalcanti", *Ecran* 30 November 1974, reproduced in ibid: 36

[3]   Forsyth Hardy, *John Grierson: A Documentary Biography* (London; Boston: Faber and Faber, 1979): 162.

[4]   Tino Balio (ed), *The American Film Industry* (Madison, WI; London: The University of Wisconsin Press, 1976): 425.

[5]   Jay Leyda, *Kino: A History of the Russian and Soviet Film*, third edition (London; Boston; Sydney: George Allen & Unwin, 1973): 400.

[6]   J P Nettl, *The Soviet Achievement* (London: Thames and Hudson, 1967): 224.

[7]   Leyda: 398.

[8]   *Neue Zeit* 11 November 1962.

[9]   Lorenzo Pellizzari, "La période internationale et le déclin" in Pellizzari and Valentinetti (eds): 52.

[10]   Translated from the French: "une volonté politique évidente". Pellizzari, in ibid (eds): 52.

[11]   Alberto Cavalcanti, "Mes relations avec Bertold Brecht", in ibid: 190.

[12]   Peter Gay, *Weimar Culture: The Outsider As Insider* (London: Secker & Warburg, 1969): 145.

[13]   Martin Walsh, *The Brechtian Aspect of Radical Cinema*, edited by Keith M Griffiths (London: British Film Institute, 1981): 7.

[14]   John Willett (ed and trans), *Brecht on Theatre: The Development of an Aesthetic* (London: Eyre Methuen, 1978): 91.

[15]   Marc Silberman, *German Cinema: Texts in Context* (Detroit: Wayne State University Press, 1995): 39.

[16]   "Kuhle Wampe", *Screen* 15: 2 (summer 1974): 41.

[17]   Walsh: 10.

[18]   Willett: 156.

[19]   John Willett (translated), *Bertolt Brecht: Mr. Puntila and His Man Matti* (London: Eyre Methuen, 1977): 6.

[20]   Willett (1978): 153.

[21]   Ibid: 154, 156.

[22]   Willett (1977): 7.

[23]   Ibid.

[24]   Ibid: 92.

[25]   Translated from the French: "*Puntila* n'est pas une pièce à thèse". Louis Marcorelles, "L'impossible gageure", *Cahiers du Cinéma* 13: 77 (December 1957): 54.

26   Willett (1977): 11.

27   Translated from the French: "le plus populaire du monde, juste après celui de Shakespeare". Cavalcanti, "Mes relations avec Bertold Brecht", in Pellizzari and Valentinetti (eds): 189.

28   Ibid: 195.

29   Translated from the French: "dans un tur pseudo-Marx Brothers terriblement guindé". Marcorelles: 54.

30   Cavalcanti, "Mes relations avec Bertold Brecht", in Pellizzari and Valentinetti (eds): 191.

31   Ibid: 194.

32   Ibid: 192.

33   Translated from the French: "commis-voyageur". Cavalcanti, "Mes relations avec Bertold Brecht", in Pellizzari and Valentinetti (eds): 193.

34   Ibid: 194.

35   Willett (1978): 99.

36   Walsh: 7.

37   *Sächsische Zeitung* 11 December 1965: 5.

38   *Der Tag* 23 December 1960.

39   *Der Tagesspiegel* 23 December 1960.

40   *Mitteldeutsche Neveste Nachrichten* 12 December 1965.

41   *Frankfurter Allgemeine Zeitung* 15 March 1961.

42   *Berliner Zeitung* 15 December 1965.

43   *Sächsische Zeitung* 11 December 1965: 5.

44   *Liberal Demokratische Zeitung* 6 December 1965.

45   Translated from the French: "échec". Bernard Dort, "Pour une critique Brechtienne du cinéma", *Cahiers du Cinéma* 19: 114 (December 1960): 35.

46   Ibid.

47   Ibid.

48   Translated from the French: "L'impossible gageure...sans conteste un échec". Marcorelles: 52.

49   Translated from the French: "Cavalcanti, en accentuant schématisme du sujet". Ibid: 55.

50   Ibid.

51   Ibid.

[52]   Translated from the French: "improvisation effrénée". Ibid: 54.

[53]   Martin Esslin, *Brecht: A Choice of Evils. A Critical Study of the Man, His Work and His Opinions*, fourth revised edition (London; New York: Methuen, 1984): 33.

[54]   Ibid: 288.

[55]   Cavalcanti, "Mes relations avec Bertold Brecht", in Pellizzari and Valentinetti (eds): 194.

[56]   Rosalind Delmar, *Joris Ivens: 50 years of film-making* (London: British Film Institute, 1979): 48-49.

[57]   Marcorelles: 54.

[58]   Quoted in Willett (1978): 269.

[59]   Pellizzari, in Pellizzari and Valentinetti (eds): 54.

[60]   Nina Hibbin, *Eastern Europe: An Illustrated Guide* (London; New York: A Zwemmer and A S Barnes, 1969): 49.

[61]   Mary Fulbrook, *A Concise History of Germany* (Cambridge; New York; Port Chester; Melbourne; Sydney: Cambridge University Press, 1990): 239.

[62]   Pellizzari, in Pellizzari and Valentinetti (eds): 55.

[63]   *Neue Zeit* 8 March 1957.

[64]   *Der Karier* 2 March 1957.

[65]   Wolfgang Klaue (ed), *Alberto Cavalcanti* (Berlin: Staatlichen Filmarchiv der Deutsches Demokratischen Republic/Club der Filmschaffenden der DDR, 1962).

[66]   Translated from the German: "Alberto Cavalcanti – er ist auch dem deutschen Publikum nicht unbekannt". *Volksricht* 10 November 1962.

[67]   Translated from the German: "treusten Gästen der Leipziger Documentarfilm". Unidentified newspaper clipping, dated 8 November 1962, from the Bundesarchiv-Filmarchiv.

[68]   *Der Demokrat* 19 November 1962.

[69]   Translated from the German: "einer Pionier". *Liberal Demokratische Zeitung* 22 October 1962.

[70]   Translated from the German: "einem Mann...dem die Filmkunst viel zu verdanken hat". *Volksricht* 10 November 1962.

[71]   Translated from the German: "eine führende Persönlichkeit auf dem ebiet des Films". *Thüringische Landeszeitung* 10 November 1962.

         Translated from the German: "sein ungemein befruchtendes Schaffe ie Dokumentarfilm-arbeit". *Neue Zeit* 11 November 1962.

         Translated from the German: "einen seiner besten Film überhaupt". ' *Zeitung* 9 November 1962.

74   Translated from the German: "antifaschistische Spielfilme". *Der Demokrat* 19 November 1962.

75   Translated from the German: "Mobilisterung der englischen Bevölkerung". *Volksricht* 10 November 1962.

76   Translated from the German: "Mit bewegenden Filmen trug er zur Stärkung kampffrontgegen den deutschen und italienischen Faschismus". Unidentified newspaper clipping, dated 8 November 1962, from the Bundesarchiv-Filmarchiv.

77   Translated from the German: "seine ganze Kraft widmete der Künstler dem Kamp gegen den Faschismus". *Volksricht* 10 November 1962.

78   Translated from the German: "ein Werk für die Völkerverständing". *Neue Zeit* 11 November 1962.

79   *National Zeitung* 9 November 1962.

80   Translated from the German: "einer der ersten im Westeuropäischen Film, der im Film soziale Probleme aufgriff". *Der Demokrat* 19 November 1962.

81   Translated from the German: "Er ging mit der Kamera mitten hinein ins Leben, filmte die menschen seiner Umwelt in realistischen Bildern". Unidentified newspaper clipping, dated 8 November 1962, from the Bundesarchiv-Filmarchiv.

82   *Neue Zeit* 11 November 1962.

83   Alberto Cavalcanti, letter to Balcon, 6 May 1956. Aileen and Michael Balcon Collection, Special Collections, British Film Institute [hereafter AMBC]: F/43.

84   Michael Balcon, letter to George Mann, 23 March 1956. AMBC: F/43.

10

Epilogue

1956, the year of *Die Windrose*, also marks the beginning of Cavalcanti's decline as a filmmaker, and none of the projects which he carried out during the 26 years from then until his death in 1982 can be compared with those brought to fruition before 1956. After *Die Windrose*, and in conjunction with Hanns Eisler, Cavalcanti attempted to develop a musical comedy based on Offenbach's opera *La Belle Hélène* (*Fair Helen*, 1864). However, various copyright and other problems soon emerged and, when these proved insurmountable, the project was abandoned. After this, Cavalcanti attempted an adaptation of Jules Verne's *Le Château des Carpathes* (*The Castle in the Carpathians*, 1892), and travelled to Romania in order to shoot the film. However, as a result of difficulties experienced with the Romanian authorities, this project was also eventually abandoned. Following these disappointments, Cavalcanti attempted to develop a version of Mozart's *Die Zauberflöte* (*The Magic Flute*, 1791), but this also failed to materialise.[1]

It is curious that Cavalcanti should have chosen to pursue projects such as these after spending the period from 1947 to 1956 preoccupied with the development of an increasingly social realist cinema. None of the interviews he gave from 1956 onwards throws any light on why he chose these subjects, apart from, perhaps, that he was fond of the works of Mozart, Offenbach and Verne.[2] The fact that these projects were all very different from each other may suggest the lack of any overall sense of direction in Cavalcanti's filmmaking after *Die Windrose*, although it does appear that, not withstanding this, he was, in fact, largely moving away from the social realist style of *O Canto do Mar* (*Song of the Sea*, 1953), and back to the more parodic form of filmmaking which he had indulged in prior to 1947.

Evidence to support this view is furnished by another of Cavalcanti's projects during this period. As a commemoration of Bertolt Brecht, who had died in August 1956, Cavalcanti proposed a project titled *Les Visions de Simone Machard*, which he conceived as an verent Brechtian version of the legend of Joan of Arc. This project onsiderable comic potential, and, if it had been realised, would enabled Cavalcanti to return to the tradition which he had successfully exploited in films such as *The Big Blockade* (1942), *Champagne Charlie* (1944) and *Simão, O Caolho* (*One-Eyed Simon*, 1952). However, Cinitel, the French production company responsible for the project, and without whom it could not be realised, eventually withdrew support, concerned about the blasphemous content of the proposed film. As a consequence, *Les Visions de Simone Machard*, like Cavalcanti's other projects during this period, failed to materialise.[3]

Cavalcanti's work from 1958 until his death in 1982 was extremely varied. In 1958, he directed the Italian-French co-production *La Prima notte/Les Noces vénitiennes* (*The First Night*, a romantic melodrama starring Martine Carol, Claudia Cardinale and Vittorio De Sica. However, Cavalcanti later disowned the film, considering it too light and commercial, and also complained about the difficulties he had experienced directing Martine Carol.[4] *The First Night* should probably be ranked alongside films such as *The First Gentleman* (1947) and *Mulher de Verdade* (*The Real Woman*, 1954) as failures, as uncharacteristic of Cavalcanti's filmmaking, and as having been primarily undertaken as a result of financial expediency. In addition to Cavalcanti's own rejection of the film, *The First Night* was criticised in both France and Italy, criticism which, coming so soon after the negative reaction to *Herr Puntila und sein Knecht Matti* (*Mr Puntila and His Hired Man Matti*, 1955), only added to the widespread perception that Cavalcanti's career had now gone into steep decline.[5]

If *The First Night* failed to advance Cavalcanti's reputation as a filmmaker of international calibre, his next film, *The Monster of Highgate Ponds* (1960), a children's film made for the Rank Film Foundation, would probably have destroyed that reputation completely if the film had ever been seen by adults. *The Monster of Highgate Ponds* must stand high in the stakes for the worst film ever made (it was apparently even regularly booed by the children who were forced to watch it at Saturday morning matinée performances), and contains no discernible trace of Cavalcanti's authorial signature whatsoever. The plot concerns a dinosaur egg brought back to Highgate by an anthropologist. The egg hatches and becomes gradually transformed into an inflated rubber dinosaur, which the child actors christen as "Beauty".

The acting throughout the film is of an appalling standard, and the dialogue is excruciatingly bad, as when, for example, the anthropologist father comments that he "did not think these things [dinosaurs] existed anymore, even in Malaysia". One can only sympathise with Cavalcanti for having been driven to make such a dire film as this – again, presumably, out of financial necessity.

Perhaps in reaction to the humbling experience of *The Monst of Highgate Ponds*, Cavalcanti then moved back into the realms of high arts in attempting to make a version of Federico García Lo epic play *Yerma* (1934). The film was to have been ma Cavalcanti's old friend Mário Audra and his Maristela co however, this project was also eventually abandoned, again b copyright and other legal problems, although Cavalcanti did complete a script. *Yerma* was to have been produced in Spain by Maristela in association with Columbia Pictures, but the film fell foul of feuding within Columbia following the death of the Cohn brothers, who had controlled the studio.

The problems experienced over the abortive production of *Yerma* also illustrate some of the less praiseworthy aspects of Cavalcanti's personality. As Audra was negotiating with Columbia, he discovered that, without informing him, Cavalcanti had also been meeting with people from within the organisation. Whether Cavalcanti was simply trying to help, or was trying to undercut Audra, will never be known. What is clear, however, is that, when the Columbia deal fell through, Cavalcanti announced that he was leaving the project, giving Audra no opportunity to find another sponsor. Cavalcanti may have been anxious about the fact that he was without any clear source of income in Spain, and had to find new commissions quickly, but his behaviour towards the loyal Audra was hardly creditable. With Cavalcanti's decision to leave the project, *Yerma* was finished, and so, according to Audra, was the friendship between the two Brazilians.[6]

Cavalcanti followed the aborted attempt to film *Yerma* with *Thus Spoke Theodore Herzl* (1967), a documentary made in Israel about the Israeli leader. Seen today, *Thus Spoke Theodore Herzl* is a strikingly modernist work, in which Cavalcanti uses non-synchronous sound, pronounced compositional devices and montage editing to produce a powerful documentary. An obscure film which is hardly ever shown, *Thus Spoke Theodore Herzl* deserves more attention. It was the only film Cavalcanti made in Israel, although, writing in 1970, he expressed a desire to return to Israel in order to make a film about Noah. However, this project, which was to be based on a script written by the Polish writer Lazar Kobrynski and on a score written by his old colleague Darius Milhaud, was never realised.[7]

Thus Spoke Theodore Herzl also illustrates Cavalcanti's continued political naïvety, and his predisposition for getting himself into political hot water. 1967, the year in which *Thus Spoke Theodore Herzl* was made, also happened to be the year of the Arab-Israeli Six Day War. The extent to which Cavalcanti's film was commissioned as part of a propaganda campaign, designed to bolster the international standing of the Israeli state during a particularly troubled period, is unclear, but the possibility remains that Israel used Cavalcanti's reputation to this end, just as the DDR had done to bolster its cultural credentials in the 1950s.

It is, at the same time, both typical of Cavalcanti and indicative of his lack of political sensibility – some might say integrity that he was capable of making both a pro-Communist film such as *Windrose* and one which celebrated the founder of modern Zionism. a long intellectual journey which encompasses working with ed colleagues such as Brecht, Pozner, Eisler and Ivens to film about Zionism, and one can only speculate on how his old comrades felt about this. Whatever the aesthetic qualities of *Thus Spoke Theodore Herzl*, Cavalcanti did himself no favours by making such a film in the same year as the Six Day War.

After *Thus Spoke Theodore Herzl*, Cavalcanti returned to France where he found employment with the state television station ORTF. There he directed three works for television: *Les Empaillés* (*The Fools*, 1969), *La Visite de la vieille dame* (*The Visit of the Old Lady*, 1970) and *Le Voyageur du silence* (1976). Unfortunately, virtually nothing is known about these works. Cavalcanti made no reference to them in any of the interviews which he gave towards the end of his career, and no recordings of them can be traced.

Ironically, the final major project of Cavalcanti's career was to be made in Brazil, the country from which he had fled in some despair in 1954. In 1976, he was approached by the Brazilian state film company Embrafilme, and was asked to make a compilation film of his life's work. The resulting work was *Um Homem e o Cinema* (*One Man and the Cinema*, 1976). Oddly, *One Man and the Cinema* does not open with any kind of introductory commentary or even sight of Cavalcanti, but launches straight into showing a number of brief extracts from Cavalcanti's early French films, organised under the title "Cenografia" ("Set Design"). The extracts shown here are from *L'Inhumaine* (*The Inhuman*, L'Herbier, 1924), *La Galerie des monstres* (*The Gallery of Monsters*, Jaque Catelain, 1924) *Feu Mathias Pascal* (*The Late Mathias Pascal*, Marcel L'Herbier, 1925) and *The Little People* (GB, George Pearson, 1925). This is followed by a section entitled "Depoimentos" ("Testimonies"), in which J B Priestley, G K Chesterton and George Bernard Shaw are seen speaking in sequences taken from *B.B.C.: The Voice of Britain* (GB, Arthur Elton, 1934)

The next section is entitled "Cenas de Amor" ("Love Scenes"), and contains brief extracts from *En rade* (*Stranded*, France, Cavalcanti, 1927), *One-Eyed Simon, The First Night, Caiçara* (Brazil, Adolfo Celi, 1950) and *Dead of Night* (GB, Cavalcanti, 1945). Interestingly, for the "love scene" in *Dead of Night* Cavalcanti chose the sequence from "The Ventriloquist's Dummy", in which Hugo is returned to Maxwell Frere's prison cell. The extract includes Hugo's declaration that he intends to abandon Frere for Kee, and Frere's frenzied destruction of Hugo, as he stamps the mannequin's face to pieces. The ascription of this as a "love scene" is clearly meant to be taken with a pinch of salt, although it does give credence to Monegal's view that "The Ventriloquist's Dummy" possessed "horrible overtones of homosexuality".[8]

The next section of *One Man and the Cinema* is entitled "Assassinatos" ("Killings"), and contains extracts from *Rien que les heures* (*Nothing But the Hours*, France, Cavalcanti, 1926), *Went the Day Well?* (GB, Cavalcanti, 1942), *For Them That Trespass* (GB, Cavalcanti, 1949) and *They Made Me a Fugitive* (GB, Cavalcanti, 1947). The scene from *Nothing But the Hours* is that of the murder of the newspaper vendor by the sailor, and, from *Went the Day Well?*, those of the a... to death of a German soldier by the postmistress Mrs Collins, a...

killing of Wilsford by Nora. The scene selected from *For Them That Trespass* is that in which Frankie is murdered by the train driver Jim, and, from *They Made Me a Fugitive*, that in which Clem Morgan is asked to kill the drunken husband of a woman whose house he has entered whilst on the run. This section of *One Man and the Cinema* illustrates Cavalcanti's own awareness of the importance of these types of sequences, with their images of brutal violence, within his films.

The following section of *One Man and the Cinema* is entitled "Dança" ("Dance"), and begins with the brief sequence from *Champagne Charlie* in which three ballerinas dance at the Mogador. This sequence, which contains no dialogue, is followed by a sequence from *Tour de chant* (*Tour of Song*, France, Cavalcanti, 1933), in which a burlesque song and dance routine is seen taking place in the elegant rooms of a bourgeois residence. Following this, Cavalcanti selects a scene from the documentary *We Live in Two Worlds* (GB, Cavalcanti, 1937), in which a Swiss peasant dance is featured. This is followed by a sequence from *Yvette* (France, Cavalcanti, 1927) featuring a costumed ball. This section of *One Man and the Cinema* then ends with sequences of native Indian dancing from *Au Pays du scalp* (*In the Country of the Scalp People*, France, Marquis de Wavrin, 1931). Despite the intrinsic interest which many of these extracts possess, there appears to be little to link them together, other than the overall theme of dance, and the end result is a rather haphazardly developed piece of filmmaking which certainly does not add up to any systematic examination of the role of dance in Cavalcanti's films.

The next section of *One Man and the Cinema* is entitled "O Absurdo da Guerra" ("The Absurdities of War"), and begins with a sequence from *The First Days* (GB, Watt, Jackson and Jennings, 1939), followed by sequences from *Greek Testament* (GB, Charles Hassé, 1943), *Squadron 992* (GB, Harry Watt, 1939), *Men of the Lightship* (GB, David Macdonald, 1940) and *Yellow Caesar* (GB, Cavalcanti, 1941). The majority of these sequences, as the title of this section of the film suggests, emphasise the absurdity, rather than the horror, of war, and this is particularly the case with the extract chosen from *Yellow Caesar*, in which the posturing Mussolini is seen to speak complete nonsense. The sequence chosen from Harry Watt's *Squadron 992* is the familiar one in which a greyhound pursues a hare whilst, in the skies above, a Spitfire pursues a German aircraft.

One Man and the Cinema is divided into two parts, and Part 2 begins with a section entitled "O Homem e o Trabalho" ("Men and Work"), which commences with a sequence from *Volta Redonda* (Brazil, John Waterhouse, 1952). This is followed by sequences from *North Sea* (GB, Harry Watt, 1938), *Line to Tcherva Hut* (GB, Cavalcanti, 1936), *Spare Time* (GB, Humphrey Jennings, 1939) and *Men in Danger* (GB, ̶at Jackson, 1938). The sequences chosen from *Spare Time* are those ̶ich feature the kazoo band and the Welsh choir. The next section of ̶ *Man and the Cinema* is entitled "Pesquisa em Comédia" ("Essays ̶omedy"), and begins with sequences from *Pett and Pott* (GB,

Cavalcanti, 1934) This is followed by sequences from *La P'tite Lilie* (France, Cavalcanti, 1927), *La Jalousie du Barbouillé* (*The Jealousy of the Barbouillé*, France, Cavalcanti, 1928), *Mr Puntila and His Hired Man Matti* (1955) and *Die Windrose*. What emerges from this part of the film in particular is the extent to which a certain eccentric and vaudevillesque form of comedy can be identified in these films.

The largest section in *One Man and the Cinema*, entitled "Pesquisa em Drama" ("Essays on Drama") begins with a sequence from *Santuário* (*Sanctuary*, Brazil, Lima Barreto, 1951). This is followed by sequences from *The Foreman Went to France* (GB, Charles Frend, 1942), *Terra é sempre Terra* (*The Earth Is Always the Earth*, Brazil, Tom Payne, 1951), *Die Windrose*, *The Life and Adventures of Nicholas Nickleby* (GB, Cavalcanti, 1947), *Song of the Sea*, *The Halfway House* (GB, Basil Dearden, 1944), *The First Gentleman* and *Thus Spoke Theodore Herzl*.

There seems little to link these episodes together, and the highly realistic episodes from *The Earth Is Always the Earth*, *Die Windrose* and *Song of the Sea*, all of which concern tragic issues of birth or death, stand out in stark contrast to the more contrived scenes from *The Life and Adventures of Nicholas Nickleby* and *The Foreman Went to France*, as well as from the didactic documentary modernism of *Thus Spoke Theodore Herzl*. It is also odd that, although Cavalcanti opted to select the final, highly symbolic scenes from *The Halfway House*, in which the inn is engulfed in flames, he also chose to select the episode from *The Life and Adventures of Nicholas Nickleby* in which Nicholas engages in an unconvincing Hollywoodesque struggle with Sir Mulberry Hawk, rather than the excellent and highly dramatic final scenes of the film, in which Ralph Nickleby commits suicide.

The final section of *One Man and the Cinema* is entitled "Pesquisa em Ritmo" ("Essays on Rhythm"), and contains excerpts from only four films: *The Earth Is Always the Earth*, *Coal Face* (GB, Cavalcanti, 1935), *Alice au pays romand* (*Alice in Switzerland*, GB/ Switzerland, Cavalcanti, 1938) and *Night Mail* (1936). All these sequences, as the title of this part of the film suggests, emphasise the role of rhythmic editing. The section from *Coal Face*, for example, is the most modernist and complexly edited in the film, in which the coal lift rises to the surface, accompanied by avant-garde music composed by Benjamin Britten. Similarly, the scenes selected from *Night Mail*, perhaps predictably, are those in which Auden's poetry and Britten's music are superimposed over images of the spinning train wheels, as the postal express speeds across open countryside towards Edinburgh. In contrast to these two modernist sequences, however, the extract selected from the little-known *Alice in Switzerland* uses music accompaniment to illustrate scenes of people skiing, and appears frankly innocuous and superficial in comparison.

In the final analysis, *One Man and the Cinema* disappointing and rambling work, and as ultimately frustrating Cavalcanti's two earlier attempts to produce comprehensive a of developments within the cinema: his 1942 film *Film and Reality* and his 1952 book *Filme e Realidade*. Like *Film and Reality, One Man and the Cinema* assiduously avoids analytical interpretation of its subject-matter, and instead presents the spectator with a loosely cohering and often random series of juxtapositions. Whilst conforming to what today might be described as a commendably postmodernist model of narrative structure, *One Man and the Cinema* appears insubstantial and unsatisfactory, and amounts to a lost opportunity on Cavalcanti's part to argue his case, and to provide a structured account of his filmmaking career. It was perhaps a blessing in disguise that, when the National Film Theatre screened a retrospective of Cavalcanti's films in February and March 1977, *One Man and the Cinema* had not yet been completed, and so could not be shown. Despite these criticisms however, *One Man and the Cinema* remains of value in that it contains a number of extracts from some extremely rare films, such as the almost unknown *Die Windrose* and *Sanctuary*.

Notes

1   Lorenzo Pellizzari, "La période internationale et le déclin", in Pellizzari and Valentinetti (eds): 55.

2   Ibid.

3   Ibid.

4   Geoffrey Minish, "Cavalcanti in Paris", *Sight and Sound* 39: 3 (summer 1970): 135.

5   Valentinetti, in Pellizzari and Valentinetti (eds): 56.

6   Mário Audra Jr, *Cinematográfica Maristela: Memórias de um Produtor* (São Paulo: Silver Hawk, 1997): 136-148.

7   Minish: 135.

8   Emir Rodriguez Monegal, "Alberto Cavalcanti", *The Quarterly of Film, Radio and Television* 9: 4 (summer 1955): 351.

11

Conclusion

The most important influence on Cavalcanti during the 1925-34 period was realism, and a clear trajectory of realist filmmaking is discernible within his films, linking *Résurrection* (1922), *L'Inondation* (*The Flood*, 1923), *Feu Mathias Pascal* (*The Late Mathias Pascal*, 1925), *The Little People* (1925), *Voyage au Congo* (*Voyage to the Congo*, 1927), *Rien que les heures* (*Nothing But the Hours*, 1926), *En rade* (*Stranded*, 1927) and *Au Pays du scalp* (*In the Country of the Scalp People*, 1931). That realist trajectory was partly taken from the impressionist cinema, but was more substantially drawn from pictorialist naturalism, and it is this latter tradition, with its emphasis on the relationship between individual and environment, which had the greatest influence on Cavalcanti's evolving filmmaking at the time.

If the French realist tradition was an important influence on Cavalcanti during this period, another was that of Surrealism, and, although Cavalcanti's relationship to the Surrealists was tenuous and often fractious, his films were nevertheless influenced by a concern for the use of incongruous juxtaposition and irrational narrative structures which stemmed from Surrealism. However, the influence of Surrealism on Cavalcanti should not be overstated, and must, on the contrary, be understood as operating in conjunction with other influences, most notably that of realism.

By 1934, Cavalcanti's filmmaking remained grounded in the French realist tradition and also exhibited a use of modernist features, melodramatic and sentimental formats, and comic, musical or folkloric elements. This complex and uneven set of stylistic characteristics did not add up to a systematic or coherent aesthetic position, although, had Cavalcanti not been so thrown off course by his involvement in the commercial film industry, it might well have eventually done so.

Cavalcanti left France for England in 1934 because he had become increasingly frustrated by the lack of opportunity available to him within the French film industry. But was his decision the right one, and is there a case for arguing that he should have remained in France? Many avant-garde filmmakers failed to survive the advent of the sound film in France, and, in many respects, Cavalcanti must b counted amongst these casualties. However, not all the avant-gar filmmakers of the period met such a fate, and some, including Jean Renoir, René Clair, Jean Vigo, Julian Duvivier, Marcel Pagnol and Jean Grémillon, went on to make valuable contributions to French cinema during the 1930s.

The question thus inevitably arises as to whether Cavalcanti might have joined the ranks of these eminent auteurs had he remained in France. Dudley Andrew has described Renoir's *La Chienne* (1931) and Grémillon's *La Petite Lise* (1930) as examples of "aesthetic heroism", in that both films were defiantly innovative in their use of the sound medium, and in that such inventiveness was achieved against a background of the increasingly normative commercial imperatives of the French film industry.[1] However, by 1931, Cavalcanti was already working for Paramount, and the "aesthetic heroism", or what Ghali has characterised as "pure cinema", of *Nothing But the Hours* and *Stranded*, had already given way to factory line productions such as *Toute sa vie* (*All His Life*, 1930).[2]

For a variety of reasons – some of them convincing – Cavalcanti was unable to emulate the aesthetic heroism of Renoir and Grémillon. Instead, and, as he himself has admitted, he chose to flee France and seek pastures new in England. In my view, this was an error. I believe that had Cavalcanti remained in France, and fought to make the type of films which he wanted to make, he would have emerged as a major French filmmaker to rank alongside Renoir, Duvivier, Carné and Vigo. I also believe that, had this taken place, the stylistic characteristics of the films which Cavalcanti would have made would be similar to those found in the films of Jean Vigo, the filmmaker whom he most admired, and to whom a chapter of *Filme e Realidade* (1952) is devoted.

However, Cavalcanti's response in the face of a troubled situation was, typically, either covertly to undermine, or snipe at, his adversaries from the sidelines, or take his leave when the opportunity presented itself. Thus, instead of going on to make what I believe would have been major films within the French poetic realist tradition, he became caught up in Grierson's megalomaniac ambitions for the creation of an "informational state" and Balcon's plans for the creation of a middlebrow English national cinema.

As I have argued earlier, Cavalcanti's contribution to both the documentary film movement and Ealing Studios was a decisive one. However, his approach to filmmaking at both organisations was often at odds with those who employed him. Consequently, although some of the films which Cavalcanti directed over the 1934-46 period remain important, that period can, in many respects, be characterised as one in which it proved difficult for him to make the kinds of films which he ideally would have liked to.

It was only with *For Them That Trespass* (1949), and, after a gap of some twenty years, that Cavalcanti was, at last, able to return to the French poetic realist tradition. However, even that film was the product of compromise, and it was, in fact, only with *O Canto do Mar*

(*Song of the Sea*, 1953) that he was able to effect a full return to poetic realism. Unfortunately for him, the expressive fatalism, or what some Brazilian critics have referred to as the "unjustified gloom and futility" of the film, was not what the film industry and film critics in Brazil either expected or wanted.[3]

Cavalcanti's films, or at least those to which he was most committed, can be divided into three main groups. Firstly, there are those which attempt, in varying degree, to subvert dominant or sanctioned values of one kind or another. In France, films such as *Nothing But the Hours* had attempted this in a spirit of avant-garde rebellion, whereas, in England, this subversive spirit was sometimes more covertly and darkly deployed in films such as *Went the Day Well?* (1942) and "The Ventriloquist's Dummy". However, although these films are important, I would argue that they do not fully represent Cavalcanti's core filmmaking concerns.

The second major group consists of transitional films such as *Champagne Charlie* (1944), *They Made Me a Fugitive* (1947) and *Simão, O Caolho* (One-Eyed Simon, 1952). Although, like the first group, these also critique official mores and conventions, they are, in addition, more intentionally constructive and positive in what they have to say concerning the relationship between individual and environment. This shift from critique to a more affirmative approach differentiates a film such as *Champagne Charlie* from the more subversive and deconstructive *Went the Day Well?*, although it also leads to the latter film appearing, perhaps superficially, as more striking, and therefore more worthy of critical attention, than the former. I believe that this misguided perception lies behind the fact that very little critical attention has been expended on films such as *Champagne Charlie*, *They Made Me a Fugitive* and *One-Eyed Simon*, and I hope that this book will go some way to reversing this situation.

Finally, there are those films which, I would argue, come closest to realising and embodying Cavalcanti's core aspirations for his own filmmaking. These include *Stranded*, *For Them That Trespass* and *Song of the Sea*, films made within the poetic realist tradition which point to the way in which Cavalcanti's filmmaking might have evolved during the 1950s, if fortune had favoured him. The mature expression of this modernist, poetic realist style is, unquestionably, *Song of the Sea*, a film which also reveals Cavalcanti's characteristic concern for the surreal.

Cavalcanti's major contribution to film culture was made in England, not as a director, but as a producer, and his production work at both the GPO Film Unit and Ealing Studios had a considerable impact on two of the most important institutions within British film culture. On the other hand, Cavalcanti's contribution to Brazilian film culture rests less with his work as a producer than with his achievements as a director, and, although the experiment with V Cruz turned out to be a failure, films such as *One-Eyed Simon* *Song of the Sea* did provide a platform upon which an indepe

Brazilian cinema would later grow.

Cavalcanti moved from country to country throughout his career, and, whilst this itinerant existence no doubt had its positive aspects, these nomadic tendencies also had their drawbacks. His custom of moving on when circumstances became difficult effectively stopped him from developing as a consistent filmmaker, because each time he moved, whether to England, France, Brazil or Germany, he had to begin, once again, at the beginning.

As I have already argued, I believe that Cavalcanti should have remained in France in 1934. On the other hand, I believe that he was correct to leave both the documentary film movement and Ealing Studios when he did. Cavalcanti was not a documentary filmmaker, and made very few documentaries after leaving the movement. His natural domain was the feature film, and he was right to move back into that genre when the opportunity presented itself. Similarly, if Cavalcanti had remained at Ealing after 1946, Balcon would have ensured that he directed few films of any real substance there. Cavalcanti also had little option but to leave Brazil in 1954, although I believe that, had he remained, he would have gone on to make other films of the stature of *Song of the Sea*, and to establish himself as the central figure within Brazilian film culture. Unfortunately, it was not to be.

None of this should deny Cavalcanti's achievements, which remain considerable, but the feeling persists that he could – and should have achieved more than he did. When I met him in Paris a few months before his death, I was impressed by a character and a bearing which struck me as both generous and dignified. However, I also believe that, at key moments in his career, such generosity and dignity were also accompanied by a failure to exercise the kind of intellectual understanding of the events around him which would have enabled him to develop as a filmmaker.

Nevertheless, I would like the final words set out here to reflect the generous and affirmative aspect of Cavalcanti's character, as well as his aspirations for both his own filmmaking and the cinema in general. Here he is, writing in 1936, and imagining what his films might achieve in the future. It is a pity that, during the course of his career, Cavalcanti was presented with so few opportunities to put such sentiments into practice:

> How much on the side of semblance of the marvellous should one try to attain in a film? The problem calls for realisation that is profound. To have reverence for life, to guard its wild freedom, to interpret it in an act of true reconstruction – this is something to look forward to in the cinema.[4]

Notes

1   Dudley Andrew, *Mists of Regret: Culture and Sensibility in Classic French Film* (Princeton, NJ: Princeton University Press, 1995): 111.

2   Noureddine Ghali, *L'Avant-Garde Cinématographique en France dans les Années Vingt: Idées, Conceptions, Théories* (Paris: Éditions Paris Expérimental, 1995): 107.

3   Catherine de la Roche, "Cavalcanti in Brazil", *Sight and Sound* 24: 3 (January-March 1955): 119.

4   Alberto Cavalcanti, "The Evolution of Cinematography in France (1936)", in Ian Aitken (ed), *The Documentary Film Movement: An Anthology* (Edinburgh: Edinburgh University Press, 1998): 204.

Filmography

The following abbreviations have been used:

AC	Alberto Cavalcanti	*p*	producer
ad	assistant director	*sc*	scenario
ap	associate producer	*snd*	sound
d	director	*sp*	screenplay
ed	editor	*std*	set design

Résurrection
France 1922 · *d* Marcel L'Herbier *std* AC *p* L'Herbier, Cinégraphic

L'Inondation
The Flood, France 1923 · *d* Louis Delluc *ad* Oscar Cornaz *std* AC *p* Marcel L'Herbier, Cinégraphic

L'Inhumaine
The Inhuman, France 1924 · *d* Marcel L'Herbier *ad* Raymond Payelle, Philippe Hériat *std* AC *p* Marcel L'Herbier, Cinégraphic

La Galerie des monstres
The Gallery of Monsters, France 1924 · *d* Jaque Catelain *ad* AC *p* Marcel L'Herbier, Cinégraphic

Feu Mathias Pascal
The Late Mathias Pascal, France 1925 · *d* Marcel L'Herbier *ad* AC *std* AC *p* Marcel L'Herbier, Cinégraphic

The Little People
GB 1925 · *d* George Pearson *std* AC *p* Thomas Welsh, George Pearson

Le Train sans yeux
The Train Without Eyes, France 1926 · *d* AC *sc* AC *ed* AC *p* Néo-Films/Films Legrand

Rien que les heures
Nothing But the Hours, France 1926 · *d* AC *sc* AC *ed* AC *p* Pierre Braunberger, Néo-Films

En rade
Stranded, France 1927 · *d* AC *sc* AC *ed* AC *p* Pierre Braunberger, Néo-Films

Voyage au Congo
Voyage to the Congo, France 1927 · *d* Marc Allégret *ed* AC *p* Pierre Braunberger

Yvette
France 1927 · *d* AC *sc* AC *ed* AC

La P'tite Lili
France 1927 · *d* AC *sc* AC *ed* AC *p* Pierre Braunberger, Néo-Films

Le Capitaine Fracasse
France 1928 · *d* Henri Wulschleger *sc* AC *ed* AC *p* Charles Schneider, Lutèce Films

La Jalousie du Barbouillé
The Jealousy of the Barbouillé, France 1928 · *d* AC *sc* AC *std* AC, Lucien Aguettand *p* Studio des Ursulines

Souvenirs de Paris
France 1928 · *d* Marcel Duhamel, Pierre Prévert *ad* AC *p* Roduick Films [film lost]

Tire-au-flanc
The Idler, France 1928 · *d* Jean Renoir *sp* Jean Renoir, Claude Heymann, André Cerf, AC *p* Pierre Braunberger, Néo-Films

Le Petit chaperon rouge
Little Red Riding Hood, France 1929 · *d* AC *sp* AC, Jean Renoir *std* AC *ed* AC *p* Jean Renoir

Vous verrez la semaine prochaine
Next Week You Will See, France 1929 · *d* AC *sc* AC *ed* AC [film lost]

Toute sa vie
All His Life, France 1930 · *d* AC *p* Paramount

A Canção do Berço
Song of the Cradle, France 1930 · *d* AC *p* Paramount

A Mi-chemin du ciel
Halfway to Heaven, France 1930 · *d* AC *sp* AC *p* Paramount

Les Vacances du diable
The Devil's Holiday, France 1930 · *d* AC *sp* AC *p* Paramount

Dans une île perdue
On an Island Lost, France 1931 · *d* AC *p* Paramount

Au Pays du scalp
In the Country of the Scalp People, France 1931 · Marquis de Wavrin *ed* AC

En lisant le journal
On Reading the Newspaper, France 1932 · *d* AC *p* Compagnie Universelle Cinématographique (CUC)

Le Jour du frotteur
The Day of the Scrubber, France 1932 · *d* AC *p* CUC

Revue montmartroise
France 1932 · *d* AC *p* Productions Marc Gelbart

Nous ne ferons jamais du cinéma
We Will Never Pretend to Make Cinema, France 1932 · *d* AC *p* Productions Marc Gelbart

Le Truc du brésilien
The Game of the Brazilian, France 1932 · *d* AC *p* Films Tenax

Le Mari garçon
The Married Batchelor, France 1933 · *d* AC *p* Amax Films

Plaisirs défendus
Forbidden Pleasures, France 1933 · *d* AC

Coralie et Cie
France 1933 · *d* AC *sc* AC *p* Jacques Haïk

Tour de chant
Tour of Song, France 1933 · *d* AC *sc* AC

Pour un piano
For a Piano, France 1934 · *d* Pierre Chanal *sc* Aman Maistre, AC *p* Eden

John Atkins Saves Up
GB 1934 · *d* Arthur Elton *p* GPO Film Unit

Votre sourire
Your Smile, France 1934 · *d* Monty Banks, Pierre Caron *sc* AC *p* Compagnie Française Cinématographique

Pett and Pott
GB 1934 · *d* AC *p* John Grierson, GPO Film Unit

S.O.S. Radio Service
GB 1934 · *p* AC, GPO Film Unit

Glorious Sixth of June: New Rates
1934 · *d* AC *p* John Grierson, GPO Film Unit

The Song of Ceylon
GB 1934 · *d* Basil Wright *snd* A E Pawley, AC

B.B.C.: The Voice of Britain
GB 1934 · *d* Stuart Legg *p* John Grierson, Stuart Legg, AC, GPO Film Unit

Book Bargain
GB 1985 · *d* Norman McLaren *p* AC, GPO Film Unit

Coal Face
GB 1935 · *d* AC *sc* AC *snd* AC *p* John Grierson, GPO Film Unit

Rainbow Dance
GB 1936 · *d* Len Lye *p* AC, Basil Wright, GPO Film Unit

Night Mail
GB 1936 · *d* Harry Watt, Basil Wright *snd* AC *p* John Grierson, GPO Film Unit

Line to Tcherva Hut
GB 1936 · *d* AC *p* John Grierson, GPO Film Unit

Calendar of the Year
GB 1936 · *d* Evelyn Spice *p* AC, GPO Film Unit

We Live in Two Worlds
GB 1937 · *d* AC *p* John Grierson, GPO Film Unit

Who Writes to Switzerland?
GB 1937 · *d* AC *sc* AC *p* GPO Film Unit

Roadways
GB 1937 · *d* Stuart Legg, William Coldstream *p* AC, GPO Film Unit

Message from Geneva
GB 1937 · *d* AC *sc* AC *p* GPO Film Unit

Four Barriers
GB 1937 · *d* AC *sc* AC *p* John Grierson, Harry Watt, GPO Film Unit

The Saving of Bill Blewitt
GB 1937 · *d* Harry Watt *p* AC, John Grierson

Mony a Pickle
GB 1938 · *d* Norman McLaren *p* AC, Richard Massingham, GPO Film Unit

N or NW
GB 1938 · *d* Len Lye *p* AC, GPO Film Unit

Happy in the Morning
GB 1938 · *d* Pat Jackson *p* AC, GPO Film Unit

Forty Million People
GB 1938 · *d* John Monck, assisted by Gordon Hales *p* Harry Watt, AC, GPO Film Unit

North Sea
GB 1938 · *d* Harry Watt *p* AC, GPO Film Unit

Men in Danger
GB 1938 · *d* Pat Jackson *p* AC, GPO Film Unit

The City
GB 1938 · *d* Ralph Elton *p* AC, GPO Film Unit

Love on the Wing
GB 1938 · *d* Norman McLaren *p* AC, GPO Film Unit

Alice au pays romand
Alice In Switzerland, GB/Switzerland 1938 · *d* AC *p* Association des Intérêts de Lausanne/Spectator Short Films, London

Men of the Alps
GB/Switzerland 1939 · *d* AC *p* GPO Film Unit/Government of Switzerland

A Midsummer Day's Work
GB 1939 · *d* AC *sc* AC *p* GPO Film Unit

Speaking from America
GB 1939 · *d* Humphrey Jennings *p* AC, GPO Film Unit

Spare Time
GB 1939 · *d* Humphrey Jennings *p* AC, GPO Film Unit

Spring Offensive
GB 1939 · *d* Humphrey Jennings *p* AC, GPO Film Unit

The Tocher
GB 1939 · *d* Lotte Reiniger *p* AC, GPO Film Unit

The HPO
GB 1939 · *d* Lotte Reiniger *p* AC, GPO Film Unit

Oh Whiskers
GB 1939 · *d* Brian Pickersgill *p* AC, GPO Film Unit

Squadron 992
GB 1939 · *d* Harry Watt *p* AC, GPO Film Unit

The First Days
GB 1939 · *d* Humphrey Jennings, Pat Jackson, Harry Watt *p* AC, GPO Film Unit

Men of the Lightship
GB 1940 · *d* David Ma. Jonald *p* AC, Ealing Studios

Kitten on the Quay
GB 1940 · *d* Robert St John Cooper *p* AC, Ealing Studios

Merchant Seaman
GB 1941 · *d* J B Holmes *p* AC, Crown Film Unit

Yellow Caesar
GB 1941 · *d* AC *p* Ealing Studios

The Young Veteran
GB 1941 · *p* AC, Ealing Studios

Mastery of the Sea
GB 1941 · *p* AC, Ealing Studios

Guests of Honour
GB 1941 · *d* Ray Pitt *p* AC, Tansy Studios

The Big Blockade
GB 1942 · *d* Charles Frend *ap* AC *p* Michael Balcon, Ealing Studios

The Foreman Went to France
GB 1942 · *d* Charles Frend *ap* AC *p* Michael Balcon, Ealing Studios

Trois chants pour la France
Three Cheers for France, GB 1942 · *d* AC [film lost]

Film and Reality
GB 1942 · *d* AC *p* The National Film Library/British Film Institute

Went the Day Well?
GB 1942 · *d* AC *p* Michael Balcon, Ealing Studios

Greek Testament
GB 1943 · *d* Charles Hassé *ap* AC *p* Michael Balcon, Ealing Studios

Watertight
GB 1943 · *d* AC *sc* AC *p* Michael Balcon, Ealing Studios

Find, Fix and Strike
GB 1943 · *d* Compton Bennett *p* AC, Ealing Studios

The Halfway House
GB 1944 · *d* Basil Dearden *ap* AC *p* Michael Balcon, Ealing Studios

Champagne Charlie
GB 1944 · *d* AC *p* Michael Balcon, Ealing Studios

Dead of Night
GB 1945 · *d* AC, Charles Crichton, Basil Dearden, Robert Hamer *p* Michael Balcon, Ealing Studios

The Captive Heart
GB 1946 · *d* Basil Dearden *location-shooting* AC *p* Michael Balcon, Ealing Studios

The Life and Adventures of Nicholas Nickleby
GB 1947 · *d* AC *p* Michael Balcon, Ealing Studios

They Made Me a Fugitive
GB 1947 · *d* AC *p* Nat Bronsten, Alliance Film Studios

The First Gentleman
GB 1947 · *d* AC *p* Joseph Friedman, Columbia British

For Them That Trespass
GB 1949 · *d* AC *p* Victor Skutezky, Associated British Pictures

Caiçara
Brazil 1950 · *d* Adolfo Celi *p* AC, Vera Cruz

Painel
Painting, Brazil 1951 · *d* Lima Barreto *p* AC, Vera Cruz

Santuário
Sanctuary, Brazil 1951 · *d* Lima Barreto *p* AC, Vera Cruz

Terra é sempre Terra
The Earth Is Always the Earth, Brazil 1951 · *d* Tom Payne *p* AC

Ângela
Brazil 1951 · *d* Eros Martim Gonçalves *p* AC, Vera Cruz

Volta Redonda
Brazil 1952 · *d* John Waterhouse *p* AC, Vera Cruz

Simão, O Caolho
One-Eyed Simon, Brazil 1952 · *d* AC *p* AC, Maristela

O Canto do Mar
Song of the Sea, Brazil 1953 · *d* AC *p* AC, Kino-Films

Mulher de Verdade
The Real Woman, Brazil 1954 · *d* AC *p* AC, Kino-Films

~r Puntila und sein Knecht Matti
~untila and His Hired Man Matti, East Germany 1955 · *d* AC *p* Bauer

Die Windrose
East Germany 1956 · *d* AC, Alex Viany, Sergej Gerasimov, Yannick Bellon, Gillo Pontecorvo, Wu Kuo-yin *ap* Joris Ivens, AC *p* Hans Wegner, DEFA Studios

La Prima notte/Les Noces vénitiennes
The First Night, France/Italy 1958 · *d* AC *p* Cinetel-Era

The Monster of Highgate Ponds
GB 1960 · *d* AC *p* John Halas, Halas Batchelor Cartoon Films

Thus Spoke Theodore Herzl
GB/France/Israel 1967 · *d* AC

Les Empaillés
The Fools, France 1969 · *d* AC *p* ORTF [film lost]

La Visite de la vieille dame
The Visit of the Old Lady, France 1970 · *d* AC *p* ORTF [film lost]

Le Voyageur du silence
France 1976 · *d* AC *p* ORTF/FR3 [film lost]

Um Homem e o Cinema
One Man and the Cinema, Brazil 1976 · *d* AC *p* Jom Tob Azulay, Embrafilme

Selected Bibliography

Writings by Alberto Cavalcanti

"Doctrine", *Cinéma* 73-74 (6 October 1922): 9-12.

"Remarques sur l'influence du cinématographie sur les arts plastiques", *Les Cahiers du Mois* 16-17 (1925): 99-103.

"Décoration et Cinéma", *Cinémagazine* 8 (16 December 1926): 363-364.

"Le metteur en scène", *Filmliga* 12 October 1927: 4-6.

"Interviews et enquêtes", *Cinégraphie* 2 (15 October 1927): 17.

"Parlons industrie", *Filmliga* 12 August 1928: 10-11.

"Evolution of Cinematography in France", *Experimental Cinema* 1: 2 (June 1930): 5-6.

"Conversation Pieces: Ethics for Movie", *Cinema Quarterly* 2: 3 (spring 1934): 166-168.

"Discussion sur le film sonore", *Intercine* 7: 8-9 (August-September 1935): 153-159 [with Alistair Cooke].

"The Function of the Art Director", *Cinema Quarterly* 3: 2 (winter 1935): 75-78.

"Jean Vigo", *Cinema Quarterly* 3: 2 (winter 1935): 86-88.

"Le mouvement néo-réaliste en Angleterre", in *Le Rôle intellectuel du cinéma* (Paris: Éditions de l'Institut International de Coopération Intellectuelle, 1937): 235-241.

"Music Can Provide Only Interior Rhythm", *World Film News* 2: 4 (July 1937): 26-27.

"Notes on the Cinema in Italy", *Sight and Sound* 6: 22 (summer 1937): 68.

"Documentari di propaganda", *Bianco e Nero* 10 (1938): 3-7.

"Comedies and Cartoons", in Charles Davy (ed), *Footnotes to the Film* (London: Lovat Dickson and Reader's Union, 1938): 71-86.

"Pioneer", *Sight and Sound* 7: 26 (summer 1938): 55-56 [on Edgar Rogers].

"A Film Director Contributes...", in M Danischewsky (ed), *Michael Balcon's 25 Years in Films* (London. World Film Publications, 1947): 46-48.

"The Producer", in Oswell Blakeston (ed), *Working for the Films* (London; New York: The Focal Press, 1947): 64-68.

"Presenting Len Lye", *Sight and Sound* 16. 64 (winter 1947-48): 134-136.

"Avant-garde française et documentaire anglais", *Ciné-Club* 8 (1948): 1.

"Kurzinformation für junge Documentarfilm-Regisseure", *DF Bulletin* 2 (1948): 1.

"Brazil: Letter from Cavalcanti", *Sight and Sound* 21: 3 (January-March 1952): 105-106.

"Il contributo straniero allo sviluppo del cinema brasiliano", *Bianco e Nero* 14: 3 (March 1953): 27-31.

"Cavalcanti in Brazil", *Sight and Sound* 22: 4 (April-June 1953): 152 [letter].

"The Big Screens", *Sight and Sound* 24: 4 (spring 1955): 209.

"Einige Gedanken zur Entwicklung des Trickfilms", *Deutsche Filmkunst* 4 (1956): 105-106.

"Die Tragödie des brasilianischen Films", *Deutsche Filmkunst* 8 (1956): 164-167.

"Entwicklungsprobleme des rumänischen Films", *Deutsche Filmkunst* 3 (1957): 89.

"Aus der Geschichte des Dokumentarfilms im Westem", *Deutsche Filmkunst* 2 (1960): 377-378.

"Dokumentarfilmschaffende der Welt über den Amateurfilm", *Film für alle* 3 (1962): 74.

"Drei Erfahrungen, die einer Verteidigung des Dokumentarfilms dienen", in Wolfgang Klaue (ed), *Alberto Cavalcanti* (Berlin: Staatlichen Filmarchiv der Deutsches Demokratiscen Republic/Club der Filmschaffenden der DDR, 1962): 7-19.

"Esboço de roteiro para um filme de 20 minutos sobre Brasília", *Filme Cultura* 28 (February 1978): 108-124.

Books

Abel, Richard. *French Cinema: The First Wave, 1915-1929* (Princeton, NJ: Princeton University Press, 1984).

——————. *French Film Theory and Criticism: A History/Anthology 1907 1939. Volume II; 1929-1939* (Princeton, NJ: Princeton University Press, 1988

Aitken, Ian. *Film and Reform: John Grierson and the Documentary Movement* (London; New York: Routledge, 1990).

—————— (ed). *The Documentary Film Movement: An Anthology* (Edi Edinburgh University Press, 1998).

Aldgate, Anthony and Jeffrey Richards. *Britain Can Take It: The British Cinema in the Second World War*, second edition (Edinburgh: Edinburgh University Press, 1994).

Andrew, Dudley. *Mists of Regret: Culture and Sensibility in Classic French Film* (Princeton, NJ: Princeton University Press, 1995).

Armes, Roy. *A Critical History of the British Cinema* (London: Secker & Warburg, 1978).

—————. *French Cinema* (London: Secker & Warburg, 1985).

—————. *Third World Film Making and the West* (Berkeley; Los Angeles; London: University of California Press, 1987).

Audra, Mário, Jr. *Cinematográfica Maristela: Memórias de um Produtor* (São Paulo: Silver Hawk, 1997).

Balázs, Béla. *Theory of the Film (Character and Growth of a New Art)*, translated by Edith Bone (London: Dennis Dobson, 1952).

Balcon, Michael. *Realism or Tinsel* (Workers Film Association, 1944).

—————. *The Producer: Being a lecture given to the British Film Institute's 1945 Summer School of Film Appreciation* (London: British Film Institute, 1945).

—————. *Michael Balcon presents... A Lifetime of Films* (London: Hutchinson, 1969).

Balcon, Michael, Ernest Lindgren, Forsyth Hardy and Roger Manvell. *Twenty Years of British Film 1925-1945* (London: The Falcon Press, 1947).

Barnouw, Erik. *Documentary: A History of the Non-Fiction Film*, second revised edition (New York; Oxford: Oxford University Press, 1993).

Barsam, Richard. *The Vision of Robert Flaherty: The Artist as Myth and Filmmaker* (Bloomington; Indianapolis: Indiana University Press, 1988).

—————. *Nonfiction Film: A Critical History*, revised and expanded edition (Bloomington; Indianapolis: Indiana University Press, 1992).

Barr, Charles. *Ealing Studios* (London: Cameron & Tayleur, in association with David & Charles, 1977).

————— (ed). *All Our Yesterdays: 90 Years of British Cinema* (London: British Film Institute, 1986).

—————. *Ealing Studios*, second edition (London: Studio Vista, 1993).

Bordwell, David. *French Impressionist Cinema: Film Culture, Film Theory and Film Style* (New York: Arno Press, 1980).

dford-Burns, E. *A History of Brazil* (New York: Columbia University Press,).

Leo. *Jean Renoir: The World of His Films* (London: Robson Books,

Brunel, Adrian. *Nice Work: The Story of Thirty Years in British Film Production* (London: Forbes Robertson, 1949).

Burns, Rob (ed). *German Cultural Studies: An Introduction* (Oxford: Oxford University Press, 1995).

Cavalcanti, Alberto. *Filme e Realidade* third edition (Rio de Janeiro: Editora Artenova, in collaboration with Empresa Brasileira de Filmes — Embrafilme, 1977) [first published in 1952].

Chapman, James. *The British At War: Cinema, State and Propaganda, 1939-1945* (London; New York: I B Tauris, 1998).

Clarke, T E B. *This is where I came in* (London: Michael Joseph, 1974).

Curran, James and Vincent Porter (eds). *British Cinema History* (London: Weidenfeld & Nicolson, 1983).

Danischewsky, Monja. *White Russian – Red Face* (London: Victor Gollancz, 1966).

Davy, Charles (ed). *Footnotes to the Film* (London: Lovat Dickson and Reader's Union, 1938).

Delmar, Rosalind. *Joris Ivens: 50 years of film-making* (London: British Film Institute, 1979).

Dickinson, Margaret and Sarah Street. *Cinema and State: The Film Industry and the Government 1927-84* (London: British Film Institute, 1985).

Drazin, Charles. *The Finest Years: British Cinema of the 1940s* (London: André Deutsch, 1998) [includes "Cavalcanti" (112-137)].

Durgnat, Raymond. *A Mirror For England. British Movies from Austerity to Affluence* (London: Faber and Faber, 1970).

Esslin, Martin. *Brecht: A Choice of Evils. A Critical Study of the Man, His Work and His Opinions*, fourth revised edition (London; New York: Methuen, 1984).

Evans, Gary. *John Grierson and the National Film Board: The Politics of Wartime Propaganda* (Toronto; Buffalo; London: University of Toronto Press, 1984).

Falk, Quentin. *Travels in Greeneland: The Cinema of Graham Greene* (London; Melbourne; New York: Quartet Books, 1984).

Fulbrook, Mary. *A Concise History of Germany* (Cambridge; New York; Port Chester; Melbourne; Sydney: Cambridge University Press, 1990).

Galvão, Maria Rita. *Burguesia e Cinema: o Caso Vera Cruz* (São Paulo: Civilização Brasileira, 1981).

Gay, Peter. *Weimar Culture: The Outsider As Insider* (London: Secker & Warburg, 1969).

Ghali, Noureddine. *L'Avant-Garde Cinématographique en France dans les Années Vingt: Idées, Conceptions, Théories* (Paris: Éditions Paris Expériment 1995).

Ginsberg, Terri and Kirsten Moana Thompson (eds). *Perspectives on German Cinema* (New York: G K Hall & Co, 1996).

Hardy, Forsyth (ed). *Grierson on Documentary* (London; Boston: Faber and Faber, 1979).

——————. *John Grierson: A Documentary Biography* (London; Boston: Faber and Faber, 1979).

Harper, Sue. *Picturing the Past: The Rise and Fall of the British Costume Film* (London: British Film Institute, 1994).

Hassard, John and Ruth Holliday (eds). *Organization Representation: Work and Organizations in Popular Culture* (London: Sage Publications, 1998).

Hibbin, Nina. *Eastern Europe: An Illustrated Guide* (London; New York: A Zwemmer and A S Barnes, 1969).

Holloway, Stanley. *Wiv a Little Bit O'Luck: The Life Story of Stanley Holloway (as told to Dick Richards)* (London: Leslie Frewin, 1967).

Houston, Penelope. *Went the Day Well?* (London: British Film Institute, 1992).

Hurd, Geoff (ed). *National Fictions: World War Two in British Films and Television* (London: British Film Institute, 1984).

Hutchings, Peter. *Hammer and beyond: the British horror film* (Manchester; New York: Manchester University Press, 1993).

Ivens, Joris. *The Camera and I* (Berlin: Seven Seas Publishers, 1969).

Jacobs, Lewis (ed). *The Documentary Tradition*, second edition (New York: W W Norton & Company, 1979).

—————— (ed). *The Emergence of Film Art: The evolution and development of the motion picture as an art, from 1900 to the present*, second edition (New York; London: W W Norton & Company, 1979) [includes Alberto Cavalcanti, "The Sound Film" (1938): 170-186].

Jackson, Kevin (ed). *The Humphrey Jennings Film Reader* (Manchester: Carcanet, 1993).

Jennings, Humphrey. *Pandæmonium 1660-1886: The Coming of the Machine as seen by contemporary observers*, edited by Mary-Lou Jennings and Charles Madge (London: André Deutsch, 1985).

Jennings, Mary-Lou (ed). *Humphrey Jennings: Film-Maker/Painter/Poet* (London: British Film Institute in association with Riverside Studios, 1982).

Johnson, Randal and Robert Stam (eds). *Brazilian Cinema*, expanded edition (New York: Columbia University Press, 1995).

Klaue, Wolfgang (ed). *Alberto Cavalcanti* (Berlin: Staatlichen Filmarchiv der Deutsches Demokratischen Republic, 1962).

Kracauer, Siegfried. *Theory of Film: The Redemption of Physical Reality* (New York: Oxford University Press, 1960).

Leyda, Jay. *Kino: A History of the Russian and Soviet Film*, third edition (London; Boston; Sydney; George Allen & Unwin, 1973).

Lovell, Alan and Jim Hillier. *Studies in Documentary* (London: Secker and Warburg, in association with the British Film Institute, 1972).

Low, Rachael. *The History of the British Film 1929-1939: Documentary and Educational Films of the 1930s* (London; Boston: Sydney: George Allen & Unwin, 1979).

McCallum, John. *Life with Googie* (London: Heinemann, 1979).

Macdonald, Kevin and Mark Cousins. *Imagining Reality: The Faber Book of the Documentary* (London; Boston: Faber and Faber, 1996).

McFarlane, Brian (ed). *Sixty Voices: Celebrities Recall the Golden Age of British Cinema* (London: British Film Institute, with the assistance of Monash University, 1992).

———————————. *An Autobiography of British Cinema: as told by the filmmakers and actors who made it* (London: Methuen, 1997).

Macnab, Geoffrey. *J. Arthur Rank and the British Film Industry* (London; New York: Routledge, 1993).

Marris, Paul (ed). *Paul Rotha* (London: British Film Institute, 1982).

Martin, John W. *The Golden Age of French Cinema 1929-1939* (London: Columbus Books, 1987).

Michael Balcon: The Pursuit of British Cinema, essays by Geoff Brown and Laurence Kardish (New York: Museum of Modern Art, 1984).

Montagu, Ivor. *Film World: a guide to cinema* (Harmondsworth: Penguin Books, 1964).

Murphy, Robert. *Realism and Tinsel: Cinema and society in Britain 1939-48* (London: Routledge, 1989).

———————————— (ed). *The British Cinema Book* (London: British Film Institute, 1997).

Nelson, Joyce. *The Colonized Eye: Rethinking the Grierson Legend* (Toronto: Between the Lines, 1988).

Nettl, J P. *The Soviet Achievement* (London: Thames and Hudson, 1967).

Orbanz, Eva. *Journey to a Legend and Back: The British Realistic Film* (Berlin: Volker Spiess, 1977).

Parkinson, David (ed). *The Graham Greene Film Reader: Mornings in the Dark* (Manchester: Carcanet, 1993).

Pellizzari, Lorenzo and Claudio M Valentinetti (eds). *Alberto Cavalc* (Locarno: Éditions du Festival international du film de Locarno, 1988).

————————————————————————————. *Alberto Ca* (São Paulo: Instituto Lina Bo e P M Bardi, 1995).

Perry, George. *Forever Ealing: A Celebration of the Great British Film Studio* (London: Pavilion/Michael Joseph, 1981).

——————. *The Great British Picture Show* (London: Pavilion Books, 1985).

Powell, Dilys. *Films Since 1939* (London: Longman Green & Co, for the British Council, 1947).

Priestley, J B. *English Journey: Being a Rambling but Truthful Account of What One Man Saw and Heard and Felt and Thought During a Journey Through England During the Autumn of the Year 1933* (London: William Heinemann, in association with Victor Gollancz, 1934).

Pronay, Nicholas and D W Spring (eds). *Propaganda, Politics and Film, 1918-45* (London: The Macmillan Press, 1982).

Redgrave, Michael. *In My Mind's Eye: An Autobiography* (London: Weidenfeld & Nicolson, 1983).

Renoir, Jean. *My Life and My Films*, translated by Norman Denny (London: Collins, 1974).

Richards, Jeffrey. *The Age of the Dream Palace: Cinema and Society in Britain 1930-1939* (London; Boston; Melbourne; Henley: Routledge & Kegan Paul, 1984).

——————. *Films and British national identity: From Dickens to Dad's Army* (Manchester; New York: Manchester University Press, 1997).

—————— and Anthony Aldgate. *Best of British: Cinema and Society 1930-1970* (Oxford: Basil Blackwell, 1983).

Rotha, Paul. *Documentary Film: The use of the film medium to interpret creatively and in social terms the life of the people as it exists in reality*, second edition (London: Faber & Faber, 1939).

——————. *Rotha on the Film: A Selection of Writings about the Cinema* (London: Faber and Faber, 1958).

——————. *Documentary Diary: An Informal History of the British Documentary Film, 1928-1939* (London: Secker and Warburg, 1973).

——————. *Robert J. Flaherty: A Biography*, edited by Jay Ruby (Philadelphia: University of Pennyslavania Press, 1983).

—————— with Richard Griffith. *The Film Till Now: A Survey of World Cinema* (London: Vision Press, 1949).

Screen: Special Number: Brecht and a Revolutionary Cinema 15: 2 (summer 1974).

Silberman, Marc. *German Cinema: Texts in Context* (Detroit: Wayne State University Press, 1995).

Sussex, Elizabeth. *The Rise and Fall of British Documentary: The Story of the Movement Founded by John Grierson* (Berkeley; Los Angeles; London: University of California Press, 1975).

Swann, Paul. *The British Documentary Film Movement, 1926-1946* (Cambridge;

Selected Bibliography · 261

New York; New Rochelle; Melbourne; Sydney: Cambridge University Press, 1989).

Tallents, Stephen, Sir. *The Projection of England* (London: Faber & Faber, 1932).

Thiher, Allen. *The Cinematic Muse: Critical Studies in the History of French Cinema* (Columbia; London: University of Missouri Press, 1979).

Thorpe, Frances and Nicholas Pronay. *British Official Films in the Second World War: a descriptive catalogue* (Oxford; Santa Barbara, CA: Clio Press, 1980).

Todd, Richard. *Caught in the Act: The Story of My Life* (London; Melbourne; Auckland; Johannesburg: Hutchinson, 1986).

Vaughan, Dai. *Portrait of an Invisible Man: The working life of Stewart McAllister, film editor* (London: British Film Institute, 1983).

Walsh, Martin. *The Brechtian Aspect of Radical Cinema*, edited by Keith M Griffiths (London: British Film Institute, 1981).

Warren, Patricia. *British Film Studios: An Illustrated History* (London: B T Batsford, 1995).

Watt, Harry. *Don't Look at the Camera* (London: Paul Elek, 1974).

Willett, John (trans). *Bertolt Brecht: Mr. Puntila and His Man Matti* (London: Eyre Methuen, 1977).

——————— (ed and trans). *Brecht on Theatre: The Development of an Aesthetic* (London: Eyre Methuen, 1978).

Williams, Alan. *Republic of Images: A History of French Filmmaking* (Cambridge, MA; London: Harvard University Press, 1992).

Winston, Brian. *Claiming the Real: The Griersonian Documentary and Its Legitimations* (London: British Film Institute, 1995).

Wright, Basil. *The Long View* (London: Paladin, 1976).

Articles

Aitken, Ian. "John Grierson, Idealism and the Inter-war Period", *Historical Journal of Film, Radio and Television* 9: 3 (1989): 247-258.

"Alberto Cavalcanti", *Film Dope* 8 (October 1975): 24d.

Baxter, Brian. "The NFA and NFT Presents...Cavalcanti", *National Film Theatre Programme* February-March 1977.

BB. "Alberto Cavalcanti", *Film Dope* 6 (November 1974): 36-38.

Beylie, Claude. "Un cinéaste entre le rêve et la réalité", *Ecran* 30 (November 1974): 50-52.

———————. Didier Lemarchand and Christian Michaud. "Entretien Alberto Cavalcanti", *Ecran* 30 (November 1974): 52-57.

Dort, Bernard. "Pour une critique Brechtienne du cinéma", *Cahiers du Cinéma* 19: 114 (December 1960): 33-43.

Harrington, John and David Paroissien. "Alberto Cavalcanti on *Nicholas Nickleby*", *Literature/Film Quarterly* 6: 1 (winter 1978): 48-56.

Lambert, Gavin. "Alberto Cavalcanti", *Screen* 13: 2 (summer 1972): 36-53.

Marcorelles, Louis. "L'impossible gageure", *Cahiers du Cinéma* 13: 77 (December 1957): 52-55.

Martialay, Félix. "'yo era un surrealista con tendencia al realismo', dice Alberto Cavalcanti", *Film Ideal* 62 (15 December 1960): 4-5, 14.

Minish, Geoffrey. "Cavalcanti in Paris", *Sight and Sound* 39: 3 (summer 1970): 134-135.

Monegal, Emir Rodriguez. "Alberto Cavalcanti", *The Quarterly of Film, Radio and Television* 9: 4 (summer 1955): 341-358.

"Obituary", *Films and Filming* 338 (November 1982): 8.

Roche, Catherine de la. "Cavalcanti in Brazil", *Sight and Sound* 24: 3 (January-March 1955): 119.

Rodrigues, Antonio and Alain Marchand. "Alberto Cavalcanti: uno 'straordinario uomo ordinario'/Alberto Cavalcanti: An 'Extraordinary Ordinary Man'", *Griffithiana* 60/61 (October 1997): 190-199.

Sadoul, Georges. "Rivelazioni e scoperte al festival di Karlovy Vary", *Cinema* 7: 141 (September 1954): 543-547.

Sussex, Elizabeth. "Cavalcanti in England", *Sight and Sound* 44: 4 (autumn 1975): 205-211.

Tynan, Kenneth. "Ealing's Way of Life", *Films and Filming* 2: 3 (December 1955): 10.

Verdone, Mario. "Cavalcanti vorrebbe fare un film sul ritorno del fascismo", *Cinema* 2: 7 (January 1949): 215.

Vesselo, Arthur. "The Quarter in Britain", *Sight and Sound* 16: 63 (autumn 1947): 120-121.

Wegner, Hans. "Alberto Cavalcanti zum 60. Geburtstag!", *Deutsche Filmkunst* 3 (1957).

Index